Obligations in Roman Law

PAPERS AND MONOGRAPHS
OF THE
AMERICAN ACADEMY
IN ROME

VOLUME XXXIII

Obligations in Roman Law

PAST, PRESENT, AND FUTURE

Thomas A. J. McGinn, Editor

THE UNIVERSITY OF MICHIGAN PRESS

ANN ARBOR

Published in the United States of America by
The University of Michigan Press
Manufactured in the United States of America
♾ Printed on acid-free paper

2017 2016 2015 2014 5 4 3 2

A CIP catalog record for this book is available from the British Library.

Library of Congress Cataloging-in-Publication Data

A Conference on Roman Law : The Future of Obligations (2008 : Rome, Italy)
Obligations in Roman law : past, present, and future / Thomas A. J. McGinn, editor.
p. cm. — (The papers and monographs of the American academy in Rome)
Includes index.
ISBN 978-0-472-11843-4 (cloth : alk. paper) — ISBN 978-0-472-02857-3 (e-book)
1. Obligations (Roman law)—Congresses. 2. Contracts (Roman law)—Congresses.
I. McGinn, Thomas A. J. II. Title.
KJA2512.O25 2008

346.02'2—dc23 2012042623

Preface

This collection of essays represents the fruits of a conference held at the American Academy in Rome on March 13–14, 2008, under the title "A Conference on Roman Law: The Future of Obligations." The conference would not have been possible without the vital support of the academy's marvelous director, Professor Carmela Vircillo Franklin. I would also like to thank my excellent staff, especially Anne Coulson and Giulia Barra, for their indispensable help with and their devotion to even the smallest detail. Thanks in no small part to their efforts, the conference was a smashing success.

I am very grateful for the financial support for the conference and this publication provided by Cleary Gottlieb Steen & Hamilton LLP. Particular thanks go to William McGurn for his unparalleled kindness and generosity. My wonderful colleague William Franklin was of great assistance, as ever, in making the impossible happen.

I would also like to thank the Publications Committee of the American Academy in Rome and especially that committee's chair, Professor Elaine Gazda, for their consistent support of this endeavor, above all for a timely grant made by them from the Lucy Shoe Meritt Fund to allay the costs of translation.

Regarding the five essays that were originally written in Italian, I am fortunate to have been able to rely on the talents of a team of translators. They are Beverly Allen (Federico Procchi), Maria Enrico (Roberto Fiori), Elisabeth Giansiracusa (Carla Masi Doria and Salvo Randazzo), and Nora Mahony (Cosimo Cascione). I am delighted to recognize the contributions of the authors themselves to this process. In fact, I am pleased to express my gratitude to all of the contributors to this volume for their kind cooperation throughout the process of publication. I would also like to thank my son, Thomas McGinn, for his superb service as a copyeditor.

I am most grateful to Vanderbilt University for a sabbatical year and other key research support. I am once more indebted to Mr. James Toplon and his excellent staff at Vanderbilt University's interlibrary loan office, in particular, Rachel Adams, David Hughett, Marilyn Pilley, and Jim Webb. I would also like to thank our bibliographer, Ramona Romero, for her energy and expertise in acquiring materials for our collection. I would also like to thank the staff at the University of Michigan Press, above all my distinguished editor, Ellen Bauerle, for invaluable assistance in getting this book to press.

T. A. J. McGinn
Vanderbilt University

Contents

CHAPTER 1

A Conference on Roman Law

The Future of Obligations

THOMAS A. J. MCGINN

In recent years, the study and teaching of Roman law have undergone fundamental transformation. Many now agree that Roman law should not be isolated from the historical context in which its norms were generated; that is, they accept the need for "historicizing" Roman law rather than treating it solely as an intellectually autonomous achievement. As a field of study, it shows an increasing affinity to social history. To a certain extent, this transformation parallels developments in other areas of legal history, but it has also arisen, in no small part, thanks to an important series of reforms in European university systems.[1] These changes, the full implications of which are still far from clear, are bound to have a lasting impact on the entire field, so much so that its future as a scholarly discipline has already been the subject of lively debate.[2]

---

1. In Italy, some of the more important reforms, which, among other things, provided for a two-track undergraduate degree (*laurea*), were enacted through a *decreto ministeriale* (n. 509) of November 3, 1999: see the "Breve guida alla riforma universitaria," found at http://www.polaris.unioncamere.it/universita/riforma.doc (accessed April 14, 2008). For an example of reaction to the Italian university reforms in the field of Roman law pedagogy, see Giachi, Stolfi, and Tamburi, "Un manuale di diritto privato romano" (2004). See also, more generally, Peppe, "Alcune riflessioni sulla storia del diritto" (2000); Guarino, "Un futuro per il diritto romano?" (2002); Capogrossi Colognesi, "Diritto romano, diritti europei" (1998–1999 [2005]); Pichonnaz, "L'insegnamento" (2008).
2. Such as with the panel held in May 2006 at the annual meetings of the Association of Ancient Historians under the provocative title "Does Roman Law Have a Scholarly Future?" See McGinn, "Crossing Boundaries" (2006–2007) for a summary. An important impetus behind the panel was Frier, "Roman Law's Descent into History" (2000).

Two questions are raised by this transformation in our understanding. First, how should we now understand the relationship between Roman legal rules when considered as intellectual achievements in themselves and these same rules when considered as historical artifacts? The tension between these two ways of approaching the subject, which might be summarized as a distinction between taking law as law and law as history, has resonated for decades now, especially in Europe.[3] Second, how should that understanding affect the way we teach and write about Roman law?

To address these issues, I organized a two-day conference, held in March 2008 at the American Academy in Rome. I invited a dozen speakers who had published substantially on related subjects and so were recognized authorities in this field. All but one were from European universities, a reflection of the diversity of interest in the subjects under discussion. By all accounts, the conference was a great success. We are now pleased to present its fruits in the form of this publication.

In what follows, I first lay out the main issues for consideration in this book and then summarize the contribution of each chapter, contextualizing each contribution with matter drawn from the Roman law itself and/or, in most cases, comparative material taken from modern U.S. law. The purpose is to offer a stimulus both for further research and for approaches to teaching. The latter subject in particular receives more attention in chapter 14.

Design of the Book

The task we set ourselves was to take one of the traditional subfields within Roman law, the law of obligations, and place this under renewed scrutiny. As is well known to students of Roman law, the law of obligations is an area of the private law that, together with property and succession, falls under the category

3. The degree of continuing disagreement on this point is suggested by the controversy in recent years over what role Roman law should play in the development of legal rules for the European Union, a controversy that has, in simplified terms, pitted those advocating a view, sometimes described as neopandectism (or even as "attualismo"), in which Roman law exists primarily as an autonomous body of rules (and so one ultimately divorced, or divorceable, from its original cultural context, the better to serve the needs of a modern one), against those who view it as more properly a historical subject: see Peppe, "Alcune riflessioni sulla storia del diritto" (2000); Mantello, "Ancora sulle smanie romanistiche" (2002); Capogrossi Colognesi, "Diritto romano, diritti europei" (1998–1999 [2005]); Scarano Ussani, "Quale diritto romano?"(2008) (see also the essays by De Giovanni and Fanizza in the same volume as this last essay).

of "things" (*res*), which itself forms one of the fundamental rubrics of private law, along with the law of persons and that of actions. "Obligations" traditionally breaks down into two subrubrics, the law of contracts (contracts are commonly defined as agreements between two or more parties that are enforceable or otherwise recognizable at law) and that of delicts, the Roman equivalent of torts (torts are civil wrongs, other than breach of contract, for which a legal remedy may be obtained). The manner in which the rules are presented in the ancient sources makes their understanding complicated, to say the least. Scholars have wrestled with these difficulties for many years, of course. Just to take one example, our most extensive single source for the classical law of obligations, the elementary textbook known as the *Institutiones* ascribed to the second-century jurist Gaius (to whom the categories of law outlined above can be traced), has a presentation of this subject that is widely acknowledged—not least in terms of its fundamental classification(s) of obligations—to be rather problematic, if not deeply flawed.[4]

In fact, this area of the law, especially as illuminated by modern scholarship, is quite dynamic, despite these traditional challenges to our understanding. Before proceeding, it is worth asking if the Romans indeed had a concept, recognizable to us, of "obligations." We should begin by clarifying to what extent our understanding of this is dependent on modern, especially nineteenth-century, scholarship. Next, we can consider how unitary are the bodies of rules devoted to the subcategories of contract and delict, respectively. Did a conceptualist desire to synthesize these categories first arise among the classical jurists, Justinian's legal experts, or modern scholars? For example, did the Romans, at any point in time, develop a single, coherent concept of nonintentional fault or negligence? The same question holds for causation. There may be some analytical level on which obligations are fruitfully regarded as a unity, but in most relevant social respects, this branch of the law might be better reduced to its constituent areas, below even the general level of *emptio venditio* (sale) or *locatio conductio* (hire/lease) or *damnum iniuria datum* (the wrongful infliction of harm to another's property), to specific topics such as the sale of wine or the construction indus-

---

4. Gaius 3.88–89, 182 (cf. Gaius [2 *aur.*] *D.* 44.7.1 pr.–1; Gaius [3 *aur.*] *D.* 44.7.4; Mod. [2 *reg.*] *D.* 44.7.52 pr.; *Inst.* 3.13). See the still useful account in de Zulueta, *"Institutes" of Gaius* (1953) 2:140–48, 196–98, as well as the fuller and more recent treatment in Nelson and Manthe, *Gai Institutiones III 88–181* (1999) 59–80. For further perspectives, see Birks, "Obligations" (1983); Zimmermann, *Law of Obligations* (1996) 10–18; Winkel, "Alcune osservazioni" (2000–2001 [2009]). For a defense of Gaius, see Biscardi, "Some Critical Remarks" (1978); Falcone, "Sistematiche gaiane" (2011).

try or medical malpractice. What kinds of tension are created by these different ways of looking at legal materials, and how can the tension be resolved?

We herein investigate what overall approaches are available to us and which ones best suit the refinement of our understanding of these matters, whether this be a materialist one, an idealist one, or something else again, such as an evaluation of transaction costs. If we accept that these rules are contingent and not inevitable, which is to say that the category "obligations" is a social construct, what does this tell us about their historical development? From there, we can attempt to draw conclusions about the particular relationship between the private law, on the one hand, and the structure and content of Roman society and the Roman economy, on the other. Next, what precisely is the interest of the state? We also want to know to what extent the rules themselves reflect upper-class values and whether it is possible to speak of them as elements of an ideology.

Plan of the Book

We were very fortunate indeed in our choice of speakers, who were well prepared to address these issues and others like them. One of the consistent themes to emerge from this collection is a critical engagement with the modern scholarship on the Roman law of obligations, above all in its more traditional aspects. We owe an immense debt to this tradition, a debt that is, I believe, fully acknowledged by our authors.

It is hardly true, of course, that all modern conceptions are equally helpful in the elucidation of the Roman law of obligations. Roberto Fiori, from the Università di Roma Tor Vergata, brings that point home in this book. Fiori's chapter, "The Roman Conception of Contract," addresses a key aspect of the doctrinal development of the Roman rules in this area. Was there a trend from an objective requirement for contracting an obligation toward a standard based on the agreement (*consensus*) of the parties? Did the Romans know a "general theory" for contracts, and what are the implications of its presence or absence? Fiori focuses particular attention on the relationship between the element of agreement and that of the contractual bond (the *vinculum iuris* or *obligatio*) itself in the formation of a contract.[5] On one level, he traces the course of the

5. On this point, see also Fiori, *La definizione della locatio conductio* (1999) 355–60; Cascione, *Consensus* (2003) 209–13.

discussion on the part of the Roman jurists over how best to accommodate the tension between the standard types of contracts and the agreements that fall outside them, a debate that has obvious resonance beyond the Roman system of law.[6] These issues go to the heart of our understanding of some of the core principles in this field of law and so have been subjected to extensive and intense discussion in the scholarship.

Fiori's essay points up the importance of placing in their proper historical context not only the ancient sources but also the long tradition of modern scholarship that has aimed to elucidate them. He offers an introduction to developments in the conception of contract on the part of both the Roman jurists and their modern interpreters. For the latter, the influence of the nineteenth century continues to loom large.

Contrary to some recent assumptions, commercial practices in that period were not inevitably a model of rationality and efficiency but were, in some respects, imbued with considerations of tradition and conservatism. The same might be said of the legal rules themselves, whose legacy continues to be felt despite their peculiarity in many respects. We might begin by pointing out that the principles of the common law of contracts were notably influenced in that century by the work of the Roman jurists, for example, the views of Ulpian on mistake invalidating an agreement, particularly the kind of mistake concerning the identity of the object of sale, known as *error in corpore*.[7] At the same time, contract enjoyed an enormous ideological significance, shaping, for example, the approach taken by Christopher Columbus Langdell in developing the case method of teaching law.[8] Such considerations informed nineteenth-century scholars' understanding of their own case law, as we see occurring, for example, with the venerable English case of *Raffles v. Wichelhaus* (1864), where the obscurity of the facts seems to have encouraged the proliferation of

---

6. Worth noting in particular is the distinction drawn between contracts that were protected with specific remedies in the praetor's edict—sometimes known as "standard" or more generally as "typical," as in "contratti tipici"— and those that were not: see, for example, Cannata, "Contratto e Causa" (1997/2006) 192.

7. Ulp. *D.* 18.1.9. Another direct influence was the thought of Friedrich Carl von Savigny, above all, Savigny's *System* (1840–1849): see Simpson, "Contracts for Cotton" (2007) 55–59. For a nineteenth-century take on this subject, see Holmes, *Common Law* (1881/2009) 279–84.

8. On the ideology of contract in the nineteenth century, see Tomlins, *Law, Labor, and Ideology* (1993); Stanley, *From Bondage to Contract* (1998). On the case method of legal pedagogy, see chapter 14 in the present volume.

theory.[9] How likely is it that the contemporary scholarly treatment of Roman law would differ in any substantial sense? And just how many of their (unexamined) assumptions have become ours?

In "Roman Contracts and the Construction of Fault in Their Formation," Federico Procchi, from the Università di Pisa, examines a specific challenge faced in the mid-nineteenth century arising from the fact that the classical Roman jurists did not, as far as we know, deal squarely with the problem of fault in precontractual liability when no contract had been concluded.[10] Some rather contingent factors, it turns out, led Rudolf von Jhering to develop a creative reconceptualization of the Roman rules in order to address the problem of how to protect the interest of a party to contractual negotiations who has acted in reliance on the conclusion of a contract that cannot be concluded thanks to the deliberately wrongful or (a more difficult case) negligent behavior of the other party.

Jhering was extraordinarily well placed, in terms of personality and experience, to play the role of mediator between the ancient and modern legal traditions.[11] In this particular instance, we see not only the vitality of the Roman tradition but of one of the many modern approaches taken to it. Procchi's essay suggests that the conflict between those who want Roman law to continue to play a role in the formation of modern law and those who view it as a historical subject may not be entirely irreconcilable. One might venture to assert, on the basis of what is shown here, that only through a correct understanding of Roman law in its proper context, both ancient and modern, can it hope to play such a role with any real chance of success. On a broader level, while recognizing the distinction between law as technology and law as culture, we may hesitate before accepting that this is always as clean as is sometimes supposed.

Common-law authorities have likewise labored to address the challenge

9. 2 H. & C. 906, 159 Eng. Rep. 375 (Ex. 1864); also in 33 L.J.N.S. 160 (Ex. 1864). See the treatment of this case in its historical context in Simpson, "Contracts for Cotton" (2007) against the ahistorical Gilmore, *Death of Contract* (1992) 39–47. See also the chapters by Ricks and Eisenberg in Barnett, *Perspectives on Contract Law* (2005); Chirelstein, *Concepts and Case Analysis* (2006) 36–38. For perspectives from English law, see Smith, *Atiyah's Introduction* (2005) 42–47, 172–82; Cartwright, *Contract Law* (2007) 89–92, 149.

10. There was recognition of liability for certain types of wrongful precontractual behavior in cases where a contract was in fact concluded: see Petrucci, "Profili di responsabilità precontrattuale" (2010).

11. See Behrends, "Rudolf von Jehring" (2003).

of precontractual liability, with partial success at best.[12] In this legal tradition, contracts have tended to be either fully enforceable or not enforceable at all.[13] There is a widespread belief that liability under promissory estoppel lies regarding investments made in reliance prior to actual agreement between parties engaged in commercial negotiations.[14] The difficulty arises that the principal case cited to justify this idea, *Hoffman v. Red Owl Stores, Inc.* (1965), seems, on close inspection, ill supported by any of the three main theories that are supposed to apply: a duty to negotiate in good faith, liability for negligent misrepresentation, and recovery in quasi contract for unjust enrichment.[15] In recent years, a more flexible standard that recognizes two types of preliminary agreement to possess binding force has gained ground, first enunciated in *Teachers Insurance and Annuity Association of America v. Tribune* (1987).[16]

The intellectual legacy of the nineteenth century continues to cast a long shadow over twenty-first-century concerns. In "Status and Contract in Ancient Rome: With Some Thoughts on the 'Future of Obligations,'" Carla Masi Doria, from the Università di Napoli Federico II, writes on a subject of critical interest, because it is one place where we can expect to trace with reasonable certainty the intersection of legal rules and social values. Not content with simply exploring that topic, Masi Doria broadens our understanding of the content and history of the Roman law of obligations by appropriating an important aspect of our common intellectual patrimony regarding this subject, namely, the thought of the famous nineteenth-century legal anthropologist Sir Henry Sumner Maine, whose methodology she employs in a novel way.[17] After introductory remarks on some peculiar aspects of Maine's contribution, Masi Doria offers useful observations on the fundamental importance of status both to the

---

12. See the discussion in Knapp, "Enforcing the Contract to Bargain" (1969/2005), recognizing two basic scenarios in precontractual negotiations, the "agreement to agree" and the "formal contract contemplated," while conceding a range of possibilities between the two.
13. The approach taken by English law in this area remains more conservative than those of the American and Australian traditions: see Smith, *Atiyah's Introduction* (2005) 68–69, 124–28; Cartwright, *Contract Law* (2007) 65–83, 129–39.
14. The standard authority is the *Restatement (Second) of Contracts* § 90 (1981). See the chapters by Yorio and Thel, Feinman, and Holmes in Barnett, *Perspectives on Contract Law* (2005).
15. 133 N.W.2d 267 (Wis. 1965).
16. 670 F. Supp. 491 (1987). For what precedes, see the discussion in Scott, "*Hoffman v. Red Owl Stores*" (2007). See also Chirelstein, *Concepts and Case Analysis* (2006) 57–58.
17. On Maine's political interests and scholarly preparation (including his paradoxically anemic knowledge of Roman law), see Kuper, "Ancestors" (1985).

historical experience of the Romans and to their law. She goes on to examine the link between status and obligation, focusing on various relations of dependency as defined by the law.

Status was regulated not only by law, of course, but also by the censors, in their operation of the *regimen morum,* the means by which they advanced appropriate men to and removed dishonored men from positions of social prominence and political responsibility. Here Masi Doria focuses on a particular instance where status is threatened because of the breaking of an oath, a conjuncture of status and obligation that is imperfectly realized in this case and eventually superseded entirely owing to the disappearance, in a strict sense, of the censorship under the Principate. This is part of a general trend, moving away from status in the direction of contract, that Masi Doria is able to trace more specifically in the law, such as in the rules governing the relations between ex-slaves and their former owners or "patrons," above all in the matter of *operae* (services) due to the latter from the former.

Masi Doria suggests the utility of Maine's thesis by demonstrating just how contingent it is. She shows that the movement from status to contract that he postulates possesses some degree of resonance for classical Roman law, though, even in this context, its explanatory power has its limits. For various reasons, the transition is not as complete or as unidirectional as the thesis by itself might suggest. Perhaps even more engaging is Masi Doria's discussion of the two historical periods, late antiquity and the recent modern era, in which she finds the flow to be reversed in important respects, in other words, where one can discern a direction moving to a significant degree from contract to status.[18] It is refreshing to see such new life breathed into the subject of nineteenth-century writing on Roman obligations.

Some light may perhaps be shed on the subject through a glimpse of the sustained contestation that played out in connection with status and contract in the history of nineteenth-century common law.[19] That century began with the legal

18. So Masi Doria's analysis runs counter to what Lawrence Friedman identifies as the master trend in the history of the family, the history of law in general, and "even perhaps the history of society" (Friedman, *Private Lives* [2004] 2; see also 10). See also Gordon, "*Britton v. Turner*" (2007) 207–10.

19. On the ideology of contract in the nineteenth century and its interplay with status concerns, see the literature cited in the notes preceding (in the discussion of Langdell's introduction of the case method) and following (in the discussion of gender and employment contracts). For a concrete example of the role status might play in contract law, see Danzig, "*Hadley v. Baxen-*

doctrine of employment firmly established as a contract relation between status unequals, much like marriage—that is, between master and servant.[20] In the United States, this doctrine was strengthened by the holding in a Massachusetts case, *Stark v. Parker* (1824), that laid the foundation for a view of the employment contract as setting up an authoritarian relationship in which the terms were set in key respects not by mutual agreement but by a preexisting prerogative of the employer, whose basic rights were deemed as implied.[21] The employer had the right to command, and the employee had the duty to obey. As the century proceeded, this idea came under increasing challenge from legal scholars, who relied on a New Hampshire case with a very different outcome, *Britton v. Turner* (1834), while at times invoking feudalism as an analogy for the dominant ideology they opposed.[22] Slavery was another popular point of comparison with the status-based employment contract, in criticism of the latter, until civil war and abolition, together with the disappearance of apprenticeship and other types of bound labor, somewhat paradoxically helped fuel a revival of the older, more favorable view.[23] Employment law, after all, sanctioned an enormous discretionary authority that was enjoyed by one party to the disadvantage of another. The courts largely resisted pressure from legislatures and social developments in the field of agricultural and industrial employment that threatened the interest of employers. Developments over time were far from linear, so that even as the partisans of equity might point to some hard-won victories, twenty-first-century American employment law is hardly free from the long shadow of status.

In a sense, the Romans had it both ways. Widespread resort to slavery meant that an unequal employment contract was hardly necessary to keep workers in thrall. One wonders whether the uncontested and uncontroversial presence of the former in that society might have facilitated a more egalitarian vision of the

---

dale" (2007) 10–11, on an 1854 English case (9 Ex. 341, 156 Eng. Rep. 145 [1854]). For a full discussion of what follows, see Gordon, "*Britton v. Turner*" (2007).

20. On marriage as both contract and status and on differential status within marriage in this period, see Stanley, *From Bondage to Contract* (1998) esp. 175–217; Cott, *Public Vows* (2000) esp. 11–13, 63–72, 160–63, 209–12; Dubler, "Wifely Behavior" (2000) 970–73; Hartog, *Man and Wife in America* (2000) esp. 11, 53–55, 113–14, 149–55, 261–62, 266.
21. 19 Mass. (2 Pick.) 267 (1824).
22. 6 N.H. 481 (1834).
23. Slavery, in its moral and ideological implications, at the same time imposed some limits on the powers of the employer, in that specific performance and the criminal law were unavailable as sanctions against the defaulting employee because of their association with "involuntary servitude": see Gordon, "*Britton v. Turner*" (2007) 199.

latter, leveling the playing field to a certain extent because the stakes were lower. The absence of social and economic pressures endemic to a modern democratic society in ferment might also have contributed to a broader self-confidence that comes to be reflected, for example, in the rules for *locatio conductio,* the contract for hire/lease. Employees hired under this agreement did low-status work, their jobs being by and large associated with the work of slaves (or, in less simplified terms, with work that was despised by members of the elite), so as to fall within the rubric of hire/lease rather than that of mandate, for example.[24] Contracts of various types might give rise to not just one or more legal obligations but a set of social ones as well, even to the point of creating dependency, sometimes in ways that might not be reasonably expected.[25] It would be quite another thing, of course, to claim that the rules themselves—in their application or, above all, in their design—reflect this imbalance in status, to the clear and consistent benefit of the socially superior.[26] Of course, the law routinely manages relations between persons of different statuses. The central question

24. For services regarded as (at least relatively) respectable, see Ulp. *D.* 50.13.1. For an extensive discussion of the distinction, see J. A. C. Thomas, "*Locatio* and *Operae*" (1961), arguing, on the basis of very uncertain evidence, for a positive revaluation of low-status work during the classical period of Roman law. On this particular point, see Y. Thomas, "Le corps de l'esclave" (2002) 230; Coppola Bisazza, *Cultura e potere* (1994) 251–90; More generally, see the literature cited in the following notes.

25. Contracts were typically concluded by individuals who were already embedded in a web of social relationships that bound them together, a fact that might not only affect the conclusion of the contract but be affected by it. Here is a vast subject. See just the different perspectives in Bürge, "Vertrag und personale Abhängigkeiten im Rom" (1980); Schermaier, "*Bona fides*"(2000) 79–80; Verboven, *Economy of Friends* (2002).

26. See, for example, Ulp. *D.* 19.2.19.9. One may usefully invoke the rules for the lease of rural and urban property in this regard. Recent work on agricultural lease law shows a degree of solicitude on the part of the legal authorities to safeguard the interests of subelite producers as against those of upper-class landlords: see Kehoe, *Law and the Rural Economy* (2007) 11, 99–109, 112–13, 123–29; see also Kehoe's essay in the present volume. The law of urban lease protected the interests of both (upper-class) landlords and tenants: see Frier, *Landlords and Tenants* (1980) 174–95; du Plessis, "Roman Concept of *Lex Contractus*" (2006) 83–84; du Plessis's essay in the present volume. This is no place for a discussion of the matter, but I wonder whether the category of "upper-class" might not be revised for this purpose to embrace the entrepreneurial middlemen who appear to have played a key role in the urban rental market: see the literature just cited, and more generally on the role of intermediaries in reducing transaction costs and in facilitating exchange, see Sanger, "Developing Markets" (2007) 143–44. We do not know much about the middlemen involved in the Roman urban rental market, but the scant evidence we have suggests subelite status at least for some: see Cic. *Att.* 12.32.2, with Frier, "Cicero's Management" (1978) 4–6; du Plessis, "Janus" (2006) 52.

is the extent to which a status differential is reflected in the rules themselves. But even if we were to determine that the Romans did not "need" a regime of contract law as explicitly embedded with considerations of status as did, evidently, nineteenth-century Americans—and especially if we decided that they did—there was still a life, beyond the law, where the rules mattered, even when not openly invoked or enforced.[27]

Status has played an important role in the modern American law of torts as well as that of contracts.[28] For many years, in virtually all U.S. jurisdictions, the duty of care owed by a property occupier to "strangers" on that property was defined according to the status-based categories of trespasser, licensee, and invitee (or social guest). This meant (typically, albeit with some confusion in some places) that no duty was owed to a social guest on one's property, to take one example, apart from that of refraining from the deliberate infliction of harm. This rule was traditionally understood in terms of the venerable distinction at common law between misfeasance and nonfeasance that essentially protected the principle of individual autonomy by refusing to enjoin no-risk interventions on bystanders. In other words, there was—and is—no duty at law to be a Good Samaritan. Another aspect of this legal tradition was to articulate a further distinction based on the status of the property in question, whether public or private, so that most states imposed a broad obligation of care in the context of business premises, a principle recognizable to any student of Roman delict familiar with the juristic case law on pit diggers and tree trimmers.[29]

The situation regarding occupiers of private property began to change through an important 1968 decision of the California Supreme Court, *Row-*

27. Further examination of this problem might profitably take a point of departure from the famous clash of opinions expressed by de Robertis in *Lavoro e lavoratori* (1963) and by Nörr in "Zur sozialen und rechtlichen Bewertung der freien Arbeit" (1965/2003). To my mind, Nörr has, by and large, the better argument; note in particular his emphasis on *locatio conductio* as a contract grounded in *bona fides* (434–35). See also Nörr, review of Visky; Martin, "*Servum Meum Mulionem Conduxisti*" (1990); Möller, *Freiheit und Schutz* (1990) 1–72; Wacke, "Faktische Arbeitsverhältnisse?" (1991); Bürge, "*Cibaria*" (1993); Möller, "Die Mercennarii" (1993); Coppola Bisazza, *Cultura e potere* (1994); Behrends, "Die Arbeit" (1999/2004); Y. Thomas, "Le corps de l'esclave" (2002).

28. Within the law of contracts, status also figures in capacity requirements. For a critique of the infancy law doctrine in U.S. law (under which minors lack the capacity to be bound under a contract), see DiMatteo, *Contract Theory* (1998) 102–7. For English law, see Cartwright, *Contract Law* (2007) 176–77.

29. Paul. *D.* 9.2.28; Mucius-Paul. *D.* 9.2.31.

land v. Christian.[30] The court abolished these status-based categories defining the duty of care of property occupiers, by declaring that the existing law was "contrary to our modern social mores and humanitarian values."[31] The decision reflects a doctrinal paradigm shift that was based on a consideration of the scope of endangerment. This was extended to other legal contexts through a fresh evaluation of the social adequacy of the existing rules, encouraged by changing social attitudes. Another motivating factor was evidently the widespread availability of inexpensive liability insurance for homeowners, which itself helped produce a reconfiguration of the relative importance of the punitive and compensatory goals of this tort regime. By 2002, nearly half of American jurisdictions had adopted the *Rowland* rule, though only partially in some cases, where the category of trespassers continued to be reserved for special treatment. This means, of course, that three decades after this decision, the older categories were far from extinct.[32]

In his contribution to this collection, Paul du Plessis, from the University of Edinburgh, takes on the subject of theory and practice in the Roman law of contracts. One major concern here is with the form in which the Roman rules have come down to us, or, to put it another way, the fruits of the almost ruthless efficiency of Justinian's compilers in severing virtually all texts from their original context. Du Plessis uses an example from the law of urban tenancy, namely, the landlord's hypothec (a form of real security in which neither ownership nor possession passes to the creditor) over the tenant's goods, to show how the state of the texts can obscure the very meaning of these rules, even as their abstract quality makes them more easily transferable to other contexts, even to other legal systems.

In my view, du Plessis is correct to argue that the recognition of an implied hypothec on certain items belonging to a tenant (those classed as *invecta et illata*), whatever the reasons for it, is not likely to be explained by a postulated ascension of the class of landlords and the triumph of their interests. For one thing, this implied term of the contract on urban lease is balanced by a tenant-friendly feature promoted by the classical juristic treatment of this contract, namely, the implied warranty of habitability.[33] For another, better explanations

30. 443 P.2d 561 (Cal.1968).

31. 443 P.2d 561, 568 (Cal.1968): quotation at Schwartz et al., *Prosser, Wade, and Schwartz's Torts* (2005) 504.

32. For what precedes, see Rabin, "*Rowland v. Christian*" (2003).

33. Frier, "Rental Market" (1977) 37; Frier, *Landlords and Tenants* (1980) 104–5, 164. For this

are available, even if, as du Plessis recognizes, absolute proof for them is lacking. One might borrow a line of analysis from the school of new institutional economics and argue that these implied features of the urban lease contract reduced transaction costs, not only for the parties, but for the courts as well, which were well placed to realize a savings in administrative expenditure through not being required to examine the presence or absence of these terms in the contract.[34] This suggests, in turn, that the true social interest served by these implied terms was more broadly conceived than the interests of the parties themselves, whether one or the other or both. Society in general had a stake in a smoothly functioning urban rental market. Insisting that, as a matter of course, landlords rented quarters fit for human habitation and that tenants paid the agreed-on price for the same represents essential aspects of this community interest. These implied terms were perhaps aimed precisely at facilitating such outcomes.

One might here adduce for comparison the implied warranty for defects in the sale of slaves (and livestock) developed by the curule aediles (the officials responsible for supervising the marketplaces for these objects) in their edict.[35] As is well known, this established liability for the disclosure of certain information about a slave on sale without regard to the seller's fault. No preponderance of the interest of one class over another is visible here, as has sometimes been claimed.[36] Instead, this implied warranty was designed to counter an asymmetry of information that privileged the seller and that thus threatened not just the integrity but the efficiency of the market.[37] In terms of its function, the aedilician edict bears comparison with a well-known trend in modern U.S. law, where the courts are often ready to supply terms that are not expressed by the parties to a contract but that the courts deem reasonable under the circum-

implied warranty in U.S. law, see Mostafa, "Implied Warranty of Habitability" (2007); For the same in English law, see Smith, *Atiyah's Introduction* (2005), 160–61; Cartwright, *Contract Law* (2007) 190.

34. On the role of transaction costs in shaping the design and application of legal rules, see the essay by Dennis Kehoe in the present volume.
35. See the recent monograph by Ortu, *Aiunt aediles* (2008).
36. This despite the deep social prejudice directed against slave dealers as a type, an attitude amply attested in the legal sources (and elsewhere): see Ortu, "*Qui venaliciariam vitam exercebat*" (2002); Bodel, "*Caveat Emptor*" (2005). At least some dealers seem to have had influential patrons, while respectable elements of society maintained an interest in the large-scale sale of slaves: see Bodel, "*Caveat Emptor,*" 183, 188–90, 195.
37. Frier and Kehoe, "Law and Economic Institutions" (2007) 119–21. See more generally, Solidoro Maruotti, *Gli obblighi* (2007).

stances. Such terms often derive from the Uniform Commercial Code, a piece of legislation that has been adopted—at times with variations—in virtually all American jurisdictions.[38] The UCC acts to derogate the common law in the sale of goods, as seen, perhaps most clearly, in its imposition of implied warranties of merchantability and of fitness for a particular purpose.[39]

Several of the contributors to this book deal either explicitly or implicitly with the creation of obligations, a subject that is studied by Ernest Metzger, from the University of Glasgow. In "Obligations in Classical Procedure," Metzger points to an interesting and often overlooked area of the law, namely, obligations created by public officials in the course of administering justice. He shows how such measures played out in the context of the Roman system of courts, as various benefits and drawbacks can be seen to emerge.

Metzger's essay may profitably be viewed in the context of what can be described as a revolution in our understanding of certain key aspects of civil procedure at Rome and elsewhere. This development has been spurred first by the appearance of what, in relative terms, is a massive amount of new evidence. This begins with the hyperfamous discovery of Gaius's *Institutes* in 1816. It continues with the uncovering of collections of tablets, originally made of wax, first at Herculaneum in the 1930s and next at Pompeii in 1959. Last, but not least, comes the unearthing of fragments of an inscription on bronze containing the *lex Irnitana* in 1981. Identifying this development as a "revolution" may seem exaggerated in light of this long arc of time, which has been prolonged through the periods necessary to produce reasonably reliable texts (that for the just-mentioned Pompeian archive appearing in 1999, for example)[40] and for the scholarship to absorb the new finds. But there is no other way to describe the difference between the state of our knowledge now and that of a couple of decades ago, let alone that at the start of the nineteenth century, when Roman civil procedure was an almost purely theoretical field. I am here obliged to cite Metzger's own book on pretrial bail and adjournment, a breakthrough in our understanding of these matters and a crystallization, in many respects, of a flurry of scholarship on the *lex Irnitana* in particular.[41]

---

38. Frier and White, *Modern Law of Contracts* (2012) 22–23, 322–23.

39. See the cases of *Vlases v. Montgomery Ward and Co.* (377 F.2d 846 [3rd Circ. 1967]) and *Massey-Ferguson, Inc. v. Utley* (439 S.W.2d. 57 [Ky. 1969]), with the discussion in Frier and White, *Modern Law of Contracts* (2012) 362–70.

40. Camodeca, *Tabulae Pompeianae Sulpiciorum* (1999).

41. Metzger, *Litigation in Roman Law* (2005).

There are, of course, a number of ways to explore the theme of the law of obligations and the interest of the state. In "Public Building Contracts in the Roman Republic," Michael Rainer, from the Universität Salzburg, shows how the censors, as part of their official duties, supervised a system of competitive bids for public contracts. By way of doing so, they generated a system of rules for such agreements that can be usefully compared with the law on private contracts. Important similarities and differences emerge from this comparison. The state had an interest in public contracts that is obvious in some respects and not so predictable in others.

From a modern perspective, certainly that of U.S. law, such a development is far from unexpected. We do find instances where government agreements are subject to the same rules and procedures that would apply between private persons or corporations. A well-known case is *Rockingham County v. Luten Bridge Co.* (1929).[42] The holding stands as a classic statement of the duty imposed on a nonbreaching party to mitigate damages when the other party has announced an intention to breach the contract. The situation of fact played out against a background of political divisiveness and partisan, even corrupt, interests that combined to raise serious questions about the fair and efficient operation of government as it performed its responsibilities, responsibilities that pertain to it alone. In its decision, the appeals court recognizes the nature of the public interest in its holding, but regardless of these contingencies, the result, especially as later enshrined in the *Restatement (Second) of the Law of Contracts* (1979), sets forth the duty of any contracting party to mitigate in certain circumstances.[43]

Elsewhere, the picture is very different, more closely resembling, in general terms, that described by Rainer for Rome. As a particular side effect of the state's role in contracts, one can cite the *vexata quaestio* of the right to recover for third-party beneficiaries of government subsidy programs.[44] But this role is at its most visible in the rules for federal contracts. There is a sizable body of law governing such agreements. This lays down, for example, first, that certain requirements be included in the contract and, second, that these requirements are still enforceable when they are omitted from the contract, which is not the rule in common law.[45] It also narrows considerably the choice of forum for

42. 35 F.2d 301 (4th Cir. 1929).

43. See the important discussion in Richman, "King of Rockingham County" (2007).

44. See Frier and White, *Modern Law of Contracts* (2012) 758–68.

45. Innis and Silberman, "Provisions and Issues Unique to Government Contracts" (2010) 173–75.

private parties to pursue claims against the state.[46] Examples could easily be multiplied.

Dennis Kehoe, from Tulane University, enters into the broad subject of the state interest in obligations in his discussion herein of the problem of Roman economic policy and the law of contracts. Kehoe examines whether Roman law, as developed and interpreted by the Roman jurists and the imperial government in responding to petitions, contributed positively to the Roman economy by facilitating economically productive contractual arrangements. To this end, he introduces a methodology that promises to encourage a better understanding of the economic implications of laws and legal institutions. The broad field of new institutional economics, he argues, provides ancient historians with new, helpful theoretical constructs with which to analyze the likely economic effects of some of the Roman government's legal policies. Kehoe takes a particular interest in exploring how this methodology can elucidate two important aspects of the Roman law of obligations especially significant for the economy, namely, the allocation of risk in agriculture and the contractual liability of property owners operating businesses through agents.

For a sense of what to expect, we may turn to the role that new institutional economics has played in the analysis of modern law. An almost paradigmatic clash of legal doctrinalism and economic functionalism can be found in the case of *ProCD, Inc. v. Zeidenberg* (1996), with the trial court opinion asserting the claims of the first and with the appeals court judgment representing a perspective drawn from the latter.[47] This clash plays out on the border between contract and property law, as the distinction between sale and license allows for the invocation of radically different sets of rules to govern the same transaction. The trial court attempts to maintain clear boundaries between different areas of the law. For the appellate court, the law of copyright allows the creation of new property rights through contracts, with the result that transaction costs are reduced through the elimination of wasteful bargaining.[48] The courts can play a considerable role in reducing transaction costs by establishing which

---

46. Bastianelli and Lange, "Litigating with the Federal Government" (2010) 451–52.
47. 908 F. Supp. 640 (W.D. Wis. 1996), rev'd and remanded, 86 F.3d 1447 (7th Cir. 1996).
48. I depend on the analysis of Epstein in "*ProCD v. Zeidenberg*" (2007), who cites (at 102) the discussion among the Roman jurists as to whether certain contracts are to be classified as sale or hire, for example, the long-term lease of municipal land where, as long as the rent continues to be paid, the property cannot be taken from the tenant or his or her heir (Gaius 3.145; see also Gaius 3.146–47; Gaius *D.* 19.2.2).

agreements or terms in agreements can be enforced. By the same token, they can hamper economic activity by defining certain activities as illegal, thereby raising those same costs.[49]

Adopting the perspective of another kind of modern methodology is the approach taken by Nikolaus Benke, from the Universität Wien, in his essay "Gender and the Roman Law of Obligations." Benke explores the implications of gender as a social construct in this area of the law. What this means in concrete terms is that a tension is easily discoverable between the law's broad claim to advance the principle of fairness and its willingness to accommodate a certain measure of "asymmetry" between women and men. Of course, if one believes, as the Romans did, that gender difference is grounded in nature rather than culture, this may not present the same problem for them as it does for us. Yet things were not quite as simple as that, as Professor Benke demonstrates.

In modern English and American law, the most obvious and persistent manifestation of gender in the law of obligations (and elsewhere) has been grounded in marital status.[50] The long-standing institution of coverture, in which a married woman's legal personality was "covered" by that of her husband, formed the basis of a long series of disabilities, the heft of which lay in the areas of property and succession, but which were felt in the area of obligations as well. Never-married women and widows (divorce has not been a factor in terms of numbers of women until relatively recently) by contrast enjoyed rights in private law similar to those enjoyed by adult males. They could make contracts for themselves, write wills, and dispose of property. A wife bound her husband by her agreements and created criminal and tort liability for him. Agreements between spouses were a nullity, and liability for tort committed against each other was a legal impossibility. The labor relation at the heart of the marital relationship resembled that between master and servant, a theme previously discussed.

Much of this picture changed over the course of the second half of the nineteenth century and the first years of the twentieth, but not all of it did. In important respects, coverture was modernized, not ended, in this period. Some

49. Sanger's "Developing Markets" (2007) has a useful discussion of these points in the context of the relatively recent and contested development of a market in surrogate motherhood.

50. In the civil law tradition, some Roman rules affecting women's status in private law persisted a long time. For example, the abrogation of the regime of the *SC Vellaeanum* was slow, late, and uneven: see Zimmermann, *Law of Obligations* (1996) 152. For what follows, see McGinn, *Widows and Patriarchy* (2008) esp. 55–59, 109–14, 128–39, with bibliography.

implications of gender in the context of marital status had to await developments in the late twentieth century for reform. In the field of obligations, we can point to a 1972 landmark Washington State case, *Freehe v. Freehe,* abrogating in its entirety the principle of interspousal immunity from liability in torts; this is now the majority rule.[51]

Both independently of and in conjunction with marital status, gender has played a role in defining the rights and duties of parties to certain contracts, namely, employment contracts. We see this most clearly perhaps in the case of actresses. In the nineteenth century, these women challenged Victorian notions about women's exalted role as the "angel in the house." There was no societal ideal, as with men, of women as free and independent employees. No other profession, however, offered women the same opportunities for personal autonomy and a high income. Female stage performers accordingly labored under a persistently adverse set of employment practices that centered on their (in)ability to abrogate a contract without unduly negative consequences. In the latter part of the nineteenth century, a rule crystallized that disallowed equitable orders to enforce performance(s) under a contract but that permitted them to prevent performance(s) under agreements with others.

The rule emerged from *Lumley v. Wagner* (1852), an English case with a checkered history.[52] At first, it was far from popular in American jurisdictions, because of associations drawn by some legal authorities with slavery—to the point of outright rejection, as in *Ford v. Jermon* (1865).[53] As we have seen above, after the abolition of slavery and the disappearance of other types of forced labor, the court-sanctioned expansion of employers' power over contract employees enjoyed a revival. Subsequent cases adopted the *Lumley* rule, whether going beyond the terms of a contract in order to subordinate women qua women (*Duff v. Russell* [1892])[54] or denying a mutuality of rights between the contracting parties to the advantage of the (male) theater owner (*Hoyt v. Fuller* [1892]).[55]

For a long period, married actresses had two masters, a theater owner and a

51. 81 Wn.2d 183 (1972), 500 P.2d 771. In completely abrogating the rule supporting interspousal immunity from liability in torts in Florida, the court in *Waite v. Waite* (618 So.2d 1360 [Fla. 1993]) noted that thirty-two other states had by then taken this step. Still others have opted for partial abrogation. See Schwartz et al., *Prosser, Wade, and Schwartz's Torts* (2005) 622–25.

52. DeG., M. & G. 604, 619, 42 Eng. Rep. 687, 693 (Ch. 1852).

53. 6 Phila. 6 (Dist. Ct. 1865).

54. 14 N.Y.S. 134 (Super. Ct. 1891), aff'd, 31 N.E. 622 (N.Y. 1892).

55. 19 N.Y.S. 962 (Super. Ct. 1892).

husband, both of whom enjoyed rights to control and profit from the actresses' labors. Male actors at first operated under a different, more equitable, set of contractual rules, though the stretching of legal logic reflected in the application and expansion of the *Lumley* holding eventually came to disadvantage them as well. The prevailing social construction of gender role did not favor independent women, casting them as suspect in terms of sexual behavior. Popular notions of actresses as prostitutes and adulteresses came to be embedded in the law. This had negative consequences not only for male performers in the long run but even for male theater owners, who seem to have been prepared to privilege their own economic interests no higher than the contemporary law system did its professed standards of logic and fairness.[56]

In "An Anthropology of Fault at Rome," Salvo Randazzo, from the Università di Bari, examines the ancient sources in light of yet another methodological perspective. He traces the anthropological aspects of the link between the concept of fault as violation of a rule and the effects of such a violation. An example is the assumption of responsibility, often realized through the infliction of a punishment, which Randazzo views through the connection that existed in archaic Rome between broad norms of social behavior, on the one hand, and religion and its precepts, on the other. In this context, religious formalism, a prototype for legal formalism, presents, in its rituals, a path for reaching a result that is itself a ritual, in its preset words and gestures. Through a process of consolidation around ritual and its defined system of shared practices, a moral community develops over time into a collective political entity.

We are here confronted with the fundamental question of the importation of social values into the law and of their subsequent articulation therein. This phenomenon is always in the background, at minimum, in discussions of fault in the law, not only in the context of the archaic period, but in that of the classical and later eras. Examination of the problem of fault in a modern context suggests that there was nothing inevitable about Roman ideas over legally defined standards of care. In other words, they are socially constructed, products of a particular society at a particular point in time.[57]

This hardly means that drawing comparisons has no utility. In a recent

---

56. For what precedes, see the essential account of VanderVelde, "Gendered Origins of the *Lumley* Doctrine" (2007).

57. One may compare the classic account by Oliver Wendell Holmes Jr. of the development of contractual liability for *assumpsit* out of a foundation in tort: see Holmes, *Common Law* (1881/2009) 247–60.

essay, Stephen Gilles lays out three possible approaches to the construction of such a standard governing the wrongful infliction of harm in the modern United States.[58] One is the so-called Hand Formula, advocated by Judge Learned Hand in an opinion offered in the case of *United States v. Carroll Towing Co.* (1947).[59] That Formula sought to define liability in terms of the relationship between probability (P), the injury or loss (L), and the burden of avoiding the latter (B). The Formula expresses the relationship in algebraic terms, so that liability results when B is less than P multiplied by L, or $B < PL$. Another approach is that of foreseeable danger, which assigns liability when the risk of loss is foreseeable, no matter how high the burden, and which refuses it when the danger is not foreseeable, no matter how low the cost. Finally, there is the community expectations standard, which rejects the cost-benefit analysis of the Hand Formula in favor of an evaluation based on prevailing expectations in the community about behaviors that best protect the safety of others. All three approaches attempt to provide content to the traditional common-law definition of negligence as the failure to do what a reasonable and prudent person (RPP) would do in similar circumstances. No matter what its precise content, the standard of the RPP continues to function as a "general coping mechanism" as the courts attempt to manage the entry of social values into decisions about tort liability.[60]

Though its implications are broader, Randazzo's essay focuses on developments in the archaic period. It sheds new light on a field that has long been dominated by two main approaches. The earlier one viewed the classical standards of care we know, broadly speaking, as the intentional and negligent infliction of harm—or harm inflicted through *dolus* or *culpa,* respectively—as arising from an original standard of strict liability based on a theory of causation. This has been largely displaced by a more recent approach based on a theory of fault, which sees classical *dolus* and *culpa* as developing out of an original standard based on a presumption of intent to cause loss and which is now the dominant thesis.[61] Randazzo's focus on religion enables him to use comparative material properly as a means of suggesting interpretative possibilities for understanding

58. Gilles, "*United States v. Carroll Towing Co.*" (2003).

59. 159 F.2d 169 (2d Cir.1947).

60. Henderson, "*MacPherson v. Buick Motor Co.*" (2003) 56–57 (quotation on 57).

61. The turning point was, in retrospect, a seminal article by Kaser, "Typisierter *Dolus*" (1962). See MacCormack, "Fault and Causation" (1981) esp. 97–101.

the (certainly meager, for this period) ancient evidence, and thus he avoids the pitfall of taking it as proof of such.[62]

Cosimo Cascione, from the Università di Napoli Federico II, introduces the subject of Roman delicts and criminal law in theory and practice. He explores the double nature of the Roman law repressing illicit acts as exemplified by the concepts of crime and delict, in part by examining the much-debated question of the origins of the idea of obligation, which, at least according to a number of scholars, can be located precisely in the area of delict. His attention is directed, beyond the rules themselves, at the manner in which illicit acts were repressed in practice, in terms of both standard and nonstandard procedure.

One of the most interesting aspects of Cascione's essay is his exploration of the frontier between delict and criminal law.[63] Given the similarity in subject matter and purpose, there are points where we might expect the boundary to be porous to the point of evanescent. So, in modern American law, the scholarship has noted the similarity between the regimes of tort and of criminal law regarding complicity, arguing that both are ultimately based on the principle of diminishing marginal returns.[64] This principle operates in another way as well. If a theory of causation has been devised for civil wrongs, why should this not apply also to criminal acts (and vice versa)?[65] Of course, in many cases, the same act can give rise to liability under both headings. The same was true at Rome, as the jurist Paul tells us.[66]

---

62. This pitfall is not, to my mind, entirely evaded by MacCormack, "Fault and Causation (1981), who, all the same, offers an interesting commentary on the anthropological evidence for cross-cultural constructions of fault.

63. Cf. Bauman, "Interface of Greek and Roman Law" (1996), postulating an original all-embracing conception of fault that extended to contracts, delicts, and crime, which he terms the *Urdelikt.* His focus is chiefly on Athenian law, with Roman material added mainly for purposes of comparison. For a comparison of the role of intent in modern criminal and contract law, see DiMatteo, *Contract Theory* (1998) 115–21. For an interesting comparative and historical discussion of the problem of transferred intent in criminal law, torts, and contracts, see Gordley, "Responsibility in Crime" (1998).

64. Katz, *Bad Acts and Guilty Minds* (1987) 253–54. This does not mean, of course, that it is always easy to distinguish between principal and accessory or that, when made, the distinction leads to different punishments (see ibid., 260).

65. See Katz, *Bad Acts and Guilty Minds* (1987) 243–46, discussing the famous torts case of *Palsgraf v. Long Island Railroad Company* (248 N.Y. 339, 162 N.E. 99 [1928]), in the context of criminal liability.

66. In some situations, the trial on delict occurs first, according to Paul. *D.* 48.1.4 (but see Harries,

At other points, the boundary seems rather better defined, as in the case of nonintentional homicide. Intentional "murder" without legal justification or excuse was famously punished by the *lex Cornelia de sicariis et veneficis* in 81 BCE, which functioned as a generalized murder statute before too long, if not from the start. Liability for nonintentional unjustified or unexcused killing was late in coming and restricted in scope, with a large measure of discretion left to public officials.[67] We find no strong evidence for a juristic elaboration of a theory of negligence in the criminal law, as with *damnum iniuria datum,* or of strict liability, as with *pauperies.*

Of course, such a development was hardly inevitable. The establishment of a strict liability regime under the *SC Silanianum,* passed in 10 CE and punishing a slave household for the killing of a master, is sufficient proof of this point.[68] If we look elsewhere in the criminal law for liability accruing to nonintentional acts, we find that the problem of negligence arises under the *lex Iulia de adulteriis* of ca. 17 BCE. In addition to adultery (*adulterium*—the offense of the respectable wife and her lover) and criminal fornication (*stuprum*—the offense of the respectable unmarried woman and her lover), the law punished criminal pimping (*lenocinium*—the offense of the husband complaisant in his wife's adultery). The statute identified two species of *lenocinium,* that of accepting payment before the fact for a wife's adultery (*quaestum facere*) and that of not divorcing a wife caught in the act of adultery (*deprehensam retinere*).[69]

Law and Crime [2007] 111–15, for complications in the field of *vis*). The point, at minimum, was to grant priority to the private interests of the victim and perhaps to avoid possible distortions arising from the interaction of criminal and civil proceedings. On such challenges in a modern context, see Schuck and Givelber, "*Tarasoff v. Regents of the University of California*" (2003) 109, a discussion of the two cases of *Tarasoff v. Regents* (529 P.2d 553 [Cal.1974] and 551 P.2d 334 [Cal.1976]).

67. See Wacke, "Fahrlässige Vergehen" (1979/2008); Höbenreich, "Verfolgung unbeabsichtigter Tötungen" (1990); Riggsby, *Crime and Community* (1999) 55, 78.

68. The *SC Silanianum* established a regime of strict liability that remained fairly robust over time, despite various limitations placed on it by juristic interpretation and imperial intervention. See, for example, Tac. *Ann.* 13.32.1, 14.42–45; Ulp. *D.* 29.5.1 pr., 17–33; Iustinianus C. 6.35.12 (532). Some see a turning point in a measure of Hadrian recorded in *HA Hadrianus* 18.11: see Wolf, *Das Senatusconsultum Silanianum* (1988) 12.

69. The jurists later grouped, as other species of *lenocinium,* the other accessory offenses identified by the statute, meaning accepting money after the fact (*pretium accipere*), furnishing a venue for the illegal act (*domum praebere*), and marrying a woman condemned for this crime (*damnatam ducere*). For a fuller discussion, including the passages discussed in the text that follows, see McGinn, *Prostitution, Sexuality, and the Law* (1998) 171–94, 220–45.

The moral significance that the jurists attributed to the two main (i.e., statutory) species of *lenocinium* is clear: . . . *nec enim mediocriter deliquit, qui lenocinium in uxore exercuit.*[70] Ulpian offers a definition of the nature of this offense that is, in some respects, strikingly expansive.

> Ulp. (4 *de adulteriis*) *D.* 48.5.30(29).4: *Quaestum autem ex adulterio uxoris facere videtur, qui quid accepit, ut adulteretur uxor: sive enim saepius sive semel accepit, non est eximendus: quaestum enim de adulterio uxoris facere proprie ille existimandus est, qui aliquid accepit, ut uxorem pateretur adulterari meretricio quodam genere. quod si patiatur uxorem delinquere non ob quaestum, sed neglegentiam vel culpam vel quandam patientiam vel nimiam credulitatem, extra legem positus videtur.*
>
> [(Ulpian in the fourth book *On Adulteries*) He is regarded as having made a profit out of the adultery of his wife who has received something in return for her committing adultery, and whether he has accepted something rather often or just once, he is not to be let off, since a man is rightly to be regarded as having made a profit from the adultery of his own wife if he has received something in return for allowing his wife to commit adultery in the manner of a prostitute. But if he tolerates the wrongdoing of his wife not for profit but out of negligence or carelessness or a certain kind of tolerance or over-credulousness, he is not regarded as being liable under the statute.]

Just as the law configures the adulteress as a prostitute, so it casts the complaisant husband as a pimp. The phrase *meretricio quodam genere* makes explicit the identification of adultery with prostitution, which is typically assumed in our sources. The wife plays the part of the prostitute who offers sex in return for payment; the husband is the pimp who arranges the sexual transaction and himself handles the money.

Criminal pimping under the *lex Iulia* is not precisely the same as the noncriminalized commercial variety, however. In one or two respects, Ulpian's definition here goes further. Only one sexual act makes a woman an adulteress, and only one monetary transaction makes her husband a pimp. This gives a broad meaning to the term *quaestus,* which more often refers to repeated or

70. Ulp. (4 *de adulteriis*) *D.* 48.5.30(29).3: ". . . for he has not committed a minor offense, who has practiced *lenocinium* with respect to his own wife."

customary behavior, the gain accruing from earning one's living. Moreover, the consideration evidently does not have to take monetary form, as would typically have been the case with noncriminal pimps, as far as we can tell. Some sort of transaction is required for there to be liability, though, as the last sentence makes clear. At this point in the text, the jurist's tone of moral condemnation is unmistakable, even as he denies liability under the law. Ulpian draws a line, in that a man's *neglegentia, culpa, patientia,* or *credulitas* does not give rise to criminal liability.

The tone of disapproval is even stronger in the following text:

> Ulp. (8 *disputationum*) *D.* 48.5.2.3: *Ceterum qui patitur uxorem suam delinquere matrimoniumque suum contemnit quique contaminationi non indignatur, poena adulteri ei*[71] *non infligitur.*
>
> [(Ulpian in the eighth book of *Disputations*) But he who allows his wife to offend and despises his marriage, and who is not angry at the defilement, is not inflicted with the punishment received by the adulterer.]

This text deals with the statutory species of *lenocinium* that I identify as *deprehensam retinere,* the refusal to divorce a wife caught in the act of adultery. A husband was not required to divorce a wife merely suspected of adultery.[72] But where was the line drawn? It seems clear that a husband guilty of negligence or the other qualities that the jurist criticizes in the context of a wife's adultery might be the object of severe social sanction. This does not mean, however, that he was liable under the adultery law. For this purpose, the statute may well have required that the act be committed *sciens dolo malo.* In any case, it is striking that, in the light of highly negative moral opinion, emperors and jurists refuse the introduction of a negligence-based standard even though one was certainly to hand. All of this suggests that the limitation on liability for nonintentional fault in the criminal law was neither casual nor unintended but was instead the product of a deliberate choice, where it occurred.

In "Roman Delicts and the Construction of Fault," Maria Floriana Cursi, from the Università di Teramo, connects important developments in the conception of fault in the Roman law of delicts with the rise, in the context of juris-

71. Mommsen reads "adulteri ei" instead of the "adulterum" in the manuscript.

72. See (Septimius) Severus, Antoninus (Caracalla) *C.* 9.9.2 (199).

tic discussion about *damnum iniuria datum* (the wrongful infliction of harm to another's property), of an emphasis on compensation for damages. This discussion took place against the background of what she views as the original function of the remedy provided under statute, the Aquilian *actio,* that of punishing the intentional infliction of harm.[73] Cursi argues that the extension of Aquilian liability to embrace negligence was grounded in the progressive emergence of an interest, on the part of the Roman slaveholding society, in the strictly material aspect of legally protected property, of which the "reification" of slaves is a prominent example. She advances her argument through an examination of the rules regarding the remedy for objects "poured out or thrown down," the *actio de effusis vel deiectis.*

Whatever view one takes of the original duty of care under the *lex Aquilia* or its date,[74] there can be no doubt that the details of this law as we know it in the classical period of Roman law depend greatly on the configuration in social, economic, and legal terms of the slave as property. The slave was in no way a

73. It is perhaps worth signaling for the reader that the terms *subjective* and *objective* can be used in different ways in the context of discussions of liability for harm to another's property. Continental legal scholarship tends to use them to distinguish what might be described broadly as forms of strict liability (*objective*) from those based on fault (*subjective*), while common-law discourse generally prefers to employ them to draw distinctions among different conceptions of fault-based liability, at bottom, that is, between one based on an objective consideration, such as how a reasonable and prudent person ought to behave, and one based on a subjective evaluation of an individual's capabilities, mental state, or behavior. See, for example, the various discussions in Holmes, *Common Law* (1881/2009) 98–103, 121, 146–47, 292–93 (he uses the term *external* more than *objective*); Lawson, *Negligence in the Civil Law* (1950) 14–20, 36–50; Talamanca, "Colpa civile" (1960); Lucrezi, "La responsabilità aquiliana" (2002). For a partial exception, see Ankum, "La responsabilità contrattuale" (2004) 143–44; more recently, Corbino, "Antigiuridicità" (2009) 88.

74. Cursi argues that the *lex Aquilia* itself might have been passed at any point between the early fourth and the early second centuries BCE and that its third chapter represents a later addition, while many scholars hold to the traditional date of ca. 287 BCE (even as they acknowledge its uncertainty) and believe that the law from the start contained all three chapters reported by the sources. As to the original duty of care under this statute, a more widely held view is that liability originally arose for acts committed "without legal right," meaning that the defendant had inflicted loss on the plaintiff without a valid legal excuse or justification: only later did liability come to be defined in terms of "wrongfulness," meaning the intentional or negligent infliction of harm. See Cursi, *Iniuria cum damno* (2002) 147–219, 271–84, with previous literature; Miglietta, review of Cursi (2002); Valditara, *Damnum iniuria datum* (2005) 5–14, 33–36; Franciosi, "Il problema delle origini del plebiscito Aquilio" (2007); Corbino, *Il danno qualificato* (2008) 41–71, 159–76; Corbino, "Antigiuridicità" (2009); Valditara, "Dalla *iniuria* alla *culpa*" (2009); Cursi, *Danno* (2010) 21–82; Cursi, "*Occidere Iniuria*?" (2011) .

new product, of course,[75] but was a complex one, rightly regarded as the most complex object of sale in the ancient world.[76] The increased emphasis over time on the slave's status as a thing was sufficient to encourage significant changes in the treatment of slaves under various headings of the law, such as the implied warranties on the sale of slaves found in the aedilician edict already mentioned.[77] In the mid- to late Republic, slaves flooded the markets as the result of Rome's wars of conquest and were merchandised on a scale not seen before.[78] These developments raised a challenge not only for the buyers of slaves, who were in a weaker position than ever before to acquire good information on the provenance, character, and health of slaves,[79] but also for the courts, which were faced with a potentially large number of unmanageable lawsuits, unmanageable precisely because of a relative deficit of information on their part.

Similar developments can perhaps be traced in other parts of the law, such as, again, in the aedilician edict, but this time with the regime of strict liability for damage caused under certain circumstances by wild animals that were not native to Roman Italy. These were perhaps more like a "new" product than slaves, after their introduction there at a date that is strictly unknown but certainly by the third century.[80] One can make a similar argument for the stan-

---

75. Though the advent of the rules for *damnum iniuria datum* reflects a fairly mature stage of this development, caution is necessary in that there is plenty of evidence as early as the Twelve Tables for the conception of slave as property and for the status of Rome as a slave society: see Bradley, *Slavery and Society at Rome* (1994) 16–19.

76. So Kehoe and Frier, "Law and Economic Institutions" (2007) 119–20.

77. Broadly similar rules existed for the sale in the marketplace of slaves in classical Athens and other Greek cities: see Jakab, *Praedicere und Cavere beim Marktkauf* (1997) 53–96. At Rome, the contractual protections afforded by the *ius civile* in the earliest period provided only for damages, not for rescission of the agreement: see Ortu, *Aiunt aediles* (2008) 1–39. For the protections afforded, thanks to the influence of the principle of "good faith," under the *actio empti*, see Schermaier, "*Bona Fides*" (2000) 85.

78. The aedilician regime was known to Plautus, as evidenced even in some of his earlier plays, and so dates to the very end of the third century at the latest: see Ortu, *Aiunt aediles* (2008) 52–63, 297.

79. Kehoe and Frier ("Law and Economic Institutions" [2007] 120) emphasize the challenge that the principle of "adverse selection" represents to buyers and, ultimately, to the market itself. As suspicious buyers demand deep discounts, sellers of sound slaves cannot realize the prices they seek and so withdraw, resulting in market failure. Kehoe and Frier cite the classic study of adverse selection by Akerlof, "Market for 'Lemons'" (1970).

80. Some think the aediles acted initially to remedy loss caused by dogs and boars (or pigs): see Jackson, "Liability for Animals" (1978) 132–33; Zimmermann, *Law of Obligations* (1996) 1106. This explanation seems less likely to me but does not affect the main point. Animals

dard of strict liability for damage caused by—at minimum—domestic animals, strictly quadrupeds, under the delict of *pauperies,* if we accept that this standard was not original to its introduction in the Twelve Tables but a later development.[81] These animals were, like slaves, not "new," but the conditions of their use in the business of agriculture in the mid-Republic had perhaps sufficiently been altered to encourage a change in legal approach in or subsequent to this period.[82]

The position in classical law with regard to the three major delicts—*furtum, iniuria,* and *damnum iniuria datum*—was that no liability accrued without fault, so that these "anomalies" beg for an explanation.[83] A similar principle holds in modern U.S. law, where, in fact, the vast majority of tort cases involve automobile accidents, the province par excellence of liability for negligence.[84]

---

such as elephants were used for display earlier than some modern authors assume, meaning by the early third century, and the practice became common by the beginning of the second century: see Beacham, *Spectacle Entertainments* (1999) 18. Even if concern with dogs and pigs/boars came first, it is likely that the aediles responded to new developments in their transportation and marketing: see Jackson, "Liability for Animals," 133. The standard introduced by the aediles in this regard is usually understood to have been one of strict liability, but there is room to argue that it was instead a negligence-based type known to modern U.S. law as *res ipsa loquitur,* in which the harm suffered by the plaintiff is deemed to have been impossible in ordinary circumstances but for the negligence of the defendant.

81. Many scholars believe that liability was (at least) originally based on attribution of fault to the animal, so that the recognition of a standard of strict liability was far from inevitable: see Zimmermann, *Law of Obligations* (1996) 1096–1100; Polojac, *Actio de Pauperie* (2003) 5–16, 37, 52–54, 92, 206–13. For a different view, see Giangrieco Pessi, *Ricerche sull'actio de pauperie* (1995) 14–36. Liability was limited by the possibility of making noxal surrender of the offending animal. Some scholars believe that strict liability came to be conditioned, at some point, in classical law by the requirement that the harm be inflicted in a manner contrary to the nature of the animal or its species (*contra naturam*), while others regard this as an innovation of the Byzantines: see Giangrieco Pessi, *Ricerche sull'actio de pauperie,* 1–83; Zimmermann, *Law of Obligations,* 1102–4; Polojac, *Actio de Pauperie,* 44–54.

82. I refer to the development of large-scale agriculture in this period, which had implications for the economic and legal status of both slaves and domestic animals. The bibliography is enormous; see Rosenstein, *Rome at War* (2004) esp. 3–25, for a recent discussion. The treatment at law of such animals as a "new product" is not inevitable, especially given the deployment of this category in the construction of a strict liability standard in modern law, discussed in the text that follows.

83. For other delicts and quasi delicts where the duty of care is identified as strict liability, see Zimmerman, *Law of Obligations* (1996) 1095–1143; see also Cursi's essay in the present volume.

84. Abraham, "*Rylands v. Fletcher*" (2003) 208. For a perspective from English law, see Cane, "Retribution" (1998) esp. 150.

The exceptions, where a standard of strict liability applies, tend to cluster in a few areas, such as abnormally dangerous activities, defective products, and (perhaps—this is controversial) vicarious liability for one's employees.[85]

It is interesting to note that the landmark case establishing strict liability regarding ultrahazardous activities, *Rylands v. Fletcher* (1866, 1868),[86] whose facts concern a reservoir flooding a coal mine, turns on a long-standing rule that may represent a medieval reception of the Roman regime for *pauperies*.[87] In the opinion of the appeals court, represented by Justice Colin Blackburn, there is language strongly reminiscent of the rules for the Roman law of delicts.[88]

> We think that the true rule of law is that the person who for his own purposes brings on his lands and collects and keeps there any thing likely to do mischief if it escapes, must keep it in at his peril, and if he does not do so, is prima facie answerable for all the damage which is the natural consequence of its escape . . . The person whose grass or corn is eaten down by the escaping cattle of his neighbor, or whose mine is flooded by the water from his neighbor's reservoir, or whose cellar is invaded by the filth of his neighbor's privy, or whose habitation is made unhealthy by the fumes and noisome vapors of his neighbor's alkali works, is damnified without any fault of his own; and it seems but reasonable and just that the neighbor, who has brought something on his own property which was not naturally there, harmless to others so long as it is con-

85. Sugarman, "*Vincent v. Lake Erie Transportation Co.*" (2003) 283.

86. 3 H. & C. 774 (Exch. 1865), rev'd, L.R. 1 Exch. 265 (Exch.Ch. 1866), rev'd, L.R. 3 H.L. 330 (1868).

87. The origins of the English regime are strictly unknown but date back to " . . . local courts from the earliest date after the Conquest of which we have record" (Williams, *Liability for Animals* [1939] 127).

88. See Ulp. *D.* 9.1.1 pr.–3, which gives strict liability (with noxal surrender possible) for damage caused by quadrupeds to another's property. Paul. *D.* 9.1.4 allows an analogous action for loss caused by nonquadrupeds; by Gaius's day, recovery was possible for bodily harm to free persons, though only for medical expenses and lost wages, not for intrinsic value (*D.* 9.1.3). In both legal systems, cattle seem to have assumed a sort of paradigmatic quality with respect to the application of the relevant rules. In a part of the modern case not quoted here, Justice Blackburn refuses liability for injury to persons, except where the owner knew the animal was vicious; this seems, albeit imprecisely, to echo the rules for *pauperies* that allow for default to the negligence-based regime of *damnum iniuria datum* in such circumstances (Servius-Ulp. *D.* 9.1.1.4–6). Of course, the infliction of harm by such animals might be ascribed to another's fault in some circumstances, such as when they were provoked (Ulp. *D.* 9.1.1.6–7; Mucius-Ulp. *D.* 9.1.1.11).

> fined to his own property, but which he knows to be mischievous if it gets on his neighbor's, should be obliged to make good the damage which ensues if he does not succeed in confining it to his own property . . . The case that has most commonly occurred and which is most frequently to be found in the books, is as to the obligation of the owner of cattle which he has brought on his land to prevent their escaping and doing mischief. The law as to them seems to be perfectly settled from early times; the owner must keep them in at his peril, or he will be answerable for the natural consequences of their escape . . . .[89]

As for defective products, modern U.S. law has seen a development from an initial reluctance to impose liability for those sold to consumers through third parties (on the theory of privity of contract), through a willingness to impose the standard known as *res ipsa loquitur,* to recognition of the standard of strict liability. The breakthrough case for the imposition of liability was *MacPherson v. Buick Motor Co.* (1916), in which Justice Benjamin Cardozo, writing for the majority, held that a manufacturer had a duty of care independent of the contract with a retailer.[90] Though Cardozo does not invoke the term *res ipsa loquitur,* he insists, construing the facts of the case perhaps a tad unrealistically, that the loss could not ordinarily have occurred without the manufacturer's negligence.[91] This was the standard received and applied by the majority of the California court some years later in a case involving an exploding soda bottle, *Escola v. Coca Cola Bottling Co.* (1944).[92] In a concurring opinion, however, Justice Roger Traynor argued instead that recovery should be based on a theory of strict liabil-

---

89. Schwartz et al., *Prosser, Wade, and Schwartz's Torts* (2005) 694–95. The defendants prevailed at trial, in the Exchequer, whose holding was reversed on appeal to Blackburn and the Exchequer Chamber, who were, in turn, upheld upon defendants' appeal to the House of Lords: see ibid., 692–99 (quotation in text on 694–95) . For developments regarding the definition of liability under *Rylands* in English law (where the standard of strict liability has been qualified) and in Australian law (which has rejected strict liability), see Schwartz, "*Rylands v. Fletcher*" (1998); Weir, "Staggering March of Negligence" (1998) 107–8; Abraham, "*Rylands v. Fletcher*" (2003) 218–19.
90. 111 N.E. 1050 (N.Y.1916).
91. On Cardozo's reading of the facts in *MacPherson,* see Henderson, "*MacPherson v. Buick Motor Co.*" (2003). Henderson's ambivalence (see ibid., 66–67) over the nature of the duty and thus the standard of liability imposed (*res ipsa* versus strict liability) is belied, to my mind, by the language of the opinion (for which see also Schwartz et al., *Prosser, Wade, and Schwartz's Torts* [2005] 409–11). For perspectives on this problem drawn from English law, see Smith, *Atiyah's Introduction* (2005) 352–74; Cartwright, *Contract Law* (2007) 220.
92. 150 P.2d 436 (Cal.1944) (No. S.F. 16951).

ity arising out of an implied warranty of merchantability.[93] Traynor's view won out over time, eventually being adopted in California and other jurisdictions (in forty-one states by 1976) and by the *Restatement (Second) of Torts* (1965).

Controversy exists as to whether the principle of vicarious liability encapsulated in the tag *respondeat superior* imposes a regime of strict liability or not.[94] Perhaps a more elegant way of looking at it is to say that it does in one respect (liability accrues to the higher-up even without fault) and does not in another (liability cannot accrue without the subordinate's negligence).[95] This analysis can be supported with reference to recent cases. In *Bussard v. Minimed, Inc.* (2003), for example, the court held that the employee's negligence while driving did not relieve the employer from liability.[96] The employer need not have acted negligently to be liable. In fact, it has long been a rule that the employer cannot escape liability by imposing safety rules or providing safety instructions.[97]

A common theme visible in the analysis of strict liability is the link between asymmetry of information and the distribution of costs. One argument for the imposition of this standard has been that the defendant—whether employer, manufacturer, or protagonist in an ultrahazardous activity—is typically in a better position to assess the risk, to know the costs and means of mitigation, and to take appropriate action.[98] It has been observed that a plaintiff is often at a disadvantage in proving negligence in such cases and that courts have an interest in avoiding the multiplication of unmanageable cases.[99] Regarding *respondeat superior*, the *Bussard* court bluntly held that "[t]he doctrine's animating principle is that a business should absorb the costs its undertakings impose on

93. See Geistfeld, "*Escola v. Coca Cola Bottling Co.*" (2003) on this and on what immediately follows.

94. Common-law authorities typically translate the Latin tag as "look to the person higher up" (*vel sim.*). A slightly more helpful version might be "the person higher up shall be liable." On the doctrine as found in the Roman and English traditions, among others, see Wicke, *Respondeat Superior* (2000). For certain aspects, see, more recently, Fercia, *La responsabilità per fatto di ausiliari* (2008).

95. Schwartz et al., *Prosser, Wade, and Schwartz's Torts* (2005) 660–61.

96. 129 Cal.Rptr.2d 675 (2003), 105 Cal.App.4th 798.

97. Schwartz et al., *Prosser, Wade, and Schwartz's Torts* (2005) 666.

98. See Abraham, "*Rylands v. Fletcher*" (2003) 222; Geistfeld, "*Escola v. Coca Cola Bottling Co.*"(2003) 245, 250; *Bussard v. Minimed,* 129 Cal.Rptr.2d 675 (2003), 105 Cal.App.4th 798, 804.

99. For the first point, see Gilles, "*United States v. Carroll Towing Co.*" (2003) 28–30; Geistfeld, "*Escola v. Coca Cola Bottling Co.*" (2003) 234. For the second, see Henderson, "*MacPherson v. Buick Motor Co.*" (2003) 52–54, 63.

others."[100] The idea is that these costs are better and more easily distributed by having them reflected in the costs charged consumers in general. At the same time, the defendant effectively becomes the insurer of the plaintiff.[101] Some or all of these issues have great potential relevance for our understanding of the Roman law of delict, and it is highly likely that an analysis based on transaction costs would have much to contribute as well.

Bernard Stolte, from the Universiteit Groningen and until recently the director of the Koninklijk Nederlands Instituut te Rome, herein addresses the Byzantine law of obligations. He begins by defining what is meant by Byzantine law, largely by describing a double transformation that took place in the age of Justinian. Stolte examines the development of the Byzantine law of contractual obligations by focusing on *nuda pacta*, "bare pacts," meaning informal agreements that, under classical law, could give rise only to an affirmative defense as a remedy.

The central issue concerns the distinction between those promises that are legally enforceable and those that are not. In U.S. law, a case often introduced to teach students the basis for this distinction is that of *Hamer v. Sidway* (1891), in which an uncle promises to give his fifteen-year-old nephew five thousand dollars on his twenty-first birthday if the latter refrains from smoking, drinking, and playing cards or billiards for money until then.[102] Nineteenth-century formalists saw the distinction turn on the presence or absence of consideration: a bargained-for exchange generated an enforceable obligation, and that was that. Twentieth-century Legal Realists, more attuned to the operation of law in its social context, looked for a serious promise subject to a condition and for reliance by the other party on that promise. A twenty-first-century critic finds that, while the doctrines of bargained-for exchange and reliance on a promise may work in the vast majority of cases, the facts of *Hamer v. Sidway* suggest the difficulty of reconciling anomalous situations to formal legal rules.[103]

A rights-based conception of law might work poorly in a family setting, for one thing. A case often cited together with *Hamer* is *Ricketts v. Scothorn* (1898).[104] In the latter, a grandfather gives his granddaughter a demand note in the hope that the interest payments on the note will enable her to quit her (wretched) job. She does quit, and she then successfully sues her grandfather's

100. 129 Cal.Rptr.2d 675 (2003), 105 Cal.App.4th 798, 803.

101. See Geistfeld, "*Escola v. Coca Cola Bottling Co.*" (2003) 252–58.

102. 124 N.Y. 538, 27 N.E. 256 (1891).

103. For all of this, see Baird, "Reconstructing Contracts" (2007), on which I rely here.

104. 77 N.W. 365 (Neb. 1898).

estate to enforce the promised gift. One scholar has characterized *Hamer* and *Ricketts* as "casebook curiosities," noting that both holdings arise from cases where the litigation was not between the promisee and promisor but between the promisee and the promisor's executor; in other words, neither promisor attempted to resist enforcement.[105] Granted, different ways of looking at these cases and the legal issues behind them are possible.[106] In any case, perhaps the most striking result lies in the fact that they illustrate how easily mores can be seen to enter the law, in contexts where legal logic is threatened, compromised, or even overturned.

Bibliography

Abraham, R. S. "*Rylands v. Fletcher:* Tort Law's Conscience." In *Torts Stories,* ed. R. L. Rabin and S. D. Sugarman, 207–28. New York: Foundation Press, 2003.

Akerlof, G. A. "The Market for 'Lemons': Quality Uncertainty and the Market Mechanism." *Quarterly Journal of Economics* 84.3 (1970): 488–500.

Ankum, A. "La responsabilità contrattuale nel diritto romano classico e nel diritto giustinianeo." In *Diritto romano e terzo millennio: Radici e prospettive dell'esperienza giuridica contemporanea (Relazioni del convegno internazionale di diritto romano—Copanello 3–7 giugno 2000),* ed. F. Milazzo, 135–52. Naples: Edizioni Scientifiche Italiane, 2004.

Atiyah, P. S. *Promises, Morals, and Law.* Oxford: Oxford University Press, 1981.

Baird, D. G., ed. *Contracts Stories.* New York: Foundation Press, 2007.

Baird, D. G. "Reconstructing Contracts: *Hamer v. Sidway.*" In *Contracts Stories,* ed. D. G. Baird, 160–85. New York: Foundation Press, 2007.

Barnett, R. E., ed. *Perspectives on Contract Law.* 3rd ed. New York: Aspen, 2005.

Bastianelli, A. L., and L. A. Lange. "Litigating with the Federal Government." In *Federal Government Construction Contracts,* ed. M. A. Branca et al., 451–76. 2nd ed. Chicago: American Bar Association, 2010.

Bauman, R. A. "The Interface of Greek and Roman Law: Contract, Delict, and Crime." *Revue internationale des droits de l'antiquité,* 3rd ser., 43 (1996): 39–62.

Beacham, R. C. *Spectacle Entertainments of Early Imperial Rome.* New Haven, CT: Yale University Press, 1999.

Behrends, O. "Die Arbeit im römischen Recht: Zur Frage ihrer rechtlichen Einordnung und moralischen Bewertung." In *Okko Behrends: Institut und Prinzip,* ed.

105. Chirelstein, *Concepts and Case Analysis* (2006) 20.

106. See the discussion in Trebilcock, *Limits of Freedom of Contract* (1993) 177–81. On the issues of reliance versus benefits to promisor, see especially Atiyah, *Promises, Morals, and Law* (1981) 212–15.

M. Avenarius, R. Meyer-Pritzel, and C. Möller, 2: 723–70. Göttingen: Wallstein Verlag, 2004. Originally published in *Le travail: Recherches historiques*, ed. J. Annequin et al., 115–62. Besançon: Presses Universitaires Franc-Comtoises, 1999.

Behrends, O. "Rudolf von Jehring mediatore fra diritto romano e diritto moderno in un momento di grande rottura culturale." *Rivista di Diritto Romano* 3 (2003): 1–19.

Birks, P. "Obligations: One Tier or Two?" In P. G. Stein and A. D. E. Lewis, eds., *Studies in Justinian's Institutes in Memory of J. A. C. Thomas*, 18–38. London: Sweet and Maxwell, 1983.

Biscardi, A. "Some Critical Remarks on the Roman Law of Obligations." *Scripta Classica Israelica* 4 (1978): 106–21.

Bodel, J. "*Caveat Emptor:* Towards a Study of Roman Slave-Traders." *Journal of Roman Archaeology* 18.1 (2005): 181–95.

Bradley, K. *Slavery and Society at Rome.* Cambridge: Cambridge University Press, 1994.

Branca, M. A., et al., eds. *Federal Government Construction Contracts.* 2nd ed. Chicago: American Bar Association, 2010.

Bürge, A. "*Cibaria*: Indiz für die soziale Stellung des römischen Arbeitnehmers?" In *Ars boni et aequi. Festschrift für Wolfgang Waldstein zum 65. Geburtstag*, ed. M. J. Schermaier und Z. Végh, 63–78. Stuttgart: Franz Steiner Verlag, 1993.

Bürge, A. "Vertrag und personale Abhängigkeiten im Rom der späten Republik und der frühen Kaiserzeit." *Zeitschrift der Savigny-Stiftung für Rechtsgeschichte (Romanistische Abteilung)* 97 (1980): 105–56.

Camodeca, G. *Tabulae Pompeianae Sulpiciorum: Edizione critica dell'archivio puteolano dei Sulpicii.* 2 vols. Rome: Edizioni Quasar, 1999.

Cane, P. "Retribution, Proportionality, and Moral Luck in Tort Law." In *The Law of Obligations: Essays in Celebration of John Fleming*, ed. P. Cane and J. Stapleton, 141–73. Oxford: Oxford University Press, 1998.

Cane, P., and J. Stapleton, eds. *The Law of Obligations: Essays in Celebration of John Fleming.* Oxford: Oxford University Press, 1998.

Cannata, C. A. "Contratto e causa nel diritto romano." In *Le dottrine del contratto nella giurisprudenza romana,* ed. A. Burdese, 187–220. Padua: CEDAM, 2006. Originally published in *Causa e contratto nella prospettiva storico-comparatistica: Il congresso internazionale Aristec, Palermo-Trapani 7–10 giugno 1995*, ed. L. Vacca (Turin: Giappichelli Editore, 1997), 35–62.

Capogrossi Colognesi, L. "Diritto romano, diritti europei: Storia della scienza giuridica e la didattica nelle nostre università." *Bullettino dell'Istituto di Diritto Romano,* 3rd ser., 40–41 (1998–99 [2005]): 743–54.

Cartwright, J. *Contract Law: An Introduction to the English Law of Contract for the Civil Lawyer.* Oxford: Hart, 2007.

Cascione, C. *Consensus: Problemi di origine, tutela processuale, prospettive sistematiche.* Naples: Editoriale Scientifica, 2003.

Chirelstein, M. A. *Concepts and Case Analysis in the Law of Contracts.* 5th ed. New York: Foundation Press, 2006.

Coppola Bisazza, G. *Cultura e potere: Il lavoro intellettuale nel mondo romano.* Milan: Giuffrè Editore, 1994.

Corbino, A. "Antigiuridicità e colpevolezza nella previsione del plebiscito aquiliano." *Studia et Documenta Historiae et Iuris* 75 (2009): 77–111.

Corbino, A. *Il danno qualificato e la lex Aquilia: Corso di diritto romano.* 2nd ed. Padua: CEDAM, 2008.

Cott, N. F. *Public Vows: A History of Marriage and the Nation.* Cambridge, MA: Harvard University Press, 2000.

Cursi, M.F. *Danno e responsabilità extracontrattuale nella storia del diritto privato.* Naples: Jovene, 2010.

Cursi, M. F. *Iniuria cum damno: Antigiuridicità e colpevolezza nella storia del danno aquiliano.* Milan: Giuffrè Editore, 2002.

Cursi, M. F. "What Did *Occidere Iniuria* in the *Lex Aquilia* Actually Mean?" *Roman Legal Tradition* 7 (2011): 16–29.

Danzig, R. "*Hadley v. Baxendale:* A Study in the Industrialization of the Law." In *Contracts Stories,* ed. D. G. Baird, 1–28. New York: Foundation Press, 2007.

de Robertis, F. M. *Lavoro e lavoratori nel mondo romano.* Bari: Adriatica Editrice, 1963.

de Zulueta, F. *The "Institutes" of Gaius.* 2 vols. Oxford: Oxford University Press, 1946–53.

DiMatteo, L. A. *Contract Theory: The Evolution of Contractual Intent.* East Lansing: Michigan State University Press, 1998.

Dubler, A. R. "Wifely Behavior: A Legal History of Acting Married." *Columbia Law Review* 100.4 (2000): 957–1021.

du Plessis, P. *Borkowski's Textbook on Roman Law.* 4th ed. Oxford: Oxford University Press, 2010.

du Plessis, P. "Janus in the Roman Law of Urban Lease." *Historia* 55.1 (2006): 48–63.

du Plessis, P. "The Roman Concept of *Lex Contractus.*" *Roman Legal Tradition* 3 (2006): 79–94.

Epstein, R. A. "*ProCD v. Zeidenberg*: Do Doctrine and Function Mix?" In *Contracts Stories,* ed. D. G. Baird, 94–126. New York: Foundation Press, 2007.

Falcone, G. "Sistematiche gaiane e definizione di *obligatio.*" In Obligatio-*obbligazione: Un confronto interdisciplinare (Atti del convegno di Roma, 23–24 Settembre 2010),* ed. L. Capogrossi Colognesi and M. F. Cursi, 17–51. Naples: Jovene Editore, 2011.

Fercia, R. *La responsabilità per fatto di ausiliari nel diritto romano.* Padua: CEDAM, 2008.

Fiori, R. *La definizione della locatio conductio: Giurisprudenza romana e tradizione romanistica.* Naples: Jovene Editore, 1999.

Franciosi, A. "Il problema delle origini del plebiscito Aquilio: Una messa a punto in tema di datazione." In *Philia: Scritti per Gennaro Franciosi,* ed. F. M. d'Ippolito, 2:935–83. Naples: Satura Editrice, 2007.

Friedman, L. M. *Private Lives: Families, Individuals, and the Law.* Cambridge, MA: Harvard University Press, 2004.

Frier, B.W. "Cicero's Management of His Urban Properties." *Classical Journal* 74.1 (1978–1979): 1–6.

Frier, B. W. *Landlords and Tenants in Imperial Rome.* Princeton: Princeton University Press, 1980.

Frier, B. W. "The Rental Market in Early Imperial Rome." *Journal of Roman Studies* 67 (1977): 27–37.

Frier, B. W. "Roman Law's Descent into History." *Journal of Roman Archaeology* 13.2 (2000): 446–48.

Frier, B. W., and D. P. Kehoe. "Law and Economic Institutions." In *The Cambridge Economic History of the Greco-Roman World,* ed. W. Scheidel, I. Morris, and R. Saller, 113–43. Cambridge: Cambridge University Press, 2007.

Frier, B. W., and J. J. White. *The Modern Law of Contracts.* 3rd ed. St. Paul, MN: Thomson/West, 2012.

Geistfeld, M. "*Escola v. Coca Cola Bottling Co.*: Strict Products Liability Unbound." In *Torts Stories,* ed. R. L. Rabin and S. D. Sugarman, 229–58. New York: Foundation Press, 2003.

Giachi, C., E. Stolfi, and F. Tamburi. "In margine alla discussione di un manuale di diritto privato romano." *Studia et Documenta Historiae et Iuris* 70 (2004): 409–39.

Giangrieco Pessi, M. V. *Ricerche sull'actio de pauperie dalle XII Tavole ad Ulpiano.* Naples: Jovene Editore, 1995.

Gilles, S. G. "*United States v. Carroll Towing Co.*: The Hand Formula's Home Port." In *Torts Stories,* ed. R. L. Rabin and S. D. Sugarman, 11–39. New York: Foundation Press, 2003.

Gilmore, G. *The Death of Contract.* Ed. R. K. L. Collins. Rev. ed. Columbus: Ohio State University Press, 1992.

Gordley, J. "Responsibility in Crime, Tort, and Contract for the Unforeseeable Consequences of an Intentional Wrong: A Once and Future Rule?" In *The Law of Obligations: Essays in Celebration of John Fleming,* ed. P. Cane and J. Stapleton, 175–208. Oxford: Oxford University Press, 1998.

Gordon, R. W. "*Britton v. Turner:* A Signpost on the Crooked Road to 'Freedom' in the Employment Contract." In *Contracts Stories,* ed. D. G. Baird, 186–228. New York: Foundation Press, 2007.

Guarino, A. "Un futuro per il diritto romano?" *Diritto romano attuale* 7 (2002): 191–97.

Harries, J. *Law and Crime in the Roman World.* Cambridge: Cambridge University Press, 2007.

Hartog, H. *Man and Wife in America: A History.* Cambridge, MA: Harvard University Press, 2000.

Henderson, J. A. "*MacPherson v. Buick Motor Co.*: Simplifying the Facts While Reshaping the Law." In *Torts Stories,* ed. R. L. Rabin and S. D. Sugarman, 41–71. New York: Foundation Press, 2003.

Höbenreich, E. "Überlegungen zur Verfolgung unbeabsichtigter Tötungen von Sulla bis Hadrian." *Zeitschrift der Savigny-Stiftung für Rechtsgeschichte (Romanistische Abteilung)* 107 (1990): 249–314.

Holmes, O. W., Jr. *The Common Law.* Cambridge, MA: Harvard University Press, 2009. Originally published in Boston: Little, Brown, 1881.

Innis, D. F., and A. P. Silberman. "Provisions and Issues Unique to Government Contracts." In *Federal Government Construction Contracts,* ed. M. A. Branca et al., 173–208. 2nd ed. Chicago: American Bar Association, 2010.

Jackson, B. S. "Liability for Animals in Roman Law: An Historical Sketch." *Cambridge Law Journal* 37 (1978): 122–43.

Jakab, É. *Praedicere und Cavere beim Marktkauf: Sachmängel im griechischen und römischen Recht.* Munich: Verlag C. H. Beck, 1997.

Kaser, M. "Typisierter *Dolus* im altrömischer Recht." *Bullettino dell'Istituto di Diritto Romano,* 3rd ser., 4 (1962): 79–104.

Katz, L. *Bad Acts and Guilty Minds: Conundrums of the Criminal Law.* Chicago: University of Chicago Press, 1987.

Knapp, C. L. "Enforcing the Contract to Bargain." In *Perspectives on Contract Law,* ed. R. E. Barnett, 93–107. 3rd ed. New York: Aspen, 2005. Adapted from *New York University Law Review* 44 (1965): 673–728.

Kuper, A. "Ancestors: Henry Maine and the Constitution of Primitive Society." *History and Anthropology* 1 (1985): 265–86.

Lawson, F. H. *Negligence in the Civil Law.* Oxford: Oxford University Press, 1950.

Lucrezi, F. "La responsabilità aquiliana tra criterio oggettivo e soggettivo nell'esperienza antica e moderna." *Index* 30 (2002): 199–203.

MacCormack, G. "Fault and Causation in Early Roman Law: An Anthropological Perspective." *Revue internationale des droits de l'antiquité,* 3rd ser., 28 (1981): 97–126.

Mantello, A. "Ancora sulle smanie romanistiche." *Labeo* 48 (2002): 7–36.

Martin, S. D. "*Servum Meum Mulionem Conduxisti:* Mules, Muleteers, and Transportation in Classical Roman Law." *Transactions of the American Philological Association* 120 (1990): 301–14.

McGinn, T. A. J. "Crossing Boundaries." *Iura* 56 (2006–7): 396–99.

McGinn, T. A. J. *Prostitution, Sexuality, and the Law in Ancient Rome.* New York: Oxford University Press, 1998.

McGinn, T. A. J. *Widows and Patriarchy: Ancient and Modern.* London: Duckworth, 2008.

Metzger, E. *Litigation in Roman Law.* Oxford: Oxford University Press, 2005.

Miglietta, M. Review of M. F. Cursi, *Iniuria cum damno* (2002). *Iura* 53 (2002): 296–323.

Möller, C. "Die Mercennarii in der römischen Arbeitswelt." *Zeitschrift der Savigny-Stiftung für Rechtsgeschichte (Romanistische Abteilung)* 110 (1993): 296–330.

Möller, C. *Freiheit und Schutz im Arbeitsrecht: Das Fortwirken des römischen Rechts in der Rechtsprechung der Reichsgerichts.* Göttingen: Muster-Schmidt Verlag, 1990 (= *Göttinger Studien zur Rechtsgechichte* 18).

Mostafa, C. "The Implied Warranty of Habitability, Foreseeability, and Landlord Liability for Third-Party Criminal Acts against Tenants." *UCLA Law Review* 54 (2007): 971–97.

Nelson, H. L. W., and U. Manthe, eds. *Gai Institutiones III 88–181: Die Kontraktsobligationen.* Berlin: Duncker und Humblot, 1999.

Nörr, D. Review of Karoly Visky, *Geistige Arbeit und die "Artes Liberales" in den Quellen des Romischen Rechts* (1977). In *Dieter Nörr: Historiae Iuris Antiqui,* ed. T. J. Chiusi et al., 2:1245–52. Goldbach: Keip Verlag, 2003. Originally published in *Iura* 28 (1980):286–93.

Nörr, D. "Zur sozialen und rechtlichen Bewertung der freien Arbeit in Rom." In *Dieter Nörr: Historiae Iuris Antiqui,* ed. T. J. Chiusi et al., 1:399–437. Goldbach: Keip Verlag, 2003. Originally published in *Zeitschrift der Savigny-Stiftung für Rechtsgeschichte (Romanistische Abteilung)* 82 (1965): 67–105.

Ortu, R. *Aiunt aediles: Dichiarazioni del venditore e vizi della cosa venduta nell'editto de mancipiis emundis vendundis.* Turin: Giappichelli Editore, 2008.

Ortu, R. "*Qui venaliciariam vitam exercebat:* Ruolo sociale e qualificazione giuridica dei venditori di schiavi." *Ius Antiquum—Drevnee Pravo* 9 (2002): 87–112. Also published in *Diritto@Storia* 1 (2002), at http://www.dirittoestoria.it.

Peppe, L. "Alcune riflessioni sulla storia del diritto ovvero della rottura della tradizione (giuridica)." *Diritto romano attuale* 4 (2000): 63–88.

Petrucci, A. "Profili di responsabilità precontrattuale nella contrattazione con gli imprenditori alla luce dell'esperienza giuridica romana." *Teoria e storia del diritto privato* 3 (2010): 1–29.

Pichonnaz, P. "L'insegnamento del diritto romano oggi." *Index* 36 (2008): 51–59.

Polojac, M. *Actio de Pauperie and Liability for Damage Caused by Animals in Roman Law.* Belgrade: Dosije, 2003.

Rabin, R. L. "*Rowland v. Christian:* Hallmark of an Expansionary Era." In *Torts Stories,* ed. R. L. Rabin and S. D. Sugarman, 73–97. New York: Foundation Press, 2003.

Rabin, R. L., and S. D. Sugarman, eds. *Torts Stories.* New York: Foundation Press, 2003.

Richman, B. D. "The King of Rockingham County and the Original Bridge to Nowhere." In *Contracts Stories,* ed. D. G. Baird, 304–34. New York: Foundation Press, 2007.

Riggsby, A. M. *Crime and Community in Ciceronian Rome.* Austin: University of Texas Press, 1999.

Rosenstein, N. *Rome at War: Farms, Families, and Death in the Middle Republic.* Chapel Hill: University of North Carolina Press, 2004.

Sanger, C. "Developing Markets in Baby-Making: *In the Matter of Baby M.*" In *Contracts Stories,* ed. D. G. Baird, 127–59. New York: Foundation Press, 2007.

Savigny, F. C. von. *System des heutigen römischen Rechts.* 8 vols. Berlin: Veit, 1840–49.

Scarano Ussani, V. "Quale diritto romano? Una disciplina in crisi di identità." *Ostraka* 17.1–2 (2008): 187–92.

Schermaier, M. J. "*Bona Fides* in Roman Contract Law." In *Good Faith in European Contract Law,* ed. R. Zimmermann and S. Whittaker, 63–92. Cambridge: Cambridge University Press, 2000. Translated as "*Bona Fides* im römischen Vertragsrecht," in *Il ruolo della buona fede oggettiva nell'esperienza giuridica storica e contemporanea,* ed. L. Garofalo, 387–416. Padua: CEDAM, 2003.

Schuck, P. H., and D. J. Givelber. "*Tarasoff v. Regents of the University of California:* The Therapist's Dilemma." In *Torts Stories,* ed. R. L. Rabin and S. D. Sugarman, 99–128. New York: Foundation Press, 2003.

Schwartz, G. "*Rylands v Fletcher,* Negligence, and Strict Liability." In *The Law of Obligations: Essays in Celebration of John Fleming,* ed. P. Cane and J. Stapleton, 209–39. Oxford: Oxford University Press, 1998.

Schwartz, V. E., et al. *Prosser, Wade, and Schwartz's Torts: Cases and Materials.* 11th ed. New York: Foundation Press, 2005.

Scott, R. E. "*Hoffman v. Red Owl Stores* and the Myth of Pre-Contractual Reliance." In *Contracts Stories,* ed. D. G. Baird, 62–93. New York: Foundation Press, 2007.

Simpson, A. W. B. "Contracts for Cotton to Arrive: The Case of the Two Ships *Peerless.*" In *Contracts Stories,* ed. D. G. Baird, 29–61. New York: Foundation Press, 2007.

Smith, S. A. *Atiyah's Introduction to the Law of Contract.* 6th ed. Oxford: Oxford University Press, 2005.

Solidoro, Maruotti L. *Gli obblighi di informazione a carico del venditore: Origini storiche e prospettive attuali.* Naples: Satura Editrice, 2007.

Stanley, A. D. *From Bondage to Contract: Wage Labor, Marriage, and the Market in the Age of Slave Emancipation.* Cambridge: Cambridge University Press, 1998.

Sugarman, S. D. "*Vincent v. Lake Erie Transportation Co.*: Liability for Harm Caused by Necessity." In *Torts Stories,* ed. R. L. Rabin and S. D. Sugarman, 259–90. New York: Foundation Press, 2003.

Talamanca, M. "Colpa civile (diritto romano e intermedio)." *Enciclopedia del diritto* 7 (1960): 517–34.

Thomas, J. A. C. "*Locatio* and *Operae*." *Bullettino dell'Istituto di Diritto Romano,* 3rd ser., 3 (1961): 231–47.

Thomas, Y. "Le corps de l'esclave et son travail à Rome: Analyse d'une dissociation juridique." In *Corps romains,* ed. P. Moreau, 225–50. Grenoble: Jérôme Millon, 2002.

Tomlins, C. L. *Law, Labor, and Ideology in the Early American Republic.* Cambridge: Cambridge University Press, 1993.

Trebilcock, M. J. *The Limits of Freedom of Contract.* Cambridge, MA: Harvard University Press, 1993.

Valditara, G. "Dalla *iniuria* alla *culpa:* Su una dibattutta questione." *Studia et Documenta Historiae et Iuris* 75 (2009): 131–45.

Valditara, G. *Damnum iniuria datum.* 2nd ed. Turin: Giappichelli Editore, 2005.

VanderVelde, L. S. "The Gendered Origins of the *Lumley* Doctrine: Binding Men's Consciences and Women's Fidelity." In *Contracts Stories,* ed. D. G. Baird, 229–64. New York: Foundation Press, 2007.

Verboven, K. *The Economy of Friends: Economic Aspects of Amicitia and Patronage in the Late Republic.* Collection Latomus 269. Brussels: Éditions Latomus, 2002.

Wacke, A. "Fahrlässige Vergehen im römischen Strafrecht." In *Unius Poena—Metus Multorum: Abhandlungen zum römischen Strafrecht,* 1–62. Naples: Jovene Editore, 2008. Originally published in *Revue internationale des droits de l'antiquité* 3rd ser., 26 (1979): 505–66.

Wacke, A. "Faktische Arbeitsverhältnisse im römischen Recht?: Zur sogenannten 'notwendigen Entgeltlichkeit,' besonders bei Arbeitsleistungen bei vermeintlichen Sklaven." *Zeitschrift der Savigny-Stiftung für Zeitschrift der Savigny-Stiftung für Rechtsgeschichte (Romanistische Abteilung)* 108 (1991): 123–54.

Weir, T. "The Staggering March of Negligence." In *The Law of Obligations: Essays in Celebration of John Fleming,* ed. P. Cane and J. Stapleton, 97–138. Oxford: Oxford University Press, 1998.

Wicke, H. *Respondeat Superior: Haftung für Verrichtungsgehilfen im römischen, römisch- holländischen, englischen, und südafrikanischen Recht.* Berlin: Duncker und Humblot, 2000.

Williams, G. L. *Liability for Animals.* Cambridge: Cambridge University Press, 1939.

Winkel, L. "Alcune osservazioni sulla classificazione delle obbligazioni e sui contratti nominati nel diritto romano." *Bullettino dell'Istituto di Diritto Romano,* 3rd ser., 42–43 (2000–2001 [2009]): 51–66.

Wolf, J. G. *Das Senatusconsultum Silanianum und die Senatsrede des C. Cassius Longinus aus dem Jahre 61 n. Chr.* Heidelberg: Carl Winter, 1988.

Zimmermann, R. *The Law of Obligations: Roman Foundations of the Civilian Tradition.* Oxford: Oxford University Press, 1996.

CHAPTER 2

*The Roman Conception of Contract**

ROBERTO FIORI

For a number of years, the scholarship on Roman law has been heading toward a profound rethinking of the Roman conception of contract.

It is well known that between the end of the nineteenth and the beginning of the twentieth centuries, Alfred Pernice and Silvio Perozzi[1] resisted the Pandectist approach—drawn from the theory of Natural Law, in which contracts are seen as a manifestation of the will of the parties—arriving at a total rejection of the relevance of *consensus* and focusing exclusively on the idea of obligation. This rather radical new conceptualization was, in turn, contested by Salvatore Riccobono, who vigorously reaffirmed the centrality of agreement.[2] During the same period, writers such as Pietro Bonfante, Emilio Betti, and Pietro de Francisci[3] put forth what we can describe as an intermediate definition: it did not totally reject the importance of agreement but placed greater emphasis on

* The principal Latin passages cited in the text are translated at the end of this article. The translations are based on Watson, *The "Digest" of Justinian* (1998) and Gordon and Robinson, *The "Institutes" of Gaius* (1988), with modifications.

1. Pernice, "Vertragslehre" (1888) 195ff.; Perozzi, "Contratto consensuale" (1898) 565ff.; Perozzi, *Le obbligazioni romane.* (1903) 311ff.; Perozzi," Dalle obbligazioni da delitto alle obbligazioni da contratto" (1915–16) 443ff.
2. Riccobono,"Dal diritto romano classico al diritto moderno" (1917) 113ff.; "La formazione della teoria generale del *contractus*" (1929) 123ff.; *Corso di diritto romano* (1935) 262ff.; "Der Wille als Entwicklungsfaktor" (1949) 55ff. Riccobono was followed, above all, by Voci (*La dottrina romana del contratto* (1946) 7, 297ff.; "La dottrina del contratto" (1946) 383ff.).
3. Bonfante, "Genesi" (1907) 107ff.; Bonfante, "Il contratto e i patti" (1920) 135ff.; Bonfante, *Corso di diritto romano* (1979) 249ff.; Bonfante, *Istituzioni di diritto romano* (1987) 327; Betti, "Valore dogmatico" (1915) 3ff.; Betti, *Istituzioni di diritto romano* (1962) 2.1:66ff.; de Francisci, Συνάλλαγμα (1916) 2:321ff.

obligation than on will, on the *contrahere* (*obligationem*) than on the "contract." This became the dominant position in the scholarship in the first half of the twentieth century.[4]

Beginning in the 1960s, a position that I will call (for the sake of convenience) "consensualist" has reasserted itself. This development is not a simple return to the theory of *Rechtsgeschäft*. It is arrived at through modern methodologies that pay attention to historical context and to the contributions of individual jurists,[5] and it involves, therefore, a more developed and nuanced approach: it is not a simple projection of modern ideas onto the past but, rather, the uncovering of a series of specific themes and issues in the work of the *prudentes*, which come to be elaborated on by later jurists, until the creation of the positivistic "theory of the will."[6] This view, consequently, cannot be countered simply by accusing it of being anachronistic: it has to be subjected to a thorough examination in an attempt to understand if the foundations for this direction in the modern scholarship— in particular, the concept of contract as an agreement that generates obligations—can be traced back to the Roman sources.[7]

---

4. Albertario, "Le fonti delle obbligazioni" (1923) 77ff.; Lenel, "Interpolationenjagd" (1925) 25; Wieacker, *Societas* 1 (1936) 80ff. (still closely tied to Perozzi; see also Wieacker, review of Wunner, *Contractus* [1967] 129ff.); Lauria, "*Contractus, delictum, obligatio*" (1938) 620ff.; Grosso, *Il sistema romano dei contratti* (1945) 42ff.; Talamanca, *Istituzioni di diritto romano* (1990) 534ff.; Talamanca, "*Conventio* e *stipulatio*" (1991) 210ff.; Sargenti, "Svolgimento dell'idea di contratto" (1988) 53, 72ff.; Martini, "Il mito del consenso" (1991) 97ff.; Melillo, *Contrahere, pacisci, transigere* (1994) 125ff., esp. 218–19.
5. Gallo, "Eredità di giuristi romani" (1991) 3ff. Gallo, *Synallagma e conventio* (1992;1995) views Ulpian's role as central. Others nominate Pedius for this: see La Pira, "Personalità scientifica" (1938) 293ff.; Schiavone, *Studi sulle logiche* (1971) esp. 131–32 with n. 178; Schiavone, *Giuristi e nobili* (1987) 240 n. 76 (suggesting at 61–62, however, that there is already in Q. Mucius "un primo nucleo di pensiero ontologico" (an early nucleus of ontological thought) that allows for the passage from the verb *contrahere* to the unitary "institution" expressed by the noun *contractus*); Schiavone, "La scrittura di Ulpiano" (1991) 125ff. For Labeo as the turning point, see Santoro, "Il contratto nel pensiero di Labeone." (1983). See also Cannata, "La '*distinctio*' *re-verbis-litteris-consensu*" (1970) 448–49 with n. 81; Cannata, "Der Vertrag als zivilrechtlicher Obligierungsgrund" (1995) 59ff.; Zimmermann, *Law of Obligations* (1996) 559ff. More cautious is Burdese ("Ancora sul contratto" [1985] 458ff; "Concetto di contratto" [1988/2006], 113; "Nozioni di patto, convenzione e contratto" [1993] 61ff.). Deserving of separate consideration is Magdelain's *Le consensualisme* (1958), theorizing a progressive rise of contractual types, after a period of unrestricted protection of agreements. See now the full discussion of these issues in Cascione, *Consensus* (2003) 194ff.
6. Schiavone, "Negozio giuridico (diritto romano)" (1977) 906ff., esp. 908.
7. The need for such an examination is suggested by the fact that the "consensualist" approach tends also to draw into its orbit other theoretical concepts of contract law, such as that of

Q. Mucius

The first relevant passage is a fragment by Pomponius, which almost certainly reports with accuracy the words of Q. Mucius Scaevola. It confirms and develops the principle that in whatever way a contractual obligation is entered in, it should be dissolved in the same manner.

> Pomp. (4 *ad Quintum Mucium*) D. 46.3.80: *Prout quidque contractum est, ita et solvi debet: ut, cum re contraxerimus, re solvi debet: veluti cum mutuum dedimus, ut retro pecuniae tantundem solvi debeat. et cum verbis aliquid contraximus, vel re vel verbis obligatio solvi debet, verbis, veluti cum acceptum promissori fit, re, veluti cum solvit quod promisit. aeque cum emptio vel venditio vel locatio contracta est, quoniam consensu nudo contrahi potest, etiam dissensu contrario dissolvi potest.*

Some have wanted to see in the passage an early form of "substantialization" of the contract in relation to the original sense of *contrahere* as a simple means of giving rise to an obligation.[8] I have elsewhere discussed problems related to the passage's undeniable authenticity and wholesale derivation from Q. Mucius.[9] I will here limit myself to some brief considerations.

It is likely that the passage was originally found in the first books of Mucius's

---

good faith. For example, recently, there has been a revival of an interpretation of *bona fides* as "respect for one's word being given." This view implies a very close tie between agreement (the "given word") and *oportere* (*ex fide bona*) that goes well beyond the confines of consensual contracts; see Talamanca, "La *bona fides* nei giuristi romani" (2003) 1ff., though Talamanca (*Istituzioni di diritto romano,* 536–37) criticizes Riccobono's position as being "giusnaturalistica e condizionata da opzioni ideologiche" (influenced by Natural Law conceptions and ideological considerations). This idea—which already appears in Schulz, *Prinzipien* (1934) 151ff.; Kunkel, "*Fides* als schöpferisches Element" (1939) 5; Condanari-Michler, "Schuld und Schaden" (1948) 90ff.; Horvat, "Osservazioni sulla *bona fides*" (1953) 423ff.; and Kaser, *Das römische Privatrecht* 1 (1971) 181— recalls the model of good faith as respect for the agreement that was prominent in Italian legal thinking under the influence of positivism and of the "theory of the will": see Fiori, "Storicità del diritto e problemi di metodo" (2007) 25ff. For criticism of this perspective, see Fiori, "*Fides* e *bona fides*" (2008) 225ff; Fiori, "*Bona Fides.*"

8. Schiavone, *Giuristi e nobili* (1987) 61–62; see also Marotta, "Tutela dello scambio" (1996) 105 n. 219.
9. Fiori "*Contrahere* e *solvere obligationem* in Q. Mucio Scevola" (2007) 1958ff.

libri iuris civilis,[10] specifically where he treats legacies. Its point of departure could be the legacy that arranges for a legatee's release from a debt (the so-called *liberatio legata*)[11] or the release from an obligation to pay out a legacy *per damnationem* and possibly *sinendi modo*.[12] In either case, it is likely that Mucius's position, as it has come down to us, was preceded by a reference to *solutio per aes et libram*.[13] Furthermore, it is clear that, under either theory, Q. Mucius's interest in definition pays less attention to *contrahere* and more to *solvere obligationem*.[14]

---

10. Schiavone, *Giuristi e nobili nella Roma repubblicana* (1987) 56, 206 nn. 79–80. See also the chart in Bremer, *Iurisprudentiae Antehadrianae quae supersunt* 1 (1896) 62–63.
11. See Lenel, *Palingenesia iuris civilis* (1889) 63 n. 5. See also Stoll, "Die formlose Vereinbarung der Aufhebung" (1924) 14; Grosso, *Il sistema romano dei contratti* (1963) 9; Knütel, *Contrarius consensus* (1968) 10; Cannata, "La *'distinctio' re-verbis-litteris-consensu*" (1970) 440–41; Schmidlin, *Die römischen Rechtsregeln* (1970) 76; Schiavone, "Labeone e la nascita dell'idea di contratto" (1987) 56, 206 n. 82. It must be pointed out that Lenel's view does not present particular difficulties when it is limited—as it was in his own publications—to the placement of the passage in the context of Pomponius's works, since there is no doubt that the institution of *liberatio legata* arose during the period in which this jurist wrote: see Santalucia, *I legati ad effetto liberatorio nel diritto romano* (1964) 64, 65ff.; see also Santalucia, "I legati ad effetto liberatorio" (1967) 151ff. Other scholars tend to backdate its origins: see Talamanca, "Intorno ad una recente ipotesi sulla *liberatio legata*" (1963–64) 679ff.; Astolfi, "Giuliano e il *legatum liberationis*" (1966) 342–43, 351ff.; see also Astolfi, *Studi sull'oggetto dei legati in diritto romano* 1 (1964) 30 ff. Greater difficulties arise with respect to Q. Mucius. If we accept that the institution of *liberatio legata* was already well known at his time—as believed possible by Schiavone (*Giuristi e nobili* [1987] 56) but rejected by Talamanca (review of Schiavone [1988] 894)—two different and equally likely views come into play. The first sees Mucius's treatment of the issue as an independent discourse, divorced from its context: see Cannata, "La *'distinctio' re-verbis-litteris-consensu* 1" (1970) 441; Schiavone, *Giuristi e nobili* (1987) 56. The second suggests that Mucius's discussion was based on a casuistic analysis of the release from debt through legacy: see Knütel, *Contrarius consensus* (1968) 10ff.
12. Talamanca, review of Schiavone, *Giuristi e nobili* (1988) 895.
13. In this respect, it does not matter that *gesta per aes et libram* were no longer practiced in Mucius's time, as he is commenting on a rule of the *ius civile* as such, without regard for its currency; see Fiori, "*Contrahere* e *solvere obligationem* in Q. Mucio Scevola" (2007) 1969. This possibility could pose problems regarding the use of the expression *contrahere obligationem* to refer to a legacy: see Talamanca, review of Schiavone, *Giuristi e nobili* (1988) 895. We must, however, keep in mind the very broad use of the verb *contrahere* in the praetor's edict: see, above all, Albanese, "*Agere, gerere* e *contrahere*" (1972/1991) 1135–36. We also should not be surprised by the fact that Mucius's examples all relate to contractual matters (*mutuum, promissio, emptio venditio, locatio conductio*), a fact that can be attributed to the juristic tendency to take a simple semantic problem as the point of departure for a general discussion.
14. This is confirmed by the discussion in the *Basilica* that translates as *katabolē* the *solutio* of *obligationes re contractae* and that uses *apochē* for *acceptilatio* of *obligationes verbis contractae* and

Given this context, the first problem the jurist faced was the broad meaning of the term *solutio*, which, in indicating a generic freeing from an obligation,[15] could refer to release (in the forms that Gaius later calls *imaginaria solutio*) as well as to fulfilled performance (which is, indeed, "the" *solutio* in a strict sense).[16] Thus, Q. Mucius chose to structure his discussion on both planes.

To understand the text, it is, in my opinion, important to highlight his uses of the verbs: *debet* is employed when treating *obligationes re* and *verbis contractae*; *potest* is instead chosen for the *obligationes consensu contractae*:

a. for *obligationes re contractae,* one "must" *solvere re,* either (a1) because there is a fulfilled performance or (a2) because the release takes place via a *solutio per aes et libram;*[17]
b. for *obligationes verbis contractae,* one "must" *solvere verbis* or *re,* either (b1) because the release from debt is accomplished *verbis,* via *acceptilatio,* or (b2) because there is a fulfilled performance (*solvere re*);[18]

---

uses *sumphōnos* for the *pactum* that dissolves the *obligationes consensu contractae* (*B.* 26.5.80 [Scheltema, A.IV.1283]): Ὡς τρόπῳ τὰ συναλλάγματα συνίσταται, τῷ αὐτῷ καὶ διαλύεται· τὰ μὲν τῆς ἐν πράγμασιν ἀγωγῆς διὰ τῆς καταβολῆς, τὰ δὲ τῆς ἐν ἐπερωτήσεσι διὰ ἀποχῆς, τὰ δὲ τῆς ἐν συναλλάγμασι κυρίως, οἷον πράσεσι καὶ τοῖς τοιούτοις, διὰ συμφώνου (in whichever way contracts are made, in the same way they are also dissolved: those that are entered in by conduct, [must be dissolved] through a formal release accomplished by conduct [*katabolē*]; those [that are entered in] by questioning [i.e., *stipulatio*], [must be dissolved] by a formal release accomplished by words [*apochē*]; those [that are entered in] by contracts in strict sense [i.e., by mutual agreement]—such as sale and such—[must be dissolved] by agreement [*sumphōnos*]"). The term *katabolē* cannot be understood as referring to the fulfillment of the performance (of the *obligationes re contractae*), because—since the Greek text does not contain any reference to an analogous form of *solutio* for the performance of the other *obligationes contractae*—this would force us to understand the commentator as saying that the *obligationes contractae verbis* or *consensu* can be dissolved only via *acceptilatio* or *contrarius consensus* and not through the fulfillment of the performance. Thus *katabolē* must be understood as release. It is clear that by interpreting the term *katabolē* in this way, it can only be understood as a reference to *solutio per aes et libram* as a means of extinguishing, under the *ius civile, obligationes re contractae.* For further discussion, see Fiori, "*Contrahere* e *solvere obligationem* in Q. Mucio Scevola" (2007) 1970ff.

15. Gaius 3.169, 173.
16. The ambiguity is noted, though with different solutions proposed, in Siber, "*Contrarius consensus*" (1921) 69; Horak, review of Behrends, *Die Wissenschaftslehre* (1978) and Schiavone, *Nascita della giurisprudenza* (1978) 419; Talamanca, review of Schiavone, *Giuristi e nobili* (1988) 894–95; and Gallo, *Synallagma e conventio nel contratto* 1 (1992) n. 12.
17. For this problem, see Fiori, "*Contrahere* e *solvere obligationem*" (2007) 1972.
18. I believe the phrase *solvere re, cum solvit quod promisit,* must be understood as meaning per-

c. for *obligationes consensu contractae,* one "can"—and not "must"—*solvere etiam dissensu contrario,* because while (c1) release takes place *consensu,* through agreement, (c2) the fulfilment of the performance (this too, as we have seen, constitutes *solvere*) takes place *re,* that is, by conduct.

Mucius's process of definition is, essentially, a *diairesis,* meaning a splitting of the genus *solvere obligationem* into two species. One of the latter is release, constituting the *quid definiendum,* while the other is performance.

Thus reconstructed, the passage does not appear to add, in any way, to the history of the concept of "contract." As for our sources, it seems that in Q. Mucius's time, *obligatio* still formed the core of the contractual relationship.

Labeo

The next step in the construction of a general theory of contract in Roman law is to be found, for some scholars, in Labeo, precisely in a fragment taken from Ulpian's commentary on the edict.

Labeo's *definitio* distinguishes among *agere, gerere,* and *contrahere.* The verb *agere,* according to the Augustan jurist, has a general import in the sense that one can act by words or by conduct, as with *stipulatio* or *numeratio,* respectively. The verb *contrahere* refers to a reciprocal obligation, what the Greeks called *sunallagma,* such as *emptio venditio, locatio conductio, societas. Gerere,* finally, indicates something accomplished without words.

Ulp. (11 *ad edictum*) *D.* 50.16.19: *Labeo libro primo praetoris urbani* [fr. 5 Lenel]

---

formance through nonverbal behavior. Labeo (see the following section of this chapter) similarly describes *gestum* as *res sine verbis facta* and describes *actum* as action taken *sive verbis sive re.* This understanding is furthermore fully consistent with the observation that *acceptilatio* was no longer required for the fulfilment of the performance of *obligationes verbis contractae* in Q. Mucius's time—if indeed it ever had been: see Knütel, *Contrarius consensus* (1968) 11; Cannata, "La *'distinctio' re-verbis-litteris-consensu*" (1970) 442; Kaser, "*Divisio obligationum*" (1983) 161. For Cannata ("La *'distinctio' re-verbis-litteris-consensu,*" 154), *acceptilatio* was, from its very origins, simply release (and was applied only in cases of release), while performance extinguished the obligation also by conduct, that is, without words (so, precisely, those *re, cum solvit quod promisit).* In a broader sense, I believe that *contrahere re* also means "contracting by conduct" and not "contracting via handing over something." Compare the rendering of *B.* 26.5.80 (Scheltema, A.IV.1283): ἐν πράγμασιν.

definit, quod quaedam 'agantur', quaedam 'gerantur', quaedam 'contrahantur': et actum quidem generale verbum esse, sive verbis sive re quid agatur, ut in stipulatione vel numeratione: contractum autem ultro citroque obligationem, quod Graeci συνάλλαγμα *vocant, veluti emptionem venditionem, locationem conductionem, societatem: gestum rem significare sine verbis factam.*

The text displays a number of obscurities: it is perhaps enough to point to the deep divergence between the restricted meaning of *contrahere* and *gerere* shown in the passage and Labeo's own broad use of the same words in other contexts.[19] Despite this, modern scholarship has consistently recognized here the definition of *contrahere* in terms of a reciprocity of obligation.

Recently, however, it has been suggested that Labeo's *definitio* places more emphasis on the "act" of the parties in order to enter into an obligation than on the obligation itself: in the passage, the word *obligatio* would still bear its (presumed) original meaning of "obligating act,"[20] and the reciprocity (*ultro citroque*) of the act (*obligatio*) would refer to the mutual agreement of the parties.[21] This usage would, in this view, extend to all contracts, including real and formal ones, since every contract is based on mutual consent: Labeo would locate both *stipulatio* and *numeratio* within the scope of *agere,* by taking into account only the manner in which the act was externalized. The *agere,* in fact, would be a genus that embraces the species *contrahere*, which is an *agere* (whether undertaken *re* or *verbis*) in which agreement between the parties (whether manifested *re* or *verbis*) is realized.[22]

According to this argument, Labeo's definition would have resulted in the

19. For the use of *contractus,* cf. Fiori, "*Contrahere* in Labeone" (2012) 319ff. This also leads us to reject the idea that Labeo wished to construct a new definition of contract, contested by the Sabinian *secta,* as suggested in Gallo, "Ai primordi del passaggio" (1997/2006) 159ff.

20. Santoro, "Il contratto nel pensiero di Labeone" (1983) 14ff.; Gallo, *Synallagma e conventio nel contratto* 1 (1992) 152ff. This view is not an entirely isolated one in the scholarship: see Dumont, "*Obligatio*" (1963) 77 ff.; Lantella, "Note semantiche sulle definizioni di *obligatio*" (1971), 165 ff.; Lantella, *Il lavoro sistematico nel discorso giuridico romano* (1975) 56 with n. 65; Benöhr, *Das sogenannte Synallagma* (1965) 11; Cerami, "*D.* 2.14.5 (Ulp. 4 *ad ed.*)" (1976) 195ff. (arguing, at 198, that *ultro citroque obligatio* should be understood as referring to a coincidence of intent that lies beyond the agreement, a position held by Pedius alone); Flume, *Rechtsakt und Rechtsverhältnis* (1990) 23ff.; Cannata, "Atto giuridico e rapporto giuridico" (1991) 335ff.; Cannata, "Contratto e causa nel diritto romano" (1997/2006) 187ff., esp. 203ff.; Falcone, *Obligatio est iuris vinculum* (2003) 166 n. 434 (see also 38–39 n. 97).

21. Santoro, "Il contratto nel pensiero di Labeone" (1983) esp. 23.

22. Santoro, "Il contratto nel pensiero di Labeone" (1983) 40–41.

recognition of a general protection for reciprocal agreements that produce obligations, including the so-called innominate contracts relying on the procedural remedy of *agere praescriptis verbis.* Once adopted by the Proculian school, it would have been deployed to oppose a Sabinian theory of contract, more closely tied to the concept of typicality of contracts, as can be found—we are told—with Aristo (see the next section in this chapter). The clash between these two views would have concluded with the victory of the Sabinian position and the near erasure from the historical record of the opposing one. According to this view, Labeo would essentially have been a precursor of modern conceptions of the contract as an agreement that generates obligations. For him, Ulpian's principle, according to which *ex nudo pacto non oritur actio,* would not have held, as even the undertaking of innominate contracts would have been protected at law on the basis of agreement alone.[23]

In my discussion of the passage and its reception in the scholarship, I limit myself to the most relevant aspects, referring the reader to a more extensive analysis published elsewhere.[24]

I believe, first of all, that it is doubtful that we can assume "act" to have been the original meaning of *obligatio,* and that Labeo relied on this. The sources do not justify understanding *ultro citroque obligatio* as an "act that generates reciprocal obligations" instead of an "obligation characterized by reciprocity," and we should not overrate the use of this term to indicate both the legal bond between the parties and the act that gave rise to it—as with *stipulatio,* which the sources often describe as *verborum obligatio:* the same could be said of the identification of *emptio venditio, locatio conductio,* and *societas* with (*ultro citroque*) *obligatio* in *D.* 50.16.19. All of this does not require the meaning of *obligatio* to be precisely "act," since it is very possible to read this word in terms that lead in the exact opposite direction, in favor of identifying contract and bond, consistently with the idea of contract as *obligatio contracta.* In other words, one can postulate that a contract at that point is subsumed into a bond so that it can itself be called *obligatio.*

Next, the theory that Labeo granted a general protection through a remedy based on mere agreement is refuted by his own use of the *agere praescriptis verbis.* This pertains not, as commonly thought, to the protection of innomi-

23. Santoro, "Il contratto nel pensiero di Labeone" (1983); Gallo, *Synallagma e conventio nel contratto* 1 (1992) 160ff., 2 (1995) 1ff.; Gallo, "Ai primordi del passaggio" (1997/2006) 162ff.; Cannata, "Contratto e causa nel diritto romano" (1997/2006) 189ff.

24. Fiori, "*Contrahere* in Labeone" (2011).

nate contracts but, instead, to protection, through a general remedy, of specific contracts that are ineffective or whose classification remains uncertain. He recommends *agere praescriptis verbis* when, within the scope of specific contracts, resort to their specific actions is not possible or may pose risks. Given that our sources seem consistently to refer to contracts where good faith is relevant, one might conclude that Labeo used the *agere praescriptis verbis* to create a general protection for *oportere ex fide bona,* even beyond the application of specific remedies, in the same way that the *actio de dolo* protected against fraudulent misconduct whenever a specific action is unavailable.[25]

It is instead probable that in *D.* 50.16.19, Labeo, far from wanting to breathe life into a general theory of contract, simply intended to clarify, in light of the very broad use of the verb *contrahere* in the edict, that the word bears the specific meaning of a bilateral bond for both parties (*ultro citroque obligatio*). He saw this bilateral sense expressed by the verbal prefix *cum-* and illustrated by its correspondence to the Greek *sunallagma,* whose etymology is analogous to Latin *contractus.* Therefore, what we have is not a revolutionary break with the past or a conceptual anticipation of developments long in the future but a simple lexical clarification.[26]

My criticism of the position just described is based on more than the fact that it is not supported by the sources. That position also emerges as overly abstract and, in concrete terms, impractical, since it suggests that Labeo granted procedural protection even to mere agreement, something that has never been accepted in the whole Western legal tradition.[27] Even in medieval canon law, where the Roman system of specific contracts still used by civilians had been discarded, the principle *ex nudo pacto oritur actio* possessed a sense that was primarily ideological in nature, given that it was tied to the need to assert the binding quality for Christians of every promise. But alongside this principle, there immediately developed a conception of *causa* that functioned as a necessary corrective of this rule, playing the same role fulfilled in Roman law by the *nomen contractus* (or *causa* with innominate contracts), by the *vestimenta* in medieval law, by consideration in English and American common law, by the notion of *causa*/*cause* in Italian and French law, and by "content" (*Inhalt*) in German law.[28]

25. See the texts in Cursi and Fiori, "Le azioni generali" (2011).
26. This point has been previously made by Beseler ("Einzelne Studien" (1932) 293ff.) and Albanese ("*Agere, gerere e contrahere*" (1972/1991) 1113ff.).
27. There is no trace of it even in the exposition by Cannata, "Contratto e causa nel diritto romano" (1997/2006), though he pays a great deal of attention to the problem of *causa.*
28. See, for all of this, Fiori, "Il problema dell'oggetto" (2003), 236–37.

The "Closure" of the Contractual System: The "Limiting Definitions" in the Debates between Sabinians and Proculians and Aristo's *Sunallagma*

I have mentioned the *communis opinio* that Labeo's work on the *agere praescriptis verbis* granted protection to the innominate contracts. I have also noted that this position is unsustainable, since the responses of this Augustan jurist proceed in an entirely different direction. It is only in the disputes between Sabinians and Proculians that a problem of innominate contracts arose.

The discussions of the *prudentes* focused, above all, on the only two specific bilateral contracts known in Roman law, as they are more difficult to distinguish from innominate contracts. Regarding sale, a well-known passage of Paul deals with the dispute, also mentioned by Gaius, over the distinction between *emptio venditio* and *permutatio.*[29] There almost certainly would have been similar discussions regarding the problem of determining the *pretium* after the conclusion of the transaction.[30] The same controversies are found with regard to the distinction between *locatio conductio* and the exchange of *res utendae fruendae,* as well the later determination of the *merces.*[31]

It is clearly not fortuitous that we see precisely in this period the fullest expression of a technique of definition that cannot be attributed to the influence of Greek philosophy.[32] Rather, it is likely the legacy of Roman sacerdotal learning that, since the archaic period, had teased out means of drawing distinctions and legal definitions not only of material realities, such as the *ager* in augural law, but also of legal phenomena, such as, for example, the definitions

29. Paul. (33 *ad edictum*) *D.* 18.1.1; Gaius 3.141. It is enough to cite Gallo, *Synallagma e conventio nel contratto* 2 (1995) 66ff.
30. For sources and literature, see Fiori, *La definizione della locatio conductio* (1999) 245ff.
31. Gaius 3.144. See Africanus (8 *quaest.*) *D.* 19.2.35.1; Ulpian (32 *ad edictum*) *D.* 10.3.23; and the discussion in Fiori, *La definizione della locatio conductio* (1999) 228ff., 245ff.
32. Albanese ("*Definitio periculosa*" [1970/1991] 701ff.) is the first to identify this technique of definition. He also notes the absence of this type of *definitio* in the Latin rhetorical sources (724–25 with n. 43). Cerami ("*Ignorantia iuris*" [1992] 72–73 with n. 52) disagrees, citing Cic. *Inv.* 2.99 (where, however, *separare,* in the rhetorical strategy under discussion, does not coincide with *definire* but instead follows it, thus amounting to a distinction drawn between phenomena that have already been defined), as does Falcone ("Ricerche sull'origine dell'interdetto *uti possidetis*" [1996] 29 n. 71), citing Cic. *Top.* 6.29 (which, however, is a case of *definitio per genus et speciem*); see also Fiori, "*Servire servitutem*" (2001) 368–69 with n. 43.

of *sacrum, sanctum,* and *religiosum* in the pontifical tradition.[33] This technique does not aim at achieving a theoretical and abstract conception of the *definiendum* but has, instead, a practical aim, since it traces the "boundaries" of the contract by identifying the peculiarities that distinguish it from other contracts in order to allow the parties and the praetor to choose the best protection available to them. An example of this can be seen in Gaius's treatment of *locatio conductio,*[34] which is entirely constructed on a comparison of hire/lease with sale and innominate contracts, that is, with the other reciprocal contracts.

During this same period—more precisely, around the middle of the second century CE—we are able to detect a link between innominate contracts and *agere praescriptis verbis.* A very well-known fragment of Ulpian is our main evidence, worth citing beginning with its *principium.*

> Ulp. (4 *ad edictum*) *D.* 2.14.7 pr.: *Iuris gentium conventiones quaedam actiones pariunt, quaedam exceptiones.* 1. *Quae pariunt actiones, in suo nomine non stant, sed transeunt in proprium nomen contractus: ut emptio venditio, locatio conductio, societas, commodatum, depositum et ceteri similes contractus.* 2. *Sed et si in alium contractum res non transeat, subsit tamen causa, eleganter Aristo* [fr. 4 Lenel] *Celso respondit esse obligationem. ut puta dedi tibi rem ut mihi aliam dares, dedi ut aliquid facias: hoc συνάλλαγμα esse et hinc nasci civilem obligationem <actionem>. et ideo puto recte Iulianum* [1 *dig.* fr. 15 Lenel] *a Mauriciano reprehensum in hoc: dedi tibi Stichum ut Pamphilum manumittas: manumisisti: evictus est Stichus. Iulianus scribit in factum actionem a praetore dandam: ille ait civilem incerti actionem, id est praescriptis verbis sufficere: esse enim contractum, quod Aristo συνάλλαγμα dicit, unde haec nascitur actio. . . .*

Aristo holds for the presence of an *obligatio civilis,* when, although the *conventio* cannot be associated with a specific contract, there is still a *causa* capable of giving rise to an obligation. This happens when, for example (*ut puta*), something has been given in exchange for something else or for a performance of some kind, like when I gave you Stichus so that you manumit Pamphilus and,

33. For this entire subject, see Fiori, *La definizione della locatio conductio* (1999) 183ff.

34. In the past, the lack of interest shown by the *prudentes* in a definition *per genus et speciem,* which identifies the "substance" of a contract and outlines its "essential elements," helped foster the theory that actual definitions are usually not found in the Roman legal sources. Schulz (*Prinzipien* [1934/1946] 38), for example, sees proof of this absence in Gaius's treatment of *locatio conductio.*

after you have manumitted him, Stichus is acquired by a third party with a better title. In these cases, while Julian limited himself to approving the grant of an *actio in factum,* Mauricianus, basing himself on Aristo's position, opted for an *actio civilis incerti,* which all scholars regard as equivalent to *agere praescriptis verbis.*

I believe, as do all modern interpreters of the text, that Aristo's discussion and the choice made by Mauricianus ought to be linked to Labeo's thought. In my view, however, later jurists merged two theories that the Augustan jurist had not necessarily connected with each other.

As we have seen, Labeo had

a. used the term *sunallagma* to denote the *ultro citroque obligatio,* that is, the bilateral obligation that coincides with a literal meaning of the word *contractus;*
b. promoted the use of the *agere praescriptis verbis* in order to provide protection in situations in which it was not possible to use specific actions, either (i) because the bargain, although corresponding to a specific contract, was uncertain in its structure or (ii) because the specific contract was ineffective with regard to the principal obligation but had given rise to a secondary obligation.

Aristo held that

a. when a *conventio* does not fall within the scope of a specific contract but still there is a *causa,* an *obligatio* arises;
b. an example of this is when something has been given in exchange for something else or for a performance: in this case, there is a *sunallagma,* from which an *obligatio* arises.

To understand Aristo's second point, we must remember that, for Labeo, the *ultro citroque obligatio* consists not in an exchange of two obligations—as we might anachronistically be led to believe by reading, in a modern key, the obligation as an "effect" of the contract—but, rather, in one single obligation that coincides with the contract and is bilateral in nature, representing a double material commitment. In my view, Aristo relied on this sense in order to arrive at his statement *b*. By merging Labeo's principles *a* and *b*, he holds that when a double material investment (*sunallagma)* is called for and when a party suffers a detriment of some kind because of it—this I would argue is the meaning of the much-discussed term *causa*[35]—there is an *obligatio* even when no specific contract occurs.

To understand the first part of Aristo's holding, however, it should be noted that he does not state in the text that the *causa* coincides with the *sunallagma*. Adopting Labeo's principle *b* as a point of departure, Aristo makes a general assertion that when there has been a material detriment within the scope of a *conventio,* there arises an *obligatio.* Then, within this general holding, he sets forth the case, not discussed by Labeo, of innominate contracts: when the bargain is based on an exchange of performances and when one (performing) party has suffered a detriment, this material loss cannot be justified but gives rise to a binding constraint imposed on the other party.

In other words, for Aristo, *sunallagma* does not coincide with *causa.* Rather, it is the bilateral nature of the bargain within which the material detriment suffered by one party—the *causa,* that is—imposes an obligation on the other. What this second-century jurist did, then, was to apply to the innominate contracts the same solution that Labeo had developed for typical contracts that were ineffective with regard to their principal obligations.

As for the remedies, we could think that Aristo was the first to suggest *agere praescriptis verbis* in connection with the innominate contracts, only if we accept the emendation of *civilem obligationem* in *civilem actionem,* as proposed by some scholars.[36] If not, we should turn to a text by Neratius[37]—a few years younger than Aristo—to find the first mention of an *actio civilis incerti* in this context. In any case, Mauricianus only reasserted a solution that had already been proposed.

If this interpretation is correct, it becomes apparent that the protection of the innominate contracts is based not on the binding quality of the *conventio,*

---

35. This is not the place to offer an analysis of the various interpretations of this expression. It suffices to say that it has been identified with the entire contract as *negotium,* with the legal qualification of the bargain, with its purpose, and—the most widely held view—with the *datio.* For an overview of the different positions, see Santoro, "La causa delle convenzioni atipiche" (1997) 225–26 (inclining toward the idea of purpose), followed by dalla Massara, *Alle origini della causa del contratto* (2004) 132–33.

36. Cf. Santoro, "Il contratto nel pensiero di Labeone" (1983) 217–18 and n. 142, with literature.

37. Nerat. (1 *resp.*) *D.* 19.5.6: *Insulam hoc modo, ut aliam insulam reficeres, vendidi. respondit nullam esse venditionem, sed civili intentione incerti agendum est* (I sold a building in the following manner: that you repair another building. He responded that there is no sale but that action must be brought with a civil-law *intentio* for an indefinite sum).

which is not operative without a *causa*, but on the existence of an *obligatio* arising from a transfer of assets that causes a detriment to one of the parties. The *conventio*, in other words, is merely the premise that allows the bargain to be treated as bilateral. It does not itself generate the obligation, but it allows the identification of the circumstances under which this bond arises.

Pedius

At first glance, the role of the *conventio*, as here reconstructed, might appear contradicted by an equally well-known passage by Ulpian reporting the view of Pedius,[38] a jurist who lived between the second half of the first century and the first half of the second century CE.[39]

> Ulp. (4 *ad edictum*) *D.* 2.14.1.3: . . . *adeo autem conventionis nomen generale est ut eleganter dicat Pedius* [*ad edictum* fr. 1 Lenel] *nullum esse contractum, nullam obligationem, quae non habeat in se conventionem, sive re sive verbis fiat: nam et stipulatio, quae verbis fit, nisi habeat consensum, nulla est.*

This fragment, too, has been used to argue for the use of *obligatio* as "act," postulating a "close connection"[40] between Labeo's ideas and those of Pedius, meaning that the latter's thinking is essentially a development of Labeo's.[41] To evaluate this position, it is necessary, first of all, to attempt to determine the context within which Pedius's holding should be placed.

Contrary to what is sometimes believed, it is not at all "obvious"[42] that the phrase *adeo autem conventionis nomen generale est* cited by Ulpian can be attributed to Pedius. It might instead be ascribed to Ulpian, on several grounds. In the first place, the later jurist develops the discussion of *conventio* as a *verbum*

38. See the full bibliography in Santoro, "Il contratto nel pensiero di Labeone" (1983) 188ff. n. 80; Giachi, *Studi su Sesto Pedio* (2005) 518ff. at n. 48.
39. See Giachi, *Studi su Sesto Pedio* (2005) 4ff.
40. Santoro, "Il contratto nel pensiero di Labeone" (1983) 56. Santoro sees a connection also with Paul. (3 *ad edictum*) *D.* 2.14.2 pr.–1.
41. Cerami, "*D.* 2.14.5 (Ulp. 4 *ad edictum*)" (1976) 198; Santoro, "Il contratto nel pensiero di Labeone" (1983) 191.
42. Santoro, "Il contratto nel pensiero di Labeone" (1983) 197. Schiavone ("La scrittura di Ulpiano" [1991] 134) is more cautious.

generale from the very beginning of the paragraph.[43] Second, the construction *adeo . . . ut* introduces a result clause that binds together the entire sentence *ut . . . fiat*:[44] only this part can be attributed to Pedius.[45] Third, we cannot conclusively assume that "if Pedius is cited by Ulpian in the fourth book of his commentary on the Edict, his own thoughts on this subject must have been expressed at the beginning of his own work by the same name."[46] We have in fact no evidence to conclude that Pedius, like Ulpian, was commenting on the *edictum de pactis* and the rubric *conventio*,[47] because the tone of the citation is such as to support even the idea of a broad reference to other places in Pedius's work.[48]

We do better to focus attention, then, on the central part of the text, precisely on the embedded sentence *nullum esse contractum, nullam obligationem, quae non habet in se conventionem, sive re sive verbis fiat*. The main difficulty in interpreting this passage is tied to the initial phrase *nullum esse contractum, nullam obligationem*. In the past, this had been viewed as meaningless verbosity and a sign of interpolation.[49] Recent studies tend, instead, to accept it as genuinely classical and to explain it in two ways.

Some scholars view the sentence as containing a hendiadys used to denote the *obligationes ex contractu*.[50] This idea has been developed further by pos-

43. This part of the text is discussed in the next section of this chapter. See also Talamanca, "*Conventio* e *stipulatio*" (1991) 211.

44. Although it is not uncommon for Ulpian to name an author in the middle of a citation: see Giachi, *Studi su Sesto Pedio* (2005) 521; see also 138ff.

45. The text should therefore be translated as follows: "so true it is that the word 'agreement' [*conventio*] has a general meaning, that as Pedius neatly says, that there is no contract" (see the translation in the appendix).

46. Santoro, "Il contratto nel pensiero di Labeone" (1983) 203.

47. Thus also the reference to Pedius seen in fragment 4 becomes very tenuous; so Santoro, "Il contratto nel pensiero di Labeone" (1983) 197–98.

48. Giachi, *Studi su Sesto Pedio* (2005) 520–21. For example, one could speculate that the subject of *stipulationes* is the main theme of his discussion (*ibid.*, 520ff.), unless we attribute the last sentence to Ulpian, as do Gallo (*Synallagma e conventio nel contratto* 2 [1995] 216; he does not, however, exclude a reference to Pedius's thought) and Garofalo ("Contratto, obbligazione e convenzione in Sesto Pedio" [2006] 352 n. 37), while Schiavone ("La scrittura di Ulpiano" [1991] 136) attributes the sentence to Pedius. An attribution to Ulpian is possible but not certain. The reference to *stipulatio* at the end of the passage, as we have it, seems to amount to nothing more than an illustration that, in substance, simply repeats the principle just given; therefore we must agree that the relationship between *conventio* and *stipulatio* is a "dialectic of distinctions drawn" (Talamanca, "*Conventio* e *stipulatio*" [1991] 214).

49. Perozzi, *Le obbligazioni romane* (1903/1948) 339 n. 1.

50. Voci, *La dottrina romana del contratto* (1946) 399; Talamanca, "*Conventio* e *stipulatio*" (1991) 211 with n. 171.

tulating that Pedius was aware of Labeo's use of *contrahere* in *D.* 50.16.19 (as reconstructed in the form I criticized earlier in this chapter) and that he took this into account by using the two expressions *contractus* and *obligatio* to indicate the bilateral act productive of an obligation. Moreover, Pedius did so, in this reconstruction, with reference both to those acts that, under Labeo's definition, come to be realized through bilateral agreement (*contractus*) and to those acts that, while based on a bilateral agreement and therefore falling within Labeo's (postulated) definition of *contractus,* Labeo had placed in the category of *agere* insofar as they are undertaken *sive verbis sive re,* meaning *stipulatio* and *mutuum.*[51] It should be noted that if this had truly been Labeo's position, Pedius's clarification would have been very opportune indeed. One can hardly deem elegant a definition of *contractus* as a bilateral "act" giving rise to an obligation, based on an agreement so to embrace all *obligationes contractae,* but in which only bilateral transactions (*emptio venditio, locatio conductio* and *societas*) are adduced as examples, while those bargains that give rise to a one-sided obligation are presented as instances of *agere,* even though—since they arise from a bilateral "act"—they too should be placed in the category of *contrahere.*[52] However, as we have seen, this is not the optimal way to interpret the Labeo passage, and the view that the original meaning of *obligatio* is "act" is unacceptable. Moreover, this very explanation of Pedius's would not clarify all that much, because the *contractus-obligatio* hendiadys could lead the reader to the mistaken impression that there is a difference between the two concepts as found in the text of Pedius and that of Labeo: why not speak only of *contractus*?

The second way of looking at the passage sees precisely a distinction in the phrase *nullum contractum, nullam obligationem*: *contractus* would be used for bilateral contracts, *obligatio* for unilateral (or, at any rate, nonreciprocal) ones, as a substitute for Labeo's *actio.*[53] While even this theory is not totally convincing—mainly because the nature of the phrase as a hendiadys is shown beyond doubt by the singular verbs *habeat* and *fiat*[54]—it is, in my view, the solution that is closest to the truth.

---

51. Santoro, "Il contratto nel pensiero di Labeone" (1983) 204ff.
52. See this chapter's earlier section on Labeo.
53. See Knütel, *La causa nella dottrina dei patti* (1997) 131ff., for the first meaning; Garofalo, "Contratto, obbligazione e convenzione in Sesto Pedio" (2006) 351–52 with n. 37, for the second.
54. Santoro, "Il contratto nel pensiero di Labeone" (1983) 193.

For my part, I believe that Pedius was responding to Labeo's definition, which distinguishes between *agere* and *contrahere* (apart from *gerere*), in the sense that the first word refers, in general, to the "manner" in which the procedures were carried out (*re* or *verbis*), while the second refers to the "effects" of these actions, with the result that *contrahere* could be used only in cases of obligations arising for both parties, as in sale, hire, and partnership. Pedius takes this terminological clarification into account and applies it to the problem of the role of *consensus* in contracts, a context that is completely different from Labeo's.

Pedius joins together the logical planes of "manner" and "effects" in a more transparent manner. In giving *contractus* Labeo's meaning of *ultro citroque obligatio,* he makes it clear that a *conventio* is required not only when there is a *contractus,* which is to say an obligation characterized by reciprocity ("effects") deriving from *consensus* ("manner"), but generally in the case of all obligations ("effects"), even when they arise *re* or *verbis* ("manner"). In my opinion, there is, indeed, a hendiadys present in this text. It is, however, what we might describe as an imperfect hendiadys, because Pedius distinguishes not between two definite conceptions on the same level of logic (reciprocal or nonreciprocal obligation) but between a specific and a generic meaning of *obligatio.* In so doing, Pedius does not in any way intend to endow the role of *conventio* in contractual obligations with the attributes of "consensualism." He is simply emphasizing that, regardless of how the *obligatio* arises and regardless of its nature, be it unilateral or bilateral, a *conventio* is always necessary,[55] even if it is not in every case sufficient to give rise to an obligation.

If one accepts this conclusion, then one must also accept what is stated previously, that the focus of the jurists is on *obligatio,* of which *contractus* is only a specific example.

Ulpian

Pedius's reasoning turns, as a *diairesis,* entirely on the dialectic between *obligatio* as a genus and *ultro citroque obligatio* (= *contractus*) as its *species.* The

55. The use of the adjective *nullus* is a warning against viewing in this holding a purely "sociological" emphasis, as argues Talamanca in "*Conventio* e *stipulatio*" (1991) 211, though one should bear in mind his comments in "Inesistenza, nullità ed inefficacia dei negozi giuridici" (1998–99) 1ff.

idea of *conventio* does not constitute a higher conceptual category.[56] Ulpian's approach is completely different. When commenting on the *edictum de pactis et conventionibus,* he proceeds with a series of *divisiones* that illustrate, through a complex pattern of classifications, the meaning of *conventio.*[57]

The first part of Ulpian's discussion deals with the problem of definition. After briefly touching on the *pactum,*[58] he describes the *conventio* as a *verbum generale* regarding any *agere* directed toward *contrahere* or *transigere.* In this regard, he echoes Pedius. Ulpian, however, emphasizes how, in cases where the *conventio* falls within a contract, it assumes the *nomen* of the *contractus* of which it serves as the basis, as in *emptio venditio, locatio conductio, pignus,* and *stipulatio.*

> Ulp. (4 *ad edictum*) *D.* 2.14.1.3: *Conventionis verbum generale est ad omnia pertinens, de quibus negotii contrahendi transigendique causa consentiunt qui inter se agunt: nam sicuti convenire dicuntur qui ex diversis locis in unum locum colliguntur et veniunt, ita et qui ex diversis animi motibus in unum consentiunt, id est in unam sententiam decurrunt. adeo autem conventionis nomen generale est, ut eleganter dicat Pedius nullum esse contractum, nullam obligationem, quae non habeat in se conventionem, sive re sive verbis fiat: nam et stipulatio, quae verbis fit, nisi habeat consensum, nulla est.* 4. *Sed conventionum pleraeque in aliud nomen transeunt: veluti in emptionem, in locationem, in pignus vel in stipulationem.*

Then the *divisiones* begin. The first identifies three *species* of the *genus conventio,* classified on the basis of a different *causa.*[59] They are (a) the *conventiones ex publica causa,* that is, the *pax* that follows warfare; (b) the *conventiones ex privata causa legitima,* the discussion of which the compilers leave to a parallel fragment from Paul's *libri ad edictum,* where the *legitima conventio* is defined as being *lege aliqua confirmatur,* so producing an *actio;*[60] and (c) the *conventiones*

56. So also Talamanca in "*Conventio* e *stipulatio*" (1991) 211.

57. The difference in approach is noticed also by Talamanca in "*Conventio* e *stipulatio*"(1991) 212.

58. Ulp. (4 *ad edictum*) *D.* 2.14.1.2.

59. There has been a natural tendency to connect the expression *causa (publica, privata, legitima, iuris gentium)* with the use of the same word a little further on in the citation of Aristo (*D.* 2.14.7.2). In my opinion, however, not too high a value ought to be placed on the meaning of the word, as perhaps happens with Schiavone, "La scrittura di Ulpiano" (1991) 140ff. It simply indicates the *causa finalis* of the *conventio.* Not coincidentally, the expression is abandoned a little later. Ulpian speaks simply of *publica conventio* (*D.* 2.14.5) and *conventiones iuris gentium* (*D.* 2.14.7 pr.), and Paul speaks of *legitima conventio* (*D.* 2.14.6; see the following note).

60. Paul. (3 ad edictum) *D.* 2.14.6: *Legitima conventio est quae lege aliqua confirmatur, et ideo*

ex privata causa iuris gentium, which, by contrast, are soon after given much broader consideration.

> Ulp. (4 *ad edictum*) *D.* 2.14.5: *Conventionum autem tres sunt species. aut enim ex publica causa fiunt aut ex privata: privata aut legitima aut iuris gentium. publica conventio est, quae fit per pacem, quotiens inter se duces belli quaedam paciscuntur.*

This part of the text is worthy of closer examination. Here, certainly, we find a more systematic perspective as well as an attempt to provide a scheme for classifying agreements.

Notwithstanding the hesitations of some scholars, there is, in my opinion, no doubt that the *divisio* should be attributed to Ulpian. Difficulties arise from the fact that from the first Byzantine commentators onward, the tripartite division has been read as a double bipartition, on the model of a *diairesis-hupodiairesis.*[61] As a result, some have felt it necessary to justify Ulpian's holding with the observation that, by adding together the different *species,* we arrive at a number of three.[62] Some subsequent scholars—starting with the humanists[63]—have criticized Ulpian's arrangement as being inelegant or erroneous.[64] Others argue for corruption of the text,[65] either because this was reworked[66]—the compilers having substituted the original binary schema with the *tres species*[67]—or because of a deletion that eliminated a reference to the third *species,* identified

---

interdum ex pacto actio nascitur vel tollitur, quotiens lege vel senatus consulto adiuvatur (A "statutory" agreement is one that receives its force from some statute. Therefore, sometimes an action arises from or is extinguished by a pact, whenever this is supported by a statute or by a decree of the Senate).

61. See *PSI* no. 55, I *verso* 1.4, a sixth-century papyrus found at Oxyrhynchus that, most probably, records a university course on the *Digest.* See Vassalli, "Frammento di un indice del Digesto" (1911) 180ff.; Vassalli, "Frammento d'un 'indice' del Digesto" (1912) 107ff.
62. Scholion 1 (ἡ κονβεντίων) ad *B.* 11.1.5 (Scheltema, B.1.184).
63. References in Cerami, "*D.* 2.14.5 (Ulp. 4 *ad ed.*)" (1976) 128 n. 9.
64. Voci, *La dottrina romana del contratto* (1946) 298; Biondi, *Contratto e stipulatio,* 134ff.; Talamanca, "Lo schema *genus-species*" (1977) 276–77; Schiavone, "La scrittura di Ulpiano" (1991) 138ff.
65. For older literature advancing arguments based on the assumption of interpolations, now substantially superseded by more recent scholarship (mainly thanks to the work of Riccobono), see Cerami, "*D.* 2.14.5 (Ulp. 4 *ad ed.*)" (1976) 125 nn. 2–3.
66. In addition to the authors cited in the notes that follow, see also Lombardi, *Ricerche in tema di ius gentium* (1946) 215ff.
67. Partsch, "Das Dogma des Synallagma" (1931) 19–20, relying on *PSI* no. 55, I *verso* 1.4.

with the *conventiones iure honorarii*[68] or *ex causa fiscali.*[69] In truth, the very fact that the *antecessores* of Byzantium, who certainly possessed Ulpian's original text, felt the need for these clarifications excludes the possibility of intervention by the compilers. One can, at the most, posit a postclassical reworking.[70] But on a correct understanding of the problem, even this idea is beside the point. The challenges to interpretation derive from the fact that the genus-species schema has been read as a *definitio per genus et speciem,* while it is—or should be—clear that Ulpian is here making a *divisio* of a kind similar to the ones explained by Cicero in the *Topica,* which was not necessarily based on a binary schema as for example, what we find in Cicero's *divisio* of *ius* into *lex, mos, aequitas.*[71]

Ulpian therefore aims at a classification of the *conventiones* within an all-comprehensive schema. His is not, in all likelihood, an isolated effort. It is probable that there was a similar treatment in the equivalent sections of Paul's *libri ad edictum.* The object, however, of both Ulpian's and Paul's commentary was not the *contractus* but the *conventio.*

This fact becomes clear as the discourse continues, when Ulpian undertakes a further *divisio* of the *conventiones iuris gentium* (D. 2.14.7 pr.-2). This, too, begins with a dichotomy that then is transformed into a tripartition.[72] Since it is a text already dealt with earlier in this chapter, it is enough here to summarize the principal points:

a. sometimes the *conventio* generates a *contractus,* and this happens when it falls within a specific (*proprium*) *nomen contractus,* generating a specific action;
b. it also happens when there is a *causa* that gives rise to an *obligatio civilis,* so that protection is achieved via an *actio civilis* to whose *intentio* are added *praescripta verba;*
c. at other times, when both the *nomen contractus* and *causa* are absent, the *conventio* does not give rise to an *obligatio* and assumes procedural

68. Riccobono, "La formazione della teoria generale del *contractus*" (1929) 146–47.
69. Cerami, "*D.* 2.14.5 (Ulp. 4 *ad ed.*)" (1976) 129ff., 188.
70. Cerami, "*D.* 2.14.5 (Ulp. 4 *ad ed.*)" (1976) 131ff.
71. Cic. *Top.* 31. It is not possible here to discuss fully Talamanca's argument in "Lo schema *genus-species*" (1997) 188 ff. that Cicero's treatment of the *divisio* (and *partitio*) was essentially irrelevant for the jurists. I will limit myself to noting that his interpretation of *divisio* as Ulpian's *definitio per genus et speciem* requires accusing the jurist of "una certa trasandatezza nella tecnica diairetica" (a certain sloppiness in his technique of diairesis) (ibid., 276).
72. Schiavone, "La scrittura di Ulpiano" (1991) 146–47.

importance only by way of allowing an affirmative defense (*exceptio*): *sed cum nulla subest causa, propter conventionem hic constat non posse constitui obligationem: igitur nuda pactio obligationem non parit, sed parit exceptionem* (§ 4).

The discussion continues with an analysis of the *exceptio pacti* and comments on the wording of the edict.

As one can easily discern, not even Ulpian offers a "general theory" of *contractus.* Rather, what we find in his writings is a general theory of *conventio,* structured on the alternative of having the agreement give rise or not to an obligation: the "contract" appears only as the means through which the obligation arises—once again as *contrahere* more than as *contractus.* Throughout, the *conventio* remains, to all appearances, hovering in the background, as though waiting in the wings, so that Ulpian, after having described its relevance in cases where the agreement corresponds to a *nomen contractus,* has to clarify the objective conditions required to speak of an *obligatio* in cases when no specific contract arises. But that the true subject of the discourse is always the *conventio* is demonstrated by paragraph 4, in which, having exhausted the themes of *nomen* and *causa,* the discussion resumes by explaining that, beyond these cases, the *conventio iuris gentium* generates not an *actio* but only an *exceptio.*

In other words, the *conventio* never assumes the role of a qualifying element for the *obligatio,* except within the limits already set by Pedius. It is a necessary, but not sufficient, condition in order to give rise to an *obligatio,* which always requires the confluence of objective elements, among which are first and foremost the *nomen* and only secondarily the *causa.* Otherwise—as has been recognized—a different solution would have resulted in "the total cancellation of the principle underlying the standard contracts."[73]

The Central Importance of *Obligatio*

The analysis, however brief, of the texts discussed so far leads us to the conclusion that the Romans did not regard *conventio* as the element that could tie together the different kinds of contracts. The category *contractus* thus is fed

73. Schiavone, "La scrittura di Ulpiano" (1991) 153: "alla totale cancellazione del principio di tipicità."

by and acquires its doctrinal legitimacy not from agreement but, rather, from other factors, such as the *nomen*—meaning the "type"—and the *causa* in the case of innominate contracts. Both *nomen* and *causa* give rise to an *obligatio*, and it is precisely the latter that amounts to the true condition required to justify an agreement as a *contractus*. Throughout the classical period in which the jurists worked, the central importance of the bond in contractual matters seems to prevail. What matters is not so much the contract as the *obligatio contracta*. It cannot be a coincidence that in a didactic work such as the *Institutiones*, Gaius does not write of *contractus* but of *obligationes quae ex contractu nascuntur* (3.89), structuring the subject matter on contracts according to the criterion of "how" the *obligatio* comes to be contracted: *consensu, re, verbis*, or *litteris*. And, as we have seen, also in Labeo's definition, *obligatio* is so all-encompassing that it tends, even in terminological terms, to embrace "contract," confirming that in the language of the jurists, *emptio venditio, locatio conductio*, and *societas* are not "contracts" that give rise to obligations but are *obligationes*, the actual bond itself (what has been "contracted").

What is the reason for the central importance attributed to *obligatio*? It is certainly not the case that the Romans ignored the importance of the *conventio*. Pedius's *dictum* previously cited, as reported and even appropriated by Ulpian, clearly shows, to the contrary, that the *prudentes* accepted that, without agreement, it was not possible to speak of a *contractus*. So why is there such insistence on the bond and consequently on the duty to perform, that is, on the elements that encourage differentiation among contracts and impede the rise of a unifying theory? The problem is a complicated one, not least because the reality of archaic law was of an entirely different nature.

As is well known, the bargains that later on were subsumed into the classical contractual system acquired their legal relevance by means of only a few—transactional and procedural—formal instruments of a "general" nature. It is often said that the contracts for sale, hire, mandate, and so on arose in the third century BCE in conjunction with Roman expansion in the Mediterranean and the resulting increase in international trade. However, this is not really the case. That moment in history gave birth not to the bargains of purchase and sale, leasing, mandate, and so on but only to the possibility of protection grounded on agreement alone. The relevant relationships, in fact, had already been identified as such not only in an economic sense but most probably also in a legal one. In the sources, we see the terms *emere, vendere*, and *locare* in contexts that evidence transactional arrangements that are not dissimilar to those later found with *obligationes consensu contractae.*[74] The formal "general" tools such as *mancipatio* or *stipulatio* were obviously adapted to a given situation through the use of *nuncupationes* or *verba* that bound the parties to the conduct that was desired in a given case. Only in this way was it possible to distinguish, through a *mancipatio,* the definitive surrender of an animal from a time-limited one or the *venum dare* of a *filius* from his submission to *nexum.* Of course, in the case of a *stipulatio,* the promisor obligated himself to a specific performance that defined the content of an otherwise empty *verborum obligatio.* In other words, archaic law recognized both formal acts and their concrete articulations, which possessed legal meaning because, according to the principle found in the Twelve Tables, *cum nexum faciet mancipiumque, uti lingua nuncupassit, ita ius esto.*[75] Thus, it is very likely that actual practice created specific "types" of acts, in the sense that some fixed transactional declarations identified the corresponding specific bargains.

As noted previously, however, these specific bargains received procedural protection only when implicated in a formal act of a "general" nature, just as acts of a "general" nature were mostly the remedies—above all, the *legis actio sacramenti,* but also the *iudicis arbitrive postulatio* and the *condictio,* though in

74. The verb *emere* was used by the Twelve Tables to indicate any *alienatio:* see Aristo (fr. 67 Lenel) = Pomponius (18 *ad Quintum Mucium*) *D.* 40.7.29.1: . . . *lex duodecim tabularum emptionis verbo omnem alienationem complexa videretur* (it seems that the law of the Twelve Tables included in the word *emptio* every kind of alienation); see also Tab. 7.11 = *Inst.* 2.1.41 e Tab. 7.12 = *Tit. Ulp.* 2.4. The usage must predate this statute, as shown by its appearance there in the compound form *coemptio.* The text of the Twelve Tables also doubtless used the verb *vendere* in the form of *venum dare.* See Tab. 4.2b = Gaius 1.132: *si pater filium ter venum du[uit] filius a patre liber esto* (if a *pater* has "sold" a *filius* three times, let the *filius* be free from the *pater*); Gaius 4.79; *Tit. Ulp.* 10.1; Tab. 3.5 = Gell. 20.1.47: . . . *trans Tiberim peregre venum ibant* (. . . were sold abroad, across the Tiber). *Locare, merces, pretium,* and *vendere* appear in Tab. 12.1 = Gaius 4.28: *Lege autem introducta est pignoris capio velut lege XII tabularum adversus eum, qui hostiam emisset nec pretium redderet; item adversus eum, qui mercedem non redderet pro eo iumento, quod quis ideo locasset, ut inde pecuniam acceptam in dapem, id est in sacrificium, inpendere* (the "taking of a pledge" has been instead introduced by statute, as, for example, by the law of the Twelve Tables against the person who had bought an animal for sacrifice but failed to pay for it, likewise against someone who failed to pay the charge for a beast of burden that another person had leased in order to use the money received for a *daps* [i.e., for a sacrifice]). For the antiquity of this terminology and an interpretation of the passage, see Fiori, *La definizione della locatio conductio* (1999) 14ff.

75. Tab. 6.1. Very important, in this regard, are the observations of Corbino, *Il formalismo negoziale,* 1ff. See also Randazzo, *Leges mancipii* (1998), though his argument for a distinction between *leges mancipii* and *nuncupationes* does not strike me as entirely convincing.

a more limited fashion. It is clear that identifying transactions by types had an effect on the form and extent of legal protection that was available, since procedural safeguards and the formulation of *certa verba* could not but take into account the parties' duties. This, however, did not result in a different choice of remedy beyond the scope of a selection among the three declaratory *legis actiones.*

So why did the Roman system of *negotia* begin, at a certain point, to structure itself on the basis of typicality?[76] I believe the answer must be sought in the genesis of the procedure *per formulas* that arose—as shown by its very procedural structure—in order to offer protection in situations beyond the scope of the *ius civile,* very likely by means of *formulae in factum.*[77] As long as the praetor was compelled to deal exclusively with the *ius civile,* he found himself operating within a well-demarcated system—albeit a constantly evolving one, thanks to *interpretatio*—and could therefore utilize "general" forms for safeguarding socially recognized interests. When, however, his goal became that of providing protection for relationships that were beyond the *ius*—we could say "non-*ius*"—the need arose for a selection from the "fact"-based relationships that he would undertake to safeguard in his court, since the praetor would otherwise have to take into consideration every single type of claim. This development was behind the origin of the edict as a "list" of edictal remedies (and, secondarily, of *formulae*) relevant for the situations guaranteed safeguarding at law, a list of procedural tools that—because bearing on specific relationships—necessarily shaped, in the sense of "typicality," the corresponding remedies. Once the formulary procedure was extended to relationships that fell within the scope of the *ius civile,* the latter were compelled, so to speak, to accept the rules established for the protection of "non-*ius,*" even if such rules were unnecessary for the actions based on *ius civile* that could not be refused to a citizen and did not need to be promised by the praetor in the so-called edictal clause.

The possibility, however, cannot be utterly excluded that the institutions of the *ius civile* underwent a slower process of "specification" and that even in the procedure *per formulas,* the corresponding claims remained as indefinite at the beginning as they were in the procedure *per legis actiones.* This may, of course, not have been true for the *actiones civiles* whose *formulae* were written with an *intentio certa*—that is, for *formulae* beginning with the words *si paret.* Their

76. For what follows, see Fiori, "Tipicità contrattuale e teoria generale del contratto" (2006) 105ff.

77. For a fuller treatment, see Fiori, *Ea res agatur* (2003) 195ff.

intentio—which was most probably created in connection with the *formulae in factum*[78] and so had to reproduce the exact wording of the edictal clause—contained, in fact, a clear and specific description of the claim. The *formulae* whose *intentio* was *incerta* contained a very general claim instead, because the description of the case was in the *demonstratio*. Since these latter *formulae* concerned situations under the *ius civile* not protected by *legis actiones* and are therefore likely to have been the most ancient *formulae in ius conceptae*,[79] it is possible that the description of the claim could be looser than what was later required, when the jurists posed the problem of a clear delimitation of the boundaries of the contracts. This could perhaps explain the oscillation in terminology found in Plautus as well as in the language used by Cato regarding the different consensual contracts and particularly those of hire and sale.[80]

Gradually, however, the structure of the different types of contracts assumed a more defined configuration. The original denotative "looseness" of the *demonstrationes* could have led the jurists of the late Republic to identify clearly the internal characteristics of individual contracts, particularly the more complex ones, such as hire or partnership. We need only think of the efforts of Servius's school at finding the right balance between the obligations of the parties in the contract of *locatio conductio*[81] or of the dispute between Servius himself and Q. Mucius over the nature of contributions by the partners in *societas*.[82] Discussion over the matter seems to have ended by Labeo's time, because he begins to take an interest in the problem of protecting contracts where it was not possible to use the typical remedies. As noted earlier in this chapter, the issue was not safeguarding innominate contracts but to protect ineffective typical contracts, where it was only possible to claim damages caused by the breach of secondary obligations or in cases where there were doubts as to which typical action should be used. This development gave rise to a nontypical "*formula* with *demonstratio*," in which the description of the fact was not binding for the judge because it was placed in a *praescriptio* outside the *formula*. These are *formulae* that, as is well known, are variously described in the sources as *actio civilis in factum, actio civilis incerti*, or *agere praescriptis verbis*.

---

78. Again, see Fiori, *Ea res agatur* (2003) esp. 233–34.

79. Fiori, *Ea res agatur* (2003) 242–43.

80. For the texts, see Fiori, *La definizione della locatio conductio* (1999) 17ff., where, however, I interpret the failure to draw distinctions as proof of the use of *legis actiones*.

81. See Fiori, *La definizione della locatio conductio* (1999) 65ff.

82. See, Fiori, "*Bona Fides*," (2011) 211ff.

It was with the work of the Sabinians and the Proculians that the concern of the *prudentes* shifted to drawing distinctions among typical contracts and addressing the problem of protecting innominate ones. Aristo (discussed earlier in this chapter) offered the theoretical schema in which to place the *nova negotia,* identifying the *causa* as a possible basis for obligation, on the same footing as the *nomen contractus.*

In this way, the jurists arrived at a "general—that is, nontypical—protection" of contracts, which, we do well to emphasize, is not at all the same thing as establishing a "general theory" for contracts. At the center of the concept of *contractus* remained always and uniquely the *obligatio,* an element that served more to distinguish among contracts than to unite them under a common category. However, even the use of this "general" remedy did not lead to the end of the "typical" system of contracts, as the praetor had to examine if conditions existed for the application of the standard forms of protection before resorting to this general one.

Subsequent jurists followed along these same lines. In repeating what Pedius and Aristo held, Ulpian (as discussed in the preceding section) offers, in his treatment of *conventio,* a *summa* of the positions elaborated by the *prudentes* who preceded him. So even in the last phase of classical jurisprudence, the picture drawn for us is that of the centrality of the *obligatio.*

Conclusion: A General Theory of Contract (at Last)

The later history of these sources led to radically different results in European law.

The "limiting definitions" and the system of typical contracts were closely tied to the formulary procedure, so that they became essentially anachronistic already in the last phase of Roman legal history, when new procedural forms replaced that *per formulas.* But the system established by the *prudentes* came to be reproduced in Justinian's *Corpus Iuris* and was passed on to later legal scholars.

The authority of the texts that contained the Roman rules helped to preserve them, but they now had to operate in a new reality, even in terms of procedure, in which their logical necessity no longer applied with the same force. In other words, while the formulary procedure imposed typical actions and therefore typical contracts, the Roman contractual types were now preserved because of tradition but were no longer indispensable. A new idea thus began to take hold, grounded in the Roman tradition but aiming at a general theory of the contract. This focuses—almost obviously, we could say—on the sole element capable of unifying the contracts while at the same time distinguishing them from all other obligations, and that is agreement.

It was a slow process, because medieval civil law jurists were still very closely tied to the Roman texts and consequently to the system expressed in them. The premises for innovation were mostly located in canon law, which saw every promise as a bond and its violation as a *peccatum,* until it became an established rule that—contrary to Roman law[83]—*ex nudo pacto oritur actio.*[84] This view, which, as I have noted earlier in this chapter, was greatly mitigated in practice by the parallel elaboration of a theory of *causa* as the "objective" counterpart of agreements,[85] amounted to a significant innovation that had an impact on the development of the civil law doctrine, particularly in the age of Natural Law, when the canonists' approach was acknowledged in civil law through the influence of Second Scholasticism in the sixteenth and seventeenth centuries.

All the same, while agreement can be a useful concept for the elaboration of a general theory, it says little about the conditions actually sought by the interested parties. Alongside the gradual development of the doctrine of consent, attention was also paid, from the Middle Ages onward, to the structural elements of the contract. This line of thought chose *emptio venditio* as a model[86] to establish the theory of essential, natural, and accidental elements in contracts. At this moment, when the contract became a "substance" to be analyzed and subdivided in organic terms, the efforts of the Roman *prudentes* to define contracts in a "limiting" sense lost all meaning, and the *definitio per genus et speciem,* the scholastic schema that, in the meantime, had become central to medieval and Western thought, prevailed for the definition of contracts.

In this new context, "defining contracts" by identifying the conditions that link a bargain with a remedy was not longer an issue. The problem was, rather, that of "defining the contract"—at most, that is, of defining the individual con-

83. Excluding exceptions that, in any event, prove the rule: see Volante, *Il sistema contrattuale* (2001) 157ff.

84. See glossa *distantiam* ad can. *Iuramenti,* c. 12, causa XXII, quaestio 5: "item hic est argumentum quod ex nudo pacto actio oritur." On this, see, for example, Calasso, *Il negozio giuridico* (1967) 267ff.

85. See, for example, Helmholz, "Contracts and the Canon Law" (1990) 51.

86. For what follows, see Fiori, *"Il problema dell'oggetto"* (2003) 182ff.

tract as the species of a wider genus. With this step, the Roman conception of contract was decisively left behind, and a path was opened to the construction of a general theory.

Appendix: Legal Passages Quoted Extensively in the Text

Pomponius (in the fourth book on Quintus Mucius) *D.* 46.3.80: In whichever way a contractual obligation is entered into, it should be dissolved in the same manner: so, when we have entered into a contractual obligation by conduct, it must be dissolved by conduct. Thus, if we give money on loan, the obligation must be dissolved by giving back the same sum. And when the contractual obligation is entered into by words, it must be dissolved either by conduct or by words: by words, when the promisor receives a formal release; by conduct, when he performs what he has promised. Equally, when a purchase and sale or a letting (and hiring) is contracted, since the contractual obligation can be entered into through bare agreement, it is also possible to dissolve it by a contrary agreement.

Ulpian (in the eleventh book on the edict) *D.* 50.16.19: Labeo, in the first book of his commentary on the urban praetor's edict, distinguishes among things that *agantur*, things that *gerantur*, things that *contrahantur*; and indeed *actum* is a general word used when something is said or done, as when making a verbal obligation or a loan; *contractum,* however, is used when there is a reciprocal obligation, what the Greeks call *sunallagma,* like purchase and sale, letting and hiring, partnership; *gestum* means something done without words.

Ulpian (in the fourth book on the edict) *D.* 2.14.1.3: The word "agreement" [*conventio*] has a general significance, being concerned with everything agreed upon by those who transact between themselves in order to reach a private arrangement about a contract or a settlement; for just as those who are collected and come from different places into one place, are said to "come together" [*convenire*], the same can be said of those who, from different motions of mind, come to an agreement on one thing, that is, reach one opinion. And so true it is that the word 'agreement' has a general meaning that, as Pedius neatly says, there is no contract, no obligation that does not contain an agreement, whether it is accomplished by conduct or by words: for even a stipulation, which is accomplished by words, cannot exist unless it contains an agreement. 4. But most agreements are classed by another term, such as sale, hire, pledge, or stipulation.

Ulpian (in the fourth book on the edict) *D.* 2.14.5: There are three types of agreements. For they are made either on a public or a private ground. A private ground is a basis in a statute or in the *ius gentium.* A public agreement is one that is made through a treaty of peace, whenever military leaders reach an accord on some terms.

Ulpian (in the fourth book on the edict) *D.* 2.14.7 pr.: Certain agreements based on the *ius gentium* give rise to actions, others to defenses. 1. Those that give rise to actions do not remain classed under this same term [i.e., "agreement"], but are categorized by a specific type of contract, as with purchase and sale, lease and hire, partnership, loan for use, deposit, and the other similar contracts. 2. But even if the transaction does not fall under the heading of another contract and yet a ground [*causa*] exists, Aristo neatly holds, in a reply to Celsus, that there is an obligation. As happens, for example, when I gave a thing to you so that you give another thing to me, or I gave so that you do something: this [he says] is a *sunallagma,* and hence a civil obligation arises. And, therefore, I think that Julian was rightly reproved by Mauricianus in the following case: I gave you Stichus so that you manumit Pamphilus. You manumitted him. Stichus is then acquired by a third party with a better title. Julian writes that the praetor ought to grant an *actio in factum.* Mauricianus says that a civil action for an uncertain amount, that is, *praescriptis verbis,* is enough. For [he writes] this is a contract, the one that Aristo calls *sunallagma,* and hence this action arises. . . . 4. But, when no ground [*causa*] exists, it is a settled principle that no obligation can arise from the agreement. Therefore a bare agreement gives rise not to an obligation but to a defense.

Bibliography

Albanese, B. "*Agere, gerere* e *contrahere* in *D.* 50.16.19: Congetture su una definizione di Labeone." In *Scritti giuridici,* 1111–70. Palermo: Palumbo, 1991. Originally published in *Studia et Documenta Historiae et Iuris* 38 (1972): 189–246.

Albanese, B. "*Definitio periculosa*: Un singolare caso di *duplex interpretatio*." In *Scritti giuridici,* 1:701–78. Palermo: Palumbo, 1991. Originally published in *Studi G. Scaduto* (Padua: Cedam, 1970), 3:299–376.

Albertario, E. "Le fonti delle obbligazioni e la genesi dell'art. 1097 del Codice civile." In *Studi di diritto romano,* 3:71–94. Milan: Giuffrè, 1936. Originally published in *Rivista di diritto commerciale* 21 (1923): 493–512.

Astolfi, R. "Giuliano e il *legatum liberationis.*" *Labeo* 12 (1966): 338–55.

Astolfi, R. *Studi sull'oggetto dei legati in diritto romano.* Vol. 1. Padua: CEDAM, 1964.

Benöhr, H. P. *Das sogenannte Synallagma in den Konsensual-kontrakten des klassischen römischen Recht.* Hamburg: de Gruyter, 1965.

Beseler, G. von. "Einzelne Studien." *Zeitschrift der Savigny-Stiftung (Romanistische Abteilung)* 52 (1932): 293–95.

Betti, E. *Istituzioni di diritto romano.* Vol. 2, part 1. Padua: CEDAM, 1962.

Betti, E. "Sul valore dogmatico della categoria *contrahere* in giuristi proculiani e sabiniani." *Bullettino dell'Istituto di Diritto Romano* 28 (1915): 3–96.

Biondi, B. *Contratto e stipulatio.* Milan: Giuffrè, 1953.

Bonfante, P. *Corso di diritto romano.* Vol. 4, *Le obbligazioni,* ed. G. Bonfante and G. Crifò. Milan: Giuffrè, 1979.

Bonfante, P. *Istituzioni di diritto romano.* 10th ed. Milan: Giuffrè, 1987.

Bonfante, P. "Sul *contractus* e sui *pacta.*" In *Scritti giuridici varii,* 3:135–49. Turin: Unione Tipografico-Editrice Torinese, 1921. Originally published as "Il contratto e i patti," *Rivista di diritto commerciale* 18.1 (1920): 353–62.

Bonfante, P. "Sulla genesi e l'evoluzione del *contractus.*" In *Scritti giuridici varii,* 3:107–24. Turin: Unione Tipografico-Editrice Torinese, 1921. Originally published in *Rendiconti dell'Istituto Lombardo di scienze e lettere* 40 (1907): 888–902.

Bremer, F. P. *Iurisprudentiae Antehadrianae quae supersunt.* Vol. 1. Leipzig: Teubner, 1896.

Burdese, A. "Ancora sul contratto nel pensiero di Labeone." *Studia et Documenta Historiae et Iuris* 51 (1985): 458–77.

Burdese, A., ed. *Le dottrine del contratto nella giurisprudenza romana.* Padua: Cedam, 2006.

Burdese, A. "Sul concetto di contratto e i contratti innominati in Labeone." In *Le dottrine del contratto nella giurisprudenza romana,* ed. A. Burdese, 111–37. Padua: Cedam, 2006. Originally published in *Atti del Seminario sulla problematica contrattuale in diritto romano (Atti Milano 1987)* (Milan: Cisalpino-Goliardica, 1988), 1:15–40.

Burdese, A. "Sulle nozioni di patto, convenzione e contratto in diritto romano." *Seminarios Complutenses de derecho romano* 5 (1993): 41–66.

Burdese, A. "Sul riconoscimento civile dei cd. contratti innominati." *Iura* 36 (1985): 14–69.

Calasso, F. *Il negozio giuridico.* 2nd ed. Milan: Giuffrè, 1967.

Cannata, C. A. "Atto giuridico e rapporto giuridico." *Studia et Documenta Historiae et Iuris* 57 (1991): 335–82.

Cannata, C. A. "Contratto e causa nel diritto romano." In *Le dottrine del contratto nella giurisprudenza romana,* ed. A. Burdese, 187–220. Padua: CEDAM, 2006. Originally published in *Causa e contratto nella prospettiva storico-comparatistica (Atti Aristec 1995),* ed. L. Vacca (Turin: Giappichelli, 1997), 35–61.

Cannata, C. A. "Der Vertrag als zivilrechtlicher Obligierungsgrund in der römischen Jurisprudenz der klassischen Zeit." In *Collatio iuris Romani: Études H. Ankum,* 1:59–70. Amsterdam: Gieben, 1995.

Cannata, C. A. "La *'distinctio' re-verbis-litteris-consensu* et les problèmes de la pratique (Études sur les obligations 1)." In *Sein und Werden im Recht: Festgabe U. von Lübtow,* 431–55. Berlin: Duncker und Humblot, 1970.

Cascione, C. *Consensus: Problemi di origine, tutela processuale, prospettive sistematiche.* Naples: Editoriale Scientifica, 2003.

Cerami, P. "Contrahere cum fisco." *Annali del Seminario Giuridico dell'Università di Palermo* 34 (1973): 277–396.

Cerami, P. "*D.* 2.14.5 (Ulp. 4 *ad ed.*): Congetture sulle *tres species conventionum.*" *Annali del Seminario Giuridico dell'Università di Palermo* 36 (1976): 123–217.

Cerami, P. "*Ignorantia iuris.*" *Seminarios Complutenses de derecho romano* 4 (1992): 57–85.

Condanari-Michler, S. "Über Schuld und Schaden in der Antike." In *Scritti C. Ferrini,* 3:28–108. Milan: Giuffrè, 1948.

Corbino, A. *Il formalismo negoziale nell'esperienza romana.* Turin: Giappichelli, 1994.

Cursi, M. F., and R. Fiori. "Le azioni generali di buona fede e di dolo nel pensiero di Labeone." *Bullettino dell'Istituto di Diritto Romano* (ser. 4) 1 (2011): 145–84.

dalla Massara, T. *Alle origini della causa del contratto.* Padua: CEDAM, 2004.

Di Paola, S. "L'opera di Giavoleno Prisco sui *libri posteriores* di Labeone." *Bullettino dell'Istituto di Diritto Romano* 49–50 (1947): 277–331.

d'Ors, A. "*Creditum* und *contractus.*" *Zeitschrift der Savigny-Stiftung (Romanistische Abteilung)* 74 (1957): 73–99.

Dumont, F. "*Obligatio.*" In *Mélanges Ph. Meylan,* 1:77–90. Lausanne: Imprimerie Centrale, 1963.

Falcone, G. *Appunti sul IV commentario delle Istituzioni di Gaio.* Turin: Giappichelli, 2003.

Falcone, G. *Obligatio est iuris vinculum.* Turin: Giappichelli, 2003.

Falcone, G. "Ricerche sull'origine dell'interdetto *uti possidetis.*" *Annali del Seminario Giuridico dell'Università di Palermo* 44 (1996): 5–360.

Favre, A. *Rationalia in Pandectas.* 5 vols. Lyons: Aurelianae, 1626.

Fiori, R. "*Bona fides*: Formazione, esecuzione ed interpretazione del contratto nella tradizione civilistica (Parte seconda)." In *Modelli teorici e metodologici nella storia del diritto privato,* ed. R. Fiori, 4: 97–242. Naples: Jovene Editore, 2011.

Fiori, R. "*Contrahere* in Labeone." In *Carmina Iuris: Mélanges M. Humbert,* 311–31. Paris: De Boccard, 2012.

Fiori, R. "*Contrahere* e *solvere obligationem* in Q. Mucio Scevola." In *Fides, Humanitas, Ius: Studi in onore di Luigi Labruna,* 3:1955–74. Naples: Editoriale Scientifica, 2007.

Fiori, R. *Ea res agatur: I due modelli del processo formulare repubblicano.* Milan: Giuffrè, 2003.

Fiori, R. "*Fides* e *bona fides:* Gerarchia sociale e categorie giuridiche." In *Modelli teorici e metodologici nella storia del diritto privato,* 3:237–59. Naples: Jovene Editore, 2008.

Fiori, R. "Il problema dell'oggetto del contratto nella tradizione civilistica." In *Modelli teorici e metodologici nella storia del diritto privato: Obbligazioni e diritti reali,* 169–238. Naples: Jovene Editore, 2003.

Fiori, R. *La definizione della locatio conductio: Giurisprudenza romana e tradizione romanistica.* Naples: Jovene Editore, 1999.

Fiori, R. "*Servire servitutem.*" In *Iuris vincula: Studi M. Talamanca,* 3:355–409. Naples: Jovene Editore, 2001.

Fiori, R. "Storicità del diritto e problemi di metodo: L'esempio della buona fede oggettiva." In *Scopi e metodi della storia del diritto e formazione del giurista europeo (Atti Padua 2005),* ed. L. Garofalo, 25–49. Naples: Jovene Editore, 2007.

Fiori, R. "Tipicità contrattuale e teoria generale del contratto: Alcuni problemi di storia e dogmatica." *Roma e America* 22 (2006): 105–15.

Flume, W. *Rechtsakt und Rechtsverhältnis: Römische Jurisprudenz und modernrechtliches Denken.* Paderborn: Schoningh, 1990.

de Francisci, P. Συνάλλαγμα: *Storia e dottrina dei cosiddetti contratti innominati.* 2 vols. Pavia: Cedam, 1916.

Gallo, F. "Eredità di giuristi romani in materia contrattuale." In *Le teorie contrattualistiche nella storiografia contemporanea (Atti Siena 1989),* ed. N. Bellocci, 3–82. Naples: Jovene Editore, 1991.

Gallo, F. *Synallagma e conventio nel contratto.* 2 vols. Turin: Giuffrè, 1992–95.

Gallo, F. "Ai primordi del passaggio dalla sinallagmaticità dal piano delle obbligazioni a quello delle prestazioni." In *Le dottrine del contratto nella giurisprudenza romana,* ed. A. Burdese, 159–85. Padua: CEDAM, 2006. Originally published in *Causa e contratto nella prospettiva storico-comparatistica (Atti Aristec 1995),* ed. L. Vacca (Turin: Giappichelli, 1997), 63–83.

Garofalo, L. "Contratto, obbligazione e convenzione in Sesto Pedio." In *Le dottrine del contratto nella giurisprudenza romana,* ed. A. Burdese, 337–78. Padua: CEDAM, 2006.

Giachi, C. *Studi su Sesto Pedio: La tradizione, l'editto.* Milan: Giuffrè, 2005.

Gordon, W. M., and O. F. Robinson, *The "Institutes" of Gaius.* London: Duckworth, 1988.

Grosso, G. "Contratto (diritto romano)." *Enciclopedia del diritto* 9 (1961): 750–59.

Grosso, G. *Il sistema romano dei contratti.* 1st ed. Turin: Giappichelli, 1945.

Grosso, G. *Il sistema romano dei contratti.* 3rd ed. Turin: Giappichelli, 1963.

Helmholz, R. H. "Contracts and the Canon Law." In *Towards a General Law of Contract,* ed. J. Barton, 49–65. Berlin: Duncker und Humblot, 1990.

Honoré, A. M. "Labeo's *Posteriora* and the Digest Commission." In *Daube Noster: Essays in Legal History for D. Daube,* ed. A. Watson, 161–81. Edinburgh: Scottish Academic Press, 1974.

Horak, F. Review of O. Behrends, *Die Wissenschaftslehre* (1976) and A. Schiavone, *Nascita della giurisprudenza* (1976). *Zeitschrift der Savigny-Stiftung (Romanistische Abteilung)* 95 (1978): 402–21.

Horvat, M. "Osservazioni sulla *bona fides* nel diritto romano obbligatorio." In *Studi V. Arangio-Ruiz,* 1:423–43. Naples: Jovene Editore, 1953.

Jörs, P. "Antistius (34)." *Realencyclopädie der classischen Altertumswissenschaft* 1.2 (1897): 2548–57.

Kaser, M. *Das römische Privatrecht.* 2nd ed. 2 vols. Munich: C. H. Beck, 1971–75.

Kaser, M. "*Divisio obligationum.*" In *Studies J. A. C. Thomas,* 73–86. London: Sweet and Maxwell, 1983. Reprinted in *Römische Rechtsquellen und angewandte Juristenmethode* (Vienna: Böhlau, 1986), 155–72.

Knütel, R. *Contrarius consensus: Studien zur Vertragsaufhebung im römischen Recht.* Cologne: Böhlau, 1968.

Knütel, R. "La causa nella dottrina dei patti." In *Causa e contratto nella prospettiva storico-comparatistica (Atti Aristec 1995),* ed. L. Vacca, 131–44. Turin: Giappichelli, 1997.

Kohlhaas, Ch. *Die Überlieferung der "libri posteriores" des Antistius Labeo.* Pfaffenweiler: Centaurus Verlag, 1986.

Kunkel, W. "*Fides* als schöpferisches Element im römischen Schuldrecht." In *Festschrift P. Koschaker,* 2:1–15. Weimar: Böhlau, 1939.

La Pira, G. "La personalità scientifica di Sesto Pedio." *Bullettino dell'Istituto di Diritto Romano* 45 (1938): 293–334.

Lantella, L. *Il lavoro sistematico nel discorso giuridico romano.* Turin: Giappichelli, 1975.

Lantella, L. "Note semantiche sulle definizioni di *obligatio.*" In *Studi G. Grosso,* 4:165–230. Turin: Giappichelli, 1971.

Lauria, M. "*Contractus, delictum, obligatio.*" *Studia et Documenta Historiae et Iuris* 4 (1938): 163–92. Reprinted in *Studii e ricordi* (Naples: Jovene Editore, 1983), 619–44.

Lenel, O. "Interpolationenjagd." *Zeitschrift der Savigny-Stiftung (Romanistische Abteilung)* 45 (1925): 17–38.
Lenel, O. *Palingenesia iuris civilis.* 2 vols. Leipzig: Tauchnitz, 1889.
Levy, E. *Der Hergang der römischen Ehescheidung.* Weimar: Bohlaus, 1925.
Lombardi, G. *Ricerche in tema di ius gentium.* Milan: Giuffrè, 1946.
Magdelain, A. *Le consensualisme dans l'édit du préteur.* Paris: Sirey, 1958.
Mantovani, D. "Sull'origine dei *libri posteriores* di Labeone." *Labeo* 34 (1988): 271–322.
Marotta, V. "Tutela dello scambio e commerci mediterranei in età arcaica e repubblicana." *Ostraka* 5 (1996): 63–138.
Martini, R. "Il mito del consenso nella dottrina del contratto." *Iura* 42 (1991): 97–109.
Melillo, G. *Contrahere, pacisci, transigere: Contributi allo studio del negozio bilaterale romano.* Naples: Liguori, 1994.
Partsch, J. "Das Dogma des Synallagma im römischen und byzantinischen Rechte." In *Aus nachgelassenen und kleineren verstreuten Schriften,* 3–95. Berlin: Springer, 1931.
Pernice, A. *Labeo. Römisches Privatrecht im ersten Jahrhundert der Kaiserzeit.* Vol. 1, part 1. Halle: Max Niemeyer, 1873.
Pernice, A. "Parerga. III. Zur Vertragslehre der römischen Juristen." *Zeitschrift der Savigny-Stiftung (Romanistische Abteilung)* 9 (1888): 195–260.
Perozzi, S. "Dalle obbligazioni da delitto alle obbligazioni da contratto." In *Scritti giuridici,* 2:441–549. Milan: Giuffrè, 1948.
Perozzi, S. "Il contratto consensuale classico." In *Scritti giuridici,* 2:563–97. Milan: Giuffrè, 1948. Originally published in *Studi F. Schupfer,* (Turin: Fratelli Bocca, 1898), 165–99.
Perozzi, S. *Le obbligazioni romane.* In *Scritti giuridici,* 2:311–439. Milan: Giuffrè, 1948. Originally published as *Le obbligazioni romane* (Bologna: Zanichelli, 1903).
Pugliese, G. *Actio e diritto subbiettivo.* Milan: Giuffrè, 1939.
Randazzo, S. *Leges mancipii: Contributo allo studio dei limiti di rilevanza dell'accordo negli atti formali di alienazione.* Milan: Giuffrè, 1998.
Riccobono, S. *Corso di diritto romano: Stipulationes, contractus, pacta.* Milan: Giuffrè, 1935.
Riccobono, S. "Dal diritto romano classico al diritto moderno: A proposito di *D.* 10, 3, 14 (Paul 3 *ad Plautium*)." In *Scritti di diritto romano,* 2:91–138. Palermo: Università degli Studi, 1964.
Riccobono, S. "Der Wille als Entwicklungsfaktor im römischen Rechte." In *Scritti C. Ferrini,* 4:55–63. Milan: Giuffrè, 1949.
Riccobono, S. "La formazione della teoria generale del *contractus* nel periodo della giurisprudenza classica." In *Studi P. Bonfante,* 1:123–73. Milan: Giuffrè, 1929.

Santalucia, B. "I legati ad effetto liberatorio fino a Giuliano." *Labeo* 13 (1967): 151–93.
Santalucia, B. *I legati ad effetto liberatorio nel diritto romano.* Naples: Jovene Editore, 1964.
Santoro, R. "Il contratto nel pensiero di Labeone." *Annali del Seminario Giuridico dell'Università di Palermo* 37 (1983): 5–304.
Santoro, R. "La causa delle convenzioni atipiche." In *Le dottrine del contratto nella giurisprudenza romana,* ed. A. Burdese, 221–77. Padua: CEDAM, 2006. Originally published in *Causa e contratto nella prospettiva storico-comparatistica (Atti Aristec 1995),* ed. L. Vacca (Turin: Giappichelli, 1997), 85–130.
Sargenti, M. "Labeone e la nascita dell'idea di contratto nel pensiero giuridico romano." *Iura* 38 (1987): 25–71.
Sargenti, M. "Svolgimento dell'idea di contratto nel pensiero giuridico romano." *Iura* 39 (1988): 24–74.
Schiavone, A. *Giuristi e nobili nella Roma repubblicana.* Rome: Laterza, 1987.
Schiavone, A. "La scrittura di Ulpiano: Storia e sistema nelle teorie contrattualistiche del quarto libro *ad edictum.*" In *Le teorie contrattualistiche nella storiografia contemporanea (Atti Siena 1989),* ed. N. Bellocci, 125–61. Naples: Jovene Editore, 1991.
Schiavone, A. "Negozio giuridico (diritto romano)." *Enciclopedia del diritto* 27 (1977): 906–21.
Schiavone, A. *Studi sulle logiche dei giuristi romani.* Naples: Jovene Editore, 1971.
Schmidlin, B. *Die römischen Rechtsregeln: Versuch einer Typologie.* Cologne: Böhlau, 1970.
Schulz, F. *Prinzipien des römischen Rechts.* Berlin: Duncker und Humblot, 1934.
Siber, H. "Contrarius consensus." *Zeitschrift der Savigny-Stiftung (Romanistische Abteilung)* 42 (1921): 68–102.
Stoll, H. "Die formlose Vereinbarung der Aufhebung eines Vertragsverhältnisses im römischen Recht." *Zeitschrift der Savigny-Stiftung (Romanistische Abteilung)* 44 (1924): 1–85.
Talamanca, M. "Contratto e patto nel diritto romano." In *Le dottrine del contratto nella giurisprudenza romana,* ed. A. Burdese, 37–83. Padua: CEDAM, 2006 Originally published in *Digesto (discipline privatistiche-sezione civile)* 4 (1989): 58–77.
Talamanca, M. "Conventio e stipulatio." In *Le teorie contrattualistiche nella storiografia contemporanea (Atti Siena 1989),* ed. N. Bellocci, 163–218. Naples: Jovene Editore, 1991.
Talamanca, M. "Inesistenza, nullità ed inefficacia dei negozi giuridici nell'esperienza romana." *Bullettino dell'Istituto di Diritto Romano* 101–2 (1998–99): 1–39.
Talamanca, M. "Intorno ad una recente ipotesi sulla *liberatio legata.*" *Studi Cagliari* 44 (1963–64): 627–92.
Talamanca, M. *Istituzioni di diritto romano.* Milan: Giuffrè, 1990.

Talamanca, M. "La *bona fides* nei giuristi romani: 'Leerformel' e valori dell'ordinamento." In *Il ruolo della buona fede oggettiva nell'esperienza giuridica storica e contemporanea: Atti in onore A. Burdese (Padova—Venezia—Treviso 2001)*, vol. 4, ed. L. Garofalo, 1–312. Padua: CEDAM, 2003.

Talamanca, M. "La tipicità dei contratti romani tra *conventio* e *stipulatio* fino a Labeone." In *Contractus e pactum: Tipicità e libertà negoziale nell'esperienza tardo-repubblicana (Atti Copanello, 1988)*, ed. F. Milazzo, 35–108. Naples: Edizioni Scientifiche Italiane, 1990.

Talamanca, M. "Lo schema *genus-species* nelle sistematiche dei giuristi romani." In *La filosofia greca e il diritto romano (Atti Roma 1973)*, 2:3–319. Rome: Accademia Nazionale dei Lincei, 1977.

Talamanca, M. Review of A. Schiavone, *Giuristi e nobili* (1987). *Bullettino dell'Istituto di Diritto Romano* 91 (1988): 881–907.

Talamanca, M. "Vendita (diritto romano)." *Enciclopedia del diritto* 46 (1993): 303–475.

Vacca, L., ed. *Causa e contratto nella prospettiva storico-comparatistica (Atti Aristec 1995)*. Turin: Giappichelli, 1997.

Vassalli, F. "Frammento di un indice del Digesto." *Bullettino dell'Istituto di Diritto Romano* 24 (1911): 180–203.

Vassalli, F. "Frammento d'un 'indice' del Digesto." In *Papiri greci e latini*, 1:107–22. Florence: Tipografia E. Ariani, 1912.

Vocabularium iurisprudentiae romanae. Vol. 1. Berlin: Reimer, 1903.

Vocabularium iurisprudentiae romanae. Vol. 4. Berlin: de Gruyter, 1914–1936–1985.

Voci, P. "La dottrina del contratto nei giuristi romani dell'età classica." In *Scritti in onore di C. Ferrini*, 383–99. Milan: Giuffrè, 1946.

Voci, P. *La dottrina romana del contratto*. Milan: Giuffrè, 1946.

Volante, R. *Il sistema contrattuale del diritto comune classico*. Milan: Giuffrè, 2001.

Watson, A., ed. *The "Digest" of Justinian*. Rev. ed. 2 vols. Philadelphia: University of Pennsylvania Press, 1998.

Wieacker, F. Review of S. E. Wunner, *Contractus* (1964). *Tijdschrift voor Rechtsgeschiedenis* 35 (1967): 129–45.

Wieacker, F. *Societas: Hausgemeinschaft und Erwerbsgesellschaft*. Vol. 1. Weimar: Bohlaus, 1936.

Wlassak, M. "Actio." *Realencyclopädie der classischen Altertumswissenschaft* 1.1 (1893): 303–25.

Wlassak, M. *Römische Prozessgesetze*. 2 vols. Leipzig: Duncker und Humblot, 1891.

Wunner, S. E. *Contractus: Sein Wortgebrauch und Willensgehalt im klassischen römischen Recht*. Cologne: Böhlau, 1964.

Zimmermann, R. *The Law of Obligations: Roman Foundations of the Civilian Tradition*. Cape Town: Juta, 1990.

CHAPTER 3

Roman Contracts and the Construction of Fault in Their Formation

FEDERICO PROCCHI

The Construction of Fault in the Formation of Contracts and the Future of Obligations

The theme of "fault" in contract formation emerges as of the greatest importance in the context of a study of a past culture that is pitched toward the "future" of obligations. This is because, as everyone knows, it involves three fundamental questions still being strongly debated today—even in the area of what has been described as "law in action"—by scholars in numerous countries.[1] These questions are

1. the nature of compensatory remedies,
2. the grounds for precontractual liability, and
3. the criterion for a judge's calculation of recoverable loss.

Since each of these issues is rooted in the problematics raised in a famous 1860 essay by Rudolf von Jhering concerning compensation for damage in contracts that are invalid or not concluded in the first place,[2] it is convenient for the mod-

1. See Ben-Dror, "Perennial Ambiguity of *Culpa in Contrahendo*" (1983) 178–98; Hondius, "Precontractual Liability" (1991) 3–28; Kessler and Fine, "*Culpa in Contrahendo*" (1964) 409–49; Kuonen, "La *culpa in contrahendo*" (2005) 267–69; Luchetti and Petrucci, *Fondamenti di diritto contrattuale europeo* (2006) 115–23; Rabello, "*Culpa in Contrahendo*" (1997) 464–98; Rabello, "Buona fede e responsabilità precontrattuale" (2003) 125–227; Solidoro Maruotti, *Gli obblighi di informazione a carico del venditore* (2007) 71–74, 125–27; Zimmermann, *Law of Obligations,* 245 and n. 77; Kuonen, *La responsabilité précontractuelle* (2007) 325–593; Solidoro Maruotti, "Annotazioni" (2010) 1–3; Procchi, *Licet emptio non teneat* (2012) 363–92.
2. The article appears in the fourth volume of the *Dogmatische Jahrbücher,* the title page of which gives the year 1861, but I believe I have demonstrated that the first number from that year,

ern interpreter to take as a point of departure a critical, even if brief, reconsideration of that article in order to examine the influence it has had, directly or indirectly, on modern scholarship regarding precontractual liability.

Loss Derived from the Apparent Conclusion of a Contract and the Denial of the Extracontractual Nature of Liability

As is well understood, eminently practical reasons induced Rudolf von Jhering to consider the possibility of recognizing a remedy on behalf of a party who had been involved in negotiations that turn out to be futile because the contract is void or not concluded. In concrete terms, the *Willenstheorie* (theory of intent)—then dominant in Germany because supported by the authority of Friedrich Carl von Savigny and the Historical School of law, among others—influenced legal authorities[3] to consider invalid all contracts characterized by a material mistake in fact[4] and thus prevented a victim of another's erroneous declaration from bringing suit to seek compensation for the loss suffered. If one wished to remain solidly anchored in the sources of Roman law, even the route of extracontractual liability was barred for a person who had suffered harm of this sort, since the application of the supplementary *actio doli* was limited only to cases of deliberate misconduct by a contracting party[5] and since resort to the *actio ex lege Aquilia* was limited to the compensation only of *damnum corpore corpori datum.*[6]

containing precisely the article dedicated to *culpa in contrahendo,* had been published at the beginning of the summer in 1860: see Procchi, "Nota di lettura" (2005) xviii–xix and n. 11.

3. See Kindereit, "Wer fühlt nicht" (2001) 122; Procchi, "Nota di lettura" (2005) xxxii. Even though Rudolf von Jhering took his distance from the Historical School of law early on and pursued an original, independent path, he never questioned the so-called *Willensdogma.* See Giaro, "*Culpa in contrahendo*" (2000) 144, which speaks of a "hypertrophy" of the theory of will on the part of the Pandectist movement .
4. See Coing, *Europäisches Privatrecht* (1989) 2:275–79; Zimmermann, *Law of Obligations* (1996) 602–4, 614–16.
5. See Kaser, *Das römische Privatrecht* (1971) 1:627–28.
6. The Pandectists had, in fact, recovered the ancient requirements for the application of the *actio legis Aquilae,* and these prevented the continued resort to it, as sometimes had happened in the old *ius commune,* as a kind of general compensatory remedy: see Coing, *Europäisches Privatrecht,* (1989) 2:440. Concerning the characteristics of the *actio legis Aquiliae:* see Kaser, *Das römische Privatrecht* (1971) 1:621–22. But also see the recent clarification of Cursi, "Per una storia critica" (2006); Cursi, *Danno* (2010) 64–91.

Jhering found such a pat solution particularly unjust,[7] above all with regard to three instances that tended to recur in the commercial practice of his day:

- that of a writing error committed in a negotiation conducted by written correspondence;[8]
- that of a commission poorly executed by a messenger who assumed, as a mere *nuntius,* the role of oral bearer of another's intent to make an agreement;[9] and
- that of a manifestation of intent entrusted to a telegraphic dispatch transmitted with errors made by the telegrapher.[10]

The Roman jurists, for their part, are not known ever to have developed case law based on this perspective,[11] and the earliest scholarship on the *ius commune* believed it had reached a satisfactory solution of the problem in question through a nonstandard, generalized application of the extracontractual remedy for loss explicitly founded by proponents of natural law on the basis of social needs linked to general notions of equity.[12] Of particular interest here is a much-debated passage in the *De iure belli ac pacis* of Hugo Grotius (1583–1645).[13]

> Hugo Grotius *De iure belli ac pacis* 2.11.6.3: *Quod si promissor negligens fuit in re exploranda, aut in senso suo exprimendo, et damnum inde alter passus sit, tenebitur id resarcire promissor, non ex vi promissionis, sed ex damno per culpam dato.*
>
> [If, however, the promissory was careless in investigating the matter or in expressing his thought, and if another suffered loss therefrom, the promissory will be bound to offer compensation not by the force of the promise but by reason of the loss suffered by his fault.]

7. See Jhering, "*Culpa in contrahendo*" (1860) 2: "the injustice and the inadequacy on a practical level of such a result leap to one's eyes; the party at fault is not held liable, and the party one can blame for nothing becomes a victim of the other's guilt!"
8. See Jhering, "*Culpa in contrahendo*" (1860) 2.
9. See Jhering, "*Culpa in contrahendo*" (1860) 4–5.
10. See Jhering, "*Culpa in contrahendo*" (1860) 6.
11. See Deroussin, "*Culpa in contrahendo*" (2004) 193–205; Procchi, "*Dolus e culpa in contrahendo* nella compravendita" (2007) 184, 218–24.
12. See Zimmermann, *Law of Obligations* (1996) 612–14.
13. See Kleinheyer-Schröder, *Deutsche und Europäische Juristen aus neun Jahrhunderten* (1996) 176–82.

Taking into consideration that the sources for *stipulatio* and *pacta* underwent a process of generalization in the seventeenth century and were then broadly employed to construct a general theory of contract, we can conclude that the *ius commune* had long ago provided a solution for the needs of practice through a generalized grant of the extracontractual remedy for loss in cases similar to those on which Jhering had focused.[14]

French legal scholarship would arrive at a similar result[15] during the course of the eighteenth century, thanks, above all, to the work of Robert-Joseph Pothier (1699–1772).[16] Pothier held that a mistake over the identity of one of the contracting parties (*error in persona*) excluded the validity of agreement only when consideration of certain characteristics of the individual had become part of the contract itself. This occurred each time the services linked to the contract were characterized by a strong *intuitus personae,* as when someone wanting to commission a painting by a great artist ("Natoire") wound up engaging, by mistake, a modest dauber ("Jacques").[17] Since this concerns an error that is not merely incidental, it is without doubt a ground for invalidating the contract. But if the case were seen this way, the painter of modest abilities, who might have rejected other work opportunities in order to accept the offer in question and who might, in actual fact, have already completed the commission, would find himself or herself deprived of any protection whatsoever and would have to bear the consequences of someone else's *error in persona.* Such an outcome seemed unfair to Pothier, who felt it necessary to offer some important clarifications.

> Pareillement, si voulant faire faire un tableau par *Natoire,* je fais marché pour faire ce tableau, avec Jacques que je prends pour *Natoire,* le marché est invalid, faute de consentement de ma part: car je n'ai pas voulu faire faire un tableau par Jacques, mais par *Natoire;* la considération de la personne de *Natoire* et de sa

14. See Choe, *"Culpa in contrahendo" bei Rudolf von Jhering* (1988) 218–20; Hutchison, "Contract Formation" (1996) 165–94. Of a different opinion is Feenstra ("De oorsprong van Hugo de Groot's leer over de dwaling" (1971) 98–101), according to whom the text in question would play a role only in the development of the theory of error.
15. See Zimmerman, *Law of Obligations* (1996) 613 n. 178. According to him, "in French law, the problem is obviated by the general clause of delictual liability (art. 1382), which, in turn, derives from the theories of natural law."
16. See Kleinheyer-Schröder, *Deutsche und Europäische Juristen aus neun Jahrhunderten* (1996) 321–24.
17. See Pothier, *Traité des obligations* (1777) 23.

> réputation entroient dans le marché que je voulois faire. Observez néanmoins que si Jacques, qui ignoroit que je le prenois pour *Natoire,* a, en conséquence de cette convention erronée, fait le tableau, je serai obligé de le prendre, et de le payer suivant le dire des experts. Mais ce n'est pas, en ce cas, la convention qui m'y oblige, cette convention, qui est nulle, ne pouvant produire aucune obligation: la cause de mon obligation est en ce cas l'équité, qui m'oblige à indemniser celui que j'ai, par mon imprudence, induit en erreur. Il nâit de cette obligation une action qui s'appelle *actio in factum.*[18]
>
> [Similarly, if I, wishing to have a painting painted by *Natoire,* arrange to have the painting done by Jacques, who I take for *Natoire,* the agreement is invalid, given the absence of consent on my part: for I did not wish to have a painting done by Jacques, but by *Natoire;* my opinion of the person of *Natoire* and of his reputation entered into the agreement that I wanted to make. Observe nonetheless that if Jacques, unaware that I had taken him for *Natoire,* had, as a consequence of this mistaken agreement, finished the painting, I would be obliged to accept it, and to pay for it according to the estimation of experts. But in this case it is not the agreement that obliges me. This agreement, which is invalid, is incapable of generating any obligation. The ground of my obligation is, in this case, fairness, which obliges me to indemnify him, whom I had, by my imprudence, induced into error. From this obligation arises a remedy that is called *actio in factum.*]

Pothier held that, in the absence of a valid contract, the client must nevertheless be made liable through an *in factum* remedy for the task entrusted to "Jacques," who did not know he was thought to be "Natoire." Our author excluded, logically, any remedy based on the contract, given the invalidity of the agreement. Agreement could produce no obligation, given the mistake, but the fault (*imprudence*) of the party who had commissioned the painting merited, nonetheless, a sanction that was, in substance, extracontractual in nature,[19] derived from considerations of equity. The price to be paid for the work done by the painter of modest talents could not, therefore, be that agreed on in the contract but would have to be determined "fairly" according to the judgment of experts.

18. Pothier, *Traité des obligations* (1777) 23–24.

19. The recognition of an *actio in factum,* instead of the *actio empti,* in cases of relative invalidity recognized by the sources constituted for Pothier the sole compromise reconcilable with his theory of the effects of invalidity. See Deroussin, "*Culpa in contrahendo*" (2004) 212.

In this way, there had developed during the seventeenth and eighteenth centuries a genuine, generalized "hypertrophy" of extracontractual liability that in Germany encountered serious challenge only with the rise of the Historical School and its call for a direct and faithful reading of the Roman legal sources.[20] The result of this development was a break in continuity with the ancient tradition of the *ius commune,* accomplished through the exclusion from the list of sources of private law of both the scholarship and the forensic practice of the *usus modernus.*[21] In any case, an application, by way of analogy, of the remedy offered by the *lex Aquilia* was at first tentatively advanced by Jhering himself in the first volume of his *Jahrbücher* (1857),[22] in an article dedicated to the distinction between de facto cooperation with the acts in the law of others ("factische Dienstleistungen bei einem fremden Rechtsgeschäft") and cooperation in a legal sense with such activities of others ("juristische Mitwirkung für fremde Rechtsgeschäfte") in order to create a basis for delictual liability (even where the requirements stipulated by Roman law were lacking) for the messenger who has erroneously transmitted the contractual intent of another, thus causing loss for the recipient of the offer.[23] But this idea came into irremediable conflict with the indispensable necessity of recovering the actual wording of the sources of Roman law and renouncing the unacceptable deviations and strained interpretations characteristic of the scholarship on the *ius commune.*

For this reason, this early position of Jhering's necessarily very soon revealed itself to be entirely unsatisfactory in the eyes of Jhering himself,[24] on a level with the recognized absence of liability on the part of the person who had chosen to rely on a third party for "de facto cooperation" in the performance of an act. To put it in Jhering's own words, "this is an outcome that outrages every notion of justice, but one that anyone wishing to stick strictly to Roman law in this area will be able to avoid only with difficulty."[25] Thus there began to appear in Jhering's writings emphasis on the centrality of that *Rechtsgefühl* (sensibility for law).[26] This slowly came to form the basis of a scholarly direction that

20. See Giaro, "*Culpa in contrahendo*" (2000) 114.
21. See Giaro, "Diritto romano attuale" (2005) 87; Pugliese, *Scritti giuridici scelti* (1985) 3:431–32, 450–51.
22. See Procchi, "Nota di lettura" (2005) xxxii–xxxiv.
23. See Jhering, "Unsere Aufgabe" (1857) 281–82.
24. See Jhering, "*Culpa in contrahendo*" (1860) 5.
25. So Jhering, "Unsere Aufgabe" (1857) 280 n. 7.
26. This centrality would reach its fullest expression at the famous Viennese conference of 1884: see Jhering, "Ueber die Entstehung des Rechtsgefühles" (1884).

wound its way "through Roman law, but surpassing it,"[27] and that came to form the basic premise of his 1860 article on *culpa in contrahendo.*[28] I have elsewhere shown how this study should be considered a kind of "intermediate stage" of Rudolf von Jhering's transition as a scholar from "juristische Konstruktion" to "praktische Jurisprudenz."[29]

The Foundations in Roman Law Scholarship of the Construction of *Culpa in Contrahendo*

It is at this point opportune to draw attention to the foundations that had been laid in modern Roman law scholarship for Jhering's theory. Since Jhering, for the reasons already stated, was compelled to recognize the invalidity of a contract compromised by error, he reviewed the sources of Roman law in order to see whether they offered any theory of contractual invalidity in which a person who had relied in vain on the effectiveness of a contract could nonetheless be assured of some kind of compensation. In the wake of a study by Heinrich Richelmann published in 1837,[30] which had substantially been ignored by subsequent literature, Jhering concentrated his attention on several sources regarding the impossibility of performance.

As is well known, if the parties set forth in a contract a performance that is impossible *ab initio,* no valid obligation can arise.[31] Such a principle is summarized in a well-known maxim of Celsus found in the title of the *Digest* known as *De diversis regulis iuris antiqui.*

> Celsus (8 *dig.*) *D.* 50.17.185: *Impossibilium nulla obligatio est.*
>
> [Celsus, in the eighth book of his *Digests*: There is no obligation to do anything that is impossible.]

---

27. See Jhering, *Geist des römischen Rechts* (1878) 1:14; Jhering, "Unsere Aufgabe" (1857) 52.
28. See Procchi, "Nota di lettura" (2005) xxxix–xli.
29. See Procchi, "Nota di lettura" (2005) xxxvi–xlvii.
30. See Richelman, *Der Einfluß des Irrthums auf Verträge* (1837) 129–38.
31. See Cuena Boy, *Estudios sobre la imposibilidad de la prestación* (1992) 9–42; Talamanca, "Vendita (diritto romano)" (1993) 329–31; Rabello, "Theory concerning *Culpa in Contrahendo*" (1994) 91–109 and further bibliography therein.

Following Richelmann, Jhering considered it necessary to invoke as authoritative the interpretation of several sources on the sale of *res extra commercium* and nonexistent inheritances.[32] The following sources in particular come into play:

Modestinus (5 *reg.*) *D.* 18.1.62.1: *Qui nesciens loca sacra vel religiosa vel publica pro privatis comparavit, licet emptio non teneat, ex empto tamen adversus venditorem experietur, ut consequatur quod interfuit eius, ne deciperetur.*

[(Modestinus, in the fifth book of his *Rules*). If a person unwittingly buys sacred, religious, or public land, then, although there is no valid purchase, he or she can nonetheless have an action against his or her seller for the damages he or she has suffered through being deceived.]

Inst. Iust. 3.23.5: *Loca sacra vel religiosa, item publica, veluti forum basilicam, frustra quis sciens emit, quas tamen si pro privatis vel profanis deceptus a venditore emerit, habebit actionem ex empto, quod non habere ei liceat, ut consequatur, quod sua interest deceptum non esse. idem iuris est, si hominem liberum pro servo emerit.*

[(Justinian in the third book of his *Institutes*). A buyer who knows he is buying a sacred or a religious place or a public one, for instance, a forum or a basilica, achieves nothing at all. However, if he is misled by the seller and buys them as if they were private or secular, he can bring an action on purchase against the seller, on the ground that he has not been allowed to remain in possession. That action will allow him to recover his interest in not being misled. The law is the same where a purchaser buys someone as a slave who turns out to be free.]

Ulpianus (25 *ad edictum*) *D.* 11.7.8.1: *Si locus religiosus pro puro venisse dicetur, praetor in factum actionem in eum dat ei ad quem ea res pertinet: quae actio et in heredem competit, cum quasi ex empto actionem contineat.*

[(Ulpian in the twenty-fifth book on the Edict): If a religious site is alleged to

32. See Talamanca,"Vendita (diritto romano) (1993) 335–37, 348–55; Trisciuoglio, "Sinallagma genetico e vendita delle *res extra commercium*" (2007) 279–310. Concerning the material nature of the remedy recognized at Ulp. (25 *ad edictum*) *D.* 11.7.8.1, see Procchi, "*Dolus e culpa in contrahendo* nella compravendita" (2007) 225–29.

have been sold as though it were an ordinary one, the praetor grants the person concerned an action *in factum* against the seller. This action is also available against an heir, since it virtually amounts to an action on sale.]

Iavolenus (2 *ex Plautio*) *D.* 18.4.8: . . . *si nulla est (hereditas), de qua actum videatur, pretium dumtaxat et si quid in eam rem impensum est emptor a venditore consequatur* . . .

[(Iavolenus in the second book from Plautius) . . . if there is no inheritance in dispute, the purchaser will recover from the seller only the price and any expenses that he has incurred in the matter . . .]

Paulus (33 *ad edictum*) *D.* 18.4.9: . . . *et si quid emptoris interest.*

[(Paul in the thirty-third book on the Edict) . . . and any damages that he has sustained.]

Jhering points out that the jurists in these texts show that they granted the action on sale to the purchaser, who had been *deceptus* (deceived) about the status of a *res extra commercium* or a nonexistent inheritance, regardless of the fact that the contract was manifestly invalid (*licet emptio non teneat*) because the bargained-for performance was impossible.[33] Later in the article, Jhering maintains that he can apply the same interpretive reasoning to sources in which the Roman jurists seem to oscillate between holding for the validity and the invalidity of the sale of a *homo liber* as a slave.[34] Regardless of the correctness or not of the arguments Jhering makes on the basis of Roman law[35] (arguments that were the target of a sharp, well-supported critique from the very start),[36] the general principle came to be established whereby a seller who "to no purpose" involved a buyer in activity resulting in an invalid contract could legitimately be sued through an *actio ex empto* aimed at the compensation of his or her interest in not being misled (the *id quod interest deceptum non esse*).

33. See Jhering, "*Culpa in contrahendo*" (1860) 28–30.
34. See Jhering, "*Culpa in contrahendo*" (1860) 63–66.
35. See Talamanca, "Vendita (diritto romano)" (1993) 439 n. 1417; Procchi, "*Dolus e culpa in contrahendo* nella compravendita" (2007) 224–46.
36. See Mommsen, *Erörterungen aus dem Obligationenrecht* (1879) 2:1–55; Brock, *Das negative Vertragsinteresse* (1902) 10, 48–58.

Bringing Liability back to "Contractual"-Type Remedies

The sources from which Jhering's analysis takes its point of departure are characterized, as I have already noted, by granting the action on sale with its compensatory function, but only to the buyer. One could not, in fact, grant any contractual remedies to the *venditor* of a *res extra commercium* or of a nonexistent inheritance. Such situations had already been used by Savigny to argue for the so-called *geschwächte Wirkung* of certain contracts: these, although valid, were characterized by "weakened effects" inasmuch as they were capable of guaranteeing to the buyer (and only to him or to her) the contractual remedy that would allow damages for failure to convey the object of sale.[37] Jhering takes a stance diametrically opposed to that of Savigny. Where Savigny recognized the existence of a valid contract, albeit one of limited efficacy, Jhering maintains that it is possible to find particular instances of invalidity that nonetheless did not exclude, given certain conditions, the availability of the *actio empti* with its compensatory function.[38]

To Jhering, this new approach seemed indispensable for the design of the theory he had set out to construct . From the rules established to guarantee compensation in connection with a valid contractual situation (albeit one with "weakened efficacy"), he could not legitimately draw any valid conclusions for resolving the problem of loss caused by contracts invalidated due to a material mistake. The availability—independently of the invalidity of the contract—of an action on sale intended to provide compensation for one's interest in not being misled represented, therefore, a kind of "squaring of the circle" by means of which Jhering could escape from the narrow confines of the Roman extracontractual liability that I have already discussed.[39]

The Construction of an Objectified *Culpa*

Contrary to the opinion of Friedrich Mommsen,[40] which was dominant at the

37. See Savigny, *Das Obligationenrecht als Theil des heutigen Römischen Rechts,* (1853) 2:284–92.
38. See Jhering, "*Culpa in contrahendo*" (1860) 28–29.
39. See Kuonen, "La *culpa in contrahendo*" (2005) 272, showing how one must deduce from this the existence of a contractual relation despite the invalidity of the contract.
40. See Mommsen, *Beiträge zum Obligationenrecht* (1853) 1:122. On this point, more generally, see Choe, *"Culpa in contrahendo" bei Rudolf von Jhering* (1988) 72–74.

time, Jhering held that liability should not be limited to situations characterized by the seller's malice (or gross negligence).[41] He bases his argument on his analysis of the verb *decipi,* which did not necessarily imply fraudulent behavior by the other party, since the same behavior can also possess an "objective" meaning, one that refers simply to the mistake made by one of the parties to the contract.[42] Savigny and Mommsen, in fact, had already put forward the thesis that the indeterminate meaning of "deceived" should be assigned to the word *deceptus* without themselves taking a position over ascribing the deception to the fraud (or the lack of fraud) of the other party.[43]

Leaving aside fraud and discarding, for obvious reasons, the issue of *custodia,* the only remaining criterion for assigning contractual liability that was useful for generalizing the principle Jhering was developing was *culpa* (fault or negligence).

> Ein allgemeines Prinzip für unsere Klage ist nur mittelst der *culpa* zu gewinnen. Nehmen wir letztere nicht zu Hülfe, so müssen wir bei den beiden Fällen der Quellen stehen bleiben, wie dies denn in der That auch bisher geschehen ist. Es fehlt hier an der Brücke, um von den zwei Fällen der Quellen zu den vielen andern zu gelangen, in denen das Bedürfniß einer Schadensersatzklage in nicht geringerem Maße vorhanden ist. Oder worin läge der *juristische* Rechtfertigungsgrund (ich meine nicht den legislativ-politischen), um, was die Quellen in jenen beiden Fällen bestimmen, auch z. B. im Fall des Irrthums eintreten zu lassen?[44]

> [It is possible to locate a general principle that justifies the grant of a remedy only through resort to *culpa.* If we do not seek assistance from the concept of negligence, we are constrained to adhere strictly to the two cases considered in the sources, and this is precisely what has happened up until today. What is missing is a bridge that allows us to connect the two cases contemplated by the sources to numerous other cases in which the need for a compensatory remedy is equally pressing. Otherwise, what would constitute the *legal* foundation (in

41. See Jhering, "*Culpa in contrahendo*" (1860) 11.
42. See Jhering, "*Culpa in contrahendo*" (1860) 11.
43. See Savigny, *Das Obligationenrecht als Theil des heutigen Römischen Rechts* (1853) 2:291–92; Mommsen, *Obligationenrecht* (1853) 1:22; Solidoro Maruotti, "La violazione degli obblighi" (2009) 618; Procchi, *Licet emptio non teneat* (2012) 200–202.
44. Jhering, "*Culpa in contrahendo*" (1860) 40–41.

no way am I speaking of the legislative-political one) for an extension analogous to the holding of the sources, for example, in cases concerning another kind of error?]

The choice of assigning liability based on negligence came to be joined inseparably, in Jhering's approach, with its contractual nature. Every other solution, in fact, would have come into irremediable conflict with the precept, canonized in his time by Savigny, that negligence could only modify an existing contractual relationship, since it was not itself in any way (unlike fraud) a general *causa obligationis.*[45]

For this very reason, Jhering struggled to connect the foundation of liability based on negligence to the "apparent" conclusion of a contract, supporting this connection by reference to the contractual nature of the action at times conceded to the buyer that he had previously postulated, as we have already had occasion to demonstrate, *licet emptio non teneat.*

> Es ist der intendirte und äußerlich oder scheinbar vollzogene Abschluß eines *Contracts,* der sich in allen Anwendungsfällen desselben wiederholt, und der uns schon von vornherein auf die Vermuthung führen muß; daß in der Verbindung, in der hier die *Verschuldung* mit dem *Contractsverhältniß* auftritt, die eigenthümliche Natur unsers Ersatzanspruches beschlossen liege.[46]

> [The conclusion of a *contract,* planned and brought to completion on the surface or in appearance, emerges repeatedly in all the cases where this question arises and should, therefore, immediately induce us to presume that it is precisely in the connection that develops in these cases between *liability* and the *contractual relationship* that one finds contained the fundamental nature of our compensatory claim.]

The precontractual aspect of negligent behavior would create a connection, even though a merely external one, with the transaction, and such a connection would also justify, apart from the grant of the *actio empti,* the application of the standard rules for contractual *culpa.* This construct is based on the postulate that contractual responsibility adheres not only to contracts already concluded

45. See Savigny, *System des heutigen Römischen Rechts* (1840) 3:295 n. d.
46. Jhering, "*Culpa in contrahendo*" (1860) 26.

but also to those still in a state of "gestation": with the beginning of negotiations, the parties would initiate a "quasi-contractual" relationship already capable on its own of creating rights and duties.[47]

In this way, Jhering created a particular theory of precontractual negligence whose rules had to be borrowed from contractual *culpa* because of the tight (though superficial) point of contact between the two cases in point.[48] According to Jhering, once negotiations begin, the contracting party emerges from the purely negative sphere of extracontractual relationships and enters the domain of contractual rules, in which come into play not only *culpa in faciendo* but also the violation of duties associated with positive diligence.[49]

> Nicht bloß die *bestehenden,* sondern bereits die *entstehenden* Contractsverhältnisse müssen unter dem Schutz der Regeln über die *culpa* stehen, wenn nicht der contractliche Verkehr nach dieser Seite hin empfindlichster Weise bloß gestellt, jeder Contrahent der Gefahr Preis gegeben werden soll, das Opfer fremder Nachlässigkeit zu werden.[50]

> [Not only *existing* contractual relationships but also relationships *coming into existence* must find themselves under the protection of the rules for *culpa,* so that the latter not be compromised and so that no contracting party will be abandoned to the risk of becoming a victim of someone else's negligence.]

For Jhering, therefore, the basis in negligence of liability *in contrahendo* was located in the behavior of whoever had involved someone else in pointless negotiations, inducing that person to trust in the apparent conclusion of a contract without, however, being able to insure that the contract would effectively come into being.[51] In this way, Jhering arrived at the point of casting blame on one of the contracting parties for having produced the result characterized as a "failure to conclude a valid contract" because of that party's own negligence and carelessness in the conduct of negotiations. From a purely dogmatic, abstract point of view, such a construct is legitimized by the fact that

47. See Ben-Dror, "Perennial Ambiguity of *Culpa in Contrahendo*" (1983) 147; Zimmermann, *Law of Obligations* (1996) 244.
48. See Jhering, "*Culpa in contrahendo*" (1860) 26–27.
49. See Jhering, "*Culpa in contrahendo*" (1860) 41–42.
50. Jhering, "*Culpa in contrahendo*" (1860) 42.
51. See Jhering, "*Culpa in contrahendo*" (1860) 41.

1. negligence and carelessness, unlike professional malpractice, have no precise configurations in the sources and are described, from time to time, in a casuistic manner; and
2. given that the theory was developed in the context of consensual *emptio venditio* and thus within the domain of the *iudicia bonae fidei,* there was no particular difficulty in constructing *culpa* in the key of omission (i.e., as the absence of all those requirements that guarantee the effective conclusion of a contract).

This *culpa* was based, all the same, on a notion of negligence and carelessness so abstract in nature that it embraced any event that prevented a valid contract from being concluded. Such interpretive convolutions of the original content of the Roman sources should not surprise the modern observer. This was typical of the method of legal constructionism that was coming to the fore during the second half of the nineteenth century[52] and of which Jhering was the uncontested master. It seems, all the same, that Jhering felt obliged to demonstrate that the compensatory payment to the *deceptus* in the case of a sale of *res extra commercium* and of nonexistent inheritance constitutes not an isolated instance but, rather, a compensatory (though rather peculiar) remedy based on negligence and, as such, one capable of generalization as a principle and through application by analogy.[53] He wrote,

> Nehmen wir letztere nicht zu Hülfe, so müssen wir bei den beiden Fällen der Quellen stehen bleiben, wie dies denn in der That auch bisher geschehen ist . . . Stützen wir einmal die Verbindlichkeit des Verkäufers zum Schadensersatz in jenen beiden Fällen auf eine *culpa* desselben, so knüpft sich daran unabweisbar die Nöthigung, in allen Fällen, wo eine gleiche *culpa* eintritt, auch eine gleiche Wirkung eintreten zu lassen.[54]

> [If we do not seek assistance from the concept of negligence, we are constrained to adhere strictly to the two cases considered in the sources, and this is precisely what has happened up until today . . . Given that, in these two cases, the seller's obligation to offer compensation for loss is based on *culpa,* we must necessarily allow the same result in all instances where a similar *culpa* is found.]

---

52. See Schanze, "*Culpa in contrahendo* bei Jhering" (1978) 331–40; Procchi, "Nota di lettura" (2005) xxi–xxxi.
53. See Jhering, "*Culpa in contrahendo*" (1860) 40.
54. Jhering, "*Culpa in contrahendo*" (1860) 40–41.

Jhering himself noted the limitations of a construct that would wind up regarding as "negligence" even the possible death of the party making the offer in contract negotiations occurring *inter absentes*. But the absolute necessity of this requirement compelled him to identify the basis in negligence for compensatory liability in the very fact of having chosen to make a contract at a distance: if one had more prudently contracted in person, with others present, death would never have been able to lead to loss for the other party as a consequence.[55] From this last example, we see clearly that, despite his chosen name for the new theory, Jhering had construed a form of liability in which the *culpa* had become so abstract and "fictive" that it seemed a mere simulacrum. He himself proposed, a few years later in his *Schuldmoment* (1867), a new formulation that was cast in more objective terms.

> Die von mir aufgestellte Theorie der *culpa in contrahendo* wird, indem sie den beschränkten Gedanken des subjectiven Unrechts zu Grunde legt, der Idee des Verhältnisses selber nicht gerecht, und meine Formulierung wird gewiss durch eine weitere, objectivere ersetz werden.[56]

> [The theory of *culpa in contrahendo* that I developed, because it has as its basis the limited concept of a subjective civil wrong, does not succeed in doing justice to the very idea of the [contractual] relationship, and my formulation will certainly have to be substituted by one that is more objective in nature.]

The Doctrinal Construction of the So-Called Negative Interest

Relying on the sources previously cited on the sale of *res extra commercium* and a nonexistent inheritance, Friedrich Mommsen[57] and, before him, Savigny[58] had already demonstrated the existence of a plaintiff's interest in something other than performance. It seemed all too obvious to them that one should speak of an interest in performance only if and inasmuch as it grew out of an obligation to perform. But this result was excluded from the start by the *impos-*

55. See Jhering, "*Culpa in contrahendo*" (1860) 92–93.
56. Jhering, *Das Schuldmoment im römischen Privatrecht* (1867) 38 n. 73. On this aspect see now also my recent discussion, Procchi, *Licet emptio non teneat* (2012) 242, 288–90.
57. See Mommsen, *Obligationenrecht* (1853) 1:107.
58. See Savigny, *Das Obligationenrecht als Theil des heutigen Römischen Rechts* (1853) 2:293 n. d.

sibilium nulla obligatio. From this derived the need to recognize a different role for the *id quod interest deceptum non esse,* through identifying in this the interest that the plaintiff had in not being deceived regarding the possibility of performance.[59] The invalidity of the obligation would not then prevent the party who has obligated himself or herself to perform something impossible from being liable, depending on the circumstances, for loss caused to the other party.

This point of departure, which had induced Friedrich Mommsen to consider the *actio empti* granted by the Roman jurists as a kind of "substitute" for the *actio doli* (extended, moreover, to the gravely negligent behavior of the seller), had to be turned to advantage by Jhering in a purely contractual key. It was Jhering, in fact, who coined the dichotomy between "positive contractual interest" ("positives Vertragsinteresse" or "Erfüllungsinteresse") and "negative contractual interest" ("negatives Vertragsinteresse").

> Das Interesse des Käufers läßt sich in unserm Verhältniß in doppelter Weise denken: einmal nämlich als ein Interesse an der *Aufrechthaltung* des Contracts, also an der *Erfüllung*—hier würde der Käufer in einem Geldäquivalent alles erhalten, was er im Fall der Gültigkeit des Contracts gehabt haben würde—und sodann als ein Interesse am *Nichtabschluß* des Contracts—hier würde er erhalten, was er haben würde, wenn die äußere Thatsache des Contractsabschlusses gar nicht vorgekommen wäre. Einige Beispiele werden diesen Unterschied, den ich der Kürze wegen mit *positivem* und *negativem Vertragsinteresse* bezeichnen will, klar machen . . . Das Interesse der ersten Art hat die *Gültigkeit,* das der zweiten die *Ungültigkeit* des Contracts zur Grundlage.[60]

> [The buyer's interest may, in our case, be considered in two different ways. On the one hand, he claims an interest in the *adherence to,* and therefore the *fulfillment of,* the contract, and in these situations the buyer would receive the monetary equivalent of all that he would have had if the contract had been valid. On the other hand, he claims an interest in the *failed conclusion* of the contract. In this case, he would receive what he would have had if there had not been the apparent fact of the conclusion of the contract. Some examples will quickly clarify this distinction, which I shall term, for the sake of brevity, the dichotomy between a *positive contractual interest* and a *negative* one . . . The interest of the

59. See Choe, *"Culpa in contrahendo" bei Rudolf von Jhering* (1988) 87–109.
60. Jhering, "*Culpa in contrahendo*" (1860) 16.

first kind has its basis in the *validity* of the contract; that of the second, in the contract's *invalidity.*]

The invalidity of the contract would mean never recognizing the plaintiff's interest in performance, because such interest would be a substitute form of performance, one inadmissible in the absence of an obligation reached in a valid manner. The failed conclusion of the contract would signify never being able to guarantee the same practical consequences that flow from a valid transaction; in such cases, one would be limited to providing compensation for associated losses (whether of *damnum emergens,* "ensuing loss," or *lucrum cessans,* "lost profit") that the other party had suffered for having, without fault of his or her own, trusted in the conclusion of the deal.[61] But Jhering thought he could take this theory further.

> Der Kutscher, der irrthümlich auf einen andern, als den beabsichtigten Tag bestellt ist, der Gastwirth, bei dem statt bei einem andern durch Versehen in der Adresse Zimmer bestellt sind, haben durch dieses Versehen keinerlei positiven Schaden gehabt, allein, wenn beide in Folge dieser Bestellung eine sich ihnen darbietende andere Gelegenheit zur Verwerthung ihres Fuhrwerks oder ihrer Zimmer abgelehnt haben, so steht dies für beide dem Verlust am baaren Gelde völlig gleich.[62]

> [The coachman engaged by mistake for a day other than the one intended, the hotel-keeper with whom one has through an error in the address reserved rooms in lieu of reserving them elsewhere, have suffered no actual loss by reason of these errors; but if either one, in the wake of this arrangement, has rejected another opportunity, which was presented, to rent out the carriage or the rooms, it is exactly the same for him as a loss in actual money.]

The basic postulate of this construct is that according to the circumstances of the concrete case, the plaintiff may obtain from an unconcluded contract a value equivalent to that he or she would have received had the transaction been valid, but never more than that.

61. See Jhering, "*Culpa in contrahendo*" (1860) 20–21.
62. Jhering, "*Culpa in contrahendo*" (1860) 21.

> Das negative Interesse kann unter Umständen die Höhe des positiven erreichen. In den beiden letzten Fällen erhalten die Kläger ganz dasselbe, was sie im Fall der Ausführung des Vertrags hätten fordern dürfen, aber, wie aus dem Bisherigen hervorgeht, aus einem ganz andern Grunde.[63]
>
> [The negative interest can, in certain cases, increase until it coincides with the positive interest. In both cases just mentioned, the parties obtain exactly what they would have been able to claim had the contract been executed; but, as we demonstrated earlier, that happens for entirely different reasons.]

The level of the interest in performance would therefore represent, according to Jhering, an unavoidable and insurmountable limit in the award of the negative interest that could, moreover, be reduced to zero each time the failed conclusion of the contract became clear to the other party before that party had suffered any damage.

The Close Interdependence of the Three "Pillars" of Rudolf von Jhering's Construct

I have here tried to demonstrate, albeit in very summary form, the narrow argumentative and doctrinal spaces in which Jhering's arguments developed, following a kind of route dictated by his respect (often more formal than substantive) for what the Roman rules contain. Caught between the two fires of transactional invalidity and the absence of a "general clause" of extracontractual liability, Jhering found himself constrained to think of liability *in contrahendo* as a *sui generis* contractual liability that had the peculiarity of granting solely to the party *deceptus* ("deceived"—to be understood, as we have seen, in an "objective" sense) the exercise of the action on sale, although only to claim compensation for loss. Proceeding in this way, however, he ran the risk of interpreting the relevant cases in point as valid contracts, even though "with weakened effects," and such a conclusion would have excluded a priori every analogous application of the remedy to instances of manifest transactional invalidity because of a failure to reach agreement.

It thus seemed indispensable to differentiate between the bases for mak-

63. Jhering, "*Culpa in contrahendo*" (1860) 21.

ing an award for loss, in order to create a clear doctrinal distinction between the *actio empti* arising from a valid sales contract and that recognized when a contract is invalid. As we have seen, Jhering believed that he could create such a doctrinal distinction by making use of the expression *id quod interest eius non deciperetur* (or words to this effect) found in the sources. Equally, the development of a basis in negligence, although fictive, turned out to be instrumental for the purpose of generalizing as a principle the liability *in contrahendo* that was now being elaborated, making it applicable in analogous cases.

Later Developments and the Impact on Modern Legal Thinking

The first two pillars described in the preceding section (the contractual nature of the compensatory remedy and its basis in negligence) were objects of a lively scholarly debate beginning in the second half of the nineteenth century. Just as many of the questions raised at that time have been transmitted in more or less exactly the same form to students of modern European civil law, the principle of the so-called negative interest as conceived by Jhering has long remained intact, perhaps partly due to the fact that it was formally received by German positive law in the original formulation of paragraph 307 of the German Civil Code (BGB) in force until December 31, 2001.[64]

(1) Wer bei der Schließung eines Vertrags, der auf eine unmögliche Leistung gerichtet ist, die Unmöglichkeit der Leistung kennt oder kennen muß, ist zum Ersatze des Schadens verpflichtet, den der andere Teil dadurch erleidet, daß er auf die Gültigkeit des Vertrags vertraut, jedoch nicht über den Betrag des Interesses hinaus, welches der andere Teil an der Gültigkeit des Vertrags hat. Die Ersatzpflicht tritt nicht ein, wenn der andere Teil die Unmöglichkeit kennt oder kennen muß.

(2) Diese Vorschriften finden entsprechende Anwendung, wenn die Leistung nur teilweise unmöglich und der Vertrag in Ansehung des möglichen Teiles gültig ist oder wenn eine von mehreren wahlweise versprochenen Leistungen unmöglich ist.

---

64. Currently the matter is governed by the second paragraph of Section 311a of the German Civil Code (BGB).

[(1) If a person, in concluding a contract, the performance of which is impossible, knew or should have known that it was impossible, he is obligated to offer compensation for any loss that the other party has sustained by relying upon the validity of the contract, not, however, beyond the value of the interest that the other party has in the validity of the same contract. The duty to offer compensation does not arise if the other party knew or should have known of the impossibility.

(2) These provisions apply *mutatis mutandis* if the performance is only partially impossible, and the contract is valid in respect of the possible part, or if only one of several promised alternative performances is impossible.]

The old paragraph 309[65] then extended the application of paragraph 307 to contracts concluded in violation of a legal prohibition.

> Verstößt ein Vertrag gegen ein gesetzliches Verbot, so finden die Vorschriften der § 307, 308 entsprechende Anwendung.

> [If a contract violates a statutory prohibition, the provisions of paragraphs 307 and 308 apply *mutatis mutandis.*]

A study that sets out to investigate the "future of obligations" by taking its point of departure in an analysis of the Roman legal experience and in what we are accustomed to define as the "Roman legal tradition" cannot, however, neglect the study of this important subject in light of the "quantity" of compensable loss, or, to use the terminology of German scholarship, of the so-called *Haftungshöhe.* As a preliminary step, it is useful to note that from the particular perspective of Roman law scholarship, the expression *quod interfuit eius ne deciperetur* used by Modestinus (and others like it) does not in itself allow an aprioristic distinction between a "positive" and a "negative" contractual interest. This is because, depending on the circumstances of the actual case, the interest in not being deceived concerning the origin of a contract might very well coincide with the interest in the effective conclusion of the same contract under the conditions that the contracting party who has been *deceptus* (deceived) had been led to believe were operative.[66] Such a result clearly arises from an analysis of the

65. The rule was abrogated and has not been in force since January 1, 2002.

66. For a different opinion, see Ben-Dror, "Perennial Ambiguity of *Culpa in Contrahendo*" (1983) 149.

Roman jurists' decisions regarding *dolus in contrahendo,* where the contract's validity is never contested and the interest in not being deceived coincides at times with that in not having concluded the transaction ("negative interest"). But it can—equally legitimately—coincide with that in having concluded the transaction according to the conditions that the contracting party had been fraudulently induced by the other party to believe had been operative.[67]

By itself, this result is already sufficient, in my view, to exclude the possibility that, from the point of view of Roman law, an equation may legitimately be drawn between the contract's validity and the award of the value of the positive interest, on one hand, and the contract's invalidity and the compensation for the value of the negative interest, on the other.[68] It must then inexorably follow that even in some cases where the conclusion of the contract has failed, the *quod sua interest eum deceptum non esse* can be understood as equivalent to the "positive interest" and not, as Jhering postulated, as a "negative interest" that rises until it coincides (and so limited in its maximum amount) with the *Erfüllungsinteresse.*

Conclusion: The Desirable Future of Judge's Calculation of Recoverable Loss in Italy

If our considerations are correct, there is no reason, from the point of view of historical or doctrinal scholarship, either to continue to maintain that precontractual liability can lead only to compensation of the negative interest or to anchor the negative interest to the unsurpassable limit represented by the interest in fulfilling the relevant performance. This ought to be an opportune time to abandon the traditional orientation of the scholarship and court holdings in the civil law tradition—still dominant to this day and not only in Italy—that currently encourages the assertion that the compensation owing in the case of the failed or invalid conclusion of a contract ought to be related to and "rendered commensurate" with the negative interest, while it emphasizes, at the same time, that this compensation could not embrace loss linked to the harm done to the positive contractual interest, understood as an interest in the valid conclusion and subsequent execution of the contract.[69] With particular

67. See Talamanca, "Vendita (diritto romano)" (1993) 441.

68. See Procchi, "*Dolus e culpa in contrahendo* nella compravendita" (2007) 202–4.

69. See Benatti, *La responsabilità precontrattuale* (1963) 149. This generally holds true for the law still prevalent in Italy today.

reference to current Italian legislation, it seems to me that at least the situation that appears in Article 1338 of the Civil Code[70] allows for the suggestion of a less "negative" reconstruction of the interest protected by precontractual duty of good faith, reconnecting it, depending on one's point of view, to a no-fault confidence in the contract's validity[71] or even to the possibility of demanding the relevant performance.[72] In such a case, it seems reasonable to me to maintain that through resort to all the requirements for the effectiveness of precontractual liability, the compensable *quantum* should guarantee in an equivalent fashion the attainment of the desired result, that is, the valid and effective conclusion of the contract.[73]

In a parallel sense, in cases where one must proceed to the award of the value of the actual "negative interest," understood as an interest "in not negotiating the terms of a contract" or "in not concluding an invalid contract," or, more generally, in not employing time and money in an activity that would later reveal itself to have been useless and productive of loss, the maximum limit represented by the comparison with the positive interest should rightly be abandoned. This conclusion should be all the more obvious for that significant sector of Italian scholarship that, supported by the decisions of lower courts (dealing more strictly with the application of law to facts) or those of higher courts (dealing with the interpretation of the law), concedes an extracontractual nature to the liability for harm to the negative interest. Once the Aquilian concept of wrongful act has been invoked as a precondition, in fact, modern scholarship should logically avoid any use of criteria and categories having to do with contractual liability, including the application of the *Erfüllungsinteresse* as an insuperable parameter for estimating loss *ab externo*.[74]

Since there no longer exists, at least in the modern civil law systems where—as in France and Italy—a choice has been made for a "general clause"

---

70. Art. 1338 Cod. Civ. It. (on knowledge of the reasons for invalidity): "La parte che, conoscendo o dovendo conoscere l'esistenza di una causa d'invalidità del contratto, non ne ha dato notizia all'altra parte è tenuta a risarcire il danno da questa risentito per aver confidato, senza sua colpa, nella validità del contratto" (The party who knows or ought to know of the existence of a reason invalidating a contract and fails to give notice of this to the other party is held responsible for compensating the loss sustained by that other party because he or she trusted, with no fault on his part, in the contract's validity).
71. See Benatti, *La responsabilità precontrattuale* (1963) 147–48.
72. See Sacco, *Il contratto* (1975) 924–25.
73. See Luminoso, "La lesione dell'interesse contrattuale negativo (e dell'interesse positivo)" (1988) 792–98.
74. See Turco, *Interesse negativo e responsabilità precontrattuale* (1990) 372–75.

of extracontractual liability, any compelling need to conceive, in the wake of Rudolf von Jhering, of liability *in contrahendo* as a principle "derived" from (and therefore, according to its inevitable nature, "subordinate" to) the true and proper contractual liability, it should not appear in any sense unfair that, in a case of the violation of precontractual duties, a party might succeed in obtaining, according to the circumstances of the individual case, a greater economic advantage than that which he or she would have gained had the contract been validly concluded. It would instead be manifestly unjust to continue to apply indiscriminately the maximum limit (as postulated by Jhering) of the total value of the positive interest every time it were concretely demonstrable that the savings in expenditures and the earnings connected to an alternative use of money, time, and energy dedicated by the *deceptus* to the pointless agreement would surely have been greater than those realizable had that agreement been successfully concluded.

Bibliography

Benatti, F. *La responsabilità precontrattuale.* Milan: Giuffrè, 1963.

Ben-Dror, Y. "The Perennial Ambiguity of *Culpa in Contrahendo.*" *American Journal of Legal History* 27 (1983): 142–98.

Brock, W. *Das negative Vertragsinteresse.* Berlin: J. Guttentag-Verlagsbuchhandlung, 1902.

Choe, B. J. *"Culpa in contrahendo" bei Rudolf von Jhering.* Göttingen: Verlag Otto Schwartz, 1988.

Coing, H. *Europäisches Privatrecht.* Vol. 2, *19. Jahrhundert: Überblick über die Entwicklung des Privatrechts in den ehemals gemeinrechtlichen Ländern.* Munich: C. H. Beck, 1989.

Cuena Boy, F. *Estudios sobre la imposibilidad de la prestación: La imposibilidad jurídica.* Valladolid: Secretariado de publicaciónes Universidad de Valladolid, 1992.

Cursi, M. F. *Danno e responsabilità extracontrattuale nella storia del diritto privato.* Naples: Jovene, 2010.

Cursi, M. F. "Per una storia critica della tutela aquiliana dei diritti assoluti." In *Modelli teorici e metodologici nella storia del diritto privato,* 2:23–126. Naples: Jovene, 2006.

Deroussin, D. "*Culpa in contrahendo:* L'indemnisation en cas d'annulation du contrat, du droit romain à la théorie classique des invalidités." *Revue historique de droit français et étranger* 82 (2004): 189–222.

Feenstra, R. "De oorsprong van Hugo de Groot's leer over de dwaling." In *Met eerbiedigende werking, Opstellen aangeboden aan Prof. Mr. L.J. Hijmans van den Bergh.* Deventer: Kluver, 1971.

Giaro, T. "*Culpa in contrahendo:* Eine Geschichte der Wiederentdeckungen." In *Das Bürgerliche Gesetzbuch und seine Richter: Zur Reaktion der Rechtsprechung auf die Kodifikation des deutschen Privatrechts (1896–1914),* ed. U. Falk and H. Mohnhaupt, 113–54. Frankfurt am Main: Vittorio Klostermann, 2000.

Giaro, T. "Diritto romano attuale." In *Le radici comuni del diritto europeo,* ed. P. G. Monateri, T. Giaro, and A. Somma, 86–167. Rome: Carocci, 2005.

Hondius, E. H. "Precontractual Liability." In *Reports to the XIIIth Congress International Academy of Comparative Law. Montreal, Canada, 18–24 August 1990,* 3–28. Deventer: Kluwer Law and Taxation Publishers, 1991.

Hutchison, D. "Contract Formation." In *Southern Cross Civil Law and Common Law in South Africa,* ed. R. Zimmermann and D. Visser, 165–94. Oxford: Clarendon, 1996.

Jhering, R. von. "*Culpa in contrahendo:* Oder Schadensersatz bei nichtigen oder nicht zur Perfection gelangten Verträgen." *Jahrbücher für die Dogmatik des heutigen römischen und deutschen Privatrechts* 4 (1860): 1–112.

Jhering, R. von. *Das Schuldmoment im römischen Privatrecht.* Giessen: Verlag von Emil Roth, 1867.

Jhering, R. von. *Geist des römischen Rechts auf den verschieden Stufen seiner Entwicklung.* Vol. 1. Leipzig: Breitkopf und Härtel, 1878.

Jhering, R. von. "Ueber die Entstehung des Rechtsgefühles." *Allgemeine Juristen-Zeitung* 7 (1884): 121–25, 133–36, 145–48, 157–61, 169–72.

Jhering, R. von. "Unsere Aufgabe." *Jahrbücher für die Dogmatik des heutigen römischen und deutschen Privatrechts* 1 (1857): 1–52.

Kaser, M. *Das römische Privatrecht.* 2nd ed. 2 vols. Munich: C. H. Beck, 1971–75.

Kessler, F., and E. Fine. "*Culpa in Contrahendo,* Bargaining in Good Faith, and Freedom of Contract: A Comparative Study." *Harvard Law Review* 77 (1964): 401–49.

Kindereit, K. "Wer fühlt nicht, dass es hier einer Schadensersatzklage bedarf—Rudolf von Jhering und die *culpa in contrahendo.*" In *Zivilrechtliche Entdecker,* ed. T. Hoeren, 107–47. Munich: C. H. Beck, 2001.

Kleinheyer, G., and J. Schröder. *Deutsche und Europäische Juristen aus neun Jahrhunderten.* Heidelberg: C. F. Müller Verlag, 1996.

Kuonen, N. "La *culpa in contrahendo:* Un colosse aux pieds d'argile?" *Revue d'histoire du droit* 73 (2005): 267–78.

Kuonen, N. *La responsabilité précontractuelle,* Zurich: Schulthess, 2007.

Luchetti, G., and A. Petrucci. *Fondamenti di diritto contrattuale europeo.* Bologna: Patrón Editore, 2006.

Luminoso, A. "La lesione dell'interesse contrattuale negativo (e dell'interesse positivo) nella responsabilità civile." *Contratto e impresa* 4 (1988): 792–803.

Mommsen, F. *Beiträge zum Obligationenrecht*. Vol. 1, *Die Unmöglichkeit der Leistung in ihrem Einfluß auf obligatorische Verhältnisse*. Braunschweig: Schwetschke und Sohn, 1853.

Mommsen, F. *Erörterungen aus dem Obligationenrecht*. Vol. 2, *Ueber die Haftung der Contrahenten bei der Abschließung von Schuldverträgen*. Braunschweig: Schwetschke und Sohn, 1879.

Pothier, R. J. *Traité des obligations, selon les regles tant du for de la conscience, que du for extérieur*. Rev. ed. Vol. 1. Paris-Orléans: Debure et Rouzeau-Montaut, 1777.

Procchi, F. "*Dolus e culpa in contrahendo* nella compravendita: Considerazioni in tema di sinallagma genetico." In *La compravendita e l'interdipendenza delle obbligazioni nel diritto romano*, ed. L. Garofalo, 1:183–246. Padua: CEDAM, 2007.

Procchi, F. Licet emptio non teneat: *Alle origini delle moderne teoriche sulla cd. "culpa in contrahendo."* Padua: CEDAM, 2012.

Procchi, F. "Nota di lettura." In *Della "culpa in contrahendo" ossia del risarcimento del danno nei contratti invalidi o non giunti a perfezione*, xv–xlvii. Naples: Jovene Editore, 2005. Italian translation of R. von Jehring, "*Culpa in contrahendo:* Oder Schadensersatz bei nichtigen oder nicht zur Perfection gelangten Verträgen," *Jahrbücher für die Dogmatik des heutigen römischen und deutschen Privatrechts* 4 (1860): 1–112.

Pugliese, G. *Scritti giuridici scelti*. Vol. 3, *Diritto romano*. Naples: Jovene Editore, 1985.

Rabello, A. M. "Buona fede e responsabilità precontrattuale nel diritto israeliano alla luce del diritto comparato." In *Il ruolo della buona fede oggettiva nell'esperienza giuridica storica e contemporanea*, ed. L. Garofalo, 3:125–227. Padua: CEDAM, 2003.

Rabello, A. M. "*Culpa in Contrahendo:* Precontractual Liability in the Italian Legal System." In *Aequitas and Equity: Equity in Civil Law and Mixed Jurisdictions*, ed. A. M. Rabello, 463–509. Jerusalem: Nevo, 1997.

Rabello, A. M. "The Theory concerning *Culpa in Contrahendo:* Precontractual Liability from Roman Law to the German Legal System." In *A Hundred Years after the Death of Jhering: European Legal Traditions and Israel*, ed. A. M. Rabello, 69–154. Jerusalem: Nevo, 1994.

Richelmann, H. *Der Einfluß des Irrthums auf Verträge*. Hannover: Helwingschen Hof-Buchhandlung, 1837.

Sacco, R. *Il contratto*. Turin: UTET, 1975. (=F. Vasalli, ed., *Trattato di diritto civile italiano* 6, ed. F. Vassalli).

Savigny, F. C. von. *Das Obligationenrecht als Theil des heutigen Römischen Rechts.* Vol. 2. Berlin: Veit und Compt, 1853.

Savigny, F. C. von. *System des heutigen Römischen Rechts.* Vol. 3. Berlin: Veit und Compt, 1840.

Schanze, E. "*Culpa in contrahendo* bei Jhering." *Ius Commune* 7 (1978): 326–58.

Solidoro Maruotti, L. "Annotazioni sui precedenti storici degli obblighi precontrattuali di informazione." *Teoria e storia del diritto privato* 3 (2010): 1–35.

Solidoro Maruotti, L. *Gli obblighi di informazione a carico del venditore: Origini storiche e prospettive attuali.* Naples: Satura Editrice, 2007.

Solidoro Maruotti, L. "La violazione degli obblighi di informazione in compravendita: un difficile recupero della prospettiva storica." In *Studi in onore di Remo Martini*, 3:609–40. Milan: Giuffrè, 2009.

Talamanca, M. "Vendita (diritto romano)." *Enciclopedia del diritto* 46 (1993): 303-475.

Trisciuoglio, A. "Sinallagma genetico e vendita delle *res extra commercium.*" In *La compravendita e l'interdipendenza delle obbligazioni nel diritto romano,* ed. L. Garofalo 1:279–310. Padua: CEDAM, 2007.

Turco, C. *Interesse negativo e responsabilità precontrattuale.* Milan: Giuffrè Editore, 1990.

Winkel, L. C. "*Culpa in contrahendo* in Roman Law and in Some Modern Dutch Court Decisions." In *Viva vox iuris romani: Essays in Honour of Johannes Emil Spruit,* ed. L. De Ligt et al., 149–57. Amsterdam: J. C. Gieben, 2002.

Zimmermann, R. *The Law of Obligations: Roman Foundations of the Civilian Tradition.* Oxford: Oxford University Press, 1996.

CHAPTER 4

*Status and Contract in Ancient Rome**

With Some Thoughts on the "Future of Obligations"

CARLA MASI DORIA

Ancient Law[1] by Henry Sumner Maine was a central point of reference for the 2008 conference on Roman law at the American Academy in Rome and especially for the topic assigned to me: "*Status and contract at Rome*." The book was published in 1861, a significant date for the history of legal culture, as Luigi Capogrossi Colognesi has more than once remarked.[2]

The nineteenth century was a normative one. It originated under the sign of legal codes, starting from the Napoleonic in 1804. The "law" determined the way in which the world had to be organized both in nature and in human society. Cause and effect were considered decisive points of the fluid geometry that gave shape to history. The influence of evolutionary theory is highlighted by the ever-increasing precision of the strictly calibrated methods of the natural sciences, as well as the "scientific" reliability of their results. The rhetorical

---

* This is the text of a lecture entitled "Status and Contract at Rome" delivered during "A Conference on Roman Law: The Future of Obligations" on March 13, 2008, at the American Academy in Rome. I thank my friend and colleague Tom McGinn and his staff for the invitation to the conference and my friend and colleague Cosimo Cascione for fruitful discussion of these themes.

1. Maine, *Ancient Law* (1931); *Diritto antico* (Italian trans. 1998), see the extensive bibliography edited by C. Faralli at pp. liii–lx in the Italian translation.

2. See the essays collected and revised in Capogrossi Colognesi, *Modelli di Stato e di famiglia* (1997), esp. 38–44, 131–252, 349–80; and now Capogrossi Colognesi, *Dalla storia di Roma* (2008), esp. 141–202, which has reintroduced Maine into the Italian scholarship of the last decades.

tradition that had dominated European culture for centuries, from Cicero to Bossuet, was on the wane. The new way of thinking was validated by the widespread progressive spirit among intellectuals in a century in which—finally and definitively—the *querelle des anciens et des modernes* no longer made any sense, because the "moderns" were now indisputably superior in the debate on nature.

Reality could now be revealed through writing and analytical procedures. *Gesetz* and *Entwicklung* became the watchwords of the philosophy of history, summarized, for example, in an important little book by the astonishingly eclectic Roman law scholar, Johann Jakob Bachofen,[3] *Die Grundgesetze der Völkerentwicklung und der Historiographie,* based on a lecture he delivered in Basel in 1864.[4]

In this context, we can place one of Henry Sumner Maine's most significant insights, a general principle, so to speak, still operative today in comparative sociology: the movement from *status* to contract. Maine considered the transformation of human societies from "static" to "progressive," from "primitive" to "modern," to be an eternally valid law. The original/ancient social order, examined in his famous book with reference, above all, to traditional Indian society and to ancient Rome, was, in his view, founded on the group, understood as the organization that regulates and determines the rights and duties of its members. This system, evolving through the disintegration of the group itself, experienced change by means of the introduction of the contract, the tool for transferring wealth, a bond founded on agreement among individuals, a source of reciprocal rights and obligations. Here Maine forces a subjective conception of the contract, based entirely on what the Pandectic legal scholarship—nearly contemporary with Maine—defined as the *Willensmoment.*[5]

The progress of society is characterized no longer by the identification of the individual with the group but through the substitution of this relation with individual obligations, a shift from *status* to contract. This thesis derives from Maine's observation of Indian society, a sort of living museum—still largely "primitive" in the eyes of the Western "civilized" observer—in which, however, the group cedes increasing space to contract. Here we might reflect on the concept of a Museum as a catalog, a *catalogue raisoné,* and therefore a rationalized

3. On this subject, see the important considerations in Capogrossi Colognesi, *Dalla storia di Roma* (2008), 107–39.
4. Bachofen, "Die Grundgesetze der Völkerentwicklung" (1864); (Italian trans. *Le leggi della storiografia* [1999]).
5. See, recently, Cascione, *Consensus* (2003) 172–201; Fiori, "Il problema dell'oggetto" (2003), 218–27.

container of the world's knowledge, as well as on its influence on nineteenth-century culture, especially in the English-speaking world.

But we cannot linger over this point, on the general thesis (which is very well known), or on the criticisms directed at Maine by Indian studies scholars. On this last issue, we can, however, point out how Maine's anthropological generalizations, without question rather vague and Eurocentric, did, in fact, capture something profound about the essence of Indian civilization, understanding its static nature and weak individualism. Maine's India is that of Sanskrit, but it is also—at least to a certain extent—the India that is represented today in popular Bollywood filmmaking.

To provide what here can be no more than a mere critical suggestion, we can refer to Louis Dumont's acute reading (one that emerges in various places in his important work), according to which Maine did not fully understand the true underlying principle of Indian civilization: hierarchy understood as structure.[6] The system composed of four *varna* and of castes would determine professional specialization, highlighting, in this way, the interdependence of the various social groups, with the aim of satisfying the needs of the entire group.[7]

The problem that most interests us, from the perspective of our conference, is the rereading, from the angle of Roman law scholarship, of the conceptual dyad *status* and contract, which serves to define a significant number of legal relations (not only under both the law of persons and that of obligations, but also beyond these two areas, for example, under public law, the law of succession, and that of procedure) from antiquity until today.

My analysis of this large problem here will be necessarily concise. I must first proceed by introducing a general framework (both historical and doctrinal) of these two concepts, which, given their synthetic nature, can function only in tandem as models that summarize historical experience.

Let us begin with *status*. All one has to do is open an introductory handbook on Roman law—and also, to some extent, one of current private law—to

6. See, in particular, Dumont's *Homo hierarchicus* (1966); and *La civilisation indienne* (1975). For discussion of the French anthropologist's work regarding the ideas expressed here, see Acquarone, "Il sistema giuridico" (2002); Acquarone, "Tendenze evolutive del diritto" (2003), esp. 103–10, with further bibliography. The hierarchical system, in relation to *fides* as a structure of the *ius civile,* played a role as well in the earliest Roman social and legal organization, as demonstrated now in Fiori, "*Fides* et *bona fides*" (2008).

7. For a summary with further bibliography, see Acquarone, "Tendenze evolutive del diritto" (2003), esp. 103–10.

find concepts such as *status libertatis, civitatis,* and *familiae*[8] that, having been forged in the full and fecund Roman law tradition, are still used today. As we shall see right away, these descriptive terms do not rest on a solid textual basis (they lack precise correspondences in ancient Roman law) but, rather, serve to group together—as Riccardo Orestano has cogently demonstrated—"with a certain idealizing faithfulness to Roman thinking and a certain unity, the rules and principles that governed personal legal status with respect to freedom, to citizenship, and to membership in an agnatic kinship group [i.e., a *familia*]."[9] The ancient sources on these topics were first manipulated by the systematizing jurisprudence of the sixteenth century, through the process of rationalizing diverse pronouncements in the texts, with the aim of clarifying the relations between *status personarum* (where the usage refers to the legal status of single individuals) and their corresponding legal treatment.[10] In later centuries, as we know, the reorientation of private law as a system of individual rights began to emerge; this led to further revisions and extensions of the doctrine on *status.* The great Savigny already noted the lack of precise textual references in Roman sources but insisted on the need to redesign the theory of *status,* by endowing it with the meaning of legal capacity.[11]

The approach taken by Savigny, we can say, created, as usual, a great deal of

8. See, in a recent volume (which comprehensively revisits the notions of *homo, caput, persona*), Negri, "Libertà e *status libertatis*" (2010); Humbert, "Le *status civitatis*" (2010); Corbino, "*Status familiae*" (2010).

9. Orestano, "*Status libertatis, civitatis, familiae*" (1971) 383, which I follow to this extent: "con una certa aderenza ideale al pensiero romano e una certa unità le norme e i principi che regolavano la condizione giuridica degli uomini in ordine alla libertà, alla cittadinanza e alla famiglia."

10. We can read this expression in Hermogenianus (1 *iuris epitomarum*) *D.* 1.5.2: *Cum igitur hominum causa omne ius constitutum sit, primo de personarum statu ac post de ceteris, ordinem edicti perpetui secuti et his proximos atque coniunctos applicantes titulos ut res patitur, dicemus* (Therefore, since all law is established for the sake of humanity, we shall speak first of the status of persons and afterward about the rest [of the law], following the order of the *edictum perpetuum* and applying titles as nearly as possible compatible with these as the nature of the case admits) (trans. A. Watson [adapted]).

11. Savigny, *System des heutigen Römischen Rechts* (1840) 2:446; *Sistema del diritto romano attuale* (Italian trans. 1888). On status in general, see Savigny, 2:443–515 (= *Sistema* [1888] 2:439–508 in the Italian trans.); for a particular, detailed analysis of the problem, see Siimets-Gross, "Die Ausdrücke *status libertatis, civitatis* und *familiae*" (2010) 217–49. See also Orestano, "*Status libertatis, civitatis, familiae*" (1971) 383–84. On *status,* in connection with the broader Roman terminology adopted for the classification of *homines* and with references also to modern scholarship on the subject, see Melillo, *Personae e status in Roma antica* (2006) 1–30.

interest among the Pandectists, conditioning their interpretive and descriptive choices and then, through them, influencing later Roman and civil law scholarship. Yet the Roman jurists were not the ones who had elaborated in a precise and distinct fashion these abstract notions that refer to the quality of being a subject at law, legal personality, and capacity. For them, *status hominis* (and also *ius personarum, status personarum, condicio hominum*) denoted the position of a person vis-à-vis the household. If the rubric of *de statu hominum* (title 1.5 in the *Digest*) invests the term with a broader meaning, the technical significance of *status* can be found in the expressions (using it in the genitive case) *status quaestio, status causa, status controversia,* "both in regard to an agnatic tie with the deceased (as a requirement for succession) and more often with respect to issues concerning freedom or slavery, freeborn or freed status."[12]

It is clear that a structure grounded in the possession of certain powers with significant limitations (both practical and legal) prevails on the individual's free management of economic resources to a great degree. As Vincenti has recently noted in the context of a broad and detailed discussion of the "confines" of law in the modern setting (but without failing to take into account the ancient Roman *ius*), "The *status* [i.e., statuses] categorize and classify the *personae* . . . individuals, qua *personae,* are not equal and their inequality is marked by their different *status* . . . the preservation of the various *status* guarantees the continued existence of these inequalities." This is how people are separated into categories, the classifications (*divisiones*) themselves creating as many personal *status.* Therefore, "not every *persona* has the capacity to *res* or *iura,*" whether absolutely (meaning no property and no rights, as with slaves) or in part ("so that some *personae,* if they are entitled to certain *res* or certain *iura,* are not on that account entitled to others")."[13]

Mario Genovese has recently published an interesting study (among the essays for Giovanni Nicosia) on the legal sources referring to persons not hav-

---

12. Orestano, "*Status libertatis, civitatis, familiae*" (1971) 383: "sia in relazione all'agnazione con un defunto (come condizione della successione) sia più frequentemente con riguardo a questioni di libertà o di servitù, di ingenuità o di libertinità."

13. Vincenti, *Diritto senza identità* (2007) 31–32: "Gli *status* classificano e censiscono le *personae* . . . Gli uomini, per quanto *personae,* non sono eguali e la loro diseguaglianza è marcata dal differente *status* . . . il mantenimento degli *status* garantisce le diseguaglianze." This is how people are separated into categories, the classifications (*divisones*) themselves creating as many personal *status.* Therefore, "non tutte le *personae* hanno l'attitudine ad avere *res* o *iura,*" whether absolutely (meaning no property and no rights, as with slaves) or in part: "(per cui talune *personae,* se possono avere certe *res* o certi *iura,* non ne possono però avere altri)."

ing *commercium* with regard to some types of property, according to the form *aliqui alicuius rei commercium non habent* (some do not have the *commercium* of some types of property).[14]

Viewed in these terms,[15] the most ancient Roman society was certainly a *status* society. The divide between patricians and plebeians (dating back, according to the sources, to the foundation of the city), the tribal legacy (probably prefoundation), and the elements of social structure based on the *gentes* attest to the original importance of groups and to the lesser political and social relevance of individuals. The divide between the orders, with all the rights of the political sphere (and authority over religion) reserved for the patricians,[16] shows a practical inequality as well as a difference of approach toward *res* and *iura*. Signs of this marked lack of social homogeneity are still evident in the historical private law. The prohibition against intermarriage (meaning the denial of the right to marry, or *conubium*), the rights to succession granted to members of the *gentes*, and the earliest management of the *ager publicus* are all proof of difference between patricians and plebeians that faded over time, in part as a consequence of the violent and revolutionary dialectic among the social groups. It was smoothed over also—and especially—thanks to a long and troubled series of political and constitutional developments that brought plebeians into the army (organized, as it was, by centuries) and into the *comitia* and then, of course (albeit slowly and with difficult moments), granted them *conubium*, entry to high political office (never separated in this ancient period from military command, as cogently reconstructed by Mommsen),[17] access to a discrete legislative power (definitively, as is well known, with the *lex Hortensia* of 287 BCE) and to the priesthoods (at least those with the greatest civic, legal, and political importance—the pontificate and augurate, above all). Then followed the emergence of a mixed patricio-plebeian *nobilitas*,[18] the waning of the *gentes*, the rise of the central role of the household *proprio iure* (albeit still primarily patriarchal), the creation of new categories of property rights based on *dominium*, the desuetude of the *ius gentilicium*, an open path to a more highly articulated conceptualization of the legal subject, one consistent with a chang-

14. Genovese, "*Res* e relative qualifiche" (2007) 95–102.
15. These terms have been restored to contemporary thinking in a theoretical construction extending from Savigny to Maine, as we have seen.
16. See, above all, De Martino, "La costituzione della città-stato" (1988/1996) 462–63.
17. Mommsen, *Römisches Staatsrecht* (1887) 1:8–161.
18. Most recently, see Goldmann, "*Nobilitas* als Status und Gruppe" (2002).

ing economy whose basis rested no longer on the relation between *heredium* and *ager gentilicius* but on the vast *possessiones,* on the "villa economy" that produced cash crops for the markets that by this time had a Mediterranean dimension.[19] This case of "globalization" of an ancient economy has recently and repeatedly been described by historians and economists, even to the point of drawing a (simplified) comparison with modern realities.[20] We should not forget how the Roman "Empire" has been inserted by modern theoreticians of the antiglobalization movement into a legal genealogy (or so, at least, they claim) in a way that would appear to have precise consequences for modernity.[21] But this is a topic that should be dealt with elsewhere.

It is clear that the framework set forth here is only a very general outline. It is important, though, to consider one issue in greater detail. Consistently with the theme of our conference, we should first look at the *modus obligandi.* In *status* societies, obligation creates a relation of personal dependence. The only model (organized in practice in various ways) is subjugation, the imposition of a subordinate status. *Potestas* and *manus* were the tools that, in principle, governed this relationship. Even the linguistic-semantic sign is identical with the physical one of the connection, tie, or bond.[22] The type of labor that today would be called "dependent employment" might be exemplified by the sale of a son or a slave, who subsequently returned to the *domus* of origin, as well as by the *operae* exchanged more or less formally (in a social context dominated by *fides*). The *nexi,*[23] described with terminology clearly suggestive of the condition of *status,* echoing the physical tie, were probably in origin simply those individuals who obtained a loan. As we know, up until 326 BCE—the date of the *lex Poetelia Papiria* according to the literary tradition (i.e., Livy: *velut aliud initium libertatis*)[24]—a creditor could keep an insolvent debtor in shackles, the

19. De Martino, *Storia economica di Roma antica* (1979) 125–42.

20. For a highly summarized description with reference to interpretive models, see Ferrarese, *Le istituzioni della globalizzazione* (2000) 16–20.

21. Hardt and Negri, *Empire* (2000); *Impero* (Italian trans. 2002), Münkler, *Imperien* (2005); *Imperi* (Italian trans. 2008) (on different grounds).

22. Recently, on the etymology and deep meaning of *obligatio,* see Brachet, "*Obligare et obnoxius*" (2005). On the same point, see also Cascione's chapter in the present volume.

23. For an acute historical contextualization of the problem of the *nexi,* see, for example, Serrao, *Diritto privato, economia e società* (2006) 179–93; he correctly deals with the topic in his discussion of *status.*

24. Liv. 8.28.1: *Eo anno plebi Romanae velut aliud initium libertatis factum est quod necti desierunt; mutatum autem ius ob unius feneratoris simul libidinem, simul crudelitatem insignem* ("In that

latter protected by minimal guarantees set out in the Twelve Tables regarding the weight of the chains and the amount of sustenance owed in the form of food.[25] The *addicti* reflected this model of obligation arising from the execution of a judicial decision (or a comparable situation). Liability—in a *status* society—lies entirely in the person, in the powers, and in the legally recognized prerogatives of the creditor. Contractual formalism insured the structural apparatus of a *status* economy,[26] with the close involvement of the *gentes*—that is, of the groups that make up the citizen community—as witnesses of the mancipation ceremonies, if not as participants in the transaction itself, as with the *testamentum calatiis comitiis* (according to the equation *comitia* = *curiae* = *gentes*) or that *in procinctu* (*exercitus* = *populus*). Furthermore, we should not forget two elements: that the context is one of a "face-to-face" society and that making provisions *mortis causa* is central to the transfer of wealth in the world of *status* (without considering its political aspects, and here I am thinking of Pietro Bonfante's reconstructions).[27] In this earliest period, social control of the legally relevant behavior of private citizens took place not only and not so much via the *iurisdictio,* the procedural forms, but also—in parallel—at a different level, that of social and political mediation. I am referring to the functions of the *censores,*[28] who carried out the census, arranging the *cives* in the different groups that made up the citizen community (*equites* and *pedites, centuriae, iuniores* and *seniores,* comitial "classes," tribes), and had a direct effect on *status,* on the actual composition of these groups, and on their position (economic, political, military) in the city. The censors conducted a peculiar kind of jurisdiction (although not jurisdictional in the sense we give the term when we think of the *iurisdictio* of the *praetor*),[29] because, via formal proceedings, they issued sanctions for actions deemed blameworthy or simply prohibited. For example, to consider an area bordering on that of obligations, the *censores* pro-

year the liberty of the Roman plebeians had as it were a new beginning, for individuals ceased to be imprisoned for debt. The change in the law, moreover, was occasioned by the notable lust and cruelty of a single moneylender") (trans. B. O. Foster [adapted]).

25. XII Tab. 3.3–4 (see also 5) in the traditional palingenesis (e.g., in *FIRA* 1^2.32–33); for an introduction to the textual and historiographical issues (with bibliography), see Flach, *Die Gesetze der frühen römischen Republik* (1994) 124–28.
26. See Corbino, *Il formalismo negoziale* (2006).
27. On which see, e.g., Capogrossi Colognesi, *Modelli di Stato e di famiglia* (1997) 67–80, 253–302.
28. See Bilz, *Die Politik des P. Cornelius Scipio Aemilianus,* 40–41; Astin, "*Regimen morum*" (1988) 21; Baltrusch, *Regimen morum* (1988) 23 n. 108.
29. "Sittengericht," "Judication," in Mommsen, *Römisches Staatsrecht* (1887) 2.1:375–88, 461–69.

nounced on broken oaths or promises, as in the famous case of Scipio Africanus the Younger,[30] who imposed the *nota censoria* for perjury on Gaius Licinius Sacerdos in connection with a *conceptio verborum* (in fact, Scipio Africanus also wanted to strip him of his horse but did not have the necessary, what we would call "political," consensus). This concerned a breach in a relationship of *fides;* the year was 142 BCE, and the episode is broadly recalled by Cicero, Valerius Maximus, and Plutarch, as well as by Quintilian in his *Institutio Oratoria.* At minimum, we can consider the following text:[31]

> Cic. *Pro Cluentio* 133–35: *[133]: At in ipsum Habitum animadverterunt. Nullam quidem ob turpitudinem, nullum ob totius vitae non dicam vitium, sed erratum; neque enim hoc homine sanctior neque probior neque in omnibus officiis retinendis diligentior esse quisquam potest. neque illi aliter dicunt, sed eandem illam famam iudicii corrupti secuti sunt: neque ipsi secus existimant quam nos existimari volumus de huius pudore, integritate, virtute, sed putarunt praetermitti accusatorem non potuisse, cum animadversum esset in iudices. qua de re si unum factum ex omni antiquitate protulero, plura non dicam. [134]: Non enim mihi exemplum summi et clarissimi viri, P. Africani, praetereundem videtur, qui cum esset censor et in equitum censu C. Licinius Sacerdos prodisset, clara voce, ut omnis contio audire posset, dixit se scire illum verbis conceptis peierasse: si qui contra vellet dicere, usurum esse eum suo testimonio: deinde cum nemo contra diceret, iussit equum traducere. ita is, cuius arbitrio et populus Romanus et exterae gentes contentae esse consuerant, ipse sua scientia ad ignominiam alterius contentus non fuit. quod si hoc Habito facere licuisset, facile illis ipsis iudicibus et falsae suspicioni et invidiae populariter excitatae restitisset. [135]: Unum etiam est quod me maxime perturbat, cui loco respondere vix videor posse, quod elogium recitasti de testamento Cn. Egnati patris, hominis honestissimi videlicet et sapientissimi: idcirco se exheredasse filium quod is ob Oppianici condemnationem pecuniam accepisset. de cuius hominis levitate et inconstantia plura non dicam: hoc testamentum ipsum, quod recitas, eius modi est ut ille, cum eum filium exheredaret quem oderat, ei filio coheredes homines alienissimos adiungeret quem diligebat. sed tu, Acci, consideres, censeo, diligenter, utrum censorum iudicium grave velis esse an Egnati. si Egnati, leve est quod censores de ceteris subscripserunt; ipsum*

30. On this episode in particular, see Astin, "*Regimen morum*" (1988) 21; Baltrusch, *Regimen morum* (1988) 23 n. 108. See also Masi Doria, "*Exemplum pessimum*" (2010) esp. 73–75.
31. See Val. Max. 4.1.10; Plut. *Apophth. Scip. Min.* 12 (200E); Quint. *Inst. Or.* 5.11.13.

enim Cn. Egnatium, quem tu gravem esse vis, ex senatu eiecerunt: sin autem censorum, hunc Egnatium, quem pater censoria subscriptione exheredavit, censores in senatu, cum patrem eicerent, retinuerunt.

(Cicero, *On Behalf of Cluentius*) [133]: But they [the censors] punished Habitus himself. Yes, but for nothing that was disgraceful, for no act in the course of his whole life that was, I will not say wrong, but even regrettable. For no one could possibly be purer than my client, or more honorable, or more scrupulous in the observance of every duty. Nor did the censors deny this; they merely followed the original rumor about the corruption of the court. It was not that they held any opinion other than we should wish concerning the honor, the blamelessness, and the high character of my client, but they thought that they could not pass over the accuser after censuring the jurors. I will quote one instance from all those that the past supplies and then will say no more on this point. [134]: I feel, indeed, that I cannot fail to mention the example of the great and famous P. Africanus. During his term as censor, he was reviewing the roll of equestrians when C. Licinius Sacerdos came forward. At that point, in a loud voice so as to be heard by the whole assembly, he said that he knew that Licinius had deliberately broken a solemn oath [*verba concepta*] and that if anyone wished to bring an accusation against him, he would give his evidence to support it. Then, as no one brought an accusation, he instructed Licinius "to lead past his horse." And so the man with whose judgment the Roman people and foreign nations had always been satisfied was not satisfied with his personal knowledge when it came to inflicting disgrace [*ignominia*] on another. But if this had been allowed to Habitus, he would easily have held his own, even if he had had the censors as his judges, against the groundless suspicion and prejudice roused against him by a demagogue. [135]: There is a further point, which troubles me greatly, an argument to which I find myself scarcely able to reply. I mean the passage, which you quote from the will of the elder Egnatius—the most honorable and intelligent of men, I need hardly say—stating that he disinherited his son for taking a bribe to secure Oppianicus's conviction. On this man's worthless and unreliable character I will not dilate: the very will that you quote has the effect of disinheriting the son whom the testator hated and, at the same time, of instituting absolute strangers as heirs conjointly with the son whom he loved. But as for you, Accius, I advise you to consider carefully whether you wish the judgment of the censors or that of Egnatius to carry weight. If that of Egnatius, then no weight can be attached to the censors' endorsements in other cases, for this very Cn. Egnatius, whose judgment you wish to carry weight, the censors expelled from the Senate. But if that of the censors, Egnatius the Younger, whose father disinherited him in the style of a censor's endorsement, was retained in the Senate by the very censors who expelled his father!] (trans. H. Grose Hodge [adapted])

According to Maine's view, perhaps a bit too rigid (but even more effective, for that reason, in its generalization), the "greatest gap in ancient civil law" was the "absence of Contract." However, an "elaborate jurisprudence of Oaths" compensated for this.[32] In the case of Scipio Africanus and Sacerdos (as in other cases mentioned in the sources), it is telling that the *censor* intervenes in the matter of disregard for a *conceptio verborum*. It is possible to regard this instance as a model of a "contractual" protection that is not strictly jurisdictional, in a world that is still (but not for long) linked to (although no longer shaped by) *status* paradigms.

This is why in earlier periods—corresponding to an attentive and pervasive activity on the part of the censors (which could only be carried out, as emerges clearly, in a small- or medium-sized context we can describe as "small-town")—there was a prevalence of *leges imperfectae*, as they are called in the much later classification of the *Tituli ex corpore Ulpiani*.[33] The infliction of the "sanction" was not assigned by the statute to an examination of the facts that was specifically jurisdictional in nature; rather, it was entrusted to the political office that naturally exercised oversight over the conduct of citizens. This took place not only through the actions of the censors themselves but also through the *coercitio* of the other officials. With the passing of time, a rationalization of the system assigned jurisdictional competence to different organs, for example, over theft (which Cicero, in his *Pro Cluentio*, shows to be subject still both to judgment by the censors and to regular civil trial).[34] Thus the overall historical con-

32. Maine, *Ancient Law* (1931/1998) 276.

33. See *Tit. Ulp.* 1.1, on which, at length, see Kaser, *Über Verbotsgesetze und verbotswidrige Geschäfte* (1977) 9–13.

34. Cic. *Pro Cluentio* 120: *Nunc si quem Cn. Lentuli aut L. Gelli libertus furti condemnarit, is omnibus ornamentis amissis numquam ullam honestatis suae partem recuperabit; quos autem ipse L. Gellius et Cn. Lentulus, duo censores, clarissimi viri sapientissimique homines, furti et captarum pecuniarum nomine notaverunt, ei non modo in senatum redierunt, sed etiam illarum ipsarum rerum iudiciis absoluti sunt* (But the fact is that while a man found guilty of theft at the instance of a freedman of Cn. Lentulus or L. Gellius will be deprived of every civil privilege and will never recover his honorable status in any particular, yet those whom our two very wise and

text diminished the importance of the censors in the community, which earlier had been enormous. The censors, in fact, were no longer elected in the future;[35] their principal duties (with the censorial *potestas*) passed, not by chance, to the *princeps*.[36] It seems to me that we are most likely dealing with a sign of change in Roman society from a structure based on *status* to an economy of contract.

A further aspect of the model I would like to propose involves the *ius patronatus,* the relationship between patrons and freedmen. From slavery, which, from various standpoints, is a structural element in a *status* society (both from the general point of view of *status libertatis* and from that status, economic and functional in nature, of subordination of the *servus* to the *dominus,* with its exclusion of legal capacity), one can move to freedom. The change took place through procedures that were, also in this case, steeped in legal formalism. The ancient *manumissiones iustae ac legitimae* were those carried out *censu, testamento,* and *vindicta*.[37] In all three of these forms, the involvement of the *dominus,* at least as a witness to the act, was a given. Very significant in these contexts is the fact that the manumission carried out with such procedures guaranteed not only *libertas* but also *civitas* and did not sever the connection between ex-*dominus* and former *servus.* A series of relationships based on *fides* persisted: *obsequium,* forensic patronage, the obligations relating to dowries, the duty to provide support to the patron in case of need (e.g., *alimenta*), the rights of succession, the procedural norms prohibiting *in ius vocatio* (extending, to a certain extent, to the patron's children and thus to his family, if not also to his *gens*).[38] The relation I would like to underscore briefly on this occasion as an example of this "movement" is that relating to *operae,* services (labor) due the patron by the freedman. From a sociological point of view, it is clear that we are dealing with the extension, albeit to a lesser degree, of the services due to the *dominus* by the slave.

Before the *manumissio,* the freedman bound himself or herself to carry out

---

distinguished censors L. Gellius and Cn. Lentulus themselves branded by name for theft and the acceptance of bribes were not only restored to the Senate but actually acquitted by the courts of those very offenses) (trans. H. Grose Hodge [adapted]).

35. For a summary discussion, with previous literature, see De Martino, *Storia della costituzione romana* (1973) 3:324.

36. See, at minimum, De Martino, *Storia della costituzione romana* (1974) 4.1:480–82.

37. Masi Doria, *Civitas, operae, obsequium* (1993) 1–15.

38. See Fabre, *Libertus* (1981) passim; Waldstein, *Operae libertorum* (1986); Masi Doria, *Civitas, operae, obsequium* (1993); Masi Doria, *Bona libertorum* (1996); Masi Doria, *Libertinitas e successione gentilizia* (1999).

certain services by an oath, *iusiurandum*. The resulting bond had a religious and moral value (as is common in *status* societies). After manumission, the oath was renewed via the so-called *promissio iurata liberti*, a solemn unilateral promise still strongly imbued with religious connotations, as the confirmation of the first oath. As Gaius notes,[39] this was the only case of a promissory oath in the Roman legal system, whose contractual nature modern experts have debated.[40] From a certain point onward, the slave who had been freed could promise services through a *stipulatio*, the so-called *stipulatio operarum*.[41] The patron was eligible for a special remedy, the *actio* or *iudicium operarum*,[42] in case of breach.

Naturally, it seems superfluous in this setting to dwell on the differences between *promissio iurata liberti* (which, like *dotis promissio*, not by chance also an institution of family law, took place *uno loquente*,[43] with *verba* pronounced only by the party who took on the obligation) and *stipulatio operarum* conducted instead *utroque loquente*, in a dialectic that led—even if not directly—to the development of contracts (here I am thinking of Arangio-Ruiz's[44] famous thesis on the genesis of consensual contracts on the basis of reciprocal *stipulationes*).[45]

The praetorian limitations on the claims of patrons, attesting to the loosening of the "ties" of *status* and the reorientation of the relationship in "contrac-

39. Gaius 3.96, integrated with Gai Ep. 2.9.4.

40. See Kaser, *Das römische Privatrecht* (1971) 1:300 and n. 31; Waldstein, *Operae libertorum* (1986) 239–47; Biscardi, *Temas de derecho romano* (1987) 40–41. See also the earlier discussion in Biscardi, "Postille gaiane" (1966) 22.

41. On this point, see the full discussion in Waldstein, *Operae libertorum* (1986) 247–51.

42. With *intentio in ius certa* (*D.* 38.1; *C.* 6.3), see, e.g., Waldstein, *Operae libertorum* (1986) 345–59.

43. Gai Ep. 2.9.3–4: 3. *Sunt et aliae obligationes, quae nulla praecedenti interrogatione contrahi possunt, id est, ut si mulier sive sponso uxor futura, sive iam marito, dotem dicat* . . . 4. *Item et alio casu, uno loquente et sine interrogatione alii promittente, contrahitur obligatio, id est, si libertus patrono aut donum aut munus aut operas se daturum esse iuravit. In qua re supradicti liberti non tam verborum solemnitate, quam iniurandi religione tenentur* (There are [verbal] obligations other [than stipulation], and these can be contracted without a preceding question, such as if a woman promises a dowry to her fiancé or husband. 4. Likewise, in another instance, when one party alone speaks and promises another without a question being asked, an obligation is contracted, such as if a freedman has sworn that he will give to his patron a gift, a favor, or services. In this case the aforementioned freedpersons are obligated not so much by the formality of the words as by respect for the oath).

44. Arangio-Ruiz, *La compravendita in diritto romano* (1956) 61–73.

45. See Cascione, *Consensus* (2003) 230–46.

tual" terms, are set forth in an exemplary way, for example, in the famous text that opens Title 38.2 of Justinian's *Digest* dedicated to *bona libertorum*.[46]

> Ulp. (42 *ad edictum*) D. 38.2.1 pr.–2: *pr. Hoc edictum a praetore propositum est honoris, quem liberti patronis habere debent, moderandi gratia. namque ut Servius scribit, antea soliti fuerunt a libertis durissimas res exigere, scilicet ad remunerandum tam grande beneficium, quod in libertos confertur, cum ex servitute ad civitatem Romanam perducuntur.* 1. *Et quidem primus praetor Rutilius edixit se amplius non daturum patrono quam operarum et societatis actionem, videlicet si hoc pepigisset, ut, nisi ei obsequium praestaret libertus, in societatem admitteretur patronus.* 2. *Posteriores praetores certae partis bonorum possessionem pollicebantur: videlicet enim imago societatis induxit eiusdem partis praestationem, ut, quod vivus solebat societatis nomine praestare, id post mortem praestaret.*
>
> [(Ulpian in the forty-second book on the Edict): pr. This edict was put forward by the praetor for the purpose of regulating the respect that freedmen ought to show to their patrons. For, as Servius observes, in former times (patrons) were accustomed to make the most severe demands on their freedmen, evidently so that they repay the enormous privilege conferred on them when they are brought out of slavery to Roman citizenship. 1. And indeed Rutilius was the first praetor to proclaim in his edict that he would not allow a patron more than an action for services and partnership, namely, where an agreement has been made that where a freedman did not show due obedience to his patron, the latter would be admitted to partnership (in his goods). 2. Subsequent praetors promised patrons *bonorum possessio* of a fixed part (of the deceased freedman's property). For evidently the idea of partnership led to a transfer of the same share with the result that what the freedman used to hand over in the name of partnership while alive he (now) supplied after his death.] (trans. A. Watson [adapted])

A restriction was introduced on the *durissimae res* that patrons used to claim from their freed slaves in an earlier period, allowing merely *operarum* and *societatis actiones*. In short, there was a move "from bondage to contract," to echo a recent felicitous recasting of Maine's *dictum* in order to describe salaried work contracts following the abolition of slavery in the United States.[47]

46. On which see Masi Doria, *Civitas, operae, obsequium* (1993); and especially Masi Doria, *Bona libertorum* (1996), the second part of which is devoted to the entire title in question.
47. Stanley, *From Bondage to Contract* (1998).

In addition, we can refer to the image—a "powerful" one, according to Dario Mantovani[48]—of the dichotomy of *ius civile* and *ius praetorium* suggested by Mario Lauria: to the former (here signifying not only the Twelve Tables but also the ancient obligatory customs of the *mos maiorum*), we should ascribe relationships of a personal nature; to the latter (created by praetorian intervention), relationships that could be assessed in monetary terms.[49]

We have seen, if only briefly, how the *status* society declined. The reasons were primarily economic, tied to the expansion of markets, but also social, connected to the weakening of archaic forms of thought and ultimately to the mastery of human fears regarding nature. These fears had long kept early human beings and then also the most ancient communities in history bound not only by the reassuring, protective ties of family groups but also by those fostered by religious beliefs (the two phenomena are closely connected).

To Maine's way of thinking, the main tool of the new economy, once this has been disengaged from the structures of *status* societies, is the contract. Contract, however, is also a sign of synthesis. Before contract in the abstract, there were—in practice—contracts, agreements that created obligations. As Burdese has recently maintained convincingly: "One type of problem that, with regard to contractual issues, the Roman legal historian is required to confront concerns the interpretation of the terminology—as an expression of thought—used by the sources, especially the writings of the jurists, to characterize individual phenomena through a range of meanings that vary over time, from jurist to jurist, or even within the work of the same jurist: language that in any case seems more consistent with common usage and less tied to doctrinal constructions compared with modern technical jargon, the use of which must when necessary be subject to qualification and its meaning calibrated to describe adequately, without distortions, the historical reality under consideration."[50]

---

48. Mantovani, "*Praetoris partes*" (2003) 51–52 n. 32.

49. Lauria, "*Ius civile—ius honorarium*" (1946/1983), (on which see Grosso, review of Lauria (1947) 236–38; d'Ippolito, "L'inquietudine dello storico" [2009] 91–99).

50. Burdese, "Panoramica sul contratto" (2007) 565: "Un primo tipo di problemi che, in ordine alla materia contrattuale, come del resto più in generale, è chiamato ad affrontare lo storico del diritto romano è quello consistente nell'interpretazione del linguaggio—quale espressione di pensiero—usato in proposito nelle fonti, in particolare giurisprudenziali, a indicare singoli fenomeni, secondo significati che variano da epoca ad epoca, da giurista a giurista, o anche da parte dello stesso giurista in accezioni diverse: terminologia che appare in ogni caso più aderente agli usi comuni e meno legata a costruzioni dogmatiche rispetto al linguaggio tecnico odierno, la cui utilizzazione necessita volta a volta di precisazioni e adattamenti di significato tali da opportunamente adeguarla a descrivere, senza travisarla, la realtà storica considerata."

This is all the more true if we follow that line of scholarship—ranging from Biondi to Kaser[51]—that sees in language itself the first expression of Roman jurists' "dogmatics" (albeit in progress). On this point, we can again refer to Burdese's recent synthesis:[52] "With regard to the term *negotium* (*contrahere*), this signifies generically (like *negotiatio*) business-related activities, especially insofar as recognized by the law (beyond its relevance in the context of trials) as financial in nature (and so not purely gratuitous) which produce effects that are not necessarily binding and that have an impact on two or more legally distinct centers of interest. To *negotium* is linked the term *contractum,* perfect passive participle of *contrahere* (*negotium*): hence the noun *contractus* (*negotii*). The former can indicate the object of the contracting activity and the latter the act of making a contract between two or more parties . . . and one designed to create a *vinculum* with effects that are typically binding, although the term *contrahere,* more than one finds with the term *contractus,* is used fully and generically in the sources, the legal sources too, not only for transactions that create (or, where relevant, extinguish) obligations, but also for financial transactions concerning acts of a personal nature (for example, *matrimonium contrahere*)."[53]

The intertwining of *negotium contractum/contractus* and the Greek *synallagma,* beginning with Labeo's famous definition,[54] offers two points of depar-

51. Biondi, "La terminologia romana" (1953); Kaser, "Zur juristischen Terminologie" (1965/1976).

52. Burdese, "Panoramica sul contratto" (2007) 565–6: "Quanto all'espressione *negotium* (*contrahere*), essa denota genericamente (come *negotiatio*) una attività di affari, specie in quanto riconosciuta dal diritto (oltre ad essere riferita ad attività processuale) come attività negoziale a contenuto patrimoniale non meramente gratuita, produttiva di effetti non necessariamente obbligatori, che incidono su due o più sfere giuridicamente distinte di interessi. Si ricollega ad essa il termine *contractum,* come participio perfetto di *contrahere* (*negotium*), donde il sostantivo *contractus* (*negotii*), laddove possono indicare l'uno ciò che si contrae e l'altro l'atto del contrarre, posto in essere tra due o più soggetti . . . e indirizzato a stringere un vincolo tra di loro con effetti normalmente obbligatori, benché la terminologia del *contrahere,* più che non il termine *contractus,* trovi maggiormente ampia e generica applicazione nelle fonti, anche giuridiche, al di là non solo di negozi costitutivi (ed eventualmente estintivi) di obbligazioni, ma pure di negozi patrimoniali, con riferimento ad atti di natura personale (ad es. *matrimonium contrahere*)." See, most recently, Fino, *L'origine della transactio* (2004) 234–48.

53. For example, *matrimonium contrahere,* or wrongful acts (e.g., *crimen contrahere*). On the terminology *contrahere, contractum, contractus,* see, among many others, the authors cited in Burdese, "Divagazioni in tema di contratto romano" (2001) 317 n. 1. See also Romano, "*Conventio* e *consensus*" (2003) 255–59.

54. Ulp. (11 *ad edictum*) *D.* 50.16.19: *Labeo libro primo praetoris urbani definit, quod quaedam 'agantur', quaedam 'gerantur', quaedam 'contrahantur': et actum quidem generale verbum esse, sive verbis sive re quid agatur, ut in stipulatione vel numeratione: contractum autem ultro citroque obligationem, quod Graeci συνάλλαγμα vocant, veluti emptionem venditionem, loca-*

ture for developing a conception that, moving beyond a narrowly legal perspective, enables us to view the contract in economic and broadly ethical terms, as a piece of business between two or more parties, the binding exchange grounded in Aristotle's theory of justice. On these issues, modern scholarship on Roman law benefits from A. Guzmán Brito's important studies, which bring together the systemic and semantic meaning of legal transactions from Roman to contemporary law (especially Latin American).[55] Contracts, especially commercial ones, seem to have provided a kind of legal infrastructure for the Roman economy of expansionism and the long *pax* of the Principate,[56] as a refashioning of the ethics of exchange. First, the contracts of the *ius gentium: emptio venditio, locatio conductio, societas, mandatum*. This may seem predictable; however, I would like to emphasize that in the juristic tradition, wealth does not circulate by means of contracts. On the contrary, according to Volterra, who wrote an important essay on the topic, "La base economica della elaborazione sistematica del diritto romano,"[57] the economy as it is treated in the fragments of the *Digest* is not that of the grand interests of individuals and groups of the empire's ruling class, who held immense wealth in land and movables and who, as the most influential economic operators (in the financial sense, as well as the agricultural, industrial, and commercial), were substantially free of the legal control exercised by the jurists and the imperial courts.[58] I would describe this as an oligarchical economy in which controversies were evidently smoothed

tionem conductionem, societatem: gestum rem significare sine verbis factam (Labeo, in the first book of his commentary on the edict of the urban praetor, distinguishes among certain things that are "done" [*agere*], certain things that are "performed" [*gerere*], and certain things that are "contracted" [*contrahere*], and [he holds that] in fact *actum* is a general word used when something is said or done, as when making a verbal obligation [*stipulatio*] or a loan; *contractum*, however, is used when there is a reciprocal obligation, what the Greeks call *sunallagma*, like sale, hire, partnership; *gestum* is used to indicate that something has been done without resort to words) (trans. A. Watson [adapted]). On this text, see Roberto Fiori's chapter in the present volume.

55. See Guzmán Brito, "Para la historia de la formación I" (1995); Guzmán Brito, "Para la historia de la formación II" (1997).

56. As in the current accounts of the history of Roman law: see, for example, Talamanca, *Lineamenti di storia* (1989), esp. 159, with appropriate caution in asserting the "Romanness" of the legal procedures that were framed "sotto la spinta delle necessità che nascevano dall'apertura al commercio internazionale" (under the pressure of needs that arose from the opening to international commerce).

57. Volterra, "La base economica" (1967/1993).

58. See, in summary form, Volterra's thinking in "La base economica" (1967/1993) 154–55.

over by mediation, a bit like our present experience with large global economic transactions.[59] This phenomenon should be taken into consideration when evaluating the "movement" from *status* to contract and the impact of the types of contracts on the actual economy of the Roman world. But I will not take this point further here, because some of the other contributors to this volume deal very specifically with the Roman consensual contracts.

I offer just one more general observation. With the crisis of the third and fourth centuries, the ancient economy changed radically, with fewer markets and a return to the land. Large rural estates and the system of land tenure known as the colonate defined the agrarian landscape of late antiquity; depopulation of the countryside accompanied an increase in brigandage.[60] The cities closed in on themselves, with the weight of taxation freezing in place the orders, professions, and trades and conditioning the transfer of patrimony from one generation to the next.[61] The *Codex Theodosianus* seems to reintroduce a *status* society. Maine's model appears to be turned on its head. If we want to trace an interpretive paradigm in Roman law scholarship comparable to Maine's in its evolutionary premises, we could look at the thesis of "regressive evolution" of legal institutions as proposed by Flaminio Mancaleoni in his 1920 inaugural lecture in Naples.[62] In this newly regressive society in which legal procedures that originated in practice have lost their driving force, privileges are now aimed at crystallizing the positions (positive or negative) of specific productive and social categories, like that of the new (and increasingly more important) category of ecclesiastics that grows out of the consolidation and the spread of Christianity.

What better characterizes the late antique world—from a legal perspective and on first impression—than the dichotomy of *honestiores* and *humiliores*?[63] Senators, equestrians, *curiales, negotiatores,* soldiers, and veterans were *honestiores* in the Principate. The members of the lower orders were not inevitably *humiliores;* the *status libertatis,* for example, was of some significance. The dichotomy may not even suffice to describe this society: it does not constitute "a

59. See, for example, Ferrarese, *Diritto sconfinato* (2006).
60. De Martino, *Uomini e terre in Occidente* (1988); De Martino, *Diritto, economia e società* (1997).
61. Mercogliano and Spagnuolo Vigorita, "Tributi (storia)" (1992) 101–4.
62. Mancaleoni, "L'evoluzione regressiva" (1921); see Reduzzi, "Flaminio Mancaleoni a Napoli" (2002).
63. On the dichotomy, with an analytical treatment that, in any case, underplays its absolute nature, see Rilinger, *Humiliores—Honestiores* (1988), to be read together with Bretone, "Fra storia sociale e storia giuridica" (1989).

'*Grundeinteilung*'. It has instead only relative value, operating together with or alongside other distinctions of personal status."[64] This holds particularly true in the area of criminal law, as Stefano Giglio has noted recently.[65] For example, in *CTh.* 16.5.52 pr., a distinction is made, for the purposes of punishment, between *inlustres, spectabiles, senatores, clarissimi, sacerdotes, principales, decuriones, negotiatores,* plebeians, and *circumcelliones.* This is the triumph of a society fragmented by *status* that reproduces itself via the hereditary nature of social position. This is not, however, the caste system of traditional India, with which we can draw only a broad parallel that, in truth, is rather weak from an analytical point of view.

A new picture of European society now begins to assert itself. That society is consolidated in new social orders and divided into different statuses. In our imaginary (general, not scientific), this picture comes to define the Europe of the Middle Ages and then of the *Ancien Régime* up until the French Revolution.

The title of our conference suggests, from a historical perspective, an opening to the "future of obligations." It seems opportune to answer this invitation—albeit briefly.

Some of the recent scholarly literature (not in Roman law, or at least not only in Roman law) sees signs that a return to *status* is occurring in the present time. Is this some kind of reversal of Maine's model? The issue is connected with the "death of contract," the title of Grant Gilmore's famous work and an image applicable to the classic common-law contract,[66] as well as to the continental law contract of ancient Roman derivation. The "crisis" of contractual models in the wake of the "ten years that knocked contract for a loop"[67] at the end of the twentieth century (and, paradoxically, after the death sentence signed by Gilmore) produced a sort of transfiguration of the contract itself. The contemporary paradigm is by now much more complex compared with the historical origins of general contract theory.[68]

If we take up a series of distinctions drawn by Vincenzo Roppo among others—and apply them to the Italian case first of all (as the most obvious application)—there are civil law contracts (of the classic model derived from the codification), consumer contracts, and contracts marked by an asymmetry

---

64. Bretone, "Fra storia sociale e storia giuridica" (1989) 49.
65. Giglio, "*Humiliores*" (2007).
66. Gilmore, *Death of Contract* (1974); *La morte del contratto* (Italian trans. 1987).
67. See Roppo, *Il contratto del duemila* (2002) 7: "I dieci anni che sconvolsero il contratto."
68. On these, see, e.g., Guzmán Brito, "Para la historia de la formación III" (2000).

of contracting power. The crisis of contract emerges especially with the idea of contract as a bond and, therefore, with the distinction between rules governing validity and rules relating to behavior/liability. The demands of the global economy reward flexibility over certainty and stability, and so it happens that the character of the contract—as Roppo affirms—"leans dangerously toward the more extreme interpretations of the radical wing of the economic analysis of law that—building on an old suggestion by Oliver Wendell Holmes, Jr.—postulates 'efficient breach.' The contract does not produce an obligation to perform; instead, it leaves open the discretion of choosing between performance and breach/compensation, between respect and violation of the contract in a zone devoid of moral evaluation. Hence it is reduced to the calculation of purely economic convenience, giving precedence to the solution that would guarantee the 'optimal' allocation of resources. In short, a contract that is increasingly less reliant on the concept of bond, on the sanctity of the principle *pacta sunt servanda,* on the metaphor 'force of law,' thus a type of contract that is more and more inconsistent with the paradigm of the legal rule, as we have customarily understood it."[69] With such perspectives on contract, patterns that are possibly dependent on a contextualization within *status* seem, in effect, to resurface.

Maine's point of view, then, seems to encounter a striking twist in the modern age as well as in late antiquity. Collective bargaining, contracts based on agreement realized through the use of forms and standard wording, and the resort to broad terms identifying the parties (like "consumer") are all elements typical of a social reality in which the contracting parties do not carry the same weight. They do not contribute in the same way to shaping the contract. In fact, in the case of the provision of services essential to modern life, such as water, electricity, gas, telephone, banking, and insurance services (especially in a system of "limited competition" in these areas, such as we have in Italy), the very option to participate or not is, at bottom, certainly very limited, if not fictitious. Safeguards established by the State, however, in favor of the weaker contracting party are being added in various fields to counterbalance the position of the party who determines the content and conditions of the contract.

Today we are well aware of how a difference in the positions of the contracting parties undercuts the dogma of mutual agreement, traditionally understood as a pure and absolute expression of individual will (in these terms, perhaps a

69. Again, Roppo, *Il contratto del duemila* (2002) 7. On the loss of unity in the contractual paradigm, see also, for example, Amadio, "Il terzo contratto" (2008).

myth).[70] In the face of this reality, legislators try to enact principles of substantive equality. Often—as in Italy—these are formally required by the constitutions of various countries.[71] To this end, they employ the tools of so-called welfare. A law of contracts founded on an idea of contract as an act concerning the parties developed and grew stronger. But this idea was, at the same time, considerably conditioned by external influences: on the one hand, through the imposition of obligations realized as a form of remuneration accruing to positions of economic strength; on the other, by means of instruments introduced by the legal system with the aim of implementing requests on a constitutional level. In short, beginning in the mid-twentieth century, contract law has been heavily influenced by social and legislative factors.[72] and the consequences have been severe erosion of individual liberties and the contract's "institutionalization." This has occasioned (at least seemingly) a sort of reestablishment of *status*.[73]

Some modern scholars recognize that "the protected *status* (tenant, operator of a family farm, woman, mother, minor, consumer etc., but also, for certain purposes, merchant, independent professional, etc.) are determined by considerations tied more to sentiment than to reason, and authorize judges to offer their opinions on the basis of emotional criteria," with the result that "from a technical-legal perspective such a dense number of protected *status* (with a corresponding number of identities) creates administrative difficulties. Their

70. Already for Roman law, see Martini, "Il mito del consenso" (1991). On the question of "contractual freedom" as it occurs in theoretical approaches in the scholarship beginning with Max Weber, see Nitsch, "*Coactus voluit*" (2007).

71. See Article 3 of the Constitution of the Republic of Italy: "Tutti i cittadini hanno pari dignità sociale e sono eguali davanti alla legge, senza distinzione di sesso, di razza, di lingua, di religione, di opinioni politiche, di condizioni personali e sociali. È compito della Repubblica rimuovere gli ostacoli di ordine economico e sociale, che, limitando di fatto la libertà e l'eguaglianza dei cittadini, impediscono il pieno sviluppo della persona umana e l'effettiva partecipazione di tutti i lavoratori all'organizzazione politica, economica e sociale del Paese" (All citizens enjoy an equivalent social dignity and are equals before the law, without distinction of sex, race, language, religion, political views, or personal and social status. It is the task of the Republic to remove the impediments of an economic and social nature which, by placing limits in actual fact on the liberty and equality of citizens, thwart the full development of the person in his or her human condition and the meaningful participation of all workers in the political, economic, and social life of the nation) (trans. T. A. J. McGinn).

72. Friedmann, *Law in a Changing Society* (1959) 95, 101.

73. See Acquarone, "Il sistema giuridico dell'India" (2002); Acquarone, "Tendenze evolutive del diritto dell'India" (2003) 116–17.

reciprocal conflict is anything but unlikely as it is logically inevitable that one protected category will be slighted to the absolute benefit of the one preferred."[74]

In sum, the movement from contract to *status* seems to have been a constant characteristic of legal developments in Italy from the 1970s onward, as if "they wanted to turn backwards over the path undertaken in the Enlightenment."[75] From Maine's perspective, it does indeed seem possible to speak of a "U-turn."

Reliance on the concept of *status* tends to emerge also at a normative level. In private law, it is regularly associated either with family relations (*status* as child, as spouse), with an economic activity (*status* as worker, businessman, professional), or with one's position in the market (producer, retailer, wholesaler/manufacturer, consumer). According to Alpa, a highly regarded civil law scholar, precisely its assimilation to family relationships or to business activity hearkens back to the ancient origins of the concept, which, in his view, derives from a tribal or caste system.[76] Without being able to examine in full the issues relating to modern interpretations of *status*, we can address the need (which is, so to speak, "positivistic') to consider the normative assumptions of this concept as a point of departure. Thus *status* expresses the specific legal position assumed by a subject within the legal system in relation to a set of rules imposed on him or her by virtue of his or her membership in a group.[77]

We can understand, therefore, how the scholarship takes for granted the concept that current labor and consumer rights law tends to postulate the recognition of individual conditions definable as *status*. But from a point of view more strictly in line with Maine, we should ask ourselves if this new notion of *status* truly transcends the individual and aims to pursue the interests of the group, understood as prevailing over the interest of the individual, or—as Acquarone has recently highlighted—if the importance of *status* might again today serve (but through nontraditional means) as a legal device deployed in

---

74. Vincenti, *Diritto senza identità* (2007) 34–35: "Gli *status* di protezione (di inquilino, di coltivatore diretto, di donna, di madre, di minore, di consumatore ecc., ma anche, almeno a certi effetti, di commerciante, di libero professionista ecc.) sono spesso dettati da ragioni legate più al sentimento che alla razionalità; e autorizzano i giudici a sentenziare sulla base di valutazioni emotive . . . dal punto di vista tecnico-giuridico una pluralità così fitta di *status* protettivi (cui corrispondono altrettante identità) crea difficoltà di amministrazione, essendo tutt'altro che improbabile il loro conflitto reciproco con la conseguente inevitabilità della posposizione di una categoria protetta a tutto vantaggio di quella preferita."

75. Rescigno, "Situazione e status" (1973) 218.

76. Alpa, *Status e capacità* (1993) 4.

77. Criscuoli, "Variazioni e scelte" (1984) 204.

service of the interest of the individual.[78] Of course, this takes the category of "individual" as arising from one's standing as a member associated with a group (not necessarily in a sense that is intuitive, automatic, or inevitable, however) but possibly as the result of an artifice that is technical or cultural or of a normative synthesis). Only in the first case, in fact, would the result be a "betrayal" of individualism and, thus, a true and proper "deviation" from or "overturning" of the law Maine formulated to explain the evolution of societies.

The revival of *status,* which might appear to be a "new path backwards,"[79] is rooted in the concern to find in the identification of the individual with the group a more effective safeguarding of those needs that would not be protected if the individual were left to interact only through his or her own discretionary power—in other words, through the means offered by the contract—in a general context in which, as we have seen, the idea of equality between contractual parties is increasingly more clearly revealed as a myth (well beyond technical knowledge).

The *ratio* that today leads to a reliance on *status* appears, in the final analysis, to be grounded not in the superior interest of a group or of the community but precisely in the protection of the person, that is, the individual. This is the same *ratio* that, in essence, has led the courts to the development of the category of class actions, recently a much-debated topic even in Italy. In these terms, Maine's evolutionary law would not, therefore, be contradicted by the apparent return to the future that is taking place today in the movement from contract to *status.*

We can, in conclusion, take note of "parochial corporate trends and a chaotic state of legal rules: even today wholesalers/manufacturers, operators of family farms, independent professionals are endowed with special *status* in the pursuit of their activities as such, *status* that, in certain circumstances, provide an excellent cover for class privileges (and which, by way of contrast, feed an institutional suspicion directed toward the categories that are protected in this way)."[80] In my view, all this does not, however, mean a return to *status,* in the

78. Acquarone, "Il sistema giuridico dell'India" (2002).

79. Criscuoli, "Variazioni e scelte" (1984) 170.

80. Vincenti, *Diritto senza identità* (2007) 45: "tendenze grettamente corporative e disuniformità di regime giuridico: ancor oggi imprenditori, coltivatori diretti, liberi professionisti sono portatori di *status* speciali nell'esplicazione delle loro attività; *status* che, almeno riguardo a certe ipotesi, forniscono un'ottima copertura a privilegi di ceto (e che, per contrappasso, alimentano il sospetto istituzionale verso le categorie così protette)."

sense preferred by Sir Henry S. Maine. Nor would such a return be productive from the perspective of legal logic and certainty. This is something we should always keep in mind, at a time of reflection, when legitimate criticism of the excesses of legal positivism risks transforming itself (in its extremist forms) into opposition to the modern system of law that has developed in continental Europe since the French Revolution and the Napoleonic Codes.[81] There is perhaps a risk of conceding, in this way, too much value to a notion of *status* that, at present, does not strengthen those groups or identities representative of their members but develops safeguards (even if at times corporate ones) concerning the positions of individuals.

Bibliography

Acquarone, L. "Il sistema giuridico dell'India dal dharma al diritto positivo, dalla gerarchia all'individuo," 2002, http://www.club.it/culture/culture2002/lorenza.acquarone/corpo.tx.acquarone.html. Revised as "Tendenze evolutive del diritto dell'India: Dallo status al contract e dal contract allo status," *Rivista di sociologia del diritto* 1 (2003): 95–119.

Alpa, G. *Status e capacità: La costruzione giuridica delle differenze individuali.* Rome: Laterza, 1993.

Amadio, G. "Il terzo contratto: Il problema." In *Il terzo contratto,* ed. G. Gitti and G. Villa, 9–30. Bologna: Il Mulino, 2008.

Arangio-Ruiz, V. *La compravendita in diritto romano.* Vol. 1. 2nd ed. Naples: Jovene Editore, 1956. Reprint, Naples: Jovene Editore, 1994.

Astin, A. E. "*Regimen morum.*" *Journal of Roman Studies* 78 (1988): 14–34.

Bachofen, J. J. "Die Grundgesetze der Völkerentwicklung und der Historiographie." In *Gesammelte Werke,* 6: 409–41. Basel: Schwabe, 1864. Reprint, Basel: Schwabe, 1951. Translated into Italian as *Le leggi della storiografia* (Naples: Guida, 1999).

Baltrusch, E. *Regimen morum: Die Reglementierung des Privatlebens der Senatoren und Ritter in der römischen Republik und frühen Kaiserzeit.* Munich: C. H. Beck, 1988.

Bilz, K. *Die Politik des P. Cornelius Scipio Aemilianus.* Stuttgart: Kohlhammer, 1935.

Biondi, B. "La terminologia romana come prima dommatica giuridica." In *Studi Vincenzo Arangio-Ruiz,* 2:73–103. Naples: Jovene Editore, 1953.

Biscardi, A. "Postille gaiane." In *Gaio nel suo tempo: Atti del Simposio romanistico,* ed. A. Guarino and L. Bove, 15–24. Naples: Jovene Editore, 1966.

81. For a summary, see Grossi, *L'Europa del diritto* (2007) *passim.*

Biscardi, A. *Temas de derecho romano.* Barcelona: Bosch, 1987.

Brachet, J.-P. "*Obligare et obnoxius:* Observations morphologiques et sémantiques." *Glotta* 81 (2005): 25–44.

Bretone, M. "Fra storia sociale e storia giuridica." *Rechtshistorisches Journal* 8 (1989): 35–51.

Burdese, A. "Divagazioni in tema di contratto romano tra forma, consenso e causa." In *Iuris vincula: Studi in onore di Mario Talamanca,* 1:315–53. Naples: Jovene Editore, 2001.

Burdese, A. "Il contratto romano tra forma, consenso e causa." In *Le dottrine del contratto nella giurisprudenza romana,* ed. A. Burdese, 85–108. Padua: CEDAM, 2006.

Burdese, A. "Panoramica sul contratto nelle dottrine della giurisprudenza romana." In *Fides, humanitas, ius: Studi in onore di Luigi Labruna,* 1:565–80. Naples: Editoriale Scientifica, 2007.

Burdese, A. "Prefazione." In *Le dottrine del contratto nella giurisprudenza romana,* ed. A. Burdese, 1–19. Padua: CEDAM, 2006.

Capogrossi Colognesi, L. *Dalla storia di Roma alle origini della società civile: Un dibattito ottocentesco.* Bologna: Il Mulino, 2008.

Capogrossi Colognesi, L. *Modelli di Stato e di famiglia nella storiografia dell'800.* 3rd ed. Rome: La Sapienza, 1997.

Cascione, C. *Consensus: Problemi di origine, tutela processuale, prospettive sistematiche.* Naples: Editoriale Scientifica, 2003.

Corbino, A. *Il formalismo negoziale nell'esperienza romana.* 2nd ed. Turin: Giappichelli, 2006.

Corbino, A. "*Status familiae.*" In *Homo, caput, persona: La costruzione giuridica dell'identità nell'esperienza romana,* 175–216. Pavia: IUSS Press, 2010.

Criscuoli, G. "Variazioni e scelte in tema di status." *Rivista di diritto civile* 30 (1984): 157–209.

De Martino, F. *Diritto, economia e società nel mondo romano.* Vol. 3, *Economia e società.* Naples: Jovene Editore, 1997.

De Martino, F. "La costituzione della città-stato." In *Diritto economia e società nel mondo romano,* vol. 2, *Diritto pubblico,* 451–71. Naples: Jovene Editore, 1996. Originally published in *Storia di Roma,* vol. 1, *Roma in Italia,* ed. A. Momigliano and A. Schiavone, 345–65 (Turin: Einaudi, 1988).

De Martino, F. *Storia della costituzione romana.* Vol. 3. 2nd ed. Naples: Jovene Editore, 1973.

De Martino, F. *Storia della costituzione romana.* Vol. 4.1. 2nd ed. Naples: Jovene Editore, 1974.

De Martino, F. *Storia economica di Roma antica.* Vol. 1. Florence: Jovene Editore, 1979.

De Martino, F. *Uomini e terre in Occidente: Tra tardo antico e Medioevo*. Naples: Jovene Editore, 1988.

d'Ippolito, F. "L'inquietudine dello storico." In *Saggi della storiografia romanistica,* 85–105. Naples: Satura, 2009.

Dumont, L. *Homo hierarchicus: Le système des castes et ses implications.* Paris: Gallimard, 1966. Translated into Italian as *Homo hierarchicus: Il sistema delle caste e le sue implicazioni* (Milan: Adelphi, 1991).

Dumont, L. *La civilisation indienne et nous.* Paris: A. Colin, 1975. Translated into Italian as *La civiltà indiana e noi* (Milan: Adelphi, 1996).

Fabre, G. *Libertus: Recherches sur les rapports patron-affranchi à la fin de la république romaine.* Rome: École française de Rome, 1981.

Ferrarese, M. R. *Diritto sconfinato: Inventiva giuridica e spazi nel mondo globale.* Rome: Laterza, 2006.

Ferrarese, M. R. *Le istituzioni della globalizzazione: Diritto e diritti nella società transnazionale.* Bologna: Il Mulino, 2000.

Fino, M. A. *L'origine della transactio: Pluralità di prospettive nella riflessione dei giuristi antoniniani.* Milan: Giuffrè Editore, 2004.

Fiori, R. "*Fides* et *bona fides:* Hiérarchie sociale et catégories juridiques." *Revue historique de droit français et étranger* 86 (2008): 465–81.

Fiori, R. "Il problema dell'oggetto del contratto nella tradizione civilistica." In *Modelli teorici e metodologici nella storia del diritto romano,* 169–238. Naples: Jovene Editore, 2003.

Flach, D. *Die Gesetze der frühen römischen Republik: Text und Kommentar.* Darmstadt: Wissenschaftliche Buchgesellschaft, 1994.

Friedmann, W. *Law in a Changing Society.* London: Stevens and Sons, 1959.

Genovese, M. "*Res* e relative qualifiche intorno al *commercium.*" In *Studi per Giovanni Nicosia,* 4:87–147. Milan: Giuffrè Editore, 2007.

Giglio, S. "*Humiliores.*" In *Studi per Giovanni Nicosia,* 4:149–65. Milan: Giuffrè Editore, 2007.

Gilmore, G. *The Death of Contract.* Columbus: Ohio State University Press, 1974. Translated into Italian as *La morte del contratto* (Milan: Giuffrè Editore, 1987).

Goldmann, F. "*Nobilitas* als Status und Gruppe: Überlegungen zum Nobilitätsbegriff der römischen Republik." In *Res publica reperta: Festschrift für J. Bleicken zum 75. Geburtstag,* ed. J. Spielvogel, 45–66. Stuttgart: F. Steiner, 2002.

Graveson, R. H. "The Movement from Status to Contract." *Modern Law Review* 4 (1941): 261–72.

Grossi, P. *L'Europa del diritto.* Rome: Laterza, 2007.

Grosso, G. Review of M. Lauria, "*Ius civile—ius honorarium.*" In *Rivista italiana per le scienze giuridiche* 84 (1943): 378–87. Reprinted in *Scritti storico giuridici,* 4:231–40. Turin: Giappichelli, 1947; reprint, 2001.

Guzmán Brito, A. "Para la historia de la formación de la teoría general del acto o negocio jurídico y del contrato." Part 1, "El vocabulario de la negocialidad jurídica en el derecho romano." *Revista de Estudios Histórico-Jurídicos* 17 (1995): 79–122.

Guzmán Brito, A. "Para la historia de la formación de la teoría general del acto o negocio jurídico y del contrato." Part 2, "El sistema y el vocabulario de la negocialidad jurídica en las codificaciones americanas." *Revista de Estudios Histórico-Jurídicos* 19 (1997): 95–106.

Guzmán Brito, A. "Para la historia de la formación de la teoría general de acto o negocio jurídico y del contrato." Part 3, "Los orígenes históricos de la teoría general del contrato." *Revista de Estudios Histórico-Jurídicos* 22 (2000): 45–60.

Hardt, M., and A. Negri. *Empire.* Cambridge, MA: Harvard University Press, 2000. Translated into Italian as *Impero: Il nuovo ordine della globalizzazione* (Milan: Rizzoli, 2002).

Humbert, M. "Le *status civitatis:* Identité et identification du *civis Romanus.*" In *Homo, caput, persona: La costruzione giuridica dell'identità nell'esperienza romana,* 139–73. Pavia: IUSS Press, 2010.

Kaser, M. *Das römische Privatrecht.* Vol. 1. 2nd ed. Munich: C. H. Beck, 1971.

Kaser, M. *Über Verbotsgesetze und verbotswidrige Geschäfte im römischen Recht.* Vienna: Verlag der österreichischen Akademie der Wissenschaften, 1977.

Kaser, M. "Zur juristischen Terminologie der Römer." In *Ausgewählte Schriften,* 1:37–82. Naples: Jovene Editore, 1976. Originally published in *Studi in onore di B. Biondi,* 1:97–142 (Milan: Giuffrè Editore, 1965).

Lauria, M. "*Ius civile—ius honorarium.*" In *Studii e ricordi,* 382–437. Naples: Jovene Editore, 1983. Originally published in *Scritti di diritto romano in onore di C. Ferrini,* ed. G. G. Archi, 597–657 (Milan: Hoepli, 1946).

Maine, H. S. *Ancient Law.* Oxford: Oxford University Press, 1931. Translated into Italian as *Diritto antico* (Milan: Giuffrè Editore, 1998).

Mancaleoni, F. "L'evoluzione regressiva degli istituti giuridici." *Studi Sassaresi* 7 (1921): 1–30.

Mantovani, D. "*Praetoris partes:* La *iurisdictio* e i suoi vincoli nel processo formulare; Un percorso negli studi." In *Il diritto fra scoperta e creazione: Giudici e giuristi nella storia della giustizia civile,* 33–151. Naples: Jovene Editore, 2003.

Martini, R. "Il mito del consenso nella dottrina del contratto." *Iura* 42 (1991): 97–109.

Masi Doria, C. *Bona libertorum: Regimi giuridici e realtà sociali.* Naples: Jovene Editore, 1996.

Masi Doria, C. *Civitas, operae obsequium: Tre studi sulla condizione giuridica dei liberti.* Naples: Jovene Editore, 1993.

Masi Doria, C. "*Exemplum pessimum:* Quinto Mucio e il *testimonium* in Val. Max. 4.1.11." *Index* 38 (2010): 70–88.

Masi Doria, C. "*Libertinitas* e successione gentilizia." *Index* 27 (1999): 251–300.

Melillo, G. *Personae e status in Roma antica.* Naples: Jovene Editore, 2006.

Mercogliano, F., and T. Spagnuolo Vigorita. "Tributi (storia)." *Enciclopedia del diritto* 45 (1992): 85–105.

Mommsen, T. *Römisches Staatsrecht.* Vol. 1. 3rd ed. Leipzig: Hirzel, 1887.

Mommsen, T. *Römisches Staatsrecht.* Vol. 2.1. 3rd ed. Leipzig: Hirzel, 1887.

Münkler, H. *Imperien: Die Logik der Weltherrschaften—vom Alten Rom bis zu den Vereinigten Staaten.* Berlin: Rowohlt, 2005. Translated into Italian as *Imperi: Il dominio del mondo dall'antica Roma agli Stati Uniti* (Bologna: Il Mulino, 2008).

Negri, G. "Libertà e *status libertatis:* Nozioni generali introduttive." In *Homo, caput, persona: La costruzione giuridica dell'identità nell'esperienza romana,* 115–38. Pavia: IUSS Press, 2010.

Nitsch, C. "*Coactus voluit:* Prospettive dalla riflessione weberiana sulle condizioni del lavoro negli Stati Uniti." In *Materiali per una storia della cultura giuridica* 37.2 (2007): 337–72.

Orestano, R. "*Status libertatis, civitatis, familiae.*" *Novissimo Digesto Italiano* 18 (1971): 383–85.

Reduzzi, F. "Flaminio Mancaleoni a Napoli." *Index* 30 (2002): 187–90.

Rescigno, P. "Situazione e status nell'esperienza del diritto." *Rivista di diritto civile* 19 (1973): 209–29.

Rilinger R. *Humiliores—Honestiores: Zu einer sozialen Dichotomie im Strafrecht der römischen Kaiserzeit.* Munich: Oldenbourg, 1988.

Romano, G. "*Conventio* e *consensus* (A proposito di Ulp. 4 *ad ed. D.* 2.14.1.3)." *Annali del Seminario giuridico dell'Università di Palermo* 48 (2003): 239–331.

Roppo, V. *Il contratto del duemila.* Turin: Giappichelli, 2002.

Savigny, F. C. *System des heutigen Römischen Rechts.* Vol. 2. Berlin: Veit und Comp, 1840. Translated into Italian as *Sistema del diritto romano attuale,* vol. 2 (Turin: UTET, 1888).

Serrao, F. *Diritto privato economia e società nella storia di Roma.* Vol. 1, *Dalla società gentilizia alle origini dell'economia schiavistica.* Napoli: Jovene Editore, 2006.

Siimets-Gross, H. "Die Ausdrücke *status libertatis, civitatis* und *familiae:* Savignys berechtigte Kritik an den neueren Juristen?" In *Homo, caput, persona: La costruzione giuridica dell'identità nell'esperienza romana,* 217–49. Pavia: IUSS Press, 2010.

Stanley, A. D. *From Bondage to Contract: Wage Labor, Marriage, and the Market in the Age of Slave Emancipation.* Cambridge: Cambridge University Press, 1998.

Stein, P. *Legal Evolution: The Story of an Idea.* Cambridge: Cambridge University Press, 1980.

Talamanca, M., ed. *Lineamenti di storia del diritto romano.* 2nd ed. Milan: Giuffrè Editore, 1989.

Vincenti, U. *Diritto senza identità.* Rome: Laterza, 2007.

Volterra, E. "La base economica della elaborazione sistematica del diritto romano." In *Scritti giuridici,* vol. 5, *Le fonti,* 123–55. Naples: Jovene Editore, 1993. Originally published in *Rivista italiana per le scienze giuridiche* 94 (1967): 239–71.

Waldstein, W. *Operae libertorum: Untersuchungen zur Dienstpflicht freigelassener Sklaven.* Stuttgart: F. Steiner, 1986.

CHAPTER 5

Theory and Practice in the Roman Law of Contracts

PAUL DU PLESSIS

The *Interdictum de Migrando*

One of the many enduring qualities of Roman law in the *Corpus Iuris Civilis* is the level of intellectual abstraction visible in the snippets of juristic writing and imperial rescripts. This is a testament not only to the Roman legal genius but also to the efficiency of Justinian's compilers in severing all texts from their original context. Although the lack of context, among other things, was largely responsible for the ease with which the legal rules and terminology of Roman law was grafted into the *ius commune* of Western Europe, it sometimes obscures the very essence of some of these rules and the remedies with which they were enforced. This essay will use a single example from the law of urban tenancy—namely, the landlord's hypothec over the tenant's goods—to demonstrate this point.

To appreciate the working of this legal remedy, we must first sketch the context in which it operated. When parties entered into a contract of urban tenancy, it would normally have contained a provision for the recovery of debt in the event of nonpayment of rent. The chief mode in which Roman law dealt with this matter was through the inclusion of an agreement in the contract whereby the landlord could attach and sell some of the tenant's property located in the rented dwelling in lieu of rent payment. The legal remedy in question operated once the landlord had already seized the tenant's goods and was threatening to sell them at auction to recover the rent. The *sedes materiae* of this legal remedy is the following text:

Ulp. (73 *ad edictum*) *D.* 43.32.1 pr.: *Praetor ait: "Si is homo, quo de agitur, non est ex his rebus, de quibus inter te et actorem convenit, ut, quae in eam habitationem qua de agitur introducta importata ibi nata factave essent, ea pignori tibi pro mercede eius habitationis essent, sive ex his rebus est et ea merces tibi soluta eove nomine satisfactum est aut per te stat, quo minus solvatur: ita quo minus ei, qui eum pignoris nomine induxit, inde abducere liceat, vim fieri veto."*[1]

[(Ulpian in the seventy-third book on the Edict): The praetor says: "If the person in question is not one of the objects included in the agreement between you and the plaintiff, according to which things introduced or imported into the dwelling in question, or born or made there, should be a hypothec to you for the rent of the dwelling; or if he is included among those things but the rent has been paid to you, or security given, or if it is your fault that security has not been given, I forbid the use of force so as to prevent the person who brought him in by way of hypothec from taking him away from there."[2]]

The *Interdictum de Migrando* was a praetorian remedy only available to tenants of urban property.[3] It was a prohibitory interdict created in the late Republic, possibly by Servius Sulpicius Rufus.[4] The text of the interdict is preserved in a single passage from the *Digest* that forms part of a short title, *De Migrando* (*D.* 43.32). It does not appear to have been altered by the compilers, though the term *actor* and the phrase *ei . . . induxit* have formerly been suspected of interpolation.[5] This remedy enabled the tenant in four circumscribed cases

1. See Lenel, *Das Edictum Perpetuum* (1927) § 265, for a full reconstruction of the text of the interdict with literature. A *utilis* version of the *Interdictum de Migrando* is mentioned in the sources, but its sphere of application seems to have been slightly different. See, for example, Ulp. (73 *ad edictum*) *D.* 43.32.1.3: *Si tamen gratuitam quis habitationem habeat, hoc interdictum utile ei competet* (But if someone should have accommodation rent free, the *utilis* interdict will be available to him). Contrast Pomp.-Marci. *D.* 20.2.5.
2. English translations of all *Digest* texts in this essay are taken from Watson's *"Digest" of Justinian* (1998), as adapted where the author does not agree with the translation. It is important to note that the texts alternate between the phrases *pignus* and *hypotheca* without discrimination. I have attempted to translate all instances of a pledge without possession as a hypothec.
3. Ulp. (73 *ad edictum*) *D.* 43.32.1.1: . . . *nam colono non competit* (. . . since it is not available to a tenant of agricultural land).
4. Frier (*Landlords and Tenants* [1980] 106–7) suggests that the interdict was created ca.27 BCE, a plausible date, given the appearance of the first commentary on it by the Augustan jurist Labeo (d. ca. 11 CE) in Labeo-Ulp. *D.* 43.32.1.4.
5. For a survey of possible interpolations, see Wubbe, *Res Aliena Pignori Data* (1960) 178–79;

to remove certain movable property detained by the landlord on account of unpaid rent.[6] The four grounds on which the tenant could invoke the interdict were as follows:

a. The object(s) detained by the landlord does not form part of an agreement with the landlord in terms of which "things introduced or imported into the dwelling in question, or born or made there," are hypothecated for the rent of the dwelling.
b. The object(s) detained by the landlord forms part of such an agreement, but the rent has been paid.
c. The rent has not been paid, but sufficient alternative security has been provided.
d. It is the defendant's [i.e., the landlord's] fault that security has not been provided.

The interdict was designed to cover a wide variety of circumstances. Logically, the first two grounds are concerned with the consequences of an agreement between landlord and tenant concerning the hypothecation of goods, while the final two grounds deal with issues of alternative security for payment of rent.

This legal remedy has featured in two important recent studies.[7] In 1980, Bruce Frier argued, in *Landlords and Tenants in Imperial Rome,* that the legal rules of urban tenancy represented a body of specialist law largely developed for upper-class tenants who had the means and the social connections to enforce their tenancy rights in a court of law.[8] Frier used the interdict to demonstrate that the Roman law of urban tenancy did not operate solely in favor of landlords but also supported (upper-class) tenants wishing to use the legal process to enforce their rights in tenancy.[9] In 1986, in the extensive study *La Pignoración de Colectividades en el Derecho Romano Clásico,* Rosa Mentxaka examined the

---

Frier, *Landlords and Tenants* (1980) 106 n. 117; Mentxaka, *La Pignoración de Colectividades* (1986) § 34; La Rosa, "La Protezione Interdittale del *Pignus*" (1987). All of the concerns about interpolations have since been resolved, and the authors agree that the text is basically sound.

6. On the prohibitory nature of the interdict, see Wubbe, *Res Aliena Pignori Data* (1960) 178, 183.
7. On this interdict, see also Betancourt, "Sobre la Pretendida Transmisbilidad de los Interdictos" (1983) 59–60; Apathy, "*Mora Creditoris* und *Pignus*" (1986) 10–11; La Rosa, "La Protezione Interdittale del *Pignus*" (1982).
8. Frier, *Landlords and Tenants* (1980) chap. 5.
9. Frier, *Landlords and Tenants* (1980) 105–35. For an alternative view, see Wubbe *Res Aliena Pignori Data* (1960) 183.

interdict in the context of a broader investigation into pledge arrangements in urban and agricultural tenancy in classical Roman law. Unlike Frier, Mentxaka's study did not use the interdict to prove a larger hypothesis, but it did much to establish the broader context in which it should be understood. While both Frier's and Mentxaka's studies have contributed greatly to modern understanding of the *Interdictum de Migrando,* both authors treated the interdict as a small component of a larger discussion, thus leaving some aspects of this interdict unexplored. More specifically, neither of these two authors sufficiently examined the relationship between the interdict as an expression of the legal rules governing urban tenancy and glimpses of everyday practice visible from the sources.[10] The aim of this essay is to revisit the *Interdictum de Migrando* in light of this unresolved issue in order to establish its scope and function in the Roman law of urban tenancy.

The argument will be developed in four stages. First, the relationship between the interdict and the contract of lease will be examined. This will be followed by an assessment of the procedure used to enforce the interdict. In third place, two cases mentioned in Roman legal sources will be analyzed. Finally, some conclusions will be drawn.

The *Interdictum de Migrando* and the Contract of Lease

The first two grounds on which the tenant could invoke the interdict referred to an agreement between the parties concerning the hypothecation of goods. It therefore seems prudent to investigate the Roman contract of lease as the larger context in which such an agreement would have functioned. Letting and hiring, being one of the four named consensual contracts in Roman law, could be created with little formality. The parties merely had to reach consensus on three essential points, namely, the object of lease, the term, and the amount of rent.[11] Details could be regulated at will, as long as such regulation did not

10. Although the interdict was never replaced, it seems to have been used less frequently in the third century CE. In *D.* 43.32.1.2, Ulpian states: *Cui rei etiam extra ordinem subveniri potest: ergo infrequens est hoc edictum* (In this matter, relief can also be granted apart from the standard procedure [*extra ordinem*], so that this edict is infrequently invoked). Frier (*Landlords and Tenants* [1980] 105–35) argues that the increasing administrative jurisdiction of the *Praefectus Vigilum* may have contributed to the decline of the interdict.

11. Consent could be expressed in a number of ways, not necessarily verbally or in the presence of the other party. See Paul. (12 *ad Sabinum*) *D.* 45.1.35.2; Paul. (16 *ad Plautium*) *D.* 44.7.48; Ulp. (71 *ad edictum*) *D.* 19.2.14.

render the agreement illegal, and ancillary agreements (e.g., penalties for non-performance) could be added in the form of contractual pacts. Writing was not a requirement for lease, and the agreement could remain entirely (or partially) unwritten. Nonlegal sources show, however, that some forms of lease (e.g., building contracts) were commonly recorded owing to their complexity.[12] No written account of a lease of urban tenancy has survived, though various legal texts allude to clauses contained in such contracts.[13] Even though Roman leases could legally exist in an unwritten form, a written version of a lease must have had some evidentiary value in a legal dispute, for example, as proof of the good faith underpinning the agreement. Consequently, it can be safely stated that the Roman conception of the "contract" (*lex contractus*) must have been rather complex and must have included both verbal and written elements.[14]

The tenant's ability to pay the rent would have been the prime concern of the landlord when entering into a contract of urban tenancy.[15] Before agreeing on the amount of rent and the dates on which the rent had to be paid, the landlord had to ensure that the tenant was solvent and possessed sufficient (future) financial means to ensure the payment of rent. One way in which Roman law protected the landlord from the potential insolvency of the tenant was to provide a legal mechanism to establish a hypothec over his or her goods. This legal device seemingly first evolved in agricultural tenancy but was already established in urban tenancy by the end of the first century BCE.[16] To understand the form and content of the hypothec, we need to understand its historical antecedent in the contract of pledge. Pledge was classified in Roman law as one of the real contracts that came into existence when a debtor handed over possession of movable property as security for the repayment of a debt. During the course

12. A prime example is the famous "contract" for the construction of a wall in Puteoli; see Du Plessis, "Protection of the Contractor" (2004) 287–314, at 291–95. For the significance of the recording of contracts and other legal instruments, see Meyer, *Legitimacy and Law in the Roman World* (2004). For an interesting example, see the letter in Greek recorded in Scaev. (57 *Digestorum*) *D.* 20.1.34.1.

13. See, for example, the clauses mentioned in Ulp. (32 *ad edictum*) *D.* 19.2.11.1; Alf.-Paul. (3 *Digestorum*) *D.* 19.2.30.4; Alf. (7 *Digestorum*) *D.* 19.2.29.

14. See Du Plessis, "Roman Concept of *Lex Contractus*" (2006) 423–37. Examples of such documents are the two Sulpicii tablets recording the lease of spaces within a warehouse, *TPSulp.* 45–46 (Camodeca, *Tabulae Pompeianae Sulpiciorum* [1999] 1:122, 125).

15. This financial concern is, for example, visible in Cicero's correspondence to Atticus about the choice of tenants for his tenement buildings; see Frier, "Cicero's Management of His Urban Properties" (1978).

16. Mentxaka, *La Pignoración de Colectividades* (1986) § 38.

of the Republic, a variant of pledge (hypothec), which did not require the transfer of possession of the movable object, came to be recognized. It is conventionally agreed that the first case of a pledge without possession occurred in agricultural tenancy when tenants pledged their farm implements and future crops for payment of rent.[17] Given the dating of the *Interdictum de Migrando*, it seems fair to conclude that this practice had migrated to the developing law of urban tenancy by the first century BCE.

Legal sources show that a hypothec could be created in one of two ways. First, the parties could make a secondary agreement in which certain goods were specified as the object of the hypothec. Thus, for example, in *D.* 20.4.9 pr.,[18] the second-century jurist Africanus recounts a case where someone rented baths and contracted that a specific slave, named Eros, would form the object of the hypothec to secure payment of rent. Similarly, in *D.* 20.3.4,[19] the third-century jurist Paul mentions a case of a money loan where the debtor listed specific assets as the object of the hypothec. Apart from an agreement listing specific goods, Gaius, a jurist of the second century CE, mentions another way in which a hypothec could be created.

> Gaius (*lib. sing. de form. hypothec.*) *D.* 20.1.15.1: *Quod dicitur creditorem probare debere, cum conveniebat, rem in bonis debitoris fuisse, ad eam conventionem pertinet, quae specialiter facta est, non ad illam, quae cottidie inseri solet cautioni-*

---

17. See Kaser and Knütel, *Römisches Privatrecht* (2003) § 31.III. An argument could be made that the hypothecation of farm implements (specific objects) together with future harvests (speculative objects) may be the origin of the two different forms of hypothec later visible in urban tenancy.

18. Afric. (8 *Quaest.*) *D.* 20.4.9 pr.: "A man who rented baths from the first of the following month agreed that a slave Eros should be hypothecated to the lessor until the rent was paid. Before the first of July he hypothecated Eros to another creditor for a loan. Asked whether the praetor should protect the landlord against the latter creditor in a suit for Eros, he answered that he should. Although, when Eros was hypothecated, nothing was yet owing for rent, even then the position of Eros was that he should not be released from the hypothec without the landlord's consent. So the landlord should have priority."

19. Paul. (5 *Resp.*) *D.* 20.3.4: "As Titius wanted to borrow money from Maevius, he promised to repay Maevius the amount, listing certain assets to be hypothecated. He sold some of the listed property and then received the loan. The question was whether the property sold before the loan was also bound to the creditor. Paul answered that since, even after he had promised to pay Maevius, the debtor was free not to take the loan, the hypothec must be taken as entered into at the time when the loan was made. Hence one must enquire what property was part of the debtor's estate at that moment."

bus, ut specialiter rebus hypothecae nomine datis cetera etiam bona teneantur debitoris, quae nunc habet et quae postea adquisierit, perinde atque si specialiter hae res fuissent obligatae.

[(Gaius in his single book on the action on mortgage) When it is said that the creditor should verify, when he makes an agreement, that the thing is *in bonis* of the debtor, this applies to a special agreement, not to the [contractual clause] commonly inserted in *cautiones* that beside the property specially hypothecated, the debtor's assets, present and future, are also bound as if especially hypothecated.]

This text does not seem to have undergone extensive alterations and reflects classical Roman law.[20] Gaius is describing two different types of hypothec: (a) one specially made where it is important to establish whether things are *in bonis* of the tenant at the time of its creation and(b) a general contractual clause that served to hypothecate the debtor's remaining assets and where the question of whether the goods are *in bonis* of the tenant did not matter.[21] There can be little doubt that the first type described by Gaius refers to a specific agreement where objects were listed by the parties as the object of the hypothec. The second type, the contractual clause, requires further investigation.

Gaius appears not to be quoting the precise wording of such a common contractual clause (inasmuch as standard contractual clauses may be said to have existed in Roman law) but merely giving the gist of it. The key to understanding this clause is the phrase *cetera . . . adquisierit*. The function of the contractual clause was to hypothecate the assets (present or future) of the tenant to ensure payment of the debt. When the content of this clause is compared to the wording Ulpian gives for the earlier *Interdictum de Migrando* (quoted previously in this essay), striking similarities appear.

Ulp. (73 *ad edictum*) *D*. 43.32.1.1: . . . *de quibus inter te et actorem convenit, ut, quae in eam habitationem qua de agitur introducta importata ibi nata, factave*

20. See Mentxaka, *La Pignoración de Colectividades* (1986) § 68.

21. For two further examples of this type of contractual clause, see Scaev. (5 *Resp.*) *D*. 20.1.32 and Gaius (*lib. sing. form. hypoth.*) *D*. 20.4.11.2. Mentxaka (*La Pignoración de Colectividades* [1986] § 34) observes that the motive for the statement about goods being *in bonis* of the tenant may be that Ulpian was drawing a comparison between the requirements for the *Interdictum de Migrando* and those for the *actio Serviana*.

> *essent, ea pignori tibi pro mercede eius habitationis essent . . .*
>
> [(Ulpian in the seventy-third book on the Edict): . . . the agreement between you and the plaintiff, according to which things introduced or imported into the dwelling in question, or born or made there, should be a hypothec to you for the rent of the dwelling . . .]

There can be little doubt that the agreement in question refers to the general contractual clause mentioned by Gaius that served to hypothecate the (current and future) assets of the urban tenant to secure payment of rent.[22]

It is not possible to date the appearance of this contractual clause, since the available sources do not provide sufficient information. At best, a rough guess may be ventured. It is conventionally assumed that the consensual contract of lease (*locatio conductio*) arose in the second half of the second century BCE, if not before (ca. 150 BCE).[23] This leaves a relatively short period of time in which much of the Roman law of letting and hiring came into existence. If the *Interdictum de Migrando* was created ca. 27 BCE and if the contractual clause on hypothec is mentioned in it, such a clause must have been created between ca. 150 and ca. 27 BCE. It is impossible to narrow down this period further, since not enough information is available, though it may be pointed out that the Roman law of urban tenancy is said to have developed mostly in the first century BCE.

It may well be asked why such a clause was required if parties could create an agreement listing specific objects hypothecated to ensure payment of rent. The listing of a specific object to be hypothecated for the payment of rent has various drawbacks. While hypothecation did not deprive the debtor of the use or ownership of his or her property, it secured a preferential real right for the creditor. This limited the debtor's ability to dispose of the property without notification. Furthermore, listing specific goods as the object of a hypothec did not take account of fluctuations in value, which could render the value of the hypothec deficient or worthless (e.g., through the death of a slave). Thus the inclusion of a contractual clause hypothecating the debtor's current and future

22. Mentxaka (*La Pignoración de Colectividades* [1986] § 34) argues that these contractual clauses reveal some similarity with those found in agricultural tenancy. Compare La Rosa, "La Protezione Interdittale del *Pignus*" (1987) 293.

23. Watson, *Law of Obligations* (1965) 100–101. Compare Watson, *Law Making in the Later Roman Republic* (1974) 31–82.

assets beside a specific agreement of hypothec would have provided added financial security for the creditor.

Given that the issue of hypothecation was not one of the essentials on which the parties had to agree for the contract of lease to come into existence, it must be assumed that the contractual clause took the form of an ancillary agreement that came into existence at the same time as the urban tenancy.[24] Initially, an explicit agreement was required, but by the end of the first century CE, the jurist Neratius (in *D.* 20.2.4 pr.) indicates that it had become an implied contractual term. Thus, in the space of approximately one century, this contractual clause had changed from an express agreement to an implied term read into all contracts. This raises two questions. First, if an explicit agreement about the hypothecation of the tenant's goods was initially required, what would the content of such an agreement have been? Second, what motivated the change from express to implied agreement?

The first question relates to the content of the contractual clause governing the hypothec. The best evidence is the wording of the interdict provided by Ulpian in *D.* 43.32.1.1. There must have been an agreement (*conventio*) between landlord and tenant whereby goods . . . *introducta importata ibi nata, factave essent, ea pignori tibi pro mercede eius habitationis essent.*[25] The text of the interdict suggests that this clause was of a general nature and that goods were not specified. Does this therefore mean that this clause served to hypothecate *all* present and future goods of the tenant to secure payment of rent? The answer to this question is no, and there are two pieces of evidence to support this view.

First, as the wording of the interdict shows, the contractual clause was concerned only with certain goods (. . . *ex his rebus* . . .). Second, the wording of the clause as visible from the text of the interdict refers to the term *invecta et illata.* Although this term was not defined in Roman legal sources, its content

24. No doubt, one reason why the pledge could be created with such ease was observed in Gaius (*lib. sing. form. hypothec.*) *D.* 20.1.4: "A pledge is made by consent, when someone agrees that his property will be bound by way of a pledge for some obligation. As in consensual contracts, it does not matter what words are used. So if an agreement for a pledge not in writing can be proved, the property will be bound as agreed. . . ."

25. The requirement of an explicit agreement also suggests that parties could opt out or could employ alternative means to secure the payment of rent: see Labeo *D.* 20.6.14. An example of such an "opt-out" is visible in a related issue on subletting, an implied contractual term from the start, which was regulated differently in the *leges horreorum* (no. 145 in Riccobono, *Fontes Iuris Romani Antejustiniani* 3 [1940–1943] 456–57).

was specific, and legal sources list various objects that did not count as such.[26] Research has also shown that this term had a specific content in urban tenancy.[27] The term *invecta et illata* etymologically referred only to movable property, but not all movable property was included per se.[28] The object described in the *Interdictum de Migrando* is a *homo*, that is, a slave belonging to the tenant. From the use of this term (and the economic function of the interdict), it may be inferred that the interdict was concerned with valuable movable property. Goods casually introduced into the rented property did not fall into this category,[29] nor did (by analogy) things that did not belong to the tenant but that were kept under contract for their owners.[30] Things that the owner was unlikely to mortgage specifically (e.g., household equipment; clothing; slaves employed in essential services or with whom the owner was on affectionate terms, including a mistress; a natural or foster child) were also excluded.[31] Finally, property that could not be privately owned and certain types of protected property (e.g., property that formed part of a dowry or belonged to a ward) also could not be hypothecated in this way.[32] Thus the term *invecta et illata* referred to a clearly circumscribed category of goods. The *conventio* mentioned in the interdict therefore must have referred to an agreement to include this provision, which referred to a circumscribed category of objects, in the contract of lease.[33]

If the contractual clause that served to hypothecate the tenants current and future assets did not list individual objects but merely referred to *invecta et illata*—an undefined but carefully circumscribed category of goods—did it affect the way in which the tenant could utilize property falling within this category? The answer to this question is visible from two texts.

---

26. For a survey of the different terms used in Roman legal sources to describe *invecta et illata*, see Mentxaka *La Pignoración de Colectividades* (1986) § 19; La Rosa, "La Protezione Interdittale del *Pignus*" (1987) 283, 290. An entire *Digest* title (*D.* 20.3) is devoted to exceptions. It seems fair to conclude that the content of this category must have settled over time as a result of legal practice.
27. La Rosa, "La Protezione Interdittale del *Pignus*" (1987) 290, 291.
28. Ulp. (73 *ad edictum*) *D.* 20.2.6.
29. Pomp. (13 *var. lectionibus*) *D.* 20.2.7.1. See Frier, *Landlords and Tenants* (1980) 109.
30. See Ulp. (73 *ad edictum*) *D.* 43.32.2; Frier, *Landlords and Tenants* (1980) 101.
31. Ulp. (73 *ad edictum*) *D.* 20.1.6, 8.
32. Ulp. (73 *ad edictum*) *D.* 20.2.6 (freed slaves).
33. Wubbe, *Res Aliena Pignori Data* (1960) 186. La Rosa ("La Protezione Interdittale del *Pignus*" [1987] 287) suggests that the content of the *conventio* was not to permit lockout in case of nonpayment.

Ulp. (73 *ad edictum*) *D.* 20.2.6: *Licet in praediis urbanis tacite solet conventum accipi, ut perinde teneantur invecta et inlata, ac si specialiter convenisset, certe libertati huiusmodi pignus non officit idque et Pomponius probat: ait enim manumissioni non officere ob habitationem obligatum.*

[(Ulpian in the seventy-third book on the Edict): Although it is understood that in urban tenancies property brought onto the premises is impliedly hypothecated as if it had been specifically agreed, yet a hypothec of this sort is no bar to the grant of liberty. Pomponius agrees. He says that security for rented accommodation is no bar to freeing a slave.]

Paul. (*lib. sing. de officio praefecti vigilum*) *D.* 20.2.9: *Est differentia obligatorum propter pensionem et eorum, quae ex conventione manifestari pignoris nomine tenentur, quod manumittere mancipia obligata pignori non possumus, inhabitantes autem manumittimus, scilicet antequam pensionis nomine percludamur: tunc enim pignoris nomine retenta mancipia non liberabimus: et derisus Nerva iuris consultus, qui per fenestram monstraverat servos detentos ob pensionem liberari posse.*

[(Paul in his single book *On the Duties of Prefect of the Vigiles*): There is a difference between property hypothecated for rent and property secured by an express agreement. We cannot free slaves subject to an express hypothec, but we can free slaves living on rented premises, until we are locked out for non-payment of rent. After that we cannot effectively free slaves detained by way of security. The jurist Nerva was mocked for holding that we can free slaves detained for rent by pointing at them through a window.]

Both *D.* 20.2.6 and *D.* 20.2.9 are basically free from interpolation.[34] These texts, attributed to Ulpian and his contemporary Paul, refer to a period when the contractual clause governing the hypothecation of the tenant's current and future assets had long since become an implied contractual term.

As both texts show, the clause created nothing more than a type of "floating charge." Even though an object fell within the agreed category of *invecta et illata,* this does not mean that the tenant could not use it or, indeed, dispose of it as he or she saw fit. Only after the tenant had been locked out on account of

34. Frier, *Landlords and Tenants* (1980) 113, 119–20.

nonpayment of rent and after the contractual clause had come into effect was the tenant no longer entitled to dispose of the property. It could be argued that Paul's reference to the early imperial jurist M. Cocceius Nerva (d. 33 CE) shows that even before this contractual clause had become an implied term, the tenant was already free to deal with the goods covered by it as he or she saw fit. It seems that Nerva was derided for not observing the proper procedure (i.e., raising the matter in front of the praetor using the *Interdictum de Migrando*).[35]

An important point in the wording of the interdict is the phrase "goods brought in as a hypothec" (. . . *ei, qui eum pignoris nomine induxit* . . .).[36] Ulpian defines this term as follows:

> Ulp. (73 *ad edictum*) *D.* 43.32.1.5: *Illud notandum est praetorem hic non exegisse, ut in bonis fuerit conductoris, nec ut esset pignori res illata, sed si pignoris nomine inducta sit. Proinde et si aliena sint et si talia, quae pignoris nomine teneri non potuerint, pignoris tamen nomine introducta sint, interdicto hoc locus erit: quod si nec pignoris nomine inducta sint, nec retineri poterunt a locatore.*
>
> [(Ulpian in the seventy-third book on the Edict): It must be noted that the praetor has not here insisted that the property should be *in bonis* of the lessee or that it should be a hypothec, but that it should have been brought in by way of hypothec. So even if the property belongs to someone else and of the kind that may not be retained by way of a hypothec, still if it has been brought in by way of hypothec, the interdict will have scope. But what has not even been brought in by way of hypothec cannot be retained by the landlord either.]

This text is generally sound, though the phrase *sed . . . sit* was at one time (wrongly) suspected of being an interpolation.[37] Ulpian states that the word-

---

35. Or properly freeing a slave, for that matter.

36. La Rosa ("La Protezione Interdittale del *Pignus*" [1987] 293–94) argues that the phrase *pignoris nomine inducere* is in opposition to the *conventio* mentioned in the *principium*. Thus, while the *conventio* still refers to the initial position where the parties had to make an explicit agreement about *invecta et illata*, the phrase *pignoris nomine inducere* refers to the later position existing in the time of Ulpian, when an explicit agreement was no longer required. While there is some merit to this argument, the wording of the text (i.e., the absence of any linguistic markers indicating that Ulpian was trying to draw a distinction between the *conventio* and the phrase *pignoris nomine inducere*) makes it difficult to prove.

37. For an overview of the debate on the supposed interpolation of this phrase, see Frier, *Landlords and Tenants* (1980) 112; La Rosa, "La Protezione Interdittale del *Pignus*" (1987) 292–93.

ing of the interdict does not require the goods (a) to be *in bonis* of the tenant or (b) to be the actual hypothec. Neither of these two examples are controversial if read in light of Gaius' statement in *D.* 20.1.15.1. The contractual clause to which the interdict referred did not require the listing of specific goods to be hypothecated for the payment of rent. The parties merely agreed on a certain "category" of objects. Thus it did not matter whether the goods were *in bonis* or were not the actual hypothecs. It was only in cases where specific objects had been hypothecated that the creditor had to ascertain whether these goods were *in bonis conductoris.*[38] Failure to ensure this would render the hypothec (of specific property) worthless.

Ulpian's final example presents more of a challenge. Goods that are (a) *aliena* and (b) of the kind that may not be retained *pignoris nomine* will still fall within the scope of the interdict's application if they have been brought into the rented property *pignoris nomine.* The term *res aliena* has been translated in the Watson edition of the *Digest* as "property which is different," but Frier's translation as "property belonging to someone else" is preferred in light of *D.* 43.32.2.[39] The second category, goods that may not be retained *pignoris nomine* but that have been introduced in such a way, is more difficult to explain. In Frier's view, this scenario referred to a case of fraud perpetrated by the tenant. Thus, for example, if goods were introduced *pignoris nomine* even though the tenant knew that they could not be held as such, since they fell outside the category of things allowed as *invecta et illata,* the tenant would still be able to use the interdict to secure their release.[40] This interpretation is mere speculation, but no other credible solution has yet been offered by modern scholarship. Thus it seems reasonable to conclude that the phrase "goods brought in by way of hypothec" referred to the "category" of goods collectively covered by the term *invecta et illata.*

The final question relates to the reasons why the contractual clause creating the hypothec changed from one requiring an explicit agreement to an implied contractual term. The change may be observed in a number of legal texts, the earliest of which is ascribed to a jurist who flourished during the early part of the second century CE, L. Neratius Priscus.

38. Compare Paul. *D.* 20.3.4, quoted in n. 19.
39. Frier, *Landlords and Tenants* (1980) 110–12. This is also the sense of *Bas.* 60.20.5, in Heimbach, *Basilicorum Libri LX* (1833–1897).
40. Frier, *Landlords and Tenants* (1980) 112.

Ner. (1 *membran.*) *D.* 20.2.4 pr.: *Eo iure utimur, ut quae in praedia urbana inducta illata sunt pignori esse credantur, quasi id tacite convenerit . . .*

[(Neratius in the first book of his *Brief Notes*): We follow that legal opinion that property brought on to an urban leasehold is hypothecated, as if it had been impliedly agreed . . .]

This text appears to be free from interpolation.[41]

Neratius' view on the matter was followed by Ulpian and his contemporary Paul in the third century CE and was also confirmed in law by an imperial rescript from the reign of Emperor Alexander Severus, in a time when Ulpian is known to have played an important role in the imperial bureaucracy.

Ulp. (73 *ad edictum*) *D.* 20.2.3: *Si horreum fuit conductum vel deversorium vel area, tacitam conventionem de invectis et illatis etiam in his locum habere putat Neratius: quod verius est.*

[(Ulpian in the seventy-third book on the Edict): If a warehouse, inn, or site is leased, Neratius thinks that there is here also an implied agreement for the hypothecation of goods brought in. This is the better view.]

Paul. (3 *ad edictum*) *D.* 2.14.4 pr.: *Item quia conventiones etiam tacite valent, placet in urbanis habitationibus locandis invecta illata pignori esse locatori, etiamsi nihil nominatim convenerit.*[42]

[(Paul in the third book on the Edict): Likewise, on the ground that even agreements by implication are valid, it is settled that in the letting of urban dwellings, the movables [of the tenant] are deemed hypothecated for the landlord even though nothing is expressly agreed.]

Alex. Sev. *C.* 4.65.5 (*Imp. Alexander A. Aurelio Petronio*): *Certi iuris est, quae voluntate dominorum coloni in fundum conductum induxerit, pignoris iure dominis praediorum teneri. Quando autem domus locatur, non est necessaria in rebus inductis vel illatis scientia domini: nam ea quoque pignoris iure tenentur.* (223)

41. Mentxaka, *La Pignoración de Colectividades* (1986) § 3.

42. Although the text is possibly abbreviated, its content does not appear interpolated; see Mentxaka, *La Pignoración de Colectividades* (1986) § 25.

> [(Emperor Alexander Severus Augustus to Aurelius Petronius; 223 C.E.): It is settled law that things which tenant farmers bring onto a farm, if their owners have agreed, are bound by the law of hypothec to the owners of the property. But where a house is leased, the owner's knowledge is not required in the case of things brought in or moved in; for these things too are held by the law of hypothec.][43]

Although there is some evidence of manipulation in *D.* 2.14.4 pr., the core of the text reflects classical Roman law.[44] *C.* 4.65.5 seems to be free from interpolation.[45]

When these texts are read chronologically, there is a suggestion that what started out as juristic opinion (. . . *eo iure utimur* . . .) in the early second century CE finally became settled law (. . . *certi iuris est* . . .) in the third century. It is also interesting that Neratius's original view is expanded by Ulpian to include warehouses, inns, and (urban) areas.[46] The fact that Ulpian ascribes the view also (*etiam*) to Neratius indicates either that he was relying on a further statement (the original of which has not been preserved in the *Digest*)[47] or that he was interpreting Neratius's use of the term *praedia urbana* to include these specific types of urban property. Ulpian's statement also contains a hint of a scholarly dispute about the matter. The fact that he deems it necessary to include the statement that Neratius's view is the better one (. . . *quod verius est* . . .) suggests that not everyone agreed with him on the matter. To that end, it may be useful to consider epigraphic evidence setting out commercial practice in Roman warehouses. Two citations from *leges horreorum* dating from the reign of the emperor Nerva (96—98 CE) state the following:

> *Quae in his horreis invecta inlata, erunt, pignori erunt horreario, si quis pro pensionibus satis ei non fecerit.*[48]

---

43. Trans. Frier (*Landlords and Tenants* [1980] 229).
44. Mentxaka, *La Pignoración de Colectividades* (1986) § 25.
45. Frier, *Landlords and Tenants* (1980) 110.
46. La Rosa ("La Protezione Interdittale del *Pignus*" [1987] 298) argues, on the basis of Scaev. (57 *Digestorum*) *D.* 20.1.34 pr., that the application of the legal rule on *invecta et illata* was extended in the classical period from cases of urban tenancy involving space rented for personal use to those involving space rented for commercial use.
47. See, for example, Ner. (*lib. prim. membranarum*) *D.* 20.2.4.1, where Neratius speculates whether stables that are not adjacent to a house classify as urban property. Compare Mentxaka, *La Pignoración de Colectividades* (1986) § 20.
48. *FIRA* 3.455–56.

[Whatever is brought or imported into these warehouses shall be regarded as being hypothecated to the *horrearius* [warehouse manager] as long as someone has not provided surety for the payment of rent.]

Quae in his horreis invecta inlata importata erunt, horreario pignori erunt donec satis ei factum non sit aut pensio solvatur.[49]

[Whatever is brought or imported into these warehouses, shall be regarded as being hypothecated to the *horrearius* as long as surety has not been provided or the rent has been paid.]

If these *leges* reflect the law of the period (and there is no reason to suspect otherwise), they provide a glimpse of the law in the time when, as Neratius stated, hypothec in urban tenancy was becoming an implied term in all contracts. It is clear that neither of these two provisions can be said to regulate the matter fully. In fact, they are nothing more than general statements. As argued elsewhere, such general statements contained in these *leges* governing the letting and hiring of stalls in a warehouse must have been supplemented by individual agreements between the *horrearius* and his or her customers containing specific issues.[50] Thus, for example, the clauses previously discussed do not mention an agreement that enabled the landlord to sell the goods in lieu of unpaid rent (the *pactum de vendendo*).[51] If this is correct, it suggests that the transition from express to implied provision is already visible in these clauses.

No clear answer can be given about why the landlord's hypothec over the tenant's goods became an implied contractual term, since the available sources do not provide any indications of the motives for legal change.[52] Any investigation into this question therefore can be little more than speculation. Mentxaka has suggested that the clause governing hypothec became an implied contractual term because the law of pledge became more generalized and because the declining socioeconomic position of tenants forced them to accept such a con-

49. *FIRA* 3.457.

50. Du Plessis, "Between Theory and Practice" (2006) 79–94.

51. It only became an implied term in the late classical period, according to Kaser and Knütel (*Römisches Privatrecht* [2003] § 31.III.5.b.bb).

52. Compare Watson, *Spirit of Roman Law* (1995) 206.

tractual term as standard.[53] The first part of this hypothesis appears to hold some elements of truth. If the contractual clause did not require the identification of specific goods and if the "categories" of permissible objects included in the scope of such a provision became fixed in law over time, a change from an explicit agreement to an implied term would not have caused any major legal complications. An explicit agreement only has value as long as there are parties choosing to modify it or to "opt out" of it. Once it becomes standard, an explicit agreement becomes unnecessary, since most parties will accept it as a matter of course. The second part of Mentxaka's hypothesis is more difficult to sustain, since it relies on a grand narrative about the declining social status of tenants and their ability to use legal remedies to protect their rights in tenancy. The link between hypothecation becoming an implied contractual term and the socioeconomic status of tenants is tenuous at best. We may list a myriad of other reasons (e.g., commercial needs, ease of use) for why this could have occurred.

Issues of Procedure

Establishing the point in the contractual process where a tenant would have used the *Interdictum de Migrando* also sheds light on the contractual clause at the heart of this legal remedy. The wording of the interdict shows that it was triggered by the nonpayment of rent.[54] Although much is known about the practice of rental payment in urban tenancy—for example, that contracts were usually concluded for a period of five years (the *lustrum*) and that rent could be paid weekly, monthly, or annually—the legal sources do not divulge whether nonpayment of rent was in itself sufficient to trigger the application of the interdict or whether the landlord was legally required to notify the tenant who went into arrears.[55] Frier has argued that since the payment of rent was one of the essentials on which the parties had to agree in order for the lease to come into existence and since the legal sources do not indicate any system

53. Mentxaka, *La Pignoración de Colectividades* (1986) § 38.

54. The application of the interdict seems to have been extended in the second century CE to include other contractual obligations that the tenant had to fulfill; see Pomp.-Marci. *D.* 20.2.2. It is difficult to see how the nonfulfillment of these would have triggered the application of this interdict, unless time limits were attached to their fulfillment.

55. See Litewski, "Die Zahlung bei der Sachmiete" (2002) 229–49.

of notification, it must be assumed that the nonpayment of rent on the agreed date constituted a sufficient breach of the contract to enable the landlord to act unilaterally.[56] Although it is not explicitly stated in the wording of the interdict, it is clear that the tenant would use it to release goods detained by the landlord. This has led to the conclusion that nonpayment of the rent on the agreed date gave the landlord the right to self-help in the form of a lockout.

Nothing is known about the general lockout procedure or the legal formalities attached to it, though it was clearly used in different areas of the law of urban tenancy, as shown by *D.* 19.2.56.

> Paul. (*lib. sing. de officio praefecti vigilum*) *D.* 19.2.56: *Cum domini horreorum insularumque desiderant diu non apparentibus nec eius temporis pensiones exsolventibus conductoribus aperire et ea quae ibi sunt describere, a publicis personis quorum interest audiendi sunt. Tempus autem in huiusmodi re biennii debet observari.*
>
> [(Paul in his single book on the *Duties of the Prefect of the Vigiles*): When lessees do not show up for a long time and do not pay the rent during this period, if the owners of storerooms and apartment buildings wish to open them and inventory what is there, they should receive a hearing before the public officials charged with this. In a matter of this kind, a period of two years should be observed.]

This text contains some traces of manipulation.[57] It is taken from Paul's commentary on the office of the *Praefectus Vigilum*, a public official who was involved in the general administration of cities. The context of this text points to the existence of an administrative forum for matters relating to urban tenancy that could deal with related matters outside the normal forum of the courtroom. Unfortunately, too little information exists to speculate about the duties of the *Praefectus Vigilum* in the context of urban tenancy.

The text focuses on the consequences of a lockout. If, after a period of two years, a tenant has not returned, the landlord may open up the locked premises to take an inventory of its contents. It is interesting to note that while the lockout apparently did not require any formality, the law required the landlord

56. His argument is largely based on a reading of Ant. (Caracalla) *C.* 4.65.3 (214 CE), which lists nonpayment of rent as a ground for expulsion of the tenant: see Frier, *Landlords and Tenants* (1980) 70–82.

57. See Frier, *Landlords and Tenants* (1980) 133.

to observe a period of two years as well as to attend a preliminary hearing in front of the *Praefectus Vigilum* before the apartment could be opened. It seems unlikely that this process was followed in all cases of nonpayment of rent, since a two-year waiting period would have affected the value of the hypothecated goods to a significant extent, but this text clearly shows that some formalities were attached to the notion of lockout.

Once the tenant had been locked out on account of unpaid rent, the next stage in the process depended on the nature of the hypothec arrangements included in the contract of lease. If the parties had made a hypothec agreement listing specific goods, these would be attached (presumably using the *actio Serviana*) and would be dealt with in terms of the agreement between landlord and tenant. The important question is whether such a hypothec agreement listing specific goods would have been supported by a general contractual clause stating that current and future assets of the tenant were hypothecated for the payment of rent. Since no written contract of urban tenancy has remained to support such a contention, it must remain little more than speculation. With that said, though, it would have made financial sense to include both in a contract of urban tenancy (especially where the agreement required the payment of a significant sum of money, e.g., the renting of baths or an entire tenement building), as suggested by Gaius in *D.* 20.1.15.1 (" . . . *etiam bona teneantur debitoris* . . . "). Merely relying on the contractual clause would have rendered the landlord financially vulnerable, since he would have had no way of establishing whether the tenant had sufficient goods to cover the debt owed until such time as nonpayment of the rent forced the landlord to lock the tenant out and to take an inventory of the goods inside the rented apartment.

A statement by Ulpian sheds light on the next stage in the process.

> Ulp. (73 *ad edictum*) *D.* 43.32.1.4: *Si pensio nondum debeatur, ait Labeo interdictum hoc cessare, nisi paratus sit eam pensionem solvere. Proinde si semenstrem solvit, sexmenstris debeatur, inutiliter interdicet, nisi solverit et sequentis sexmenstris, ita tamen, si conventio specialis facta est in conductione domus, ut non liceat ante finitum annum vel centum tempus migrare, idem est et si quis in plures annos conduxerit et nondum praeterierit tempus. Nam cum in universam conductionem pignora sunt obligata, consequens erit dicere interdicto locum non fore, nisi liberata fuerint.*[58]

58. There is evidence of some manipulation in this text; see Frier, *Landlords and Tenants* (1980) 116.

> [(Ulpian in the seventy-third book on the Edict): Even if the rent is not yet due, Labeo says that this interdict is inapplicable unless the lodger is prepared to pay the rent. Furthermore, if he has paid the rent for six months and six months' rent is owing, he will not effectively invoke the interdict unless he pays the following, always provided that a special agreement has been made in renting the house that he may not move before the end of a year, or of a certain period. The same applies if someone has rented a house for several years and the time has not yet elapsed. For since pledges are given for the entire lease, it follows that one should say the interdict does not apply unless they are released.]

Thus, following the lockout, the tenant must pay the rent before he or she will be entitled to use the interdict. The text also makes clear the need to pay not only the rent owing but all the rent outstanding for the remaining period of the lease.[59] The reason for this lies in the purpose of the interdict as stated in *D.* 43.32.1.1. The function of the interdict was to aid those tenants who had paid the rent and who wished to move. Thus, by paying not only the rent due but also the rent outstanding for the remainder of the term of lease, the tenant indicated his or her intention to terminate the contract and to move elsewhere. This would also entitle the tenant to invoke the *Interdictum de Migrando* in order to obtain the release of the goods detained by the landlord.

Two Examples

The *Interdictum de Migrando* lists four grounds on which a tenant of urban property could invoke it. Three of these grounds involve claims (a) that the rent has in fact been paid, (b) that the rent has not been paid but that alternative security has been provided, or (c) that it is the defendant's (i.e., the landlord's) fault that security has not been provided. When these three grounds are read together, there is a suggestion that the wording of the interdict may have been drafted to deal with complex contractual chains involving not only landlord and tenant but also third parties. More specifically, claims that the rent had in fact been paid (to a third party, e.g., a contractual middleman or a slave collector) without the knowledge of the owner of the rented property, who then proceeded to lock the tenant out, or that a third party (*actor*) had taken alterna-

---

59. Compare Ulp. *D.* 20.1.14 pr.

tive security for the payment of rent from the tenant (or had neglected to do so when offered) without relaying the state of affairs to the owner of the property may conceivably fall within the scope of these three grounds. To that end, I will here attempt to shed light on the working of the interdict by analyzing two "cases" mentioned in the legal texts.

The first example is taken from *D.* 13.7.11.5, a difficult text attributed to the late classical jurist Ulpian.[60]

> Ulp. (28 *ad edictum*) *D.* 13.7.11.5: *Solutam autem pecuniam accipiendum non solum, si ipsi, cui obligata res est, ed et si alii sit soluta voluntate eius, vel ei cui heres exstitit, vel procuratori eius, vel servo pecuniis exigendis praeposito. Unde si domum conduxeris et eius partem mihi locaveris egoque locatori tuo pensionem solvero, pigneraticia adversus te potero experiri (nam Iulianus scribit solvi ei posse): et si partem tibi, partem ei solvero, tantundem erit dicendum. Plane in eam dumtaxat summam invecta mea et illata tenebuntur, in quam cenaculum conduxi: non enim credibile est hoc convenisse, ut ad universam pensionem insulae frivola mea tenebuntur. Videtur autem tacite et cum domino aedium hoc convenisse, ut non pactio cenacularii proficiat domino, sed sua propria.*[61]
>
> [(Ulpian in the twenty-eighth book on the Edict): It is correct to say that the money is paid not only where it is paid to the creditor himself to whom the thing is charged but also when it is paid with his consent either to someone whose heir he is or to his *procurator* or to a slave in charge of collecting debts. Hence, if you rent a house and sublet part of it to me and I pay my rent to your lessor, I will have an action on *pignus* against you (for Julian writes that it is permissible to pay him). And if I pay part to you and part to him, the same will be clear *pro tanto.* It is clear that my own furniture and movables will be charged only with the sum for which I took my lodging; for it is not to be believed that my odds and ends were agreed to be charged for the rent of the whole block. However, this agreement is impliedly taken to have been made with the owner of the building as well, so that it is not from the bargain of the primary tenant that the owner derives advantage, but from his own.]

60. See Frier, *Landlords and Tenants* (1980) 124–32, for an extensive discussion of this text with an overview of earlier literature on its interpretation.
61. There is some evidence of manipulation in the text, see Frier, *Landlords and Tenants* (1980) 124–32.

The first part of this text states a general rule, namely, that money is deemed to have been paid by law if it is paid either to the creditor personally or with the creditor's consent to persons legally bound to him or her. This is followed by two examples from the realm of urban tenancy, one where someone had rented a room within a house rented by a third party from the owner, the other where someone had rented an apartment within an apartment building that had been rented *en bloc* by a primary tenant, with the view to make a profit by renting the spaces to individual secondary tenants at a profit. This text explores whether the *invecta et illata* of secondary tenants (with whom the owner/landlord had no contractual relationship) may be said to be pledged for the payment of the primary tenant's rent. Ulpian concludes that the goods of secondary tenants are only bound in proportion to their liability for rent of their respective flats. His rationale, stated at the very end of the text, is both a financial and a legal one. The owner/landlord should derive benefit from his or her contract with the primary tenant, not from the latter's contracts with secondary tenants.

While it seems likely that Ulpian's example is a theoretical one, the practical consequences of this business arrangement require closer inspection. For the purposes of this essay, the second example will be given more prominence. Primary tenants generally rented the entire tenement building for a period of five years (the normal duration of such contracts), with an agreement to pay the annual rental installment at the start of the Roman "financial year" (July 1).[62] The contracts between the middleman and the secondary tenants could stipulate diverse dates of rental payment (daily, weekly, monthly), but the cumulative effect of this was that the primary tenant paid out a significant amount of rent to the owner at the start of the year and then had to ensure that he or she collected sufficient rent (and profit) during the course of this year to pay next year's installment as well as to recover his or her expenditure. This was part and parcel of the "financial risk" inherent in such contracts and was a method whereby the owner/landlord ensured a steady income on his or her investment.

At this point, it becomes necessary to investigate the nature of the hypothec to which Ulpian is referring in this text. This essay has argued that in the context of urban tenancy, a hypothec could be created in one of two ways, namely, either by entering into an agreement listing a specific object to be hypothecated to secure the repayment of the debt or by including a general contractual clause into a tenancy agreement whereby certain categories of goods were deemed to

62. Frier, *Landlords and Tenants* (1980) 34–39.

be hypothecated for the payment of rent. The text under discussion does not provide sufficient information to establish with certainty what the hypothec arrangements between owner and primary tenant were, but Ulpian's use of the term *frivola mea* (my odds and ends) would suggest that a general contractual clause existed in contracts between primary and secondary tenants. If we assume that such general hypothecs over the *invecta et illata* had become implied contractual terms by the time of Ulpian in the third century CE, the primary tenant would therefore have secured a hypothetical right over the movables of his or her (secondary) tenants residing in the tenement building to the extent of their debts for rent owed through the working of the implied contractual term. The question remains whether such a theoretical right would have served any purpose to the owner.

This is where the text becomes ambivalent, as it stresses that the owner should obtain benefit from his contract with the primary tenant, not indirectly from the contracts between primary and secondary tenants. It seems reasonable to conclude that such a right would not have been of any value to the owner, nor would it have been to the owner's benefit to rely purely on such a contractual clause in any contract between him or her and the primary tenant. It seems unlikely that the personal goods of the primary tenant would have been sufficiently valuable to cover a significant annual rental payment due to the owner at the start of the financial year. While, in theory, the owner/landlord would, of course, have a hypothec indirectly over the cumulative goods of all the secondary tenants, it is debatable how readily enforceable such a hypothec would have been, especially since the value of the goods would not have been known until the hypothec were enforced through lockout. The hypothec that the owner/landlord had over the *invecta et illata* of the primary tenant was nothing more than a theoretical right.

In practice, the security for the payment of rent would have been obtained in a different manner, as demonstrated by the following text:

> Ulp. (32 *ad edictum*) D. 19.2.13.11: *Qui impleto tempore conductionis remansit in conductione, non solum reconduxisse videbitur, sed etiam pignora videntur durare obligata. Sed hoc ita verum est, si non alius pro eo in priore conductione res obligaverat: huius enim novus consensus erit necessarius . . .* [63]

---

63. There is some evidence of manipulation in this text; see Frier, *Landlords and Tenants* (1980) 165–67.

> [(Ulpian in the thirty-second book on the Edict): When a man remains in the leasehold after the term of hire is over, not only will he be construed as having rehired, his pledges are considered to remain obligated. This is true except if a third party obligated property on his behalf during the earlier lease; his agreement will be required afresh . . .]

Nothing in the palingenetic context of this text suggests that it is in any way concerned specifically with urban tenancy or, indeed, with the case of subletting mentioned in the previous text.[64] However, the possibility that third parties could have guaranteed rental payment on behalf of the tenant as described in this text may have served as one of the alternatives to securing a general hypothec over the (potentially valueless) property of the primary tenant or indirectly over the cumulative property of the secondary tenants living in the tenement building.

The final example to be examined is *D.* 20.4.13.

> Nerva-Proc.-Paul. (5 *ad Plautium*) *D.* 20.4.13: *Insulam tibi vendidi et dixi prioris anni pensionem mihi, sequentium tibi accessuram pignorumque ab inquilino datorum ius utrumque secuturum. Nerva Proculus, nisi ad utramque pensionem pignora sufficerent, ius omnium pignorum primum ad me pertinere, quia nihi aperte dictum esset, an communiter ex omnibus pignoribus summa pro rata servetur: si quid superesset ad te. PAULUS: facti quaestio est, sed verisimile est id actum, ut primam quamque pensionem pignorum causa sequatur.*[65]

> [(Paul in the fifth book on Plautius): I sold you an apartment block on terms that the first year's rent accrued to me, the second to you, and that we should both have the benefit of the securities [pledges/hypothecs] given by the tenants. Nerva and Proculus hold that unless the securities are sufficient for the rents of both years, the whole goes to me, because there was no express agreement that the amounts should be secured proportionally on all the property secured. If anything is left over, it goes to you. Paul: It is a question of fact, but probably the intention was that the rents should be secured in the order in which they fell due.]

64. See Lenel, *Das Edictum Perpetuum* (1927).

65. Although there is some evidence of manipulation in this text, its core seems sound; see Mentxaka, *La Pignoración de Colectividades* (1986) § 28.

This text deals with a provision in a contract of sale of a tenement building. A clause in the contract provided that the income generated by the tenement building in the year following the sale should go to the seller, while the income of the year thereafter would go to the purchaser. The question occupying the jurists is the interpretation of this clause. Nerva and Proculus make two observations on the matter, both of which rely on the premise that the parties had not regulated the matter in detail. Where the cumulative value of the pledges of the tenants living in the tenement is sufficient to cover the rental income of the tenement for two years, there will be no issue. Where the cumulative value of the pledges is insufficient, however, it should cover the loss of the seller first; if anything is left over, the purchaser's loss will be covered. Paul adds that the interpretation of this verbal provision will be a question of fact.

One point made obliquely in this text is the issue of the cumulative value of the pledges of the tenants residing in the tenement. It may well be asked what the nature of the pledge arrangement in this example would have been. As explained in this essay, it could have been either an agreement listing a specific object or merely a contractual clause. That the text contains the phrase *pignorumque ab inquilino datorum* suggests that the pledge arrangement referred to in this case is not one involving a contractual clause. In fact, the reference to *pignoris datio* suggests that actual pledges were physically handed over as security for the payment of rent. This text is therefore important for at least two reasons. First, it demonstrates a different commercial practice whereby actual pledges were handed over instead of relying on a general contractual clause. Second, it shows that an agreement lacking detail could be detrimental to one of the parties.

Conclusions

An investigation into the relationship between the *Interdictum de Migrando* as an expression of the legal rules governing urban tenancy and the glimpses of everyday practice preserved in both legal and nonlegal sources has brought new information to light. It has shown that this interdict was, among other things, introduced to deal with difficulties arising from a contractual clause generally inserted in contracts of urban tenancy that served to hypothecate the tenant's current and future assets for the payment of rent. Although the precise date when this clause was first introduced into urban tenancy cannot be established, it seems to have been created somewhere in the period ca. 150–27 BCE, possibly from an earlier model used in agricultural tenancy.

Such a clause did not list specific goods to be hypothecated for the payment of rent. Instead, it merely referred to *invecta et illata,* a circumscribed category of goods that could be introduced into a rented property *pignoris nomine.* Although the parties agreed that such a category of goods would be hypothecated for the payment of rent, this did not affect the tenant's ability to dispose of goods falling within this category during the course of the term of lease. It was therefore nothing more than a "floating charge." Only after the tenant defaulted on the payment of rent and after the landlord enforced his or her right of lockout did it become impossible for the tenant to dispose of objects falling within this category. A tenant wishing to liberate objects from the rented property had to use the *Interdictum de Migrando.*

The contractual clause hypothecating the tenant's current and future assets did not exist *in vacuo.* There is evidence to suggest that it was always included alongside an agreement listing specific goods to be hypothecated. This would suggest that it only ever came into effect when the sale of the goods listed in the primary agreement did not yield enough money to cover the tenant's debt. By the mid-second century CE, this contractual clause had become an implied term. The reason for this change cannot be fully explained, but it seems to be related to the concretization of the category of *invecta et illata.*

Glimpses of legal practice visible from Roman legal sources may provide new insight into the scope and function of legal rules and the remedies with which they were enforced. Unfortunately, the paucity of source material leaves many tantalizing questions unanswered. These questions include the effectiveness of this interdict, the scale of its application, and the extent to which all (as opposed to some upper-class) tenants had access to it.

Bibliography

Apathy, P. "*Mora Creditoris* und *Pignus.*" In *Iuris Professio: Festgabe für Max Kaser,* ed. H. P. Benöhr et al., 9–20. Vienna: Böhlau, 1986.

Betancourt, F. "Sobre la Pretendida Transmisbilidad de los Interdictos." *Anuario de Historia del Derecho Español* 53 (1983): 45–76.

Camodeca, G. *Tabulae Pompeianae Sulpiciorum (TPSulp.): Edizione critica dell'archivio puteolano dei Sulpicii.* 2 vols. Rome: Edizioni Quasar, 1999.

Du Plessis, P. J. "Between Theory and Practice: New Perspectives on the Roman Law of Letting and Hiring." *Cambridge Law Journal* 65 (2006): 423–37.

Du Plessis, P. J. "The Protection of the Contractor in Public Works in the Roman Republic and Early Empire." *Journal of Legal History* 25.3 (2004): 287–314.

Du Plessis, P. J. "The Roman Concept of *Lex Contractus*." *Roman Legal Tradition* 3.1 (2006): 79–94.

Frier, B. W. "Cicero's Management of His Urban Properties." *Classical Journal* 74.1 (1978): 1–6.

Frier, B. W. *Landlords and Tenants in Imperial Rome*. Princeton: Princeton University Press, 1980.

Heimbach, G., ed. *Basilicorum Libri LX*. 7 vols. Leipzig: J. A. Barth, 1833–97.

Kaser, M., and R. Knütel. *Römisches Privatrecht*. 17th ed. Munich: C. H. Beck, 2003.

La Rosa, F. "La Protezione Interdittale del *Pignus* e L'*Actio Serviana*." In *Studi in onore di Cesare Sanfilippo*, 7:281–317. Milan: Giuffrè Editore, 1987.

Lenel, O. *Das Edictum Perpetuum*. 3rd. ed. Leipzig: Bernard Tauchnitz, 1927.

Lenel, O. *Palingenesia Iuris Civilis*. 2 vols. Leipzig: Bernard Tauchnitz, 1889.

Litewski, W. "Die Zahlung bei der Sachmiete (vor oder nach Ablauf der Mietzeit) im römischen Recht." *Tijdschrift voor Rechtsgeschiedenis* 70 (2002): 229–49.

Mentxaka, R. *La Pignoración de Colectividades en el Derecho Romano Clásico*. Bilbao: Servicio Editorial Universidad País Vasco, 1986.

Meyer, E. A. *Legitimacy and Law in the Roman World: Tabulae in Roman Belief and Practice*. Cambridge: Cambridge University Press, 2004.

Riccobono, S., et al., eds. *Fontes Iuris Romani Antejustiniani*. 3 vols. Florence: S. A. G. Barbèra, 1940–43.

Watson, A., ed. *The "Digest" of Justinian*. Rev. English ed. 2 vols. Philadelphia: University of Pennsylvania Press, 1998.

Watson, A. *Law Making in the Later Roman Republic*. Oxford: Oxford University Press, 1974.

Watson, A. *The Law of Obligations in the Later Roman Republic*. Oxford: Oxford University Press, 1965.

Watson, A. *The Spirit of Roman Law*. Athens: University of Georgia Press, 1995.

Wubbe, F. B. J. *Res Aliena Pignori Data*. Leiden: Universitaire Pers, 1960.

CHAPTER 6

Obligations in Classical Procedure

ERNEST METZGER

The Praetor's Court

Roman civil procedure developed and evolved like any other body of law, with perhaps one unique difference: the pressures for reform regularly took place under the very gaze of the praetor. He was witness to the wasted time, the over-eager plaintiffs, the reluctant defendants, and the shameless airing of private affairs. He was uniquely placed to see, understand, and respond to problems. His responses took the form of various tools or "devices," such as stipulations, actions, defenses, and oaths. With such devices, he could enforce or encourage appropriate behavior toward his tribunal.

This essay discusses the use of obligations as a device to reform civil procedure. The thesis is a very simple one. First, the civil law equipped the praetor with relatively few rules of procedure. He made up the deficiency in the civil law by actively creating rules of procedure himself. Second, the praetor's lawmaking frequently took the form of actions and stipulations, which is to say, obligations. Accordingly, the discussion that follows offers a selection of examples in which the law of procedure was reformed with the aid of obligations. Given the scarcity of evidence on procedure, the examples offered are some of the few in which both the earlier state of the law and the "remedial" obligation are discernible to us. The discussion closes with a few comments on the usefulness of obligations as against other devices.

Foreword on the Law of Procedure

This exercise—isolating obligations within the law of procedure—rests on the mild anachronism that classical Roman law contained a "law of procedure." In the modern day, we speak of a law of procedure simply because it suits us to set apart rules that deal with litigation. We do so for the benefit of practitioners or as an aid to law reform or for developing principles.[1] These were never priorities for the Romans.[2] We are also more comfortable than the classics at least with the notion of abstract rights that exist separately from the machinery of justice;[3] wherever the two are still engaged, it is harder to find a law of procedure.

Yet even without a law of procedure, the praetor knew perfectly well that tribunals needed to be managed, that litigants misbehaved, and that rules and devices could help to avoid disruption. This is why it makes sense to discuss how the praetor responded to procedural problems, notwithstanding the absence of a law of procedure. Admittedly, using modern categories tends to make discussions like the present one somewhat artificial. For example, the penal stipulations described by Gaius in the fourth book of his *Institutes* are treated as procedural in this essay because they were intended to discourage vexatious litigation.[4] These stipulations are not so different in formulation from the (nonprocedural) *actio depensi,* which gave an *actio in duplum* to a surety who was not reimbursed by the principal debtor within six months.[5] But there is no error of anachronism in calling the one procedural and the other non-procedural, unless we allow ourselves to believe that the praetor, in carrying out his reforms, was prompted to do so by peculiarly modern motives or priorities.[6] It would be wrong, for example, to assume that the praetor reformed the law in order to make it more systematic or to champion some principle of modern procedural law. But there is none of this sort of anachronism in this essay. To the contrary, this essay suggests that the praetor reformed the law in response to the changing character of Roman litigation.

---

1. On the last of these, see Kaser and Hackl, *Das römische Zivilprozessrecht* (1996) 8–11; Seidl, *Römische Rechtsgeschichte* (1971) 162–67.
2. The Romans themselves did not cultivate a law of procedure. Book 4 of Gaius's *Institutes,* though lucid and informative on procedure, is not a systematic work. It was not until the twelfth century that systematic study of procedure based on Roman law began: see van Caenegem, *History of European Civil Procedure* (1973) 11, 16–17.
3. See Metzger, "Actions" (1998) 214–17; Donahue, "Ius in the Subjective Sense in Roman Law" (2001); Jolowicz, *Roman Foundations of Modern Law* (1957) 66–81.
4. Gaius 4.171.
5. Gaius 3.127, 4.9; *Pauli Sententiae* 1.19.1.
6. See Hoetink, "Les notions anachroniques dans l'historiographie du droit" (1955) 10. See also n. 6 and the accompanying text in the present chapter.

Summons

From at least the time of the Twelve Tables and through the period of the classical law, a plaintiff brought his opponent to the praetor by *in ius vocatio*. Generally speaking, it served as the commencement of the lawsuit, though in practice, a defendant might first learn of the suit through *editio actionis*,[7] and stubborn defendants might require more than one *vocatio*.[8] The civil law machinery was very rudimentary.[9] The summons itself was a purely private affair; a person who had a grievance against another person was responsible for bringing that person to the praetor. Force could be used, but there are doubts about whether any amount of force could ensure the defendant's presence in every case.[10] The law required the defendant either to come immediately or to offer a so-called *vindex* in his place. If he offered a *vindex*, then the *vindex* was responsible for bringing the defendant before the magistrate at some time in the future.[11]

The main shortcoming in the summons procedure is the lack of any means, in the last resort, for compelling a defendant to come *in ius*. Loosely speaking, a defendant's participation at this stage was voluntary.[12] Hence the praetor

7. See Kaser and Hackl, *Das römische Zivilprozessrecht* (1996) 220.
8. See Horace *Serm.* 1.9; Cicero *Quinct.* 61. The second is a somewhat more involved example, where the plaintiff has changed his strategy after the lawsuit had been alive for some time; he summons the defendant's *procurator in ius* in order to lodge a different claim. See Metzger, *Litigation in Roman Law* (2005) 36–43.
9. XII Tab. 1.1–4. The full sources for modern reconstructions of these provisions are given in Crawford, *Roman Statutes* (1996) 2:584–90.
10. See the extended discussion in Kelly, *Roman Litigation* (1966) 6–12.
11. This, at least, is believed to be the duty of the *vindex*. See Kaser and Hackl, *Das römische Zivilprozessrecht* (1996) 66, 224; see also the literature cited in Domingo, *Estudios sobre el primer título del edicto pretorio* (1993) 56 n. 140. The difficult text is Gaius (1 *ad legem duodecim tabularum*) *D.* 2.4.22.1, which suggests a wider role for the *vindex*. On the other hand, the sources make it clear that certain defendants were obliged to put forward a sufficiently wealthy *vindex*. See XII Tab. 1.4 and the authorities cited in Crawford, *Roman Statutes* (1996) 2:588–89; Paul. (1 *ad edictum*) *D.* 2.6.1 (interpolated).
12. In the classical procedure, there was a threat of *missio* and bankruptcy against any defendant who hid himself away or who was adjudged "absent and undefended." See *D.* 42.4.7.1 (Ulp. 59 *ad edictum*); Gaius 3.78; Lenel, *Das Edictum Perpetuum* (1927) tit. 38. Kaser is confident on the point that this edict (or edicts) applied to a defendant resisting summons. See Kaser and Hackl, *Das römische Zivilprozessrecht* (1996) 222; compare Kelly, *Roman Litigation* (1966) 10–11. This interpretation rests very substantially on a series of events recounted in Cicero in *Pro Quinctio*, where Cicero's client has himself had his goods seized and where, according to a widely held

stepped in to innovate, and he did so with the help of obligations. He created an *actio in factum*, a so-called action on the facts, which he offered to grant against a defendant who neither came when summoned nor gave a *vindex* to vouch for his future appearance. If the action were successful, the defendant would pay the plaintiff under some unknown formula. Our source is Gaius.

> Gaius 4.46: *Ceterae quoque formulae quae sub titulo "de in ius vocando" propositae sunt, in factum conceptae sunt, velut adversus eum qui in ius vocatus neque venerit neque vindicem dederit.*
>
> [(Gaius in the fourth book of his *Institutes*). The other *formulae* published under the title "*de in ius vocando*" are also framed on the facts, as for instance the formula granted against one who, summoned *in ius*, neither comes nor gives a *vindex*.]

The action achieved two goals. The first is the rather obvious, procedural goal of encouraging appropriate behavior toward the tribunal. The second is remedial: the action created a debt between the plaintiff and the defendant. This was an acknowledgment that if the defendant did not come when summoned, the plaintiff was the one who directly suffered. In this respect, it was superior to a remedy that would punish the recalcitrant party without recognizing the plaintiff's loss in the matter.[13]

---

view, the "absence" took place before any proceedings had been initiated. I have argued, to the contrary, that *missio* (the authorized seizure of property) there took place after a compulsory order to reappear had been ignored by Cicero's client or his client's erstwhile procurator: see Metzger, *Litigation in Roman Law* (2005) 30–38, 163–66. With this essential piece of evidence removed, there is a serious question about whether these remedies were available against defendants who resisted summons. On the powers of municipal magistrates to exact a fine for failing to appear when summoned, see the following note in the present chapter.

13. See Paul. (1 *ad edictum*) *D.* 2.5.2.1: *Si quis in ius vocatus non ierit, ex causa a competenti iudice multa pro iurisdictione iudicis damnabitur: rusticitati enim hominis parcendum erit: item si nihil intersit actoris eo tempore in ius adversarium venisse, remittit praetor poenam, puta quia feriatus dies fuit* (If a person who is summoned *in ius* shall not come, he shall be condemned by a competent judge [sc. magistrate] for cause to pay a fine within the power of the judge [sc. magistrate] to impose: of course a simple man ought to be spared this. Similarly if it did not matter to the plaintiff whether the defendant came at the time he was summoned, the praetor remits the penalty, for example when the day of appearance was a holiday). Ignoring interpolations, the text describes the powers of municipal magistrates to fine certain *vocati*, at least where real harm is done by their delays.

This remedial goal is worth remarking, particularly because this action has been criticized as ineffective, as it requires a second *in ius vocatio* with no more guarantee of success than the first.[14] Yet there is a significant advantage in creating a debt between plaintiff and defendant in circumstances like these. Some defendants are motivated by a specific desire to "run out the clock" or otherwise gain a permanent victory by delaying an action until it can no longer be brought. For example, there were advantages to a would-be usucaptor in delaying an action; some delictual actions did not survive the death of the wrongdoer; and rules on limitation of actions might rob the plaintiff of any opportunity to sue.[15] Hence, to create a debt between plaintiff and defendant may have given the plaintiff a recovery that was not otherwise possible. It would serve (roughly speaking) as a kind of restitutionary remedy.

The broader point is that the praetor innovated in order to make up for the shortcomings of the civil law in getting defendants to court. His innovation took the form of a threat to create a debt between the plaintiff and the defendant. He hoped to persuade the defendant to behave in the proper way.

Postponement

In early Roman procedure, under the so-called *legis actio* procedure, it was sometimes necessary to postpone the proceedings before the praetor. A plaintiff would bring his defendant *in iure,* but they did not necessarily finish all their business on that day. Shortness of time was sometimes the cause; postponement was also an intrinsic feature of certain forms of action that observed periods of delay. In either event, the postponement created a problem: a defendant might be reluctant to return. To give some degree of security to the plaintiff, the defendant was sometimes required to provide a surety, called a *vas,* for his return. The sources are spotty, but it seems that the procedure operated as follows: the defendant put forward a person who would promise to produce the defendant at the necessary time. If that person, the *vas,* failed to produce the defendant, the plaintiff could proceed against the *vas,* and the *vas* could absolve himself by paying a sum.[16]

14. See the discussion in Buti, *Il praetor e le formalità introduttive del processo formulare* (1984) 296–98.

15. See the authorities cited in Metzger, *Litigation in Roman Law* (2005) 117–18.

16. See generally Kaser and Hackl, *Das römische Zivilprozessrecht* (1996) 68–69.

Varro *Lingua Latina* 6.74: *Vas appellatus, qui pro altero vadimonium promittebat. Consuetudo erat, cum reus parum esset idoneus inceptis rebus, ut pro se alium daret.*

[(Varro, in the sixth book of his *Lingua Latina*) The so-called *vas* was one who promised a bond for another person. It was the custom for a defendant to give another for himself when he was not sufficiently capable of managing his affairs.]

There was also the person of the *subvas*. Aulus Gellius describes how, in his own time, both *vades* and *subvades* were unimportant as subjects of study. The observations are given through a supposed friend, one *ius civile callens* (skilled in the *ius civile*).

Aulus Gellius *Noctes Atticae* 16.10.8: *Sed enim cum . . . "vades" et "subvades" . . . evanuerint omnisque illa Duodecim Tabularum antiquitas, nisi in legis actionibus centumviralium causarum lege Aebutia lata consopita sit, studium scientiamque ego praestare debeo iuris et legum vocumque earum quibus utimur.*

[(Aulus Gellius in the sixteenth book of his *Attic Nights*) But frankly since "*vades*" and "*subvades*" have disappeared and all those fossils of the Twelve Tables have been laid to rest (except for the *legis actiones*, which the *lex Aebutia* preserved for centumviral cases), I ought to apply my attention and knowledge to the law and statutes (and their terms) still in use.]

The role of the *subvas* is unknown. A passage in Livy may help: he describes multiple *vades* being used to secure the appearance of a man to be tried for homicide in the middle fifth century BCE. Each *vas* was bound to pay a fixed sum,[17] suggesting the possibility that some *vades* were reliable sureties only up to some (assessed?) ceiling. These may bear some relation to the *subvades* Gellius speaks of, though the context is utterly different. On this conjecture, some defendants were obliged to put forward several *subvades* in order to cover their liability fully.[18]

17. Livy 3.13.8: *Vades dari placuit; unum vadem tribus milibus aeris obligarunt.* ([The Senate] resolved to provide sureties, each surety bound to pay three thousand *asses*).

18. But it is only conjecture. Other suggestions are offered in Kaser and Hackl, *Das römische Zivilprozessrecht* (1996) 68 n. 39.

It is difficult to criticize this institution confidently, as we know so little about it, though one particular shortcoming is clear enough: security for reappearance required the participation of a third party, and this was undoubtedly awkward at times. The defendant had to find one or more individuals under pressure of time. Those individuals whom he found might be challenged as persons without sufficient property. It could be time-consuming to discover the true state of affairs and, if necessary, locate another individual.

The reform of the law on postponements was effected by both statute (as Gellius notes) and praetorian intervention. At some unknown time, the praetor adopted the practice of ordering litigants to perform stipulations and promises with one another. These were the so-called praetorian stipulations. They were a diverse group of transactions, including *vadimonium* (a stipulation to appear), *cautio damni infecti* (a stipulation against impending damage), *operis novi nuntiatio* (a stipulation for assurance from a neighbor who contemplates a threatening work), and others. The meaning of *stipulatio praetoria* and its classifications are disputed, for what the matter is worth.[19] So far as postponements are concerned, the introduction of praetorian stipulations and the disappearance of *vades* with the *lex Aebutia* (late second century BCE) were enormous improvements: it was no longer necessary for a defendant to find suitable *vades*. He could serve as his own surety by using *vadimonium*.[20]

The substance (though not the words) of the praetorian edict on *vadimonium* is preserved in Gaius.[21] At the center of every *vadimonium* was a simple stipulation and promise to reappear (e.g., *Spondesne* [*in diem loco hora*] *te sisti? Spondeo*), but the edict specified various cases in which the transaction could be enhanced to give additional assurance to the plaintiff. Most of the alternatives offered in the edict did not require a surety; indeed, the examples that survive to us in documents have no surety.[22] The typical stipulation was

19. See especially Giomaro, "Ulpiano e le *stipulationes praetoriae*" (1983) 413–40. Two groups of texts classify the stipulations in different ways, Pomponius (26 *ad Sabinum*) *D.* 45.1.5 pr. and *Inst.* 3.18 pr., on the one hand, and Ulp. (70 *ad edictum*) *D.* 46.5.1, on the other.

20. Ulp. (70 *ad edictum*) *D.* 46.5.1 pr., 3: *Praetoriarum stipulationum tres videntur esse species, iudiciales cautionales communes* . . . 3. *Communes sunt stipulationes quae fiunt iudicio sistendi* [sc. *vadimonii*] *causa* (There appear to be three kinds of praetorian stipulation: judicial, by way of undertaking, and common . . . 3. Those called "common" are stipulations that are made for the sake of appearance at trial [sc. *vadimonium*]).

21. Gaius 4.184–87. The contents of the edict are considered in detail in Metzger, *Litigation in Roman Law* (2005) 68–94.

22. The documents are listed as numbers 9–27 and 33–37 in Metzger, *Litigation in Roman Law* (2005) appendix.

"double-barreled": the plaintiff demanded, first, an unconditional promise to appear and, second, a conditional promise to pay a sum of money to him in the event the promisor (the defendant or his representative)[23] did not appear as promised. The sting was in the debt, but only if the promisor failed to appear.

The advantages of the new procedure over the use of *vades* are quite clear. No third person had to be found; the person from whom the plaintiff needed assurances was already present. Also, there was very little to argue about on the day of postponement: the new procedure put off most opportunities for disagreement until the defendant's absence actually put those disagreements in issue.[24] Last, the breach of a duty to appear—formerly resolved in a roundabout way through the *vades*—was reduced to a simple action for debt. There is a strong resemblance to the *actio in factum* previously described, brought against a defendant who failed to come or give a *vindex*. Here again, the praetor threatened to create a debt between the parties in the event that one party did not obey, and the praetor hoped that the threat alone would persuade the defendant to behave in the proper way.

Vexatious Litigation

A third example in which the law of procedure was reformed with the aid of obligations concerns claims for *certa pecunia* and, in particular, vexatious litigation over *certa pecunia*.[25] There are times when a defendant clearly has no

23. The promisor might be the defendant himself, his *procurator*, or his *cognitor*. Cicero's speech for Publius Quinctius gives an example of a promise by a *procurator*. See Cicero *Quinct*. 57, with the discussion in Metzger, *Litigation in Roman Law* (2005) 33–34. A settlement agreement from Puteoli, dated 48 CE, gives an example of a promise by a *cognitor*: *TPSulp*. 27. One suspects that the use of representatives, allowed in the new formulary procedure, was a strong inducement to abandon the use of *vades*.

24. One opportunity for disagreement remained: the amount of the sum to be paid as a penalty if the promisor does not return. Ulpian describes how the praetor deals with the charge of *calumnia* in putting the stipulation. Ulp. (77 *ad edictum*) D. 46.5.1.9: *Quod si sit aliqua controversia, ut puta si dicatur per calumniam desiderari, ut stipulatio interponatur, ipse praetor debet super ea re summatim cognoscere et cautum iubere aut denegare* (But if there is any dispute, if for example the claim is made that the stipulation was put forward out of a desire to be vexatious, the praetor himself ought to investigate the matter summarily and order, or deny, the undertaking). In other words, the reforms brought by praetorian stipulations streamlined the process of postponements, but the problem of the plaintiff's "exposure" remained.

25. For the discussion immediately following, see Liebs, "History of the Roman *Condictio*" (1986) 164–65.

warrant denying that he owes the debt; similarly, there are times when a plaintiff clearly has no warrant demanding the debt. For such cases, there were two early and not wholly effective remedies. One was found in the *legis actio per condictionem,* from the third century BCE.[26] This form of action—established by two statutes, for *certa pecunia* and *certa res,* respectively[27]—created a thirty-day period of reflection between the defendant's denial of the debt and the trial. A second remedy, perhaps introduced at the same time, gave the parties the opportunity to avoid litigation by using oaths. There are a few references in Plautus that serve to show how these oaths were used near to the time of their introduction.[28] We are better informed about the uses of these oaths in the late classical law, and there is some danger in projecting the rules backwards, but the following appears to be the usual course of events in Plautus's time.[29]

The defendant is in court before the praetor. If the defendant denies that he owes the debt to the plaintiff, the plaintiff may elect to ask the defendant whether he would deny the debt on oath. If the defendant denies the debt on oath, the debt is absolved. If the defendant declines to deny on oath, he is condemned. The defendant also had the further choice of asking the plaintiff to affirm the debt on oath. A plaintiff who affirms on oath would obtain a condemnation against the defendant. A plaintiff who declines to take the oath is nonsuited.

The oath procedure puts the matter of vexatious suits squarely into the hands of the parties, particularly the plaintiff. A plaintiff could choose to end the litigation, one way or the other, by electing to put the defendant to an oath. If he trusted the defendant to act with propriety, he would give the defendant that choice. But if he misjudged the honesty of the defendant, he lost the action. The figure of the defendant who abjures dishonestly was familiar to Plautus's audience.[30]

Plautus *Rudens* 13–20: [Arcturus:] *Qui falsas litis falsis testimoniis / petunt*

26. Gaius 4.17b.
27. The *leges Silia* and *Calpurnia* (Gaius 4.19).
28. See the following note in the present chapter.
29. *Digest* 12.2 treats several categories of oath, most pertinently the voluntary *iusiurandum,* treated in Ulpian 22 and Paul 18 *ad edictum,* and the compulsory *iusiurandum,* treated in Ulpian 26 and Paul 28 *ad edictum.* The compulsory oath, permitted in a restricted number of actions including actions for *certa pecunia,* is the more probable successor to the early practice of oath tendering attested in Plautus. For details of the compulsory oath, with literature, see Kaser and Hackl, *Das römische Zivilprozessrecht* (1996) 268–69.
30. See also *Persa* 478; *Curculio* 496.

> *quique in iure abiurant pecuniam, / eorum referimus nomina exscripta ad Iovem; / cotidie ille scit quis hic quaerat malum: / qui hic litem apisci postulant peiurio / mali, res falsas qui impetrant apud iudicem, / iterum ille eam rem iudicatam iudicat; / maiore multa multat quam litem auferunt.*
>
> [(Plautus in *The Rope*). [Arcturus:] Those who use false witnesses to bring false cases, those who swear away what they owe: their names are taken down and brought to Jupiter; he has a daily update on those who do evil here: when those here expect to win a case by perjury or get a trial on a false claim, he reopens the case; he exacts a penalty greater than the spoils of litigation.]

The oath system, as this passage suggests, did not solve the problem of vexatious litigation in debt actions, doubtless because debtors had nothing to lose by denying the debt on oath, at least as far as liability was concerned. This was, therefore, an area ripe for innovation. At some unknown time (and the time is very much disputed),[31] the praetor innovated with the help of so-called penal stipulations. There are a generous number of sources for the practice, some recently discovered.[32] Gaius gives a textbook description.

> Gaius 4.171. *[Adversus infitiantes] ex quibusdam causis sponsionem facere permittitur, velut de pecunia certa credita et pecunia constituta, sed certae quidem creditae pecuniae tertiae partis, constitutae vero pecuniae partis dimidiae.*
>
> [(Gaius in the third book of his *Institutes*). In certain cases an opponent is permitted to make a *sponsio* against those who deny liability, such as cases for *certa pecunia* and *pecunia constituta*, though in *certa pecunia* the *sponsio* is for one-third, while in *pecunia constituta* the *sponsio* is for one-half.]

What Gaius describes are somewhat ruthless but effective devices for keep-

---

31. See Liebs, "History of the Roman *Condictio*" (1986) 165 n. 9.
32. The outstanding item of recent evidence is a document from Puteoli recording a formula seeking a debt and an additional one-third of the debt (*TPSulp.* 31). Two *vadimonia* from Puteoli, recently discovered, record promises to pay two sums, the first sum being one-third of the second (*TPSulp.* 1 bis and 7, both from CE 40). It is possible that the defendants in those lawsuits were reluctant to appear on earlier occasions and that the plaintiff has now secured a penalty to be paid if the defendant again does not appear and refuses also to pay the judgment debt. For other sources, see *lex de Gall. Cisalp.* 21; Cicero *Q. Rosc.* 10, 14.

ing meritless debt cases out of litigation.[33] A meritless defense in a suit for *certa pecunia* would be discouraged by the so-called *sponsio tertiae partis*. The praetor would allow the plaintiff to stipulate to the defendant in words something like the following:[34]

> *Spondesne si secundum me iudicatum erit, tertiam partem pecuniae quae petetur dare?*
>
> [If judgment [in the debt action] is in my favor, do you promise to give me an additional one-third of what I am seeking?]

There was also a companion stipulation, the *restipulatio tertiae partis*, with which the defendant made a corresponding challenge to the plaintiff.[35] A wise litigant would know better than to press or contest a claim vexatiously in a suit where a penal stipulation had been permitted.

This final example of reform, involving vexatious litigation, is similar to the two examples previously discussed. Since the praetor lacked the means to force the litigants to behave, he created a procedural device that encouraged the behavior he desired. The device he chose was the threat to impose a debt on the misbehaving litigant.

The Novelty of Using Obligations in Procedure

To us, obligations might seem to be an easy and obvious choice of device for a praetor seeking to encourage appropriate behavior. But there is reason to think that it was a more novel choice than it seems. In private affairs, obligations are created with certain expectations. One or both parties actively hopes the obligation will come into existence, and if the obligation is conditional, one or both parties actively hopes the condition will be satisfied. Procedural obligations of

---

33. Gaius speaks of suits both for *certa pecunia* and for *pecunia constituta;* the present discussion is concerned only with *certa pecunia*. Where the parties had agreed by stipulation to confirm an existing debt (*pecunia constituta*), to raise a meritless defense was a greater outrage and attracted a greater penalty.
34. See Lenel, *Das Edictum Perpetuum* (1927) 238; Mantovani, *Le formule del processo privato romano* (1999) 103.
35. Gaius 4.13, 4.180.

the kind previously described carry very different expectations: the obligation is not actively sought, and the satisfaction of the condition is usually something to be avoided.

There is a rule of conditions that highlights this difference of expectations. If a condition fails as a result of the conduct of the party who would lose or be bound were the condition satisfied, the condition is treated as satisfied.[36] This is the so-called fictitious satisfaction rule. There is the well-known case of the seller who will sell his library to a certain buyer on the condition that the buyer secures from the local council a place to put the books. When the buyer fails to pursue the matter with the local council, Ulpian gives the opinion that the seller may sue "as if the condition were satisfied."[37] This is an example from sale, but the rule operated in conditional stipulations as well;[38] apparently, the *stricti iuris* nature of the contract was no hindrance. The point, however, is that the fictitious satisfaction rule could not possibly operate in any of the procedural obligations previously described. No disapproval attaches to the frustration of a condition that the parties hoped would not be satisfied in the first place.[39] Even in the case of penal stipulations for vexatious litigation, which very nearly fall within the letter of rule ("when through the act of the promissor the promisee does not comply with the condition"[40]), application of the rule is unthinkable.

These differences in character between the procedural obligations and their private equivalents suggest that the praetor's decision to use obligations was a less obvious choice than it might seem to us. We can only guess at whether their introduction shocked or surprised litigants.[41]

---

36. Iulian. (55 *digestorum*) *D.* 35.1.24; Ulp. (77 *ad edictum*) *D.* 50.17.161. See Daube, "Condition Prevented from Materializing" (1960) 271–96; Thomas, "Fictitious Satisfaction and Conditional Sales in Roman Law" (1966) 116–27; Zimmermann, *Law of Obligations* (1996) 729–31.
37. Ulp. (11 *ad edictum*) *D.* 18.1.50.
38. See the passages cited in n. 36 in the present chapter. Daube ("Condition Prevented from Materializing" [1960] 274–76) argues that as far as stipulations were concerned, the classical rule was confined to the case described by Julian and Ulpian: the promisor hinders the promisee from fulfilling the condition.
39. Oddly, the principal passages for the rule, cited in n. 36 in the present chapter, are apparently part of a discussion of *vadimonium*. Daube ("Condition Prevented from Materializing" [1960] 280) argues that the fictitious satisfaction rule must have been brought in by way of contrast, since "helping a defendant to appear" could not possibly trigger the rule.
40. These are the words of both Iulianus (55 *digestorum*) *D.* 35.1.24 and Ulp. (77 *ad edictum*) *D.* 50.17.161.
41. Gaius (4.13) happens to mention the similarity between the wager created by penal stipulations in his own day and the wager created by certain early forms of action. The praetor's

Reforming Civil Procedure

The praetor actively reformed the law of procedure with the aid of not only obligations (in the form of stipulations and actions) but several other devices as well: for example, oaths, popular actions, and defenses. To understand the role of obligations in procedure, it would be desirable to know why, in some instances, obligations were chosen as an instrument of reform in preference to other devices. We can avoid an overambitious answer, but still chip away at the question, by citing the features that made obligations attractive to the praetor. First, it is very simple, as a matter of formulation, to attach a condition to an obligation. If the praetor's aim is to persuade a litigant to behave in a certain way, a conditional obligation gives the praetor the behavior he desires, with the sting of the obligation being felt only if the litigant is foolish enough to satisfy the condition. Second, where the condition is satisfied, the remedy goes directly to the party who was injured by his opponent's misbehavior, rather than to the public treasury.

Obligations were therefore used as a means of compulsion, but there is a risk here of oversimplifying the development of praetorian reforms. We could easily conclude that the early law did a poor job of compelling litigants to behave and that the praetor rose to the occasion and found for himself the means to do so. But this conclusion has, at its root, a narrow and possibly anachronistic[42] view of the early law. It is a view that was championed some years ago by John Kelly.[43] Very briefly, Kelly argued that state sanctions against reluctant litigants were noticeably weak from the time of the Twelve Tables through most of the classical law. Its weakness was especially evident in cases of summons and execution, where the outcome could depend substantially on the relative strengths of the contending parties: "[T]he average Roman lawsuit up to the mid-second century CE was one in which the plaintiff either commanded physical superiority over the defendant, or at least was a good match for him."[44] If Kelly is right, then praetorian reforms in the law of procedure will reduce to a simple story: the

---

introduction of risks and wagers would, in any event, have shocked no one at all.

42. Following Hoetink, I would call this view genuinely anachronistic, because it attributes modern motives or states of mind to the ancient actors. See n. 6 in the present chapter.

43. Kelly, *Roman Litigation* (1966) chap. 1 ("The Underlying Sanctions of Roman Litigation"), especially 4–20.

44. Kelly, *Roman Litigation* (1966) 20.

praetor perceived the weakness of the law and actively sought out new means of compulsion, among them conditional obligations. Is this the right story?

Some years ago, Geoffrey MacCormack criticized Kelly's account for reasons that are especially relevant to this essay.[45] MacCormack argued that in early Roman procedure, the magistrate[46] was less concerned with compelling obedience to rules and more concerned with mediating and bringing about the settlement of disputes. This is not a thesis unique to MacCormack;[47] his contribution is in showing how the system of dispute resolution evident in the Twelve Tables was peculiarly suited to the nature of early Roman society. At the time of the Twelve Tables, MacCormack says, a typical litigant would have had a whole series of ongoing connections and relationships with the person he was suing. The litigants might be connected by family or other kinship, might also be neighbors, and might also be participants in various private and commercial transactions. Thus, when a litigant presents himself to the magistrate, the magistrate's immediate and most pressing worry is not "how to resolve the claims in accordance with the law." It is, instead, "how to avoid the disruption to the community which might be caused by these two parties falling out with one another." MacCormack is led to this conclusion by comparing early Rome with certain modern African communities. In his opinion, these modern communities and their systems of dispute resolution resemble the communities of early Rome and the system of dispute resolution one finds in the Twelve Tables.[48]

We can expand what McCormack is saying. The central mistake in Kelly's reading of the sources is his assumption that the magistrate's first instinct when presented with a dispute was to parse the dispute into claims. From this, adjudication becomes important as a matter of course, leading Kelly to observe how

---

45. MacCormack, "Roman and African Litigation" (1971) 221–55.

46. That is, the respective magistrates in charge of administering justice, being first a consul, until the creation of the praetorship in the mid-fourth century BCE.

47. At one time, the arbitral nature of early procedure was discussed alongside the hard historical question of whether litigation was originally unitary in origin, with the king and then the consul exercising full judicial powers rather than delegating the trial to another. The prevailing opinion at present is that the procedure was divided at least from the time of the Twelve Tables, if not before. This would seem to make arbitration—and, by extension, MacCormack's mediation—a not implausible model for early procedure. Kaser, however, has argued strenuously that state compulsion is evident in the early procedure, and if this is correct, then both the arbitration model and the mediation model must suffer. On all of this, see Kaser and Hackl, *Das römische Zivilprozessrecht* (1996) 29–30, 79; Kaser, "Novi studi sul processo civile Romano" (1969) 190–98; Metzger, "Litigation" (forthcoming).

48. MacCormack, "Roman and African Litigation" (1971) 225–54.

the rules failed to funnel litigants efficiently through an adjudicative process. But to parse a dispute into claims is not an inclination we should attribute a priori to every magistrate in every period, and MacCormack is suggesting that in the early law the magistrate, faced with a dispute, perceived instead a kind of "general falling out" on perhaps one or more indistinct matters. This is why his aim was to mediate and reconcile rather than to compel one side to perform. If this was the true state of affairs in the early law, then what Kelly observed is true but not remarkable.

We know that, in time, the praetor was moved to innovate and equipped himself with better rules of procedure, rules that the civil law had not provided. In equipping himself with rules of procedure, he turned repeatedly to obligations. In contrast to what came before, these obligations did an excellent job in funneling litigants through an adjudicative process. Kelly would say that the praetor was waking up to the realities of litigation. We might read it instead as a sign that Roman procedure was adjusting itself to a new, more adjudicative role.

Bibliography

Buti, I. *Il "praetor" e le formalità introduttive del processo formulare.* Naples: Jovene Editore, 1984.

Caenegem, R. C. van. *History of European Civil Procedure.* International Encyclopedia of Comparative Law 16.2. Tübingen: J. C. B. Mohr, 1973.

Crawford, M., ed. *Roman Statutes.* 2 vols. London: Institute of Classical Studies, 1996.

Daube, D. "Condition Prevented from Materializing." *Tijdschrift voor Rechtsgeschiedenis* 28 (1960): 271–96.

Donahue, C. "Ius in the Subjective Sense in Roman Law: Reflections on Villey and Tierney." In *A Ennio Cortese,* ed. D. Maffei, 1:506–35. Rome: Il Cigno, 2001.

Domingo, R. *Estudios sobre el primer título del edicto pretorio.* Santiago de Compostela: Universidad de Santiago de Compostela, 1993.

Giomaro, A. M. "Ulpiano e le stipulationes praetoriae." In *Studi in onore di Arnaldo Biscardi,* 4:413–40. Milan: Cisalpino-La Goliardica, 1983.

Hoetink, H. R. "Les notions anachroniques dans l'historiographie du droit." *Tijdschrift voor Rechtsgeschiedenis* 23 (1955): 1–20.

Jolowicz, H. F. *Roman Foundations of Modern Law.* Oxford: Oxford University Press, 1957.

Kaser, M. "Novi studi sul processo civile Romano." *Labeo* 15 (1969): 190–98.

Kaser, M, and K. Hackl. *Das römische Zivilprozessrecht.* 2nd ed. Munich: C. H. Beck, 1996.

Kelly, J. *Roman Litigation.* Oxford: Oxford University Press, 1966.

Lenel, O. *Das Edictum Perpetuum.* 3rd ed. Leipzig: B. Tauchnitz, 1927.

Liebs, D. "The History of the Roman *Condictio* up to Justinian." In *The Legal Mind: Essays for Tony Honoré,* ed. N. MacCormick and P. Birks, 163–83. Oxford: Oxford University Press, 1986.

MacCormack, G. "Roman and African Litigation." *Tijdschrift voor Rechtsgeschiedenis* 39 (1971): 221–55.

Mantovani, D. *Le formule del processo privato romano.* 2nd ed. Padua: CEDAM, 1999.

Metzger, E. "Actions." In *A Companion to Justinian's "Institutes,"* ed. E. Metzger. London: Duckworth, 1998.

Metzger, E. "Litigation." In *The Cambridge Companion to Roman Law,* ed. D. Johnson. Cambridge: Cambridge University Press, forthcoming.

Metzger, E. *Litigation in Roman Law.* Oxford: Oxford University Press, 2005.

Seidl, E. *Römische Rechtsgeschichte und römisches Zivilprozessrecht.* Cologne: Carl Heymann, 1971.

Thomas, J. A. C. "Fictitious Satisfaction and Conditional Sales in Roman Law." *Irish Jurist.* n.s., 1 (1966): 116–27.

Zimmermann, R. *The Law of Obligations: Roman Foundations of the Civilian Tradition.* Oxford: Oxford University Press, 1996.

CHAPTER 7

Public Building Contracts in the Roman Republic

J. MICHAEL RAINER

The Interest of the State

The subject suggested to me by the host of the conference serving as the basis for this volume is of enormous dimensions, making it necessary to limit my contribution to topics already investigated by me relating to private as well as to constitutional law.[1] There can be no doubt that the state intervened and interfered closely in the field of obligations, encouraging a complex pattern to develop over time. As so often in Roman law, we are able to discern some systematic aspects, some order even without concluding that such aspects were intended from the start.

It is rather difficult to discover and set forth a history of the state's interest in obligations. The oldest legal sources, the Twelve Tables, do not mention any direct activity or participation of the state in this area, but they do show the interest of the state in enabling a peaceful cohabitation of all the citizens. So the state was keen to guarantee through the law of contracts and the law of torts—both relating to the term obligation—the functioning of society as a whole. It had created decision-making procedures and imposed these on the citizens through the political power exercised by the *praetores*. But when was the state directly involved as a party and even as a partner in an obligation? Was it in the form of contracts or delicts, and did it participate on a level of equality, or was it always an unequal partner in the sense that it played a predominant role? It can

1. The best introduction to Roman constitutional law in the English language is Lintott, *Constitution of the Roman Republic* (1999). See also Rainer, *Römisches Staatsrecht* (2006).

categorically be emphasized that contrary to the private law, the sources that are able to shed light on our topic are the historians (above all Livy); middle or late republican authors like Cato, Varro, and Cicero (mainly the speeches against Verres); and the municipal *leges* of the *municipia* attested by inscriptions.

Before starting a more detailed review, I would like to give a survey regarding those aspects where we can find a direct interest and direct involvement of the state. First of all, the Roman state was interested in the construction, the restoration, and the maintenance of public buildings. In remoter times, these buildings were, above all, temples, but as the Servian Wall shows, they were also fortifications, streets, aqueducts, and sewage facilities. Illuminating in this context is a list of works hired out during the famous censorship of M. Porcius Cato in the year 184 BCE.[2] Together with his colleague L. Valerius Flaccus, he let out contracts for important works regarding sewage. But the censors did not necessarily act together; they could also hold auctions for public contracts as individuals. Cato's contracting activities concerned two *atria* (halls), four *tabernae* (shops), and one basilica, which bore his name for many years. The conquest of large parts of Italy made it necessary to find a use for the conquered land. This necessity grew stronger as the Romans started crossing the borders of Italy and accumulating one province after the other.

The Role of the Censors

We do not know when the state began conceptualizing in a legal sense the problems that arose in the fields just mentioned, though this is attested in our sources from the second century onward. It can be assumed that the state began very early to develop rules involving private citizens as partners and not as subjects obliged to compulsory labor, as we find happened so often in the European Middle Ages. A very old-fashioned terminology still in use during the first century CE supports this assumption.

The state was normally represented by the censor, a fact that raises a fair number of questions, the most important concerning the limitation of the censors' magistracy to one and a half years within a *lustrum* of five years. It has

2. Livy 39.44.4–8. Cato's colleague as censor was L. Valerius Flaccus. See Milazzo, *La realizzazione delle opere pubbliche* (1993) 76–83; Gast, "Bauberichte" (1965) 17–18; Richter, "Zum censorischen Baubericht von 184 v. Chr" (1964) 181–85; Bodei Giglioni, *Lavori pubblici ed occupazione nell'antichità classica* (1974) 74.

been noted that the intervals between censorial elections were not so strictly maintained as modern introductions to Roman constitutional law would suggest, but there can be no doubt that while in office, the pair of censors were in charge without interruption. Their sphere of competence concerning the *lustrum* itself, the *census,* the *cura morum,* and the *lectiones senatus* never shifted to another public official, meaning neither a *consul* nor a *praetor* could fulfill those duties.

But with regard to restoring temples, building aqueducts, and so on, we are entitled to ask, could all these activities be restricted to just one and a half years? Before answering this question, which is of central interest, I here offer a brief introduction to the activities of the censors in this area. In a very technical sense, the censors assigned public land and public services to private citizens in a special contractual way.

All these activities could, in the traditional sense of Roman private law, easily have been assigned to the sphere of *locatio conductio,* meaning contracts of lease in which a lessor lets property or services to a lessee. Indeed, it is perfectly true that the procedure in which the state participated, although we can note some crucial differences, was called *locatio conductio.* The lease of land and houses as well as the hire of services were the most prominent contents of the *locatio conductio,* a classical contract that arose by mere agreement, or "*consensus.*" The pattern developed by the censors was only partly comparable to and compatible with this well-known consensual contract.

As far as our sources are concerned, the terminology regarding the censorial activities is more flexible and less certain. Together with the *locare* just mentioned, we can find also the terms *vendere* and *redimere,* terminology normally associated with the contract of sales. In the contractual terms proposed by Cato the censor, the lessee is sometimes called *redemptor.*[3] In Festus,[4] we can find explanations for the changing terminology, and even if these attempts do not convince in a historical sense, they prove that the experts were conscious of the problem.

But it has been noted that no earlier period had a clearly defined distinction between the contract of sales and the contract of lease. The rules regarding such contracts as well as the terminology used for them were the product of a long

3. Cato *Agr.* 144.3, 145.3.

4. Festus 516L, 332L; Kunkel and Wittmann, *Staatsordnung und Staatspraxis in der Römischen Republik* (1995) 446 n. 189.

and interesting development.[5] As far as contracts between private citizens were concerned, the concepts of *emptio venditio* and *locatio conductio* were clearly and distinctively defined, and such terms were exclusively used, by the end of the second century BCE and the beginning of the first century, thanks to the intellectual capacities of such jurists of the period as the Mucii Scaevolae and the influence of Greek categories. Even in the late Republic—when, as pointed out, there could be no doubt concerning the presuppositions of formation, execution, and nonperformance of typical contracts—the censors remained bound by an old but translaticious language as far as the patterns laid down in the *leges censoriae* were concerned, so that they could not follow the new, rationalized terminology. The *lex agraria* of the year 111 again proves that as far as public activities were taken into consideration, the exact terminology prescribed when the state was contracting was simply to resort to doublets, writing *redimere* and *conducere* or *vendere* and *locare*.[6]

In the late Republic, every kind of public land was leased to contractors by public auction, as well as the collection of taxes and the undertaking of public works. Before auctioning the land, the taxes, or the projects in question, these were registered in a public register known as the *tabulae censoriae*.[7] The conditions—that is, the presuppositions under which the censors would accept offers—were laid down in the *leges censoriae* and made public. The *leges censoriae* contained in detail all the duties and rights of the future contractor. Most probably a general pattern concerning the particular content of the contract was taken as a common base, but every contract had, of course, to assume a concrete form. All the auctions took place in the Forum, and an employee of the censors, the *praeco,* after having read the *lex censoria,* passed to the concrete procedure. As is well known, the contract itself was drafted exclusively by the censors. The prospective contractors had no chance of changing the content, and without mentioning the reasons, the censors could exclude former lessees or anybody else. This exclusion[8] had to be made known through an edict. The censors also established the bases on which the auction had to start. Obviously,

5. Kaser, *Das römische Privatrecht* (1971) 564–65; Mayer-Maly, *Locatio-Conductio* (1956) 111; Kaufmann, *Die altrömischen Miete* (1964) above all 248–51; Mommsen, "Die römischen Anfänge von Kauf und Miete" (1885) 265.

6. *Lex agraria* 25, 85, 87.

7. Mommsen, *Römisches Staatsrecht* (1887) 2.1:434–36; Kunkel and Wittmann, *Staatsordnung und Staatspraxis* (1995) 446–52; Cicero *Leg. Agr.* 1.3; *Nat. Deor.* 3.49; Pliny *NH* 33.78; Alfenus *D.* 50.16.203.

8. Cicero *Verr.* 2.1.143; Livy 39.44.8, 43.16.2.

the contract was assigned to the highest bidder as far as the lease of public land and the tax collection were concerned, and to the lowest bidder in the case of public works projects. Cato the censor succeeded during the public auctions of the year 184 BCE in achieving very favorable terms for the state.[9]

Before the assignation (*addictio*) could take place, the contractor had to promise guarantees following the instructions of the censors. Contrary to the usage with private contracts, the securities had to be both real and personal in nature. Persons acting as sureties were called *praedes*, and the real securities pledged to the state were known as *praedia*. Again we can emphasize that as far as public contracting was concerned, very old and old-fashioned patterns survived well into the classical period. To guarantee performance of a duty by nominating *praedes* was the original form the Romans had used in archaic times. It meant that if the duty was not duly fulfilled by the contractor himself, the surety was bound in a personal way: he was obligated through *nexum* or *mancipium* to the creditor. For the later period that concerns us, this form of surety had been abandoned in private law and was replaced by the principle that the surety was a second debtor who guaranteed the debt with his means (i.e., his entire estate) but not with his person. The surety was no longer called *praes* but was referred to as *sponsor* or *fideipromissor* or *fideiiussor*, in accordance with the formal legal act that established this special relationship between the creditor and the person willing to guarantee for a debtor.

If the contractor was in a position to nominate a possible *praes*,[10] the censor would ask that person if he was ready to become a *praes*. In this case, the *praes* would be a debtor exactly as the contractor was; here was no subsidiarity, no proportionality or division of the debt, but a direct responsibility, an immediate liability in the case of nonperformance. Of course, if the work was subsequently approved by the employer (i.e., the state), the sureties were released along with the contractor, and the real *praedia* perforce disappeared, probably through cancellation of the registration.

Very curiously, however, the presuppositions changed, though not exactly in the same way as in the private law, which succeeded in creating a very modern system of sureties. Notwithstanding the attachment to old rules and formalisms, it became accepted that the contractor himself could stand also as *praes*, as a surety, a procedure totally unknown—and even useless—in private law. We

9. Livy 39.44.7–8.

10. The term *praes* is used exclusively for sureties in public contracting: see Varro *Lingua Latina* 5.40, 6.74; Festus 249L s.v. *praes* (see also Festus 35L, 137L).

do not know if this "self-surety" was very common or favored either by contractors or the state, but our only relevant source encourages us to take it seriously into consideration. In Festus, we are told that the lessee is also called surety, because in the same way as those who had made guarantees on his behalf, he also had to perform his duties or else indemnify the state.[11]

The Inscription from Puteoli

At the roots of this development, we find, on the one hand, that the tax collectors known as *publicani* were themselves wealthy and trustworthy enough to be treated *ipso iure* as *praedes* and, on the other hand, that building contracts blossomed in the area of euergetism, as prominent people preferred to contribute to the welfare of the community by financing public buildings. A possible example of such an undertaking emerges from a document from Puteoli in which C. Blossius had accepted fifteen hundred sesterces to erect an important public building. He was also accepted as a surety.[12] In this case, the names of four more guarantors are added. The amount of money paid to the builder does not, at first sight, strike one as enormous, but it might be regarded as significant compensation all the same.[13] Even nearly two hundred years later in Pompeii, few persons among the higher reaches of society kept such a sum at home. During the middle and late Republic, a sesterce weighed 1.137 grams of silver (*scrupulum*) and was worth three *asses*. At Cato's time, a relatively large farm might be valued at about 100,000 sesterces,[14] while the level of wealth required for enrollment in the first census class was about 333,000 sesterces.

The inscription[15] dates from the year 105 BCE and can be considered of the

---

11. Festus 137L: . . . *quia idem praes est . . . quia tam debet praestare populo quod promisit, quam is, qui pro eo praes factus est* (. . . because equally he is called guarantor [*praes*], as he is bound to perform on behalf of the people what he has promised in the same way as the person who has given a guarantee on his behalf). See Kunkel and Wittmann, *Staatsordnung und Staatspraxis* (1995) 449.
12. Martin, *Roman Jurists* (1989) 131–36; Badian, *Publicans and Sinners* (1972) 68–69. See also Kaden, "Études sur l'origine du contrat d'enterprise" (1938) 204–7.
13. Kunkel and Wittmann (*Staatsordnung und Staatspraxis* [1995] 449 n. 199) are certain that the amount was far too low and that this was a case of euergetism.
14. Livy 24.11.7–8; De Martino, *Storia della costituzione romana* (1972) 1:185–88.
15. *FIRA* 3.153; *CIL* 1^2.524–26; *CIL* 10.1009; Wiegand, "Die puteolanische Bauinschrift" (1894) 678–93; Badian, *Publicans and Sinners* (1972) 31 n. 18; Ries, *Bauverträge im römischen Reich* (1989) 7–14; du Plessis, "Protection of the Contractor" (2004) 291–95.

utmost interest. One first notes that the public contracts were registered and conserved in a public archive. The inscription probably was placed on the wall built by Blossius in order to commemorate the sponsor, but it happens to contain the original wording of the contract itself.[16] The contract thus preserved—one of very few dating to the Republic—was the second stipulated during the current year. The contract is correctly described as *lex,* and so it can be identified as a contract between a private entrepreneur and the state, the state being, in this case, a Roman colony administered following the rules normally and universally given to autonomous towns inhabited by Roman citizens. The law in force in all those numerous colonies was undoubtedly Roman law, and the political structures were reproduced, on a smaller scale, from the institutions of the Roman Republic. Thus the *duoviri* stood in for the consuls, remaining in office an entire year as chief executives of the community. The *ordo decurionum* composed of former officials exercised the functions comparable to (some of) those of the Senate. The *lex* concerned the erection of a wall near the temple of Serapis. Whoever obligates himself as a contractor—the Latin text uses the legally correct terminology *redemerit*—must offer personal and real sureties in accord with the instructions given by those contracting for the state, namely, the *duoviri.* The real sureties had to be documented and registered, a formality that is still practiced in our time.[17] This text teaches us also that in self-administered towns, the office of the *duoviri*[18] exercised aspects of the duties enjoyed by the Roman censors.

An important step toward the conclusion of the contractual relation

---

16. Du Plessis ("Protection of the Contractor" [2004] 292) argues that the text does not embody the actual contract and that it was erected to commemorate the successful completion of the project. Of course, the fragment we possess was erected for precisely this purpose, but nonetheless this commemoration contains the exact text of the original contract under which the work was performed. Whereas the legal validity of a written text was indeed less developed in private contracts, we can be sure that as far as public contracting and, above all, building contracts are concerned, the literal form itself was a sine qua non. The idea was that every citizen should know the details of how public works were contracted.
17. Du Plessis ("Protection of the Contractor" [2004] 292–93), in translating the text, interprets it in the sense that the sureties themselves had to sign for real guarantees. I cannot agree, as I believe that the contractor was compelled to look for real guarantees above all in his property. The sureties, in any case, as personal guarantors, were liable up to the value of their entire estates, that is, with all of their real and personal property: see Hardy, *Roman Laws and Charters* (1912) 77–82.
18. Mommsen, *Römisches Staatsrecht* (1887) 2.1:596–99.

between the state and the contractor was the *probatio*.[19] We know every single aspect of this procedure in the field of private contracts. Typically, upon completion of the work, the builder (*conductor/ redemptor*) had to present the results to the employer (*locator/venditor*) for inspection. Above all, the inspection was designed to check the builder's conformity to the contract, meaning, in the case of a public contract, his conformity to the *lex censoria*. A technical inspection was then made in order to assure the employer that the work had been accomplished following commonly accepted standards of architecture and engineering. Only if the *probatio* was successful would the employer (in our case, the state) proceed to the final payment. In the case of faults, irregularities, and technical problems, the employer would delay the payment, asking the builder to make the appropriate corrections. If the builder was not, in the end, able to present the work as requested, he would not receive full or perhaps even partial payment. If he had already received a part of the payment in form of a lump sum, he could be sued to compel him to return this money in whole or in part. In private contracts, all these legal issues could be addressed in a trial between the parties where the parties stood on the same level and were judged by an independent judge. In the case of public contracts, the procedure was normally conducted by the public official who had let the contract or by another official if the former was no longer in office.

In Puteoli, the work was to be supervised and, in the end, approved by the *duoviri* and all the members of the local council, the assembly of ex-officials. A deliberation concerning a specific building contract was valid only if a minimum of twenty councillors were present. The same quorum was necessary to ratify the *probatio*, which had to be expressed by oath.[20] Du Plessis[21] is perfectly right to emphasize that the measure was included to prevent corruption and to foster transparency. Transparency not only discourages dishonest officials from squandering public money and obtaining undue benefit but also can be seen as a way of protecting the private contractor. A public discussion in the assembly of the former *duoviri* made it possible to bring into the open all the aspects necessary for approval or disapproval. A fixed date and the payment modalities

19. Martin, "Reconsideration of *Probatio Operis*" (1986) 321–37; Martin, *Roman Jurists* (1989) 103–12.

20. Du Plessis ("Protection of the Contractor" [2004] 294) thinks that the number of favorable votes was not made public, that is, that only the quorum of twenty was recorded and, of course, that a majority of them sufficed to carry the measure.

21. Du Plessis, "Protection of the Contractor" (2004) 294.

were inserted into the agreement. In this case, the work had to be completed by the first of November; half of the compensation was to be paid when the contractor had fulfilled all the guarantees concerning the real sureties, and the other half would be paid as soon as the work had been approved.

Security

Normally, as I have pointed out, real security had to be offered together with sureties:[22] all our sources show that it was standard procedure to offer both forms of guarantees. Mommsen's[23] opinion that normally the sureties themselves would have been obliged to pledge also their property cannot be accepted, as it is evident that they were liable up to the value of their entire estate. But were the contractors obliged to pledge land, or could the censor establish that the personal guarantee would be sufficient? The testimony of the *lex Flavia municipalis* could be interpreted in yet another sense. This law makes it necessary to provide real *praedia* only when the guaranty of the *praedes* appeared to be insufficient.[24] But the premises were different, as these guaranties were to be pledged in case a citizen stood for election to the highest local offices. Guaranties in case of public contracting might be considered a more serious matter. In any case, we can assert with certainty that real *praedia,* meaning land, normally had to be pledged. The way the real security came into existence is quite striking: it had to be registered in a censorial protocol, perhaps as a *subsignatio* in the *lex censoria* itself. The real security could be created only on land owned by a Roman citizen. The pledge on the state's behalf was similar in some ways to *fiducia,* a form of real security deriving from ancient Roman private law, and it undoubtedly arose in a period before the more recent form of real security represented by *hypotheca* emerged. At all events, the possession and even the use and enjoyment of the land remained with the guarantor. Only in the case of nonperformance was the land taken by the state. The censor could also involve

22. In the sources, we consistently find the conjunction *et* or *ac* or *-que*—never *vel* or *ve*—in the context of *praes* and *praedia:* Livy 22.60.4; Cicero *Verr.* 2.1.142; *lex agraria* (111 BCE) 46; *lex Tarentina* 9; *lex Malacitana* 63–65. The distinction also appears at Polybius 6.17.4.

23. Mommsen, "Die Stadrechte der latinischen Gemeinden Salpensa und Malaca" (1905) 307–8, followed by du Plessis, "Protection of the Contractor" (2004) 292–93, against Kunkel and Wittmann, *Staatsordnung und Staatspraxis* (1995) 450.

24. *Lex Flavia municipalis* 60.

experts (*cognitores*)[25] to determine the exact value of the pledged land. If their assessment turned out to be erroneous, they were responsible to the state for the difference in price received during a public auction following the rules of the *lex praediatoria*.[26]

Quite amazingly, in the case of failure to perform, the standard procedure excluded a civil trial. Even if, by the late Republic, the sureties were no longer liable in a strictly personal sense, a special executory procedure against them took place under the terms of a general *lex praediatoria*. This led to a forced sale of the goods up to the value of the loss caused by the nonperformance.

Why did the state not follow the development of private law? In the first place, I think this can be ascribed to a certain conservative approach to the spheres of competence assigned to public officials. Second, the established procedure seemed to cater more effectively to the interest of the state in the security of public money. Nonperformance in cases of contracts stipulating payment to the public treasury would be prosecuted in a direct and severe way to compel the contractors to adhere to the premises and the explicit contents of the *lex censoria*, which could lead to a direct seizure of the goods of the *praes* and to personal liability as well. Following the usage of guarantees in private law would have meant accepting pledges in the form of *pignus*, signifying a transfer of possession of the property in question to the state and possibly (in fact, the likelihood is great) incurring high costs for the state in fulfillment of its duty to safeguard the real securities.

The End of a System

It is very difficult to say when the system of censorial leases disappeared. I think deep changes took place already under the reign of Augustus. While the very conservative first *princeps* did not formally abolish the position of censor, it survived only very theoretically, as part of the powers of the *princeps*.

The administration of Rome was restructured, the *ager publicus* in the republican sense disappeared due to the creation of new colonies and the demilitarization of the Roman state, and the collection of taxes soon became largely the responsibility of a centralized administration informed by more

25. *Lex Malacitana* 64.

26. *Lex Malacitana* 64; Wesener, "Praediatura" (1974).

rational principles. Of course, some contracting with the state continued, but, as we see with the *fiscus*, this happened very differently from before.

The republican system survived, however, for a long period in the *municipia*.[27] The *leges municipales* show that the Roman towns outside Rome had adopted the republican approach wholesale. The *lex Flavia municipalis* evinces exactly the same legal premises as I have described just now.[28] Obviously, the censor was substituted by the *duoviri* insofar as they were the most prominent officials of the *municipia*.

We have seen how the Roman state operated in its guise as a public administration contracting and creating obligations. What were the benefits and what were the weaknesses of this system? To my mind, the most outstanding weakness was the lack of a standard legal procedure to follow when failure to perform was claimed by the state. The special executory procedure was far too heavily weighted in favor of the state to guarantee equal rights to the lessee. The immunity from prosecution enjoyed by holders of public office (buttressed by *imperium* in the case of consuls and praetors) prevented contractors from suing public officials and prevented the latter from suing a contractor in a civil trial deriving from a contract of *locatio conductio*. Instead, the rules established customarily (meaning that they were constituted by constitutionally accepted *mores*) regarding contracting by the state led to the development of a particular species of contracts as well as the special executory procedure and the *leges praediatoriae*.

The duration of the censors' term of office represented another serious problem. This had lesser consequences regarding the lease of public land and the collection of taxes, since these could be leased out for longer terms. But other contractual arrangements, particularly the building contracts, required strict supervision and, in the latter case, inspection and approval of the project. Who approved the buildings? We know only that a request by the censors in the year 168 BCE for the prolongation of their term in order that they might see to the carrying out of the building repairs and oversee the performance of the contracts they had let was vetoed by a tribune.[29] Of course, the procedure of inspection and approval is of crucial importance because it determined whether a contract had been completed or not. Two solutions can be proposed. Either the censors fixed the termination of the contracts to coincide with their own

27. See the excellent analysis by du Plessis, "Protection of the Contractor" (2004) 300–303.

28. *Lex Flavia municipalis* 63–64.

29. Livy 45.15.9.

period of office, which is when failure to perform produced the consequences established in the *lex praediatoria,* or we should try to identify another public representative competent to decide on the *probatio.* There are few indications in the sources regarding other officials. Even if the *aediles*[30] could and should have been involved,[31] and though we hear of a consul, too,[32] a more plausible solution can be found in the Senate. As we have seen with the inscription of Puteoli, at least in the *municipia,* the institution that was modeled on the Roman Senate, that is, the council of the former *duoviri,* played an active role in the procedure of inspection and approval. We know from Polybius that, at least during the Second Punic War, the Senate had the ultimate authority[33] regarding public works and could decide, for example, on the extent of a contractor's liability and the extension of the period of completion for a building project.[34] There can be no doubt that in referring to the responsibilities of the Senate, Polybius was influenced by the actual way the Senate proceeded, so that we might assume that, at least during the second half of the second century BCE, the Senate was involved in public contracting. According to Cicero,[35] the Senate at the beginning of Verres's praetorship gave instructions through a *senatusconsultum* governing cases in which the approval and inspection of works authorized through public building contracts had not yet followed through,[36] but Cicero does not mention any deeper involvement in the approval and inspection procedure. The text shows that, at least in the provinces and, subsequently, Italy itself (with the exception of Rome), consuls, praetors, and promagistrates exercised the functions of the censors in Rome. The *senatusconsultum* had to be decreed because neither the consuls who had hired out the building contracts nor the praetors to whom the supervision had been delegated had found the time to inspect and approve the works performed.[37] Cicero's second speech against Verres[38] indeed

30. *CIL* 1^2.1560.
31. Robinson, *Ancient Rome* (1993) 49.
32. *CIL* 1^2.694.
33. Polybius 6.17: " . . . all these transactions came under the authority of the Senate."
34. Du Plessis, "Protection of the Contractor" (2004) 295.
35. Cicero *Verr.* 2.1.130; Mommsen, *Römisches Staatsrecht* (1887) 2.1: § 444.
36. Cicero *Verr.* 2.1.130–50 cites the old and technically correct terminology as far as the maintenance of temples were concerned: *sarta tecta aedium sacrarum locorumque publicorum tueri* (to protect the roofs of the holy temples and of all the public buildings).
37. Du Plessis ("Protection of the Contractor" [2004] 309 n. 55) takes this evidence as a proof that in the years without censors, the consuls had to provide for building contracts.
38. See the excellent summary of the relevant aspects of the case in du Plessis, "Protection of the Contractor" (2004) 295–300.

offers general proof that Roman officials with *imperium* exercised exactly the same functions in the provinces as the censors did in Rome. Above all, the appropriate official had the responsibility of inspecting and approving,[39] and if he judged that the work done so far did not conform to the contract, he could unilaterally terminate the contract and further call for new tenders in an auction procedure.

As far as the functions of the Senate are concerned, we can certainly assume a constitutional competence regarding building contracts, but not a direct involvement in the procedure of inspection and approval. Only twice do our sources make reference to the Senate's activities. In 184 BCE, the Senate cancelled existing contracts, because the censors had auctioned them off at exceptionally low rates.[40] In 155 BCE, the censors were prevented by the Senate from auctioning off a contract for building a permanent theater on the Palatine Hill, because of a cited lack of public utility.[41] Both interventions are political in nature, in that the Senate felt compelled to preserve the public welfare, which it felt was not being observed. But the Senate did not review either the content of the contract itself or the final inspection and approval.

Conclusion

This discussion should conclude by emphasizing the main points of the procedure regarding the public building contracts in the Roman Republic. In the first place, I would like to underline the formal legal aspects of the procedure. The state itself decided in favor of a well-structured and transparent procedure: the *leges censoriae* were public and could be inspected by every citizen. We find not arbitrariness but the clear will of the state to lease land, the collection of taxes, and the performance of services in a publicly controlled procedure. Due to the extremely high reputation of the censors, to whom the moral oversight of the entire citizen body and of admission to the Senate were entrusted, we can be sure that censorial contracts and the sums requested of contracting parties were totally fair. The same must be stressed as far as the process of inspection and approval is concerned. The trial against Verres is the best proof that mischief of this kind was severely prosecuted. The long survival of these rules in the

39. Martin, *Roman Jurists* (1989) 104.
40. Livy 39.44.8.
41. Velleius 1.15.3.

municipia proves their substantial correctness. With the only known exception of the famous Verres trial, no complaints have survived, either in legal texts or in our historical or rhetorical sources, as far as public contracting is concerned. In conclusion, I think the lesson we can learn is that in the Republic, for the first time in history, a state took part in a rational way as a partner in contracting, through the adaptation of patterns in use between private citizens, and subordinated its procedures and its behavior to the principle of legality.

Bibliography

Badian, E. *Publicans and Sinners: Private Enterprise in the Service of the Roman Republic.* Ithaca, NY: Cornell University Press, 1972.

Bodei Giglioni, G. *Lavori pubblici ed occupazione nell'antichità classica.* Bologna: Pàtron, 1974.

Coarelli, F. "Public Building in Rome between the Second Punic War and Sulla." *Papers of the British School in Rome* 45 (1977): 1–19.

De Martino, F. *Storia della costituzione romana.* 2nd ed. 6 vols. Naples: Jovene Editore, 1972–1975.

du Plessis, P. "The Protection of the Contractor in Public Works Contracts in the Roman Republic and Early Empire." *Journal of Legal History* 15 (2004): 287–314.

Gast, K. "Die zensorischen Bauberichte bei Livius und die römischen Bauinschriften." PhD diss., University of Göttingen, 1965.

Hardy, E. G. *Roman Laws and Charters.* Aalen: Scientia Verlag, 1977. Originally published in Oxford: Oxford University Press, 1912.

Kaden, E. "Études sur l'origine du contrat d'entreprise dans le droit romain." In *Recueil des travaux publiés par la Facolté du Droit de l'Université de Genève,* 198–217. Geneva: University of Geneva, 1938.

Kaser, M. *Das römische Privatrecht.* 2nd ed. 2 vols. Munich: C. H. Beck, 1971–75.

Kaufmann, H. *Die altrömische Miete: Ihre Zusammenhänge mit Gesellschaft, Wirtschaft, und staatlicher Vermögensverwaltung.* Cologne: Böhlau, 1964.

Kunkel, W., and R. Wittmann. *Staatsordnung und Staatspraxis in der Römischen Republik.* Vol. 2, *Die Magistratur.* Munich: C. H. Beck, 1995.

Lintott, A. *The Constitution of the Roman Republic.* Oxford: Oxford University Press, 1999.

Martin, S. D. "A Reconsideration of *Probatio Operis.*" *Zeitschrift der Savigny-Stiftung für Rechtsgeschichte (Romanistische Abteilung)* 103 (1986): 321–37.

Martin, S. D. *The Roman Jurists and the Organization of Private Building in the Late Republic and Early Empire.* Collection Latomus 204. Brussels: Latomus, 1989.

Mayer-Maly, T. *Locatio Conductio: Eine Untersuchung zum klassischen römischen Recht.* Vienna: Herold, 1956.

Milazzo, F. *La realizzazione delle opere pubbliche in Roma arcaica e repubblicana: Munera e ultro tributa.* Pubblicazioni della facoltà di Giurisprudenza di Catanzaro 23. Naples: Edizioni Scientifiche Italiane, 1993.

Mommsen, T. "Die römischen Anfänge von Kauf und Miete." *Zeitschrift der Savigny-Stiftung für Rechtsgeschichte (Romanistische Abteilung)* 6 (1885): 260–75.

Mommsen, T. "Die Stadtrechte der latinischen Gemeinden Salpensa und Malaca in der Provinz Baetica." In *Juristische Schriften* 1:265–382. Berlin: Weidmann, 1905.

Mommsen, T. *Römisches Staatsrecht.* 3rd ed. 3 vols. Leipzig: S. Hirzel, 1887–88.

Rainer, J. M. *Römisches Staatsrecht: Republik und Kaiserzeit.* Darmstadt: Wissenschaftliche Buchgesellschaft, 2006.

Richter, W. "Zum censorischen Baubericht von 184 v. Chr." *Wiener Studien* 77 (1964): 183–85.

Ries, P. "Bauverträge im römischen Reich." PhD diss., University of Munich, 1989.

Robinson, O. F. *Ancient Rome: City Planning and Administration.* London: Routledge, 1993.

Strong, D. E. "The Administration of Public Building in Rome during the Late Republic and the Early Empire." *Bulletin of the Institute of Classical Studies* 15 (1968): 97–107.

Wesener, G. "Praediatura." *RE Suppl.* 14 (1974): 447–55.

Wiegand, T. "Die puteolanische Bauinschrift sachlich erläutert." In *Sonderdruck aus dem XX Supplementbande der Jahrbücher für klassische Philologie,* 661–778. Leipzig: B. G. Teubner, 1894.

CHAPTER 8

Roman Economic Policy and the Law of Contracts

DENNIS KEHOE

The Ancient Economy

Population and technology established the basic constraints within which an ancient economy could develop, as is emphasized in many chapters in the recently published *Cambridge Economic History of the Greco-Roman World.*[1] In recent years, however, scholars have recognized the potentially complex role that law and legal institutions could play in an ancient economy. The Roman law of obligations is clearly important in this connection, since it established the basic parameters within which countless economic transactions were conducted. So the question is whether Roman law, as developed and interpreted by the Roman jurists and the imperial government in responding to petitions, enhanced the performance of the Roman economy within the overall constraints posed by population and technology. It would have done so by fostering governance structures surrounding contracts that created incentives for people to enter into mutually beneficial business arrangements. The alternative is that the principal sectors of the Roman economy, agriculture and commerce, limped along with inefficient forms of organization that restrained economic activity. Roman law and legal institutions could simply have preserved the privileges of the elite at the expense of others, without fostering growth. Another possibility is that the law was too weak to have had much of an effect on the economy, so that economic actors in the Roman world found ways to enforce contracts in which formal legal institutions played only a modest role.

1. Scheidel, Morris, and Saller, *Cambridge Economic History of the Greco-Roman World* (2007).

Analyzing the role of legal institutions in the Roman economy is a difficult undertaking, but I believe that we can learn a great deal about the economic implications of Roman contract law by exploring the methodologies used in the current debate about the relationship between law and the economy in the fields of law and economics and the new institutional economics (NIE).[2] The debate in these fields provides ancient historians with a useful perspective for evaluating the likely effects of the Roman government's legal policies. This methodology has its limits for analyzing an ancient economy (or even a better-documented modern economy), since the available evidence usually makes it impossible to verify hypotheses about the likely incentives resulting from various property rights regimes. Still, analyzing ancient legal institutions helps us to predict the economic incentives created by Roman legal institutions, including property rights as defined by the state, contractual arrangements, or even the customary arrangements affecting the organization of private business. After sketching out some of the basic assumptions of NIE, I will then take some time to apply this methodology to two areas of legal policy that had important implications for the economy, namely, the allocation of risk in agriculture and the contractual liability of property owners running businesses through agents.

The development of Roman law as a legal system with wide application in the Mediterranean world had potentially enormous consequences for the Roman economy. In the best-case scenario, the Romans would have succeeded in imposing a more uniform system of law across the empire, which would have made it easier to develop legal institutions that protected property rights and facilitated commerce. Certainly, the Roman government took many steps to accomplish this goal. In the west, at least, it established Roman law and procedures as the basis for the legal systems of countless towns and cities. Throughout the empire, moreover, provincial governors spent much of their time fulfilling a basic responsibility to hear cases involving both Roman and local law. Perhaps the best indication of the Roman government's efforts to create a more uniform and equitable legal system is the development of a system to respond to petitions. The petitions that the office of the *a libellis* handled came from people all across the empire representing a variety of social statuses. Petitioners would receive authoritative responses about the law applicable to their cases,

2. In this essay, I am applying the methodology that I developed in Kehoe, *Law and the Rural Economy* (2007); for a discussion of the application of the methodologies of law and economics and NIE to the ancient economy, see Frier and Kehoe, "Law and Economic Institutions" (2007).

and they could then take these rescripts to local courts, whose judges would be obligated to follow them.[3] People also sent petitions to officials of lower rank, from local magistrates to provincial governors. The willingness of so many people to submit to this process suggests the effectiveness of the Romans in establishing authoritative legal institutions to resolve disputes. Responding to petitions at the level of the *a libellis,* moreover, provided the state with one way, albeit reactive, to intervene in the economy by establishing new interpretations of areas of the law significant for the economy.

The allocation of risk in agriculture and the contractual liability of property owners running businesses through agents are crucial areas for testing the intersection of law and the economy, for several reasons. To begin with farm tenancy, it was an institution basic to the Roman agrarian economy and one, moreover, where it is possible to trace how the Roman legal authorities mediated between the interests of large-scale landowners and the more modest farmers on whose production the Roman agrarian economy depended. This focus on farm tenancy is not to overlook the other ways of exploiting land, including through slave labor and wage labor hired on a long-term or casual basis or even through owner cultivation.[4] Farm tenancy remained a widespread institution in the Roman Empire throughout the period of the Principate, and to a large degree, it provided the institutional basis on which the fiscal system of the later empire was built.[5] The issue of allocating the costs associated with risk was one of the most important and difficult issues in farm tenancy with which the Roman legal authorities had to contend. Agriculture in the Mediterranean world was subject to serious risk resulting from periodic droughts and locally catastrophic weather conditions, and it stands to reason that allocating the costs of this risk was a constant and contentious issue affecting the interests of both landowners and tenants.[6] The approach that the legal authorities took to this issue represented one of the principal ways in which they could influence the rural economy.

3. On the rescript process, see Nörr, "Zur Reskriptenpraxis" (1981); Peachin, *Iudex vice Caesaris* (1996); Corcoran, *Empire of the Tetrarchs* (1996).

4. Rathbone, *Economic Rationalism and Rural Society* (1991); Banaji, *Agrarian Change in Late Antiquity* (2001).

5. For discussion of the connections between tenancy in the early empire and the bound colonate of the later empire, see, e.g., the essays in Lo Cascio, *Terre, proprietari e contadini dell'impero romano* (1997).

6. For the risks in Mediterranean agriculture, see especially Horden and Purcell, *Corrupting Sea* (2000) 175–230.

Agency is likewise of fundamental importance to the Roman economy. Any economy faces the challenge of creating effective incentive and enforcement mechanisms to allow people to enter into contractual relationships with confidence that their contracts are enforceable.[7] As the economists Avinash Dixit and Avner Greif emphasize, from quite different perspectives, the availability of resources that can be exchanged does not in and of itself create commercial markets, and both of these scholars examine how economic actors or groups can establish mechanisms to promote commerce in the absence of strong state enforcement of contracts.[8]

Greif explores how, in various settings in the medieval world, groups of merchants or communities developed governance structures for contracts that were crucial for commerce and for the emergence of markets.[9] The medieval world, with numerous political units and systems of law, is not directly comparable with the Roman Empire, which had a more uniform system of laws and stronger state-sanctioned legal institutions to enforce property rights. Of course, only a tiny fraction of disputes ever resulted in lawsuits heard in Roman courts, but the existence of strong legal institutions that enforced property rights provided merchants and other people involved in commerce at all levels with a kind of legal endowment on the basis of which they could negotiate and enforce contracts. The possibility of using courts whose decisions were authoritative, then, meant that negotiations were carried out in the "shadow of the law."[10] Providing legal institutions to enforce contracts and the resolution of disputes, however, represented only part of the solution to creating the institutional infrastructure to support commerce. In addition, Roman property owners required governance systems that allowed them to manage businesses, especially ones that were geographically scattered across the Mediterranean. This involved developing appropriate incentive systems to make sure that the activities of their agents would also serve their own interests.

The questions that I am addressing in this essay involve two very different aspects of the role that Roman law and legal institutions played in the Roman economy. The first concerns the degree to which the jurists and the office of

---

7. On agency, see Furubotn and Richter, *Institutions and Economic Theory* (2005) 162–70.
8. Dixit, *Lawlessness and Economics* (2004); Greif, *Institutions and the Path to the Modern Economy* (2006).
9. Greif, *Institutions and the Path to the Modern Economy* (2006).
10. For the use of this concept to refer to divorce settlements in U.S. courts, see Mnookin and Kornhauser, "Bargaining in the Shadow of the Law" (1979). For theoretical discussion of this concept, see Dixit, *Lawlessness and Economics* (2004) 25–58.

the *a libellis* interpreted the law surrounding tenancy in an economically efficient and productive manner. In this connection, economic efficiency means that the application of the law encouraged landowners and tenants to bargain in a mutually beneficial fashion to promote productive and profitable agriculture. It is certainly possible that the law could discourage such bargaining, with the result that the costs associated with risk would be imposed on one party or the other without bargaining or even on society as a whole. This is a form of market failure, something that efficient legal rules would be designed to avoid. With agency, the issue to be examined is somewhat different, since it concerns how social institutions fundamental to Roman society influenced the organization of economic activity and the forms that legal rules took. The hierarchical structure of the Roman *familia* was one of the basic building blocks of Roman society. It provided the setting within which many forms of economic activity were organized, not just the management of businesses, but also the training of people in skills vital to commercial activity. As Greif emphasizes in his analysis of trading mechanisms in the medieval economy, social institutions impose constraints on the possibility for economic change, since they help to shape not only the values of society but also the ways in which people perceive and order the world around them.[11] Thus the institution of agency in Roman business organization, grounded as it was in the Roman slave system, provides an opportunity to explore the complex issue of the capacity of Roman society to develop governance structures that would foster dynamic economic change and even growth.

New Institutional Economics and the Ancient Economy

Before proceeding with an analysis of Roman institutions, it will be helpful to explore some of the assumptions underlying the NIE approach to analyzing economic institutions. NIE builds on neoclassical economics by taking into account the constraints affecting economic activity and decision making.[12] Neoclassical economics analyzes the relationships among economic actors

11. Greif, *Institutions and the Path to the Modern Economy* (2006) 190–91.
12. For fuller discussions of applying the approaches of law and economics and NIE to relationship between ancient law and society, see Frier and Kehoe, "Law and Economic Institutions" (2007), as well as Kehoe, *Law and the Rural Economy* (2007) chap. 1. For a basic introduction to NIE, see Mercuro and Medema, *Economics and the Law* (1997) 130–56; P. G. Klein, "New Institutional Economics" (2000), Furubotn and Richter, *Institutions and Economic Theory* (2005); Eggertsson, *Economic Behavior and Institutions* (1990).

who are assumed to seek to maximize their wealth or utility. These actors make rational decisions, based on complete information on their own welfare and the effects of various contractual arrangements on it, in pursuit of clearly defined and well-understood goals. This approach, while abstract, provides an analytic basis from which to evaluate the relative efficiency of contractual arrangements and the likely economic implications of various distributions of property rights. But for a broader analysis of legal institutions surrounding the economy, this way of evaluating economic relationships seems too idealized.

Recognizing the same basic incentives that represent the premise of neoclassical economics, scholars working in the neoinstitutional tradition seek to analyze how real-world conditions affect the incentives for engaging in the type of bargaining that would promote economic growth and, on the basis of analyzing these constraints, to explain the development of institutions and institutional arrangements. Making more realistic assumptions about the real world, NIE posits that economic activity is subject to all sorts of constraints, or *transaction costs.* This term refers to the costs involved in just about any activity connected with an economic transaction, such as acquiring information or negotiating and enforcing contracts. This approach to analyzing institutional arrangements privileges private bargaining, and it evaluates institutions that affect private bargaining in terms of the Coase Theorem, the work of Ronald Coase.[13] According to the Coase Theorem, the precise legal definition of property rights is not important as long as property rights are defined fully, since economic actors will find a way to bargain around any allocation of property rights to produce an economically efficient result, that is, one in which resources find their highest valued use. This holds true as long as transaction costs are zero. Of course, in the real world, transaction costs are never actually zero. Rather, the Coase Theorem provides an analytical basis on which to assess forms of economic organization in terms of the transaction costs that they create, since these transaction costs represent an impediment to the gains that parties might achieve from exchange. The success of institutions, then, can be measured in the degree to which they reduce the transaction costs surrounding private bargaining.

---

13. See Coase, "Problem of Social Cost" (1960). For discussion of the literature on the Coase theorem, see Field, "New Economic History and Law and Economics" (2000) especially 737–38; Medema and Zerbe, "Coase Theorem" (2000). The discussion in this section is based on Frier and Kehoe, "Law and Economic Institutions" (2007); and Kehoe, *Law and the Rural Economy* (2007) chap. 1.

This observation of the theoretical efficacy of institutions leaves unanswered the question of how institutions come into existence in the first place. In the field of institutional economics (a field related to but distinct from NIE), economic institutions are viewed as subject to the influence of political and legal institutions and social values.[14] Certainly, the influence of powerful forces can be keenly felt, but economic institutions do not necessarily evolve to achieve greater efficiency. In the field of NIE, many scholars view institutions as "instrumental," in the sense that they are the result of the efforts of well-connected people to serve some positive end.[15] But even from this perspective, institutional change is subject to severe constraints, as Greif emphasizes. Powerful people seeking to enact substantial change in economic institutions have to act on the basis of the institutions that they inherit. Not only do such institutions carry with them a whole set of interests and procedures that can make change prohibitively expensive, but they also shape the values of economic actors and the ways in which they perceive the world.[16]

Greif's notion of the importance of the values and perceptions that people internalize from existing institutions builds on an emphasis, in much of NIE scholarship, on the role that uncertainty plays in economic decision making. One perspective on the role of uncertainty is to see economic institutions as evolving, with weaker or inadequate ones falling by the wayside as better-suited institutions flourish and even reenforce themselves. This "evolutionary" approach, which is inspired by evolutionary biology, finds expression in the very influential 1950 article of Armen A. Alchian.[17] In Alchian's view, people find their economic way in a world fraught with uncertainty, and it is practically impossible for an economic actor to know fully the consequences of any economic decision. Consequently, we cannot analyze economic decision making simply in terms of the rational pursuit of wealth or utility maximization, since it will be impossible for any individual to know fully how to attain this or even to recognize when he or she has achieved this goal. Under this circumstance, economic actors are subject to "bounded rationality," a concept

---

14. Rutherford, *Institutions in Economics* (1994); and Ogilvie, "Economic Institutions in Pre-Industrial Europe" (2007).
15. Greif, *Institutions and the Path to the Modern Economy* (2006) 153–54, 188, and elsewhere, citing especially Williamson, *Economic Institutions of Capitalism* (1985).
16. Greif, *Institutions and the Path to the Modern Economy* (2006) 188.
17. Alchian, "Uncertainty, Evolution, and Economic Theory" (1950).

developed by Herbert Simon.[18] In Simon's view, our limited ability to make rational decisions means not that we make irrational decisions but that our rationality is bounded by our limited understanding of the world in which we live. Consequently, we make what Simon terms "satisficing decisions" to solve problems on the basis of this type of rationality. These are decisions that enable a person to achieve a desired goal in terms of the means available, which ultimately depend on the knowledge at his or her disposal. At the same time, "rational" behavior is subject to the rules generated by institutions that affect how people understand the world.[19] The upshot is that given the limits on our ability to measure the value of one type of arrangement against another—say, in the ancient world, various forms of land tenure—we often rely on time-honored solutions. Institutional change is likely to occur when we perceive that these choices have begun to fail.

Neither Alchian's nor Simon's approach fully explains the origins or development of institutions, but we can learn a great deal from Greif's analysis of the constraints imposed by existing institutional structures. Such constraints can be seen as producing what is termed *institutional path dependence.* Institutions, once established, provide the basic starting point for any future economic development.[20] Changing to a more efficient allocation of resources, even if one can be determined, can be prohibitively expensive, since it would involve altering a host of existing arrangements. The process of institutional change, barring some exogenous event like a catastrophe or revolution, is likely to be gradual and incremental. The point that emerges from Greif's discussion, however, is that the range of possible institutional arrangements is further limited by the perceptions and even the ideologies that people internalize from existing ones. Past institutional settings become pervasive and powerful, since they shape not only our information but the way we process information, which is in terms of deep-seated moral values, shared beliefs, and social expectations. At the very least, such perceptions shape what we believe to be permissible and desirable in economic transactions. So our "rationality" is constrained not simply by the limits on our ability to collect and synthesize information but, much more fundamentally, by the values and cognitive framework within which we organize what is possible or thinkable.

18. See especially Simon, *Reason in Human Affairs* (1983).

19. Greif, *Institutions and the Path to the Modern Economy* (2006) 127.

20. For the concept of institutional path dependence, see especially North, *Institutions, Institutional Change, and Economic Performance* (1990).

This approach to understanding institutions provides a valuable theoretical basis for analyzing the economic aspects of Roman legal institutions. To turn to Roman legal policies surrounding contract law, my hypothesis is that the Roman legal authorities were acutely aware of the concerns of upper-class property owners and sought to respond to them. As Yan Zelener has sought to demonstrate formally in his 2003 Columbia University dissertation, commerce and manufacturing played a limited, albeit significant, role in the Roman economy.[21] Consequently, Roman property owners had no choice but to invest the bulk of their wealth in agriculture. This situation necessarily shaped the investment strategies of Roman property owners, but it also informed the approach of the Roman legal authorities in areas of the law that directly impinged on the economy. With many exceptions, of course, Roman property owners tended to be risk-averse, since, given the overall constraints on the economy and the lack of short-term growth, it made more sense for them to preserve their sources of income rather than to take risks to increase them.[22] This risk aversion was not simply a reaction to the economic conditions as Roman property owners understood them but can also plausibly be regarded as a self-enforcing social norm, with far-reaching (though difficult to determine) consequences for how property owners interacted with their trading partners, whether they were tenants or merchants.

Risk and Tenancy

To turn to farm tenancy, we can place Roman legal policy in a useful perspective by considering the concept of the "relational contract." This concept is used by contemporary legal scholars to analyze long-term, dynamic business relationships (including employment), when the contracting parties at the outset are unable to anticipate or provide for all the future contingencies but when both sides have a vested interest in the continuation of the relationship.[23] The theory

21. Zelener, "Smallpox and the Disintegration of the Roman Economy" (2003).
22. I argue this view in Kehoe, *Law and the Rural Economy* (2007). For arguments that members of the Roman upper classes were more aggressive and enterprising in pursuing profits, see Rathbone, *Economic Rationalism and Rural Society* (1991) on agriculture; Wilson, "Machines, Power, and the Ancient Economy" (2002) on investing in technology.
23. For discussion of the relational contract, see Macneil, "The Many Futures of Contracts" (1974); Macneil, "Contracts: Adjustment of Long-Term Economic Relations" (1978); Goetz and Scott,

of the relational contract is grounded in the assumptions of NIE about the limits on our ability to make fully informed, rational decisions. This conception of a contract is to be contrasted to that of neoclassical economics, which views the contract as a "discrete transaction" negotiated by parties with full knowledge of future contingencies. As I will argue, the notion of the relational contract helps to explain the principles guiding the Roman legal authorities as they responded to legal disputes involving risk in farm tenancy. The legal authorities did not prescribe terms of land tenure but instead encouraged landowners and tenants to readjust the terms of lease arrangements in reaction to changing circumstances. This process of mutually advantageous renegotiation, or private ordering, provided a way to achieve overarching goals and to preserve beneficial long-term tenure arrangements. It was impossible for anyone to know whether this approach represented the most economically efficient allocation of resources, since there was simply no way to test alternatives, but it did promote economic security by preserving sources of income for landowners.

The classical lease contract is often analyzed as an agency relationship that is in some ways ideally designed to serve the needs of risk-averse landowners.[24] It was of short duration, generally five years, with the obligations of landowner and tenant defined clearly. The landowner leased out a working farm, or *fundus,* and was generally expected to provide fixed capital, such as buildings, storage facilities, and olive and wine presses. The landowner's main obligation was to provide a farm that the tenant could cultivate. The tenant, in turn, paid the landowner a cash rent (*merces*) and was expected to return the farm in good working order at the end of the lease. In addition, the tenant typically supplied movable capital, such as tools, livestock, and even slaves. The landowner's costs at the outset of the lease were predictable, as was the income he would receive. The tenant, for his part, had every incentive to work productively, since he would be able to reap the full reward of any extra expenditure of labor or investment of resources in the farm under lease. The landowner could enforce the tenant's obligations by holding a lien over the property that the tenant brought

"Principles of Relational Contracts" (1981); Schwartz, "Relational Contracts in the Courts" (1992). Those sources provide the basis for my discussion in Kehoe, *Law and the Rural Economy* (2007) 95–109.

24. For discussion of the normative Roman lease contract, see Kehoe, *Investment, Profit and Tenancy* (1997) chap. 3, relying on Frier, "Law, Technology, and Social Change" (1979), and Johne, *Die Kolonen in Italien und den westlichen Provinzen des Römischen Reiches* (1983). For more general treatment of lease, see Zimmermann, *Law of Obligations* (1990) 338–83.

onto the farm, the *invecta aut illata*.[25] To enforce this lien, the landowner could call on several procedural remedies.

While the classical lease contract can be analyzed in this way from a neoclassical economic perspective, this mode of analysis has limitations. Consider, for example, the much-discussed rescript that the emperor Antoninus Pius issued to a tenant seeking remission of rent because of the age of the vines on the farm he was leasing.

> (Ulpian in the thirty-second book on the Edict)
> When someone complained about the meagerness of his crops, it is stated in a rescript of the divine Antoninus that the basis for his claim should not be considered. Again it is stated in another rescript as follows: "You want something revolutionary [*novam rem desideras*], that a remission be given you on account of the age of the vines."[26]

In the neoclassical perspective, the lease in question can be viewed as a "discrete transaction," in which the tenant, before negotiating the contract, should have taken into account the age of the vines, clearly a foreseeable circumstance that would affect the value of the lease. This perspective takes no account of the prior relationship between the landowner and the tenant or of any future one. The circumstances of the tenant's petition suggest an ongoing lease relationship, but one that had broken down beyond repair, since the tenant was seeking through legal channels what ordinarily would be a matter for negotiation. Having failed to obtain a reduction in rent from his landowner, he probably refused to pay some of his rent. In response, the landlord must have sued, so now the tenant appealed to the emperor for a legal opinion that would support his view of the case. The whole lawsuit only makes sense in the context of an ongoing lease relationship of some duration.

The Roman court—in this case, the emperor—was in no position to resolve a gap in the original contract, that is, a provision that was not negotiated. It is possible that the two parties had reached some sort of understanding about who was to pay for the upkeep of the vines, but it would be difficult for either

25. See the essay by du Plessis in this volume.

26. Ulp. (32 *ad edictum*) *D.* 19.2.15.5: *Cum quidam de fructuum exiguitate quereretur, non esse rationem eius habendam rescripto divi Antonini continetur. item alio rescripto ita continetur: 'Novam rem desideras, ut propter vetustatem vinearum remissio tibi detur.'* I discuss this and the texts that follow in Kehoe, *Law and the Rural Economy* (2007) 101–3.

one to prove the noncompliance of the other in court.[27] The tenant sought to use traditional lease law to impose on the landowner the costs of maintaining the vines, presumably by claiming that the landowner had failed to provide him with a farm that he could cultivate. For his part, the emperor responded on the same terms, those of a purely conventional Roman lease, which contained no provision for the gradual replacement of aging vines. But the inability of the Roman government to resolve gaps in contracts does not mean that it was unaware of the "relational" aspect of many tenancy arrangements. Instead of resolving gaps and, in effect, putting itself in the position of deciding issues of facts that it had no way to verify, the Roman government sought to adopt legal policies that encouraged private negotiation between landowners and tenants. We can see this especially in its flexibility in sorting out the legal issues that arose when landowners granted tenants remissions of rent on the basis of poor crops, or *sterilitas.* In this situation, the Roman government responded to the substantial risks imposed by Mediterranean agriculture by seeking to preserve the lease contract. It did this by carefully defining the rights and duties of landowners and tenants when the former group went beyond the strict requirements of conventional Roman lease law and granted remissions because of poor crops. This policy served a larger purpose, one based on the way in which upper-class landowners conceived of their economic interests. For them, the continued presence of productive tenants was central to the estate economy of the Roman Empire.

The Roman legal authorities showed some flexibility, at least by the late classical age, in their willingness to modify the allocation of risk under the classical lease contract. In that contract, the tenant bore the bulk of the risk. Since he paid a rent in cash, he was responsible both for the size of the harvest and for the market price of the crops.[28] He was entitled to a remission of rent only when an unforeseeable disaster (*vis maior*) made it impossible for him to fulfill his contractual obligations.[29] The types of disasters that qualified as *vis maior* included an invasion of an army, an unusual infestation by predatory birds, or an unforeseeable natural disaster, such as an earthquake or an unaccustomed

27. This argument draws on Schwartz, "Relational Contracts in the Courts" (1992).

28. For discussion of the Roman doctrine of *remissio mercedis,* see now especially Frier, "Law, Economics, and Disasters down on the Farm" (1989–1990); du Plessis, *History of* Remissio Mercedis *and Related Legal Institutions* (2003); Capogrossi Colognesi, *Remissio mercedis* (2005).

29. Servius-Ulp. *D.* 19.2.15.2; cf. Gaius *D.* 19.2.25.6.

heat wave. But the tenant was expected to bear the costs for the foreseeable risks associated with agriculture (*vitia ex re*). In the passage previously quoted, the emperor Antoninus Pius viewed a poor crop, not to mention aging vines, as just such a risk, whose costs the tenant had to bear.

To some extent, the allocation of risk in the classical Roman lease contract was economically efficient, at least in the approach advocated by Richard Posner and Andrew Rosenfield, since it encouraged landowners and tenants to "internalize" the costs associated with risk, that is, to factor them into the bargaining process.[30] Consequently, it encouraged both parties to take the appropriate steps to reduce their exposure to risk. The tenant, who was in the best position to reduce the risk directly connected with the cultivation of the crops, had an incentive to take such risk-reducing steps as storing surpluses, engaging in polyculture, and cultivating crops (e.g., barley) that are more resistant to drought. The landowner, who would generally be more able to shoulder the costs arising from a larger catastrophe, bore the risk for unforeseeable disasters. The landowner could reduce his exposure to such risk by owning land in different geographical locations.

The problem with this approach is that it oversimplified the nature of risk in agriculture, since there were many disasters that could wipe out a tenant's crop but that would also be regarded as *vitia ex re*. Landowners responded to this situation, motivated either by social considerations or by the need to retain tenants who were otherwise difficult to replace, by granting tenants remissions of rent. Such remissions for *sterilitas*, granted informally, amounted to a renegotiation of the lease, carried out outside the framework of any judicial proceeding. This "private ordering" could be economically beneficial, since it provided a way for landowner and tenant to renegotiate terms of land tenure in response to changing conditions that neither party was in a position to foresee. The contribution of the Roman legal authorities to this effort was simple but significant. It did not define what constituted *sterilitas*, a disastrously poor harvest; we only have Gaius's formulation that the crops had to be "damaged beyond what is tolerable."[31] Rather, the legal authorities encouraged productive private ordering by defining clearly the rights and obligations of both parties when the landowner granted the tenant a remission on the basis of *sterilitas*. The termination of the lease contract was not a remedy, as it would be in later

30. Posner and Rosenfield, "Impossibility and Related Doctrines in Contract Law" (1977).

31. Gaius (10 *ad edictum provinciale*) *D.* 19.2.25.6: *si plus, quam tolerabile est, laesi fuerint fructus.*

civilian systems; rather, its goal was to define property rights on the assumption that the lease would endure beyond the individual growing season.[32] We can see this approach in the response of the early third-century jurist Papinian, as cited by Ulpian.

> (Ulpian in the thirty-second book on the Edict)
> Papinian says in his fourth book of *Responses* that if someone has granted a tenant a remission in one year on account of a poor crop, and then an abundant harvest occurs in subsequent years, the remission does not prejudice the claims of the landlord, but the payment is to be demanded also for the year in which he remitted the rent. He made the same response concerning the loss on land leased from a town. But if the landlord remitted the rent on account of the poor crop of a year as a gift, the same thing will have to be maintained, as if it were not a gift but a transaction [*transactio*]. What happens, however, if the last year of the lease, in which he granted the tenant a remission, was sterile? The better view is that [*verius dicetur*] if the previous years had abundant crops and the lessor knows, this year should not be included in the computation.[33]

In Papinian's interpretation, the grant of remission of rent represented a provisional settlement of contractual claims, since the loss in income represented by the remission of rent could be balanced against his continuing claim for the rent due for the lease period in its entirety. The principle formulated by Papinian guided the imperial government in its subsequent treatment of requests for remissions of rent. For instance, the emperor Alexander Severus, in responding to a tenant's claim for a remission of rent in 231 CE, would only allow such a remission if the tenant could demonstrate that the poor crops caused by a weather-related disaster were not balanced out by plentiful crops in other years.

---

32. For the termination of the lease in later civilian systems, see Kehoe, "Roman-Law Influence on Louisiana's Landlord-Tenant Law" (1995). For their treatment of remission of rent, see Zimmermann, *Law of Obligations* (1990) 373–74.

33. Pap.-Ulp. (32 *ad edictum*) *D.* 19.2.15.4: *Papinianus libro quarto responsorum ait, si uno anno remissionem quis colono dederit ob sterilitatem, deinde sequentibus annis contigit uberitas, nihil obesse domino remissionem, sed integram pensionem etiam eius anni quo remisit exigendam. hoc idem et in vectigalis damno respondit. sed et si verbo donationis dominus ob sterilitatem anni remiserit, idem erit dicendum, quasi non sit donatio, sed transactio. quod tamen, si novissimus erat annus sterilis, in quo ei remiserit? verius dicetur et si superiores uberes fuerunt et scit locator, non deberi eum ad computationem vocari.*

(Emperor Alexander Severus to Sabinianus Hyginus; 231 CE)
Assuming that you have leased a farm for fixed annual payments, if, however, it has not been expressed in the lease or the custom of the region does not require that, if any losses had occurred because of disastrous weather or another climatic problem, they should be your burden, and if the poor crops that have happened will be proved not to have been balanced by the abundant crops of the other years, you will rightly demand that your request be considered in accordance with good faith, and the judge who will hear the case on appeal will follow this principle.[34]

The doctrine formulated by Papinian and followed by Alexander Severus was not particularly favorable to tenants, since it allowed the landowner to exercise a continuing claim for the rent under certain circumstances. But it did define property rights more precisely and, in so doing, would have given landowners an additional incentive to grant remissions in circumstances that went beyond the classical interpretation of *remissio mercedis,* under which the tenant bore the risk for all the normal hazards of farming. The somewhat artificial distinction between fully foreseeable risks (*vitia ex re*) and unforeseeable hazards (*vis maior*) in the classical rule would leave a great deal of ambiguity about the rights of landowners who granted remissions. The insistence on the continuing validity of the landowner's claim established a firm legal basis for any renegotiation of the lease. Moreover, it did so without removing the incentives that tenants had under classical doctrine to internalize the costs associated with agricultural risk by pursuing risk-reducing strategies, since they could not simply impose these costs on the landowner.

The willingness of the Roman legal authorities to accommodate within *remissio mercedis* arrangements that did not fall under this legal principle as strictly defined raises the question about the relationship between the development of law and social institutions. Certainly, there were social norms that affected the ways in which landowners and tenants dealt with one another, and these are likely to have varied from one region of the empire to another. But if the Roman legal authorities were concerned to find a legal mechanism to

34. Alexander Severus C. 4.65.8: *Licet certis annuis quantitatibus fundum conduxeris, si tamen expressum non est in locatione aut mos regionis postulat, ut, si qua labe tempestatis vel alio caeli vitio damna accidissent, ad onus tuum pertinerent, et quae evenerunt sterilitates ubertate aliorum annorum repensatae non probabuntur, rationem tui iuxta bonam fidem haberi recte postulabis, eamque formam qui ex appellatione cognoscet sequetur.*

preserve lease arrangements, this suggests that landowners, at least, had similar considerations. The Roman legal authorities were concerned to accommodate within Roman law what was likely to have been a widespread practice of landowners to grant remissions of rent for poor crops, and this practice must have been rooted, to some extent, in the ways in which landowners were expected to treat their tenants. Pliny the Younger, for his part, seems to discuss granting remissions of rent as something that landowners might regularly do, and Columella earlier saw granting a remission of rent as something that a landowner might be forced into, even when he was not legally required to do so.[35] This attitude could be explained as economically rational if replacing suitable tenants (especially those with substantial resources at their disposal) was difficult. But this type of rationality was also grounded in norms of behavior that guided upper-class landowners. From this perspective, the efforts of the Roman legal authorities centered around accommodating social practice within the law. It is possible to explain the law surrounding tenancy as reflecting the economic interests of upper-class landowners, but the relationship between law and social practice is likely to have been a bit more complicated.[36]

Roman property owners identified their economic interests against the backdrop of shared social values, ones that helped to shape how they perceived their choices in economic matters and defined what was appropriate behavior for their class.[37] If they viewed tenure arrangements as "relational," they could not simply discard tenants who had fallen behind on their rent. In a similar manner, as I will argue in connection with agency in business relationships, property owners had to be trustworthy both with agents who were social dependents and with trading partners. But we must also consider remissions of rent from the tenant's point of view, which is even harder to reconstruct than that of landowners. One central aspect of Roman imperial ideology was that the Roman state brought justice to the empire's subjects. The state promoted this ideology with carefully managed communications with the empire, as Clifford Ando emphasizes, and the state certainly invested a great deal of its prestige, as well as its resources, in the process of responding to petitions.[38] As part of this policy, the imperial government discouraged self-help as a means of

35. Pliny *Ep.* 9.37, 10.8.5; Columella *Re Rust.* 1.7.1.

36. For the "agency" perspective on the development of economic institutions, see the text accompanying n. 15 earlier in the present chapter.

37. See Greif, *Institutions and the Path to the Modern Economy* (2006) 190–91.

38. Ando, *Imperial Ideology and Provincial Loyalty* (2000). On petitions, see n. 3 earlier in the present chapter.

resolving debts and other legal disputes, and it sought to keep these under the watchful eye of the courts.[39] The state's ideology and legal policy surely had an effect on the perceptions of the people ruled. This can be seen in the rhetoric of petitions, in which a common theme is that the plaintiffs are of moderate means, contributing to imperial revenues by cultivating their land productively, whereas their opponents have exercised force (*vis* or *bia*). It seems clear that, in many cases, terms meaning "force" were used to characterize actions taken without the sanction of a court or other competent legal authority. From the perspective of tenants or other people of moderate means, problems were not to be settled by self-help or resorting to force but, rather, within the lawfully established procedures of courts. In Roman ideology, bargaining was to be done in the shadow of the law.

Agency and Commercial Transactions

An economic analysis of the jurisprudence on the crucial issue of risk in agriculture suggests two overriding concerns: first, to promote private bargaining by defining property rights clearly and so offering the affected parties an incentive to bargain; second, to respond to the needs of risk-averse property owners who sought financial stability above all. We can trace a similar effort to respond to such concerns in other areas of the law, particularly in the legal institutions surrounding the ways in which Romans managed their often diverse and far-flung business interests.

An analysis of Roman commercial institutions must take into account some of the basic constraints affecting commerce in the empire. To be sure, the late Republican period and the early Principate saw the impressive commercial networks in the Mediterranean area, to the extent that it is possible to consider the question whether markets in the Roman economy were "integrated" across the Mediterranean world.[40] However, the growing integration of markets in the Roman world does not mean that property owners did not face substantial difficulties in enforcing contracts and managing their business arrangements,

---

39. Kehoe, *Law and the Rural Economy* (2007) chap. 4.
40. On this issue, see Lo Cascio, "Forme dell'economia imperiale" (1991). For the sophistication of Roman financial institutions in comparison to those of premodern Europe, see Temin, "Financial Intermediation in the Early Roman Empire" (2004) For basic discussion of commerce in the Roman Empire, see Morley, "Early Roman Empire" (2007).

particularly when they could not be personally present for long periods of time in order to do so. The establishment of authoritative legal institutions in the Roman Empire made the task of enforcing contracts easier. For instance, in the case of Roman Egypt, it was clearly possible to enforce a contract beyond the confines of an individual city, as lawsuits involving people from Alexandria with property concerns in the *chora* amply illustrate.[41] But going to court is costly and, we should imagine, a last resort. The possibility of taking this step does not solve the problem of creating governance systems for commerce.

One of the major questions that remains is how people in the Roman world overcame problems arising from a deficit in information to establish credit relationships that were necessary for commerce on anything other than a purely local scale. In the medieval world, in Greif's analysis, Jewish merchants from Old Cairo in the eleventh century overcame some of these difficulties by creating trading networks overseas with merchants sharing a similar ethnic and cultural background. The challenges that these merchants faced were more complicated than in the Roman world, since the Mediterranean world in the Middle Ages was fragmented politically, so that there was no single legal system to which merchants could have recourse. Instead, these merchants developed their own "merchants' law."[42] In developing countries in the contemporary world, as Dixit observes, business arrangements are characteristically made within networks of people who have personal connections with one another. Business people invest substantially to create and maintain these networks, and they often prefer to do business within them than to seek potentially more remunerative arrangements outside. This is one reason why, today, Chinese firms have an easier time doing business in the United States, where commerce is open and subject to universally applicable rules, than U.S. firms have in China, where business often depends on long-cultivated relationships.[43] To turn to the Roman world, it would be naive to think that markets were as open as they are in the United States or in the European Union, and it is likely that many activities of business enterprises, including the furnishing of capital through loans, came about as a result of personal connections.[44]

41. Enforcing contracts beyond the confines of an individual city is one of the major problems in the development of medieval commerce that Greif investigates in *Institutions and the Path to the Modern Economy* (2006) 309–49.

42. Greif, *Institutions and the Path to the Modern Economy* (2006) 58–90.

43. Dixit, *Lawlessness and Economics* (2004) 59–95, especially 79–80.

44. For discussion of the role of friendship in Roman business, see Verboven, *Economy of Friends* (2002).

This aspect of the Roman economy is illustrated by the figure of Trimalchio in Petronius's *Satyricon*, as studied by John D'Arms.[45] Trimalchio has a variety of business interests, including commerce and agriculture and, finally, lending money through (or to) freedmen. The assumption underlying this portrayal is that a business enterprise for a wealthy Roman would involve not a coherent strategy to expand on a base of expertise and production but simply exploring profit-making ventures as they might arise. So the question to be addressed for the Roman world concerns the ways in which the governance structures developed by the Romans addressed commercial and social needs, given the likely personal nature of many business arrangements and the restricted nature of the capital market.

In the Roman world, the formal legal institutions that governed commerce were limited. One problem was the absence of a firm that had a legal personality distinct from the persons who might be involved in a business undertaking. In the Roman law of partnership (*societas*), the relationship, with the exception of the *societates* that collected state revenues, would dissolve upon the death or withdrawal of one of the partners.[46] It is not necessarily the case that this situation would have crippled Roman commerce, if credit for commercial transactions was driven by supply rather than by demand, in the sense that property owners would invest their money in commercial ventures as opportunities arose. The opposite would be enduring commercial enterprises that created a constant demand for credit.[47]

More important for commerce in the Roman world was the development of agency laws that made it possible for agents to act with some authority on behalf of property owners, but the Roman law of agency was also incomplete in this respect. Such agency law as did exist consisted of six legal remedies introduced in the third or second century BCE and later, called the *actiones adiecticiae qualitatis*.[48] These remedies gave protection to people engaging in contracts with agents representing principals. Such agents would include sons-in-power and slaves, who operated their businesses with the *peculia* set at their

45. D'Arms, *Commerce and Social Standing in Ancient Rome* (1981) 97–120.

46. See Frier and Kehoe, "Law and Economic Institutions" (2007) 126–34; Plescia, "Development of Agency in Roman Law" (1984); Kaser, *Das römische Privatrecht* (1971) 1.572–76; Zimmermann, *Law of Obligations* (1990) 451–76.

47. On this distinction and its applicability to modern developing countries, see Dixit, *Lawlessness and Economics* (2004) 79–80.

48. For the development of these remedies, see De Ligt, "Legal History and Economic History" (1999); Aubert, *Business Managers in Ancient Rome* (1994) 46–91.

disposal. Through these actions, the praetor granted people who were owed money by agents or who had otherwise entered into contractual relationships a way to recover their losses by suing the principal, often a *pater familias* or a slave owner.

These legal remedies established the parameters of liability on the part of the principal for actions done by an agent. It is significant that Roman law substantially limited the liability of the principal; in most cases, this liability was restricted to the amount of the *peculium* granted the agent. In addition, the agent usually had to have the permission of the principal to enter into a contract, although such permission could be assumed in many circumstances. These rules reduced the property owners' exposure in potentially lucrative but also risky business ventures. To some extent, the law codified the very cautious orientation toward risk on the part of upper-class Romans that I have already discussed. Roman law enforced the obligations created by agents, but only to a limited extent; the interests of the principal generally took precedence over those of the person conducting business with an agent. The Roman law of agency thus established a basic endowment of legal rights that formed the starting point for bargaining when people did business with agents.

A key issue for understanding the economic contribution of the law in the Roman world is to determine the extent of the social cost created by the protection against risk accorded principals. This social cost is likely to have been substantial, since some potential economic activity was lost as a result of people's unwillingness to enter into business relationships from which they could only recover part of their investment if they had to resort to the courts. After all, one of the advantages enjoyed by modern corporations and, on a much humbler level, licensed contractors is that they can be sued. This means that they can make a promise and be counted on to fulfill it.[49] Of course, in the Roman world, people could always bargain around the restricted liability of a principal, and it seems likely that to maintain ongoing business relationships, property owners would have to stand behind the obligations entered into by their agents, even if they were not formally required to do so.

The law of agency represented by the *actiones adiecticiae qualitatis* was largely the product of broader social institutions that shaped virtually all aspects of Roman economic life. It seems very difficult to separate this law from the institutional setting that helped to create it and that it, in turn, fostered—

---

49. For this point, see Dixit, *Lawlessness and Economics* (2004) 100.

namely, the hierarchical structure of the Roman *familia,* with its principals, slaves, and freedmen. Its economic effects are difficult to assess but certainly important. For one, it helped Roman property owners to create incentives for business managers to engage in the type of activity that promoted the interests of the principals. This is one of the chief problems that analysts of the modern firm have identified. One of the fundamental problems is the asymmetries of information that exist between principals and agents: the agent in managing a business has a great deal more knowledge about day-to-day affairs and will be in a position to make profits for himself without necessarily benefiting his employer. In the Roman world, the problem of monitoring performance was especially difficult when a principal was employing an agent in a distant location; the slowness of communication would make it very challenging for a property owner to monitor the activities of an agent on a regular basis.

Assigning the slave manager a *peculium* and allowing him to manage his business independently solved this problem to some degree. The slave manager acting with a *peculium* became an independent businessman in his own right and so had every incentive to monitor efficiently and rigorously the employees (including slaves) in his charge. The recourse that the property owner might exercise against an unsatisfactory agent, however, would likely take place outside the law of contracts. The slave manager would have to have confidence that he would be rewarded for his efforts, whereas the property owner could only punish the agent by withholding eventual freedom or imposing other penalties that had little to do directly with the management of the business. The chief cost to property owners would be that they would surrender a great deal of control over businesses, no doubt sacrificing some income that they would otherwise receive from a more centralized system of managing their business interests.

Using the *familia* structure to manage businesses provided a second advantage, in terms of the costs of acquiring information about potential trading partners, which would have been considerable. If it is unsurprising that business in the Roman world would often revolve around personal relationships, the implications are still interesting. The *familia* system would have made it easier for new people to enter the commercial world and to build up their reputations, as they would gain from the prestige and backing of the property owner employing them. This would help to mitigate some of the difficulties involved in entering a business world oriented around "relation-based" contracts, to use Dixit's term.

At the same time, the use of slaves or freedmen as agents in business depended on the consistency of property owners in observing unwritten laws that were part of the ideology of Roman slavery. No one could force Roman property owners to grant freedom or other rewards to slaves who had served them well, and slaves were always subject to arbitrary treatment by their owners.[50] Still, the whole system would have failed if slaves could not rely on their masters' rewarding them, and this, in turn, depended on masters' internalizing a set of values for the proper treatment of slaves and other social dependents. The implication is that for slavery to be fully understood as an institution central to the Roman economy, it must be studied from the perspective of the obligations and restrictions it imposed on owners.

For society as a whole, the incentive for property owners to manage their business interests in a decentralized manner would have militated against large-scale undertakings that required substantial investment of capital and coordination. But the cost that society bore resulted not so much from the failure of Roman law to develop adequate governance structures to allow the development of complex firms but, rather, from the economic preferences of property owners. Above all, they sought stability from their investments, and Roman law created legal mechanisms that facilitated their pursuit of this goal. The Roman law of agency, then, represented a reasonable solution to problems faced by property owners operating businesses within the constraints imposed by conditions in the Roman Empire. It served not necessarily to maximize economic activity but, rather, to help Roman property owners to achieve overriding economic goals.

Conclusion

To conclude, I hope that this brief examination of two areas of the law crucial to the economy helps to show how a comparative legal and economic methodology can help us to understand better the complex relationship between the law and the economy in the Roman Empire. An analysis of Roman legal institutions from an economic perspective does not allow us to estimate the scale of the Roman economy. But it does allow us to understand better the complex factors surrounding the economy and how such factors promoted or impeded particular forms of economic activity. Ultimately, an economic analysis of legal insti-

50. See Bradley, *Slavery and Society at Rome* (1994); this point is challenged, to some extent, by Roth in *Thinking Tools* (2007); and Mouritsen, *Freedman in the Roman World* (2011).

tutions can help us to understand the basic character of the Roman Empire, whether it was a society that promoted the privileges of an elite few or, rather, provided legal protections and the possibility for economic advancement to a broader public.

Bibliography

Alchian, A. A. "Uncertainty, Evolution, and Economic Theory." *Journal of Political Economy* 58.3 (1950): 211–21.

Ando, C. *Imperial Ideology and Provincial Loyalty in the Roman Empire.* Berkeley: University of California Press, 2000.

Aubert, J. J. *Business Managers in Ancient Rome: A Social and Economic Study of* Institores, *200 B.C.—A.D. 250.* Leiden: E. J. Brill, 1994.

Banaji, J. *Agrarian Change in Late Antiquity: Gold, Labour and Aristocratic Dominance.* Oxford: Oxford University Press, 2001.

Bouckaert, B., and G. De Geest, eds. *Encyclopedia of Law and Economics.* 5 vols. Cheltenham, UK: Edward Elgar, 2000. (On-line edition [1999] encyclo.findlaw.com/tablebib.html).

Bradley, K. R. *Slavery and Society at Rome.* Cambridge: Cambridge University Press, 1994.

Capogrossi Colognesi, L. *Remissio mercedis: Una storia tra logiche di sistema e autorità della norma.* Naples: Jovene Editore, 2005.

Coase, R. H. "The Problem of Social Cost." In *The Firm, the Market, and the Law,* 95–156. Chicago: University of Chicago Press, 1988. Originally published in *Journal of Law and Economics* 3 (1960): 1–44.

Corcoran, S. *The Empire of the Tetrarchs: Imperial Pronouncements and Government AD 284–324.* Oxford: Oxford University Press, 1996.

D'Arms, J. H. *Commerce and Social Standing in Ancient Rome.* Cambridge, MA: Harvard University Press, 1981.

De Ligt, L. "Legal History and Economic History: The Case of the *Actiones Adiecticiae Qualitatis.*" *Tijdschrift voor Rechtsgeschiedenis* 47 (1999): 205–26.

De Neeve, P. W. "Remissio mercedis." *Zeitschrift der Savigny-Stiftung für Rechtsgeschichte (Romanistiche Abteilung)* 100 (1983): 296–339.

Dixit, A. K. *Lawlessness and Economics: Alternative Modes of Governance.* Princeton, NJ: Princeton University Press, 2004.

du Plessis, P. J. *A History of* Remission Mercedis *and Related Legal Institutions.* Rotterdam: Erasmus University, 2003.

Eggertsson, T. *Economic Behavior and Institutions.* Cambridge: Cambridge University Press, 1990.

Field, A. J. "New Economic History and Law and Economics." In *Encyclopedia of Law and Economics*, ed. B. Bouckaert and G. De Geest, 1:728–53. Cheltenham, UK: Edward Elgar, 2000.

Frier, B. W. "Law, Economics, and Disasters down on the Farm: *Remissio Mercedis* Revisited." *Bulletino dell'Istituto di Diritto Romano*, 3rd ser., 31–32 (1989–90): 237–70.

Frier, B. W. "Law, Technology, and Social Change: The Equipping of Italian Farm Tenancies." *Zeitschrift der Savigny-Stiftung für Rechtsgeschichte (Romanistiche Abteilung)* 96 (1979): 204–28.

Frier, B. W., and D. P. Kehoe. "Law and Economic Institutions." In *The Cambridge Economic History of the Greco-Roman World*, ed. W. Scheidel, I. Morris, and R. Saller, 113–43. Cambridge: Cambridge University Press, 2007.

Furubotn, E. G., and R. Richter. *Institutions and Economic Theory: The Contribution of New Institutional Economics*. 2nd ed. Ann Arbor: University of Michigan Press, 2005.

Goetz, C. J., and R. E. Scott. "Principles of Relational Contracts." *Virginia Law Review* 67.6 (1981): 1089–1150.

Greif, A. *Institutions and the Path to the Modern Economy: Lessons from Medieval Trade*. Political Economy of Institutions and Decisions. Cambridge: Cambridge University Press, 2006.

Horden, P., and N. Purcell. *The Corrupting Sea: A Study of Mediterranean History*. Oxford: Blackwell, 2000.

Johne, K. P., V. Weber, and J. Köhn. *Die Kolonen in Italien und den westlichen Provinzen des Römischen Reiches: Eine Untersuchung der literarischen, juristischen und epigraphischen Quellen vom 2. Jahrhundert v.u.Z. bis zu den Severern*. Berlin: Akademie-Verlag, 1983.

Kaser, M. *Das römische Privatrecht*. 2nd ed. 2 vols. Munich: C. H. Beck, 1971–75.

Katz, A. W., ed. *Foundations of the Economic Approach to Law*. New York: Oxford University Press, 1998.

Kehoe, D. P. *Investment, Profit, and Tenancy: The Jurists and the Roman Agrarian Economy*. Ann Arbor: University of Michigan Press, 1997.

Kehoe, D. P. *Law and the Rural Economy in the Roman Empire*. Ann Arbor: University of Michigan Press, 2007.

Kehoe, D. P. "Roman-Law Influence on Louisiana's Landlord-Tenant Law: The Question of Risk in Agriculture." *Tulane Law Review* 70.4 (1996): 1053–68.

Klein, P. G. "New Institutional Economics." In *Encyclopedia of Law and Economics*, ed. B. Bouckaert and G. De Geest, 1:456–89. Cheltenham, UK: Edward Elgar, 2000.

Lo Cascio, E. "Forme dell'economia imperiale." In *Storia di Roma*, ed. A. Schiavone, 2.2:313–65. Turin: G. Einaudi, 1991.

Lo Cascio, E., ed. *Terre, proprietari e contadini dell'impero romano: Dall'affitto agrario al colonato tardoantico.* Rome: La Nuova Italia Scientifica, 1997.

Macneil, I. R. "Contracts: Adjustment of Long-Term Economic Relations under Classical, Neoclassical, and Relational Contract Law." *Northwestern University Law Review* 72.6 (1978): 854–905.

Macneil, I. R. "The Many Futures of Contracts." *Southern California Law Review* 47.3 (1974): 691–816.

Medema, S. G., and R. O. Zerbe, Jr. "The Coase Theorem." In *Encyclopedia of Law and Economics,* ed. B. Bouckaert and G. De Geest, 1:836–92. Cheltenham, UK: Edward Elgar, 2000.

Mercuro, N., and S. G. Medema. *Economics and the Law: From Posner to Post-Modernism.* Princeton, NJ: Princeton University Press, 1997.

Mnookin, R. H., and L. Kornhauser. "Bargaining in the Shadow of the Law: The Case of Divorce." *Yale Law Journal* 88 (1979): 950–97.

Morley, N. "The Early Roman Empire: Distribution." In *The Cambridge Economic History of the Greco-Roman World,* ed. W. Scheidel, I. Morris, and R. Saller, 570–91. Cambridge: Cambridge University Press, 2007.

Mouritsen, H. *The Freedman in the Roman World.* Cambridge: Cambridge University Press, 2011.

Nörr, D. "Zur Reskriptenpraxis in der hohen Prinzipatszeit." *Zeitschrift der Savigny-Stiftung für Rechtsgeschichte (Romanistiche Abteilung)* 98 (1981): 1–46.

North, D. C. *Institutions, Institutional Change, and Economic Performance.* Cambridge: Cambridge University Press, 1990.

Ogilvie, S. "'Whatever Is, Is Right'? Economic Institutions in Pre-Industrial Europe." *Economic History Review* 60.4 (2007): 649–84.

Peachin, M. *Iudex vice Caesaris: Deputy Emperors and the Administration of Justice during the Principate.* Heidelberger Althistorische und Epigraphische Beiträge 21. Stuttgart: F. Steiner, 1996.

Plescia, J. "The Development of Agency in Roman Law." *Labeo* 30 (1984): 171–90.

Posner, R. A., and A. M. Rosenfield. "Impossibility and Related Doctrines in Contract Law: An Economic Analysis." *Journal of Legal Studies* 6 (1977): 813–18. Excerpted in *Foundations of the Economic Approach to Law,* ed. A. W. Katz, 227–36 (New York: Oxford University Press, 1998).

Rathbone, D. *Economic Rationalism and Rural Society in Third-Century A.D. Egypt: The Heroninos Archive and the Appianus Estate.* Cambridge: Cambridge University Press, 1991.

Roth, U. *Thinking Tools: Agricultural Slavery between Evidence and Models.* Bulletin of the Institute of Classical Studies Supplement 92. London: University of London, 2007.

Rutherford, M. *Institutions in Economics: The Old and the New Institutionalism.* Cambridge: Cambridge University Press, 1994.

Scheidel, W., I. Morris, and R. Saller, eds. *The Cambridge Economic History of the Greco-Roman World.* Cambridge: Cambridge University Press, 2007.

Schwartz, A. "Relational Contracts in the Courts: An Analysis of Incomplete Agreements and Judicial Strategies." *Journal of Legal Studies* 21 (1992): 271–318.

Simon, H. *Reason in Human Affairs.* Stanford: Stanford University Press, 1983.

Temin, P. "Financial Intermediation in the Early Roman Empire." *Journal of Economic History* 64.3 (2004): 705–33.

Verboven, K. *The Economy of Friends: Economic Aspects of* Amicitia *and Patronage in the Late Republic.* Collection Latomus 269. Brussels: Editions Latomus, 2002.

Williamson, O. E. *The Economic Institutions of Capitalism: Firms, Markets, Relational Contracting.* New York: Free Press, 1985.

Wilson, A. "Machines, Power, and the Ancient Economy." *Journal of Roman Studies* 92 (2002): 1–32.

Zelener, Y. "Smallpox and the Disintegration of the Roman Economy after 165 AD." PhD diss., Columbia University, 2003.

Zimmermann, R. *The Law of Obligations: Roman Foundations of the Civilian Tradition.* Cape Town: Juta, 1990.

CHAPTER 9

*Gender and the Roman Law of Obligations**

NIKOLAUS BENKE

Framework of This Chapter

The topic of gender and the Roman law of obligations requires exploring the relationship of two normative systems: gender consists of normative constructions, and so does law. The two normative systems are closely interrelated; one reflects and influences the other. This chapter analyzes legal cases and provisions within the framework of gender constructions in ancient Rome.

On Gender as a Means of Structuring Society

Gender is understood as the set of rules that makes us perceive a person as a woman or as a man and that makes us assume that certain qualities are feminine whereas others are masculine. The genders are rooted in what we call the male sex and the female sex, but they are not confined to the biology of the sexes.[1] This becomes obvious when a person deviates from what is considered

---

* I would like to express my deep gratitude to Tom McGinn for inviting me to the 2008 conference on Roman law held at the American Academy in Rome, for being a wonderful host, and for effecting the publication of our papers in this volume. My special thanks go to Margaretha Debrunner, Viktor Falschlehner, Birgit Forgó-Feldner, Verena Halbwachs, Elisabeth Holzleithner, Philipp Klausberger, and Peter Steindl, who contributed substantially to this essay. A few exemplary sources are mentioned in the main text. A selection of other relevant sources and translations can be found in the appendix at the end of this chapter.

1. Academia fosters a lively debate on the meanings and the relationship of gender and sex. This is not the place to enter that debate. A quite instructive (although simplifying) sketch of the meanings of sex and gender can be found on the website of the World Health Organization, http://www.who.int/gender/whatisgender/en/index.html.

a "regular" man or a "regular" woman—either in physical terms (e.g., due to a disorder of sexual differentiation)[2] or in performative terms (e.g., being transgender[3] or homosexual).[4]

There are various cultural techniques available to structure society.[5] One way of structuring consists in creating classes and class differences—social classes and/or legal classes.[6] Another way of structuring society consists in creating gender and gender differences.[7] Like class, gender positions a person in society and thus directs or determines to what extent the individual will enjoy freedom, power, and equality.

In modern gender studies, the so-called intersectional approach has

---

2. Roman law provides that a hermaphrodite be classified as a man or as a woman according to the majority of physical features indicating male or female sex. See Ulp. (1 *ad Sabinum*) *D.* 1.5.10 (see appendix).
3. Three definitions of transgender are offered at the website of the Transgender Education Network of Texas, https://transtexas.org/index.php?option=com_content&view=article&id=46&Itemid=56>&view=article&id=46&Itemid=56: "Transgender Education Network of Texas defines the term transgender as a community of people whose gender identity, expression or behavior is different from those typically associated with their assigned sex at birth, including but not limited to transsexuals, crossdressers, androgynous people, genderqueers, and gender non conforming people. Transgender does not imply any specific form of sexual orientation; transgender people may identify as heterosexual, homosexual, bisexual, pansexual, polysexual, or asexual."
4. See the "deviation" issue in the famous criminalization of male homosexuality by Constantius and Constans at *CTh.* 9.7.3 (342). According to these emperors, the conjunction of a man with a man creates a situation in which the (male) sex has lost its stance (*ubi sexus perdidit locum*), in which emerges an outrage that there is no benefit to know (*ubi scelus est id, quod non proficit, scire*), in which Venus changes to another form (*ubi Venus mutatur in alteram formam*) in which love is sought after but does not appear (*ubi amor quaeritur, nec videtur*).
5. For example, age can be used as a criterion of inclusion and exclusion. In the recent past, discrimination on the grounds of age has become an issue. Since 2000, the directive 2000/78/EG forbids (among other things) discrimination on the grounds of age in the European Union. See, for example, a recent decision of the European Court of Justice: ECJ 19.01.2010 C-555/07 Seda Kücükdeveci v Swedex GmbH & Co. KG.
6. For example, when it comes to sanctions, Roman criminal law often makes a distinction between *humiliores* and *honestiores;* see, for example, Paul. (5 *sententiarum*) *D.* 48.19.38.3 (see appendix).
7. Originally, Roman women were generally entitled to *postulare*—making applications before a magistrate—but according to Ulpian, a shameless person called Carfania kept the magistrate frivolously on the run, and therefore women were excluded from *postulare* for others. Similarly excluded were men who practiced passive homosexual intercourse—*qui corpore suo muliebria passus est* (Ulp. [6 *ad edictum*] *D.* 3.1.1.5–6 [see appendix]). See Benke, "Women in the Courts" (1995) 203–12, 244–50.

become prominent.[8] The intersectional approach combines exploring gender with exploring other features that might be used to marginalize a person—such as ethnic origin or class. As far as Roman antiquity is concerned, a substantial difference should be kept in mind. Like the present, Roman antiquity shows class and gender intertwined in manifold ways[9]—whereas ethnic origin was a category of much less significance than it has become in modern times.[10]

Identifying Equality and Domination

The structuring of society is a phenomenon we can observe in history as well as in the present.[11] Yet, to accept that societies need to be structured says nothing

---

8. The intersectional approach puts the aspect of gender in perspective with other aspects possibly used for discrimination—such as race and religion—and investigates the impact and the interrelationship of such various aspects relevant in different settings. See, for example, Shields, "Gender" (2008).
9. If a reputable woman ignored the Roman rules of *pudicitia*—the code of women's sexual conduct—she would suffer significant loss of social and legal standing. McGinn (*Prostitution, Sexuality, and the Law* [1998] 156–57) explains, "As part of the established penalty, a woman convicted of adultery was to be publicly humiliated through open identification as a prostitute. This was mainly achieved by stipulating that the *adultera damnata* should wear the toga, which heretofore only prostitutes among women had been accustomed to wear." See also Höbenreich and Rizzelli, *Scylla* (2003) 236–39. The relationship of a freeborn (unmarried) woman with a slave was felt to be such a disgrace that the *senatusconsultum Claudianum* provided for legal sanctions: the woman was requested to terminate the relationship; if she went on, she herself would become a slave of her lover's *dominus* (see Gaius 1.91, 160). If a (reputable) woman was harassed, the law would diminish her protection for sexual harassment—*adtemptata pudicitia*—in case she was not dressed like a reputable woman (Ulp. [77 *ad edictum*] *D.* 47.10.15.15). See the discussion later in this chapter.
10. This is noted, for example, by Thompson in *Romans and Blacks* (1989) 157: " . . . Roman attitudes towards *Aethiopes,* even at their most negative, have nothing to do with the familiar modern phenomenon of *race* and are of a kind very different from those commonly described by social scientists by the terms 'racist,' 'racial prejudice,' 'color prejudice,' and 'racism'" (157); "The structures of society carried no inherent prejudice against blacks qua blacks . . ." (162); "In any case, blacks who were humble folks suffered, *qua* humble folk, the various privations of humble folk in a society structured on the premise of inequality of rank and class . . . Equally, well-to-do blacks lived lives characteristic of the well-to-do generally" (163). The work of Frank Snowden on this subject (*Blacks in Antiquity* [1970] and *Before Color Prejudice* [1983]) remains fundamental. See, more recently and with different perspectives, Isaac, *Invention of Racism* (2004); Eliav-Feldon, *Origins of Racism* (2009).
11. Radically refusing societal distinctions has never been an option. Individual and collective identities require a discourse of differences and definitions. At the same time, a concept of a society and its individuals that is carried by enough consensus requires a profound culture of

about the question of justification and hence legitimacy: what makes one differentiation legitimate and another differentiation discriminating?

Any scholarly answer to this question requires considering a number of conditions. These conditions depend on the respective historical setting. When exploring a situation in history, one has to ascertain the historical criteria in those days that produced the legitimacy of such differentiations in those days—and to examine whether the criteria were applied in a consistent way.[12]

Referring to historical concepts of difference, legitimacy, and equality does not, however, prohibit our assessment that some societal designs achieved gender equality[13] whereas others supported an illegitimate gender bias. In the light of a society's concepts of liberty and equality, a problematic gender imbalance appears as soon as one gender employs the other gender for its purposes, thus denying the other gender the status of liberty that it claims for itself.[14] As a rule, such hegemonic practice will lack legitimacy.

A most common technique to establish domination is that of excluding people from the societal discourse that is relevant for holding power. The dominant gender usually effectuates this by isolating and silencing the other gender.[15] Isolating means keeping people (physically) out of certain places; silencing means

---

justice. Justice and social peace largely depend on the people's belief that the distinctions are well founded, adequate, and fair.

12. It would be an unhistorical approach to apply today's criteria of gender equality to the cultural settings of Roman antiquity. Still, there were distinct concepts of liberty and equality in those days. That becomes most obvious in the debate on the status of slavery. Scholars subscribe to historical methods by exploring how the gender differences complied with those concepts of liberty and equality. See, for example, the definitions of liberty and slavery given by the Roman jurist Florentinus and his critical remark that slavery is *contra naturam* (Florentinus [9 *institutionum*] *D.* 1.5.4 pr.–1 [see appendix]). Of particular interest, not surprisingly, are statements that criticize gender differences, as in Pap. (31 *quaestionum*) *D.* 1.5.9: *In multis iuris nostri articulis deterior est condicio feminarum quam masculorum* (There are many points in our law in which the condition of females is worse than that of males). See, among others, the critical remarks at Cicero *De re publica* 3.10.17 and Gaius 1.190 (see appendix). A representative evaluation of Rome's gender scenarios is not easy to achieve, since the Roman literary documents were almost exclusively produced by men.
13. Since the formal legal rules of equality proved insufficient to overcome "glass ceilings" and other structural obstacles to substantial gender equality, 20th-century gender politics developed concepts of affirmative action.
14. Two aspects to illustrate this: First, traditionally, housework and looking after family members are mostly women's domain and done as unpaid labor. Second, to perform domination, Roman patriarchs repeatedly alleged that women were weak—*infirmitas* or *imbecillitas sexus* or *levitas animi*. See *infra* nn. 40–41, 46, 49, 70.
15. See Benke, "Women in the Courts" (1995) 210–11.

denying people opportunity to express themselves either with significance or at all.[16] Thus repression curtails the life options of the dominated. In its most aggressive guise, domination can even turn to eradicating the members of the other gender.[17]

On the Gender Scenario in Roman Antiquity and the Role of the Law as Regards Gender

Under the heading "Gender and the Roman Law of Obligations," one might compose a long catalog of legal texts showing women as creditors or debtors. However, such a catalog would not be rewarding in the limited space of this essay. So I will take another approach. In accordance with the preceding observations on gender differences, legitimacy, and equality, I am going to pursue three questions. First, in what way was the Roman law of obligations gender neutral? Second, in what way did the Roman law of obligations support or even effect the subordination of women?[18] Third, in what way did the Roman law of obligations empower women and thus enable them to get compensation for patriarchal drawbacks?

In the period that supplies us with the most prolific and significant legal sources—the late Republic and the Principate up to the end of the third century CE—the Roman culture of gender appears quite ambivalent.[19] On the one hand, Roman society is distinctly patriarchal. Law reflects this in addressing its restrictive regime on sexual behavior to women, not to men.[20] In addition,

---

16. See, for example, the title of Valerius Maximus 8.3: *Ne de his quidem feminis tacendum est, quas condicio naturae et verecundia stolae ut in foro et iudiciis tacerent cohibere non valuit* (We also should not be silent about those women whose natural condition and the modesty of traditional woman's dress [the *stola*] could not confine them to being silent in the forum and in court).
17. In the present, we speak of hate crimes. Gender-related hate crimes are usually directed against women and homosexual people. See, for example, http://www.humanrightsfirst.org/wp-con tent/uploads/pdf/everyday-fears-080805.pdf.
18. See supra n. 12.
19. See the instructive overview of different aspects of Roman women's lives by Cantarella in *Pandora's Daughters* (1987) 135–70. See also Benke, "Slave Infants and Dowries" (2006) 36–37.
20. See Gardner, *Women in Roman Law and Society* (1986) 117–36. According to the Augustan *lex Iulia de adulteriis coercendis,* if a reputable married woman had sex with a man other than her husband, she would have committed *adulterium* against her husband and might have been prosecuted, by her husband and possibly by others. If a married man had sex with a woman other than his wife, his own wife could not, as a rule, prosecute him. If the mistress was a prostitute or slave or otherwise of low status, no sanction would ensue; if the partner was a

women are formally excluded from suffrage, from holding office in the state, from official positions in the army, and from positions in public politics.[21] The following text lists some of those positions under the notion of *officia civilia:*

> Ulp. (1 *ad Sabinum*) *D.* 50.17.2 pr.–1: *Feminae ab omnibus officiis civilibus vel publicis remotae sunt et ideo nec iudices esse possunt nec magistratum gerere nec postulare nec pro alio intervenire nec procuratores existere.* 1. *Item impubes omnibus officiis civilibus debet abstinere.*
>
> [(Ulpian in the first book on Sabinus) pr. Women are debarred from all civic and public duties [*officia civilia vel publica*] and therefore cannot be judges [*iudices*], hold magistracies, bring legal claims for others [*postulare*], represent others in court, or make applications or intervene on behalf of another person, or act as *procuratores* [for others in lawsuits]. 1. Likewise, minor-age children must abstain from all civic duties.][22]

On the other hand, an adult Roman woman *sui iuris*—a woman became *sui iuris* when she escaped *patria potestas* and successfully avoided submission under her husband's *manus*—is able to hold property, to negotiate, to enter contracts,[23] to dispose of her property,[24] and to become liable for her tortuous

---

reputable married woman, he would commit *adulterium,* though again not *versus* his own wife but *versus* the partner's husband and family. See, for example, (Septimius) Severus et Antoninus (Caracalla) (to Cassia) *C.* 9.9.1 (197). See also McGinn, *Prostitution, Sexuality, and the Law* (1998) 144–45, 194–202; Höbenreich and Rizzelli, *Scylla* (2003) 237.

21. See Forgó-Feldner, "Zur Vermögensverwaltung von Frauen im klassischen römischen Recht" (2002). Drawing a more complete and detailed picture of the Roman legal gender landscape would require a closer look at provisions like those excluding women from adopting children (see Ulp. [5 *opinionum*] *D.* 5.2.29.3 [see appendix]), from being witnesses when testaments were established (*Tit. Ulp.* 20.7), or from making *publica accusatio* in criminal trials (Pomp. [1 *ad Sabinum*] *D.* 48.2.1; Pap. [1 *de adulteriis*] *D.* 48.2.2 pr.).

22. Trans. Frier and McGinn, *Casebook on Roman Family Law* (2004) 457. See also Paul. (17 *ad edictum*) *D.* 5.1.12.2 (see appendix).

23. For example, Claudia Diotima of *C.* 4.54.1 was the winner when selling a piece of land and negotiating a *lex commissoria,* which finally enabled her to reclaim her piece of land and keep the buyer's forfeited installments. Here, too, the purchaser was a woman: see appendix.

    Antoninus (Caracalla) (to Claudia Diotima) *C.* 4.54.1 (216): *Si ea lege praedium vendidisti, ut, nisi intra certum tempus pretium fuisset exsolutum, emptrix arras perderet et dominium ad te pertineret, fides contractus servanda est.*

    [If you sold the piece of land under the condition that, if the price was not paid on time, the buyer would lose the installments [already paid] and you would be entitled to the land, the provision of the contract must be observed.]

conduct.[25] If one compares the specific fields of private law, the rules of property and the rules of obligations largely support women's autonomy, the Roman law of succession handicaps women in some respects,[26] and the law of persons creates significant differences in status based on gender.

At this point, a few remarks on the legal statuses effected by *patria potestas, manus,* and *tutela mulieris* seem expedient.

Patria potestas profoundly determined the nucleus of the Roman society, the *familia.*[27] The *pater familias* enjoyed full legal capacity,[28] whereas any person under his *potestas—personae alieni iuris*—had legal capacity only in a limited range.[29] In particular, the *personae alieni iuris* were not able to own property.[30] They could establish valid contracts, but the property conveyed by the other party to the contract was only able to be acquired for the *pater familias.*[31] At the

24. See, for example, Halbwachs, "Ipsae sibi negotia tractant" (1999); Benke, "Aemilia Pudentilla" (2005).

25. See, for example, the liability of the midwife whose patient died on consuming a *medicamentum* the midwife had prepared or even administered personally (Ulp. [18 *ad edictum*] *D.* 9.2.9 pr.). A free person who fraudulently let himself or herself be sold as a slave would be denied a trial for asserting his or her liberty, as noted in Paul (51 *ad edictum*) *D.* 40.12.15: *id est sive virilis sexus sive feminini sit, dummodo eius aetatis sit, ut dolum capiat* (that is the case, be the person of male or female sex, if only he/she is of full age, so that he/she is capable of fraud).

26. See, for example, the *lex Voconia* (discussed later in this chapter), the formal requirements that women were supposed to observe when making a testament (Gaius 1.115a, 2.112, 2.118), the customary tendency of testaments to appoint men as heirs and women only as legatees, and the gender-biased provisions on disinheritance (Gaius 2.127–28).

27. See, for example, Ulp. (46 *ad edictum*) *D.* 50.16.195. See Gardner, *Family and* Familia *in Roman Law* (1998).

28. Gaius 1.48: " . . . *Nam quaedam personae sui iuris sunt, quaedam alieno iuri subiectae sunt* (Some people are *sui iuris* [of their own right], some *alieni iuris* [submitted to another person]).

29. For example, children under *patria potestas* needed the fathers' consent for getting married. See, for example, *Tit. Ulp.* 5.2. As to property, see *infra* nn. 30–31.

30. Gaius 2.87: . . . *ipse enim, qui in potestate nostra est, nihil suum habere potest* . . . (. . . someone who is in our *potestas* can own nothing by himself . . .). See also Gaius 2.96. As an exception, *peculium castrense* enabled a *filius familias* to enjoy an owner-like position as regards the *peculium* property that he acquired from or during his military service (see *D.* 49.17). In addition, a *filius familias* was able to hold public office; see, for example, Pomponius (16 *ad Quintum Mucium*) *D.* 1.6.9: *Filius familias in publicis causis loco patris familias habetur, veluti ut magistratum gerat, ut tutor detur* (In public affairs the *filius familias* is regarded as in the place of a *pater familias,* so that he, for example, holds magistracy or is appointed *tutor*).

31. Gaius 1.55: *Item in potestate nostra sunt liberi nostri, quos iustis nuptiis procreavimus* . . . (Likewise in our *potestas* are our children who we have procreated in legitimate matrimony . . .). Gaius 1.52: . . . *quodcumque per servum adquiritur, id domino adquiritur* (. . . any acquisition through a slave is made for the *dominus*). Gaius 2.86: *Adquiritur autem nobis non solum per*

same time, the *pater familias* was liable in delict for the wrongful conduct of his family members, including his slaves,[32] and was, under certain conditions, also liable for the contractual debts of those persons.[33] On the whole, *patria potestas* made the *pater familias* the superior and agent of his family. The very essence of *patria potestas* is expressed in the father's *ius vitae necisque*—the right to decide over the life and death of his family members.[34]

The disempowerment to which women were submitted when they were under *patria potestas* or even slaves seems balanced by the fact that men likewise might be subject to *patria potestas*[35] or slavery.[36] Yet a gender difference was produced by the institution of *manus*[37]—the legal power a husband might possess over his wife. A wife in her husband's *manus* stood *filiae loco,* a position like that of her husband's legitimate daughter.[38] *Manus,* however, seems not to have been a regular implication of marriage from the end of the Republic onward.[39]

The same holds true for what followed the *patria potestas* and *manus* in a woman's life, namely, the *tutela mulieris.*[40] According to the Roman jurist

---

nosmet ipsos, sed etiam per eos, quos in potestate manu mancipiove habemus . . . (We can make acquisitions for us not only by ourselves but also by those whom we have in our *potestas* or in our *manus* or in our *mancipium* . . .).

32. As a rule, the *pater familias* could either pay damages or surrender the perpetrator to the wronged person—*noxae deditio.* See Gaius 4.75; *D.* 9.4. *Noxae deditio* would not have been an option if the *pater familias* knew about the act and could have prevented it or if he instigated it. The same would apply to a *dominus* or a *domina* if his or her slave committed a delict. See Ulp. (18 *ad edictum*) *D.* 9.4.2; Paul. (3 *ad edictum*) *D.* 9.4.4 pr.
33. See *D.* 14.1, 14.3, 15.1–4; *C.* 4.25.
34. See, for example, Gaius 1.52.; Pap. (*libro singulari de adulteris*) *Collatio* 4.8.1.
35. See Gardner, *Women in Roman Law and Society* (1986) 5–11. Another remarkable example of Roman legal gender balance can be found in the intestacy rules of *ius civile,* which provide for equal treatment of sons and daughters under *patria potestas* (Gaius 2.156; *Pauli Sententiae* 4.8.20).
36. For the possible hardship suffered by slave mothers who could not keep their children when creditors claimed those children like cattle, see Benke, "Slave Infants and Dowries" (2006) 28–30.
37. Gaius 1.109: *Sed in potestate quidem et masculi et feminae esse solent; in manum autem feminae tantum conveniunt* (Men and women are accustomed to be in *patria potestas.* Only women, however, enter into *manus*). See also Gaius 1.118.
38. Women cannot hold *patria potestas.* This is pointedly articulated in Ulp. (46 *ad edictum*) *D.* 50.16.195.5: *Mulier autem familiae suae et caput et finis est* (But a woman is both the beginning and the end of her *familia*) (trans. Frier and McGinn, *Casebook on Roman Family Law* [2004] 19). See also Gaius (10 *ad legem Iuliam et Papiam*) *D.* 38.16.13 (see appendix).
39. See Gardner, *Women in Roman Law and Society* (1986) 11–15.
40. Gaius 1.144. See *infra* appendix.

Gaius, the law requires adult women *sui iuris* to be under *tutela mulieris.*[41] In the period we are exploring (from the first century BCE to the late third century CE), this institution was still of some legal significance, but its practical importance seems to have been increasingly marginal.[42] Women could choose to compel their *tutores*[43] and, in fact, often conducted business without involving them.[44] Thus, the regime of *tutela mulieris* had faded to a mainly symbolic existence.[45] Gaius pronounces this clearly in his famous remark *mulieres enim, quae perfectae aetatis sunt, ipsae sibi negotia tractant* (since adult women do business personally and for themselves).[46] I see no reason to disbelieve Gaius. So, as a rule, *tutela mulieris* could be neglected when a woman practiced business to acquire or to alienate property.[47]

The *tutela mulieris* worked, however, to bar women from assuming the guardianship over minors, the *tutela impuberis:* a person under guardianship lacks the capacity to be a guardian. Unless the emperor had granted her a privilege for *tutela,*[48] a Roman woman could not hold the guardianship over *impuberes*—even if the *impuberes* were her own children.[49]

This handicap demonstrates again the construction of the Roman family, which evolves around the concept of *patria potestas.* The *pater familias* is the superior and the agent of the *familia;* he is the one to administer and represent the *familia,* particularly in public.[50] Women are legally excluded from holding

41. Gaius 1.143–45 (see appendix). See also Cicero *Pro Murena* 12.27: *Mulieres omnes propter infirmitatem consilii maiores in tutorum potestate esse voluerunt* (Because of [women's] weakness of deliberation the forefathers wanted all women in the *potestas* of *tutores*).
42. See Gardner, *Women in Roman Law and Society* (1986) 14–22.
43. See Gaius 1.150–54, 190, 192.
44. From the late Republic onward, a large number of legal and nonlegal sources report women's transactions without mentioning a *tutor mulieris.* See also *supra* nn. 24, 43.
45. Contrary to *tutela impuberis,* which holds the former *tutor* liable for correct administration and rendering account, no liability is imposed on the *tutor mulieris.* Gaius 1.191 (see the following note).
46. Gaius 1.190–91 (see appendix).
47. See McGinn, *Prostitution, Sexuality, and the Law* (1998) 27, 29, 31.
48. Neratius (3 *regularum*) *D.* 26.1.18 (see appendix). See Forgó-Feldner, "Zur Vermögensverwaltung von Frauen im klassischen römischen Recht" (2006) 12–14.
49. See Gaius (12 *ad edictum provinciale*) *D.* 26.1.16 pr.: *Tutela plerumque virile officium est* (Tutelage is generally a male duty [*virile officium*]) (trans. Frier and McGinn, *Casebook on Roman Family Law* [2004] 461). See Alexander (Severus) (to Otacilia) *C.* 5.35.1 (224) (see appendix). See Forgó-Feldner, "Zur Vermögensverwaltung von Frauen im klassischen römischen Recht" (2006) 12–14.
50. See *supra* nn. 27–34.

patria potestas.[51] Consequently, *tutela impuberis,* which substitutes for *patria potestas* in many respects, cannot be held by a woman.[52]

Corresponding with their *status familiae*—being a *filia familias* or an *uxor in manu* and even when *sui iuris* under *tutela mulieris*—Roman women were prevented from representing others.[53] This exerted a strong petrifying impact. Representation is a key element for autonomy and subordination. Being incapable of acting for others constitutes and preserves isolation; it is an efficient obstacle to gaining power in the societal network and thus enhancing one's social standing in the community. In that respect, women's exclusion from *tutela* highly resembles the regimes of the *Senatusconsultum Velleianum*[54] and the *lex Voconia.*[55]

In What Way Was the Roman Law of Obligations Gender Neutral?

The principle of gender neutrality is distinctly expressed in Roman law: *Verbum hoc "si quis" tam masculos quam feminas complectitur* (The expression "if someone" comprises male as well as female persons).[56]

Certainly, this idea applies also to the law of obligations. However, to assess its bearing is not easy. What we can discern are two important characteristics. First, it responds to an understanding of the law that does not automatically include women.[57] That understanding must have been quite present in the Roman legal mind. This becomes obvious in repeated remarks by Gaius that a provision on which he is reporting will also apply to females.

> Gaius *Institutiones* 1.72: *Quaecumque de filio esse diximus, eadem et de filia dicta intellegemus.*

---

51. See *supra* n. 38. As a rule, women were also not able to adopt. See Ulp. (5 *opinionum*) *D.* 5.2.29.3 (see appendix).
52. For the exception by imperial privilege, see *supra* n. 48. For ways of circumventing the prohibition, see *infra* n. 98.
53. See *supra* n. 7 and the discussion later in this chapter.
54. See the discussion later in this chapter. In a certain way, the intercessionary acts for the primary debtor already when entering a *fideiussio* promise, because he puts the debtor's obligation into perspective by doing so: the creditor may choose not to address the original debtor but the *fideiussor* instead, who will then direct his claim for reimbursement against the debtor.
55. See the discussion later in this chapter.
56. Ulp. (1 *ad edictum*) *D.* 50.16.1. See Benke, "In Sola Prudentium Interpretatione" (2000) 43–45.
57. Remarkably enough, *D.* 50.16.1 does not claim a masculine expression to be gender neutral. In fact, it states that *quis,* which is a masculine as well as feminine pronoun, refers to both genders when used as a legal term and must not be reduced to the masculine. See Benke, "In Sola Prudentium Interpretatione" (2000) 44.

> [(Gaius in the first book of his *Institutes*) All what we have said about the son [*filius*], the same we will understand as said about the daughter [*filia*].][58]

An observation by Ulpian describes the understanding in a more accurate way, explicitly allowing for exceptions—*plerumque*—to the rule of gender neutrality.

> Ulp. (46 *ad edictum*) *D.* 50.16.195 pr.: *Pronuntiatio sermonis in sexu masculino ad utrumque sexum plerumque porrigitur.*

> [(Ulpian in the forty-sixth book on the Edict) The articulation of a statement using the masculine gender extends mostly to either gender.]

Second, Roman law claims to be gender neutral but falls short of gender symmetry. The masculine form is claimed to be gender neutral, whereas the opposite operation—interpreting the feminine form as comprising either gender—is utterly rejected by the Roman jurist Pomponius in *D.* 31.45 pr.[59] In the testament, *filiis meis* means not only "for my sons" but "for my children," whereas *filiabus meis* should only mean "for my daughters." This reflects the very well known cultural concept that "man" stands for "human being" and is thus general, whereas the feminine gender ranks as the "other," the "exception."

> Pomponius (8 *ad Quintum Mucium*) *D.* 31.45 pr.: *Si ita sit scriptum: 'filiabus meis centum aureos do', an et masculini generis et feminini liberis legatum videatur? nam si ita scriptum esset: 'filiis meis hosce tutores do', responsum est etiam filiabus tutores datos esse. quod non est ex contrario accipiendum, ut filiarum nomine etiam masculi contineantur: exemplo enim pessimum est feminino vocabulo etiam masculos contineri.*

> [(Pomponius in the eighth book on Quintus Mucius) If it is written, "I give a hundred *aurei* to my daughters," does the legacy appear to have been given to children of both the male and female gender? For if it had been written, "I assign these *tutores* to my *filiis*," an authoritative legal response [*responsum*] provided that the *tutores* were also assigned to the daughters. But it is not to be

58. See Ulp. (10 *ad edictum*) *D.* 3.5.3.1; Iulianus (*liber singularis de ambiguitatibus*) *D.* 32.62; Ulp. (29 *ad edictum*) *D.* 15.1.1.3; Gaius (10 *ad legem Iuliam et Papiam*) *D.* 50.16.152 (see appendix).

59. See Benke, "In Sola Prudentium Interpretatione" (2000) 45–48. On the interpretation of *liber* and *liberi*, see, for example, *Ulp.* (5 *ad edictum*) *D.* 2.4.10.5; Ulp. (71 *ad edictum*) *D.* 43.29.3.1; Ulp. (62 *ad edictum*) *D.* 50.16.56.1 (see appendix).

held applicable the other way round so as to include males under the designation of daughters. For males to be included under a word describing females would set a very bad precedent.][60]

In What Way Did the Roman Law of Obligations Support or Even Effect the Subordination of Women?

Under this heading, three legal institutions seem most significant: (1) the exclusion of women from the antique predecessor of banking business, the *officium argentarii;* (2) the *Senatusconsultum Velleianum;* and (3) the *actio iniuriarum* in case of *pudicitia ademptata.* An excursus will be devoted to the *lex Voconia,* because the statute reflects and supports the policy of the *Senatusconsultum Velleianum.*

Argentarii

The exclusion from the *officium argentarii* is reported in one text, which lacks substantial reasoning.

> Callistratus (1 *edicti monitorii*) *D.* 2.13.12: *Feminae remotae videntur ab officio argentarii, cum ea opera virilis sit.*
>
> [(Callistratus in the first book *On the Monitory Edict*) Women are held to be excluded from the position of banker (*officium argentarii*), since this is a male job [*opera virilis*].][61]

I suspect a primary reason for this holding was the goal of keeping women from the increased social standing and control that would have ensued from successful performance as a banker.[62]

Once again, however, the Roman gender scenario seems varied.[63] Prohibiting women from becoming *argentarii* did not prevent them from getting involved in another part of the financial market: two of four *rescripta* in the

60. Likewise Modestinus (9 *differentiarum*) *D.* 32.81 pr. (see appendix).

61. Trans. Frier and McGinn, *Casebook on Roman Family Law* (2004) 461. See the concept of *virile munus* in Gaius (12 *ad edictum provinciale*) *D.* 26.1.16 pr. (*supra* n. 49) and Alexander (Severus) (to Otacilia) *C.* 5.35.1 (224) (*supra* n. 49 and appendix) and that of *virile officium* in Ulp. (6 *ad edictum*) *D.* 3.1.1.5 (*supra* n. 7 and appendix).

62. See the discussions later in this chapter concerning the *SC Velleianum* and the *lex Voconia.*

63. See *supra* n. 19.

Codex Iustinianus concerning the high-risk maritime loan—*nauticum fenus*—are addressed to women.[64]

According to these sources, the *nauticum fenus* seems not to have counted as *argentarii* business. Perhaps this was due to the specific conditions and rules of maritime transport. Perhaps there was a public interest in motivating the merchants of maritime transport not to withdraw their expertise and their money. In his *Life of Claudius,* Suetonius mentions such a reason for the administration of Rome's grain supply: one of the ship managers to whom Claudius grants a privilege for good services supporting the *cura annonae* is a freedwoman.[65] Thus it seems quite likely that the women moneylenders of the *Codex* had learned the business of maritime trade as slaves and were then freed. At any rate, the *rescripta* give the sense that they knew their business very well and pursued determined strategies when appealing to the emperors concerning their disputes.[66]

> Diocletianus et Maximianus Aureliae Cosmianae *C.* 4.33.3 (286): *Cum dicas pecuniam te ea lege dedisse, ut in sacra urbe tibi restitueretur, nec incertum periculum, quod ex navigatione maris metui solet, ad te pertinuisse profitearis, non dubium est pecuniae creditae ultra licitum te usuras exigere non posse.*
>
> [(Emperors Diocletian and Maximian to Aurelia Cosmiana; 286 CE) As you say that you granted money under the condition that it shall be repaid in the holy

64. Diocletian and Maximian (to Aurelia Cosmiana) *C.* 4.33.3 (286) (after n. 66 in the text that follows); Diocletian and Maximian (to Aurelia Iuliana) *C.* 4.33.4 (see appendix). See Halbwachs, "Ipsae sibi negotia tractant" (1999) 359–62. If the recipient of a *nauticum fenus* (*D.* 22.2; *C.* 4.33) engaged in maritime transport and accidentally—that is, without his fault—suffered loss, he would be freed from his obligation to repay the loan. To balance this risk economically, the grantor was not bound to the legal limit of 12 percent interest (see, for example, Cicero *Ad Atticum* 5.21.13; *Fragmenta Vaticana* [Pap. 3 *responsorum*] 11) but could take any amount of interest agreed on with the recipient (see, for example, Diocletian and Maximian [to Scribonius Honoratus] *C.* 4.33.3).
65. The status of the person is clearly indicated by the *ius quattuor liberorum,* a position reserved for freedwomen, whereas for freeborn women the *ius trium liberorum* would be relevant, as indicated in Suet. *Claudius* 18–19: *Urbis annonaeque curam sollicitissime semper egit . . . et naves mercaturae causa fabricantibus magna commoda constituit, pro condicione cuiusque: civi, vacationem legis Papiae Poppaeae; Latino ius Quiritium, feminis ius quattuor liberorum; quae constituta hodieque servantur* (He always managed Rome's grain supply with utmost solicitude. And to the shipbuilders he granted great benefits, relating to the status of each: the citizen he exempted from the *lex Papia Poppaea,* to the *Latinus* gave the Roman citizenship, to women the *ius quattuor liberorum.* These enactments are still valid today).
66. See *supra* nn. 23, 24.

city [Rome] and that the uncertainty of the risk due to the perils of navigation has not been assumed by you, there is no doubt that you are not entitled to collect interest above the legal rate on the money loaned.]

Senatusconsultum Velleianum

The *Senatusconsultum Velleianum* provides that a woman must not engage in an *intercessio. Intercessio* means "stepping in" and denotes a transaction by which a person assumes legal responsibility for the fulfillment of another's debt.[67] This is the case when somebody stands surety mainly by giving a pledge (*pignus*) or a formal promise (*fideiussio*).[68] The security given affects the creditor, who then has better chances that his claim will be fulfilled. But it affects the debtor primarily. In case of *fideiussio*, he will not know whether the creditor will address him or the *fideiussor*.[69] If the *fideiussor* fulfills his promise, he settles the debtor's obligation. Subsequently, he will request the debtor to reimburse him.

To justify the prohibition on women's *intercessio*, the jurists resort to *imbecillitas* and *infirmitas sexus*,[70] which would require supervising them—otherwise, the *res familiaris*, the family's household and property, would be jeopardized.[71]

Taking into account that Gaius clearly rejects the point of *infirmitas sexus* as unrealistic, we must think of another reason.[72] I suspect the root lies in the idea that the Roman woman ought to be attached to one man—first her *pater familias*, then her husband[73]—and ought not to be a player in a complex social constellation, ought not to act *promiscue*.[74]

---

67. See Ulp. (29 *ad edictum*) *D.* 16.1.2.5: . . . *intercedit: suscipit enim in se alienam obligationem* . . . (. . . she intercedes in that she makes herself liable for another's obligation . . .).

68. See, for example, Ulp. (29 *ad edictum*) *D.* 16.1.8 pr.; Pap. (10 *quaestionum*) *D.* 46.1.48 pr.; Alexander (Severus) (to Torquatus) *C.* 4.29.6 pr. (228). For *C.* 4.29.6 pr., see *infra* n. 98 and appendix.

69. The creditor is not obliged to seek redress first with the original debtor but has an option—*eligere*—concerning whom he addresses for performance. See *Pauli Sententiae* 2.17.16; Antoninus (Caracalla) (to Potamo) *C.* 8.40.5 (214).

70. Ulp. (29 *ad edictum*) *D.* 16.1.2.2 (see appendix). The following fragment draws on women's *infirmitas* (Ulp. [29 *ad edictum*] *D.* 16.1.2.3). See Dixon, "*Infirmitas sexus*" (1984); Halbwachs, "Ipsae sibi negotia tractant" (1999) 349–50.

71. Paul. (30 *ad edictum*) *D.* 16.1.1.1 (see appendix).

72. *Supra* n. 46.

73. This concept is also expressed in the Roman ideal of the *mulier univira*—the woman who does not remarry after her husband's death but remains faithful to him. See McGinn, *Prostitution, Sexuality, and the Law* (1998) 74.

74. See *D.* 3.1.1.5: . . . *ne contra pudicitiam sexui congruentem alienis causis se immisceant*. . . . (*supra* n. 7).

Acting *promiscue* is likely to have been felt as contrary to the gender construction of the reputable Roman woman.[75] To put it metaphorically, *intercessio* creates a constellation that resembles adultery. The woman intercessionary is obliged to the main creditor; at the same time, she does a favor to a third person, namely, the debtor.[76] Accepting her fully as an intercessionary turns her into an eminent player in a triangle where debtor and creditor compete in pursuing different interests and where the woman may choose between different alliances.[77]

The sources on the *SC Velleianum* produce the impression that the Roman patriarchs efficiently marginalized women in the security market. At the same time, they confined the prohibition to the core of intercessionary business like *fideiussio;* they took care that women remained reliable debtors in other constellations, even if such constellations involved three people and if the woman's acting in the business implied some kind of representation. There is a repeated debate of this question, and the jurists assert constantly that a woman's liability would not be impeded by her sex.[78] Not surprisingly, the issue often arises in the field of *actiones adiecticiae qualitatis*[79]—in the field of business activities conducted mainly by a *person alieni iuris* for his or her *pater familias, dominus,* or *domina.*[80]

---

75. See Benke and Halbwachs, review of Rizzelli (2002). Remarkably enough, edicts by Augustus and Claudius, which preceded the *SC Velleianum,* forbade women to intercede for their husbands. See Ulp. (29 *ad edictum*) *D.* 16.1.2 pr. (see appendix).
76. Interestingly, the *SC Velleianum* was not regarded as rendering the woman's intercession absolutely void but had to be pleaded by way of *exceptio.* Thus the application of the *SC Velleianum* seems to have been (partly) a matter of how power was balanced between the creditor, the debtor, and the woman intercessionary. See Benke, "Why Should the Law Protect Roman Women?" (2001) 47–48, 52–53.
77. On the legal level, it is her choice to move for an *exceptio Senatusconsulti Velleiani* or to perform her *fideiussio* and require the debtor to reimburse her. See Paul. (1 *ad Neratium*) *D.* 16.1.31 (see appendix). See Benke, "Why Should the Law Protect Roman Women?" (2001) 52–55.
78. Numerous texts confirm the irrelevance of being a woman in order to be contractually liable. On the one hand, this debate seems to have derived from masculine terminology that sometimes suggested that it would not refer to women (see the discussion earlier in this chapter). On the other hand, there seems to have been a repeated debate whether business activity that resorted to some form of representation—as, for instance, the *actiones adiecticiae qualitatis*—implied *intercessio* and would therefore prevent women's liability.
79. *Supra* n. 33.
80. As regards the status of the agent, *actio institoria* and *actio exercitoria* worked even with business managers and captains who were *sui iuris* and with foreign slaves (even without *ususfructus*). *Actio de peculio, actio quod iussu,* and *actio de in rem verso* required the agent to be *alieni*

Ulp. (28 *ad edictum*) *D.* 14.3.7.1: *Parvi autem refert, quis sit institor, masculus an femina, liber an servus proprius vel alienus. item quisquis praeposuit: nam et si mulier praeposuit, competet institoria exemplo exercitoriae actionis, et si mulier sit praeposita, tenebitur etiam ipsa. sed et si filia familias sit vel ancilla praeposita, competit institoria actio.*

[(Ulpian in the twenty-eighth book on the Edict) But it is of little importance, who the *institor* [business manager] is, a man or a woman, a freeborn person or one's own slave or another's slave; likewise, who appointed [the *institor*]: for also if a woman appointed the *institor,* the *actio institoria* will lie, following the example of the *exercitoria actio;* and if a woman is appointed, she herself will also be liable. But likewise if a *filia familias* or a slave woman is appointed, the *institoria actio* lies.][81]

Excursus: *Lex Voconia*

Even if the aforementioned analogy of *intercessio* with adultery is too daring, the *promiscue* acting of an intercessionary doubtless entails networking and thus enhances social standing in a public discourse.[82] The same patriarchal strategy seems to be pursued in the *lex Voconia.* So this statute should be briefly highlighted here, although it refers to the law of succession, not the law of obligations.

The *lex Voconia* forbade the first census class—people whose property was worth one hundred thousand sesterces or more—to institute women as heiresses.[83] This looks like a policy aimed at a gender-biased property regime of the wealthiest group in Roman society. In fact, a tradition among Romanist scholars subscribes to that idea.[84]

---

iuris as to the master—hence in the master's *patria potestas, manus,* or *dominium;* they worked also with the *servus usufructuarius* and the *liber bona fide serviens* (a free person acting erroneously in the belief that he or she is a slave).

81. See, for example, Ulp. (29 *ad edictum*) *D.* 15.1.3.2; Ulp. (28 *ad edictum*) *D.* 14.1.1.16; Diocletian and Maximian (to Antigone) *C.* 4.25.4 (293) (see appendix).

82. For the analogy, see *supra* nn. 75–78. On the *lex Voconia,* see Benke, review of Weishaupt (2002).

83. Gaius 2.274 (see appendix).

84. [Quintil.] *Decl. Min.* 264, 12–13: . . . *Quid enim putas voluisse legis latorem cum hoc ius constitueret? Ne feminae nimias opes possiderent, ne potentia earum civitas premeretur* . . . . (. . . So what do you think did the legislator intend when he established this law? [He intended] that women should not have enormous fortunes in order to prevent their power from bringing pressure on the state . . .). See Benke, review of Weishaupt (2002) 498–500.

There was, however, an easy way to overcome the prohibition of the *lex Voconia*. When establishing his or her testament, a person of the first census class could choose the form of a *fideicommissum*[85] and let the woman thus receive his or her wealth whatever its extent.[86] This is a crucial point in the understanding of the *lex Voconia:* since the prohibition could be circumvented easily, the *lex Voconia* must have had another basis. As elaborated in my review on the book by Arnd Weishaupt on the *lex Voconia,*[87] I think that the issue is a possible increase of social standing. Being heir or heiress means becoming the administrator of the estate—a role not provided for the recipient of a *fideicommissum*. Being the administrator of the estate means achieving and performing a socially challenging and prestigious function, because it implies negotiating with all the people who the deceased had addressed in his testament. (In later times, this function appears often in the competence of courts, administrators, or notaries.)[88] Since the hereditary estates of the first census class were complex and of extended volume, being the administrator was all the more challenging and prestigious[89]—and it implied the chance to gain the reputation of being a prudent manager and a skillful negotiator.

Actio Iniuriarum for *Adtemptata Pudicitia*

A different perspective on our question is provided by the *actio iniuriarum* for *adtemptata pudicitia*. This law entitles a woman to sue a man because of sexual harassment.[90] One may wonder why I mention this in the section on norms that handicap women. Although devising the delict of sexual harassment is a truly remarkable achievement in legal history, this *actio iniuriarum* remains highly ambivalent as regards gender. Basically, the *actio* does not aim only at protecting women's individual integrity and agency. In substance, the remedy reflects too much of a regime that works against women's self-determination. Safeguarding the Roman value of female *pudicitia,* it represents the pointedly gender-biased code of sexual conduct. External interest in a woman's chastity appears dominant—as documented by the concept that the woman is not the

---

85. Gaius 2.274 (see appendix).

86. See Cicero on the *lex Voconia,* at *de re publica* 3.10.17: *Cur enim pecuniam non habeat mulier?* (So why should a woman not have money?).

87. See *supra* n. 82.

88. See, for example, the U.S. Uniform Probate Code, http://www.law.upenn.edu/bll/archives/ulc/upc/Final2005.htm

89. See Benke, review of Weishaupt (2002) 506–7, 510.

90. Gaius 3.220–21; Ulp. (77 *ad edictum*) *D.* 47.10.15.15–26.

only possible claimant; the others are her *pater,* her husband, or her fiancé.[91] Thus the *actio iniuriarum* seems an expression less of personal autonomy than of the restrictive sexual conduct code imposed on women.[92]

In What Way Did the Roman Law of Obligations Empower Women, So That They Could Compensate for Patriarchal Drawbacks?

Marriage and dowry—*dos*[93]—went hand in hand for the Romans. During marriage, the husband was entitled to administer the *dos* and reap its revenues. Once widowed or divorced, a Roman woman could file the *actio rei uxoriae* to recover her *dos.* Except for retentions by the divorced husband or for specifically stipulated claims in favor of the grantor,[94] the dowry then went to the woman *sui iuris.*

The *actio rei uxoriae* appears as the most important component of a woman's material autonomy. The acquisition of the *dos* by the woman is designed to cover her living expenses[95] and allows her to contemplate a new marriage.[96] One

91. Gaius 3.221; Ulp. (56 *ad edictum*) *D.* 47.10.1.2–3; Ulp. (77 *ad edictum*) *D.* 47.10.15.24; Paul. (55 *ad edictum*) *D.* 47.10.18.2.

92. The regime of female *pudicitia* subordinates women to severe external control and, at the same time, makes them liable for disobedience. This resembles very much a "double bind" situation, because the patriarchal design of womanly *pudicitia* promises some autonomy to women. Yet autonomy that lapses as soon as a strict code of external requirements is not fulfilled reveals itself as the opposite of autonomy—as domination, in fact.

93. See Gardner, *Women in Roman Law and Society* (1986) 97–114; Treggiari, *Roman Marriage* (1991) 323–64.

94. The dowry would have to be restored to a third-party giver if this person had stipulated its return (*dos recepticia, Tit. Ulp.* 6.5). On the wife's death, either the dowry either had to be restored to the deceased wife's father who granted it (*dos profecticia, Tit. Ulp.* 6.3–4, 6), or it would remain with the widower (*dos adventicia, Tit. Ulp.* 6.5, 6). On its return, the *dos* could be reduced by certain deductions in favor of the former husband, or *retentiones*—typically *propter liberos* (for maintaining the children), *propter mores* (sanctioning to the former wife's indecent conduct), *propter impensas* (for investments into the *dos* property), *propter res donatas* (for donations made by the husband to his wife, contrary to the prohibition of donations between spouses), and *propter res amotas* (for things taken away by the wife). See, for example, *Tit. Ulp.* 6.9, 10, 12.

95. This is expressed by the institute of *collatio dotis:* When determining the shares of an estate to be distributed by way of succession, a married woman's share was reduced by the amount of *dos* she had already received. See *D.* 37.7; *C.* 6.20. See Treggiari, *Roman Marriage* (1991) 350–57.

96. Paul. (60 *ad edictum*) *D.* 23.3.2 (see appendix); Pomponius (15 *ad Sabinum*) *D.* 24.3.1 (see appendix). See Treggiari, *Roman Marriage* (1991) 361–64.

may contend morally that the dowry is simply the share for what she contributes to society—being a wife and a mother. This is true, but in many societies—historically and globally speaking—that contribution is not rewarded, and women are simply put at high risk to end up in destitution.[97]

Women having access to contractual instruments such as *stipulatio*, which perfectly represent the liberal and individual Roman societal order, devise strategies against their exclusion based on gender. This is clearly documented in the field of *tutela*. Women actually administrate their children's property issues, thus arrogating substantially the business of guardianship. By promising *cautiones*, they succeed in appeasing the *tutores*. Receiving these *cautiones*, the "formal" *tutores* are sure to be indemnified for liabilities they might be exposed to under an *actio tutelae*.[98]

Conclusions

First, the Roman law of obligations is liberal, individual, and largely gender neutral.[99] In principle, a woman *sui iuris* is able to enter any contract, as a debtor as well as a creditor. She is able to effectuate her claims and become liable for her debts ensuing from such contracts. In addition, a Roman woman has in principle the same position as a Roman man in the field of delicts and unjustified enrichment.[100]

Second, where a position based on private law promises to enhance a person's social standing significantly, enabling that person to establish an influential position in a public discourse, Roman patriarchy bars women. This bias could

97. On the regimes of matrimonial property in England and Germany and the fact that women's rights under those regimes deteriorated in late medieval and early modern times, see McGinn, *Widows and Patriarchy* (2008) 56–59, 80–83. Remarkably enough, the "Rezeption" of the Roman law of dowry—*dos*—in early modern Germany did not empower women, since the German jurists interpreted the rules of dowry in a way less advantageous to women than the Roman antique original; see McGinn, *Widows and Patriarchy* (2008) 82.

98. Alexander (Severus) (to Torquatus) *C.* 4.29.6 (228) (see appendix). See Forgó-Feldner, "Zur Vermögensverwaltung von Frauen im klassischen römischen Recht" (2006) 17–19; see Chiusi, "Babatha vs. the Guardians of Her Son" (2005). For other ways that women found to involve themselves in the administration of the property of their minor-age children, see Gardner, *Family and* Familia *in Roman Law* (1998) 249–52.

99. See *supra* nn. 23–25.

100. See *supra* n. 99 and section 4.1.

explain women's exclusion from the *officium argentarii*,[101] from *intercessio*,[102] from being instituted as an heiress in the first census class (*lex Voconia*),[103] and from *tutela*.[104] As regards the reasons produced for these gender differentiations, four types can be distinguished. Some sources state the difference without offering any justification at all[105] or call it a matter of general acceptance,[106] some resort to an idea of masculine tasks or functions,[107] and some patronize women by alleging that womanly weakness would call for protection[108]—a protection that, in fact, paralyzes them.

On the whole, the Roman law of obligations appears to have been in consistent interaction with the Roman constructions of gender. On the one hand, it reflects a fundamentally patriarchal society, which is particularly male dominated in the public sphere.[109] On the other hand, women enjoy quite extended possibilities of self-expression when it comes to economic activities. Here, their agency seems equal to that of men in many respects. Yet the demarcation line is clear. Women are excluded from economic activities that could strengthen their societal presence in a way that would consequently lead to their becoming significant players in the state's politics and administration.

Bibliography

Benke, N. "Aemilia Pudentilla—a Landowning Lady." In *Ex iusta causa traditum: Essays in Honour of Eric H. Pool*, ed. R. van den Bergh, 19–31. Pretoria: Fundamina Editio specialis, 2005.

Benke, N. "In Sola Prudentium Interpretatione: Zur Methodik und Methodologie römischer Juristen." In *Norm und Entscheidung: Prolegomena zur Theorie des Falls*, ed. B. Feldner and N. Forgó, 1–85. Vienna: Springer, 2000.

Benke, N. Review of A. Weishaupt, *Die lex Voconia. Zeitschrift der Savigny-Stiftung für Rechtsgeschichte (Romanistische Abteilung)* 119 (2002): 506–10.

Benke, N. "Slave Infants and Dowries for Defrauded Creditors? Economic Sense

101. See the discussion earlier in this chapter.
102. See the discussion earlier in this chapter.
103. See the discussion earlier in this chapter.
104. See *supra* at nn. 48–52.
105. See *supra* n. 22.
106. See *supra* n. 22.
107. See *supra* n. 61.
108. See *supra* nn. 40–41, 46, 49, 70.
109. See *supra* at nn. 20–22.

Challenging Women's Fortune in *Digest* 42.8." In *Festschrift Herbert Hausmaninger,* ed. R. Gamauf, 25–40. Vienna: Manzsche Verlags- und Universitätsbuchhandlung, 2006.

Benke, N. "Why Should the Law Protect Roman Women? Some Remarks on the *Senatus Consultum Velleianum* (ca. 50 A.D.)." In *Gender and Religion in Europe: European Studies,* ed. K. Børresen, S. Cabbibo, and E. Specht, 41–56. Rome: Carocci Editore, 2001.

Benke, N. "Women in the Courts: An Old Thorn in Men's Sides." *Michigan Journal of Gender and Law* 3.1 (1995): 195–256.

Benke, N., and V. T. Halbwachs. Review of G. Rizzelli, *Le donne nell'esperienza giuridica di Roma antica. Zeitschrift der Savigny-Stiftung für Rechtsgeschichte (Romanistische Abteilung)* 119 (2002): 469–87.

Cantarella, E. *Pandora's Daughters: The Role and Status of Women in Greek and Roman Antiquity.* Trans. M. B. Fant. Baltimore: John's Hopkins University Press, 1987.

Chiusi, T. J. "Babatha vs. the Guardians of Her Son—A Struggle for Guardianship: Legal and Practical Aspects of P. Yadin 12–15, 27." In *Law in the Documents of the Judaean Desert,* ed. R. Katzoff and D. Schaps, 105–32. Leiden: Brill Academic, 2005.

Dixon, S. "*Infirmitas sexus:* Womanly Weakness in Roman Law." *Tijdschrift voor Rechtsgeschiedenis* 52 (1984): 343–71.

Eliav-Feldon, M., et al., eds. *The Origins of Racism in the West.* Cambridge: Cambridge University Press, 2009.

Forgó-Feldner, B. "Women's Exclusion from the Roman *Officium.*" Berlin: forum historiae iuris, 2002. http://www.rewi.hu-berlin.de/online/fhi/articles/pdf-files/0209feldner.pdf.

Forgó-Feldner, B. "Zur Vermögensverwaltung von Frauen im klassischen römischen Recht." In *Frauenrecht und Rechtsgeschichte: Die Rechtskämpfe der deutschen Frauenbewegung,* ed. S. Meder, A. Duncker, and A. Czelk, 1–20. Cologne: Böhlau, 2006.

Frier, B. W., and T. A. J. McGinn. *A Casebook on Roman Family Law.* New York: Oxford University Press, 2004.

Gardner, J. F. *Family and* Familia *in Roman Law and Life.* Oxford: Oxford University Press, 1998.

Gardner, J. F. *Women in Roman Law and Society.* London: Routledge, 1986.

Halbwachs, V. T. "Ipsae sibi negotia tractant: Zur Frau als Geschäftspartnerin im Spiegel römischrechtlicher Quellen." In *Atti della 51a Sessione della SIHDA, Crotone-Messina 16–20 settembre 1997,* 349–63. Soveria Mannelli: Rubbettino, 1999.

Höbenreich, E., and G. Rizzelli. *Scylla: Fragmente einer juristischen Geschichte der Frauen im antiken Rom.* Vienna: Böhlau, 2003.

Isaac, B. *The Invention of Racism in Classical Antiquity.* Princeton: Princeton University Press, 2004.

McClintock, M. "Everyday Fears: A Survey of Violent Hate Crimes in Europe and North America." September 1, 2005. http://www.humanrightsfirst.org/wp-content/uploads/pdf/everyday-fears-080805.pdf, 2005.

McGinn, T. A. J. *Prostitution, Sexuality, and the Law in Ancient Rome.* New York and Oxford: Oxford University Press, 1998.

McGinn, T. A. J. *Widows and Patriarchy: Ancient and Modern.* London: Duckworth, 2008.

Shields, S. A. "Gender: An Intersectionality Perspective," July 18, 2008. http://www.springerlink.com/content/dl8gn23l052j14w7/fulltext.pdf.

Snowden, F. M. *Before Color Prejudice: The Ancient View of Blacks.* Cambridge, MA: Harvard University Press, 1983.

Snowden, F. M. *Blacks in Antiquity: Ethiopians in the Greco-Roman Experience.* Cambridge, MA: Harvard University Press, 1970.

Thompson, L. A. *Romans and Blacks.* London: Routledge; Norman: University of Oklahoma Press, 1989.

Treggiari, S. *Roman Marriage: Iusti Coniuges from the Time of Cicero to the Time of Ulpian.* Oxford: Oxford University Press, 1991.

Appendix

C. 4.25.4 *Diocletianus et Maximianus Antigonae* (293) (n. 81)

Et si a muliere magister navis praepositus fuerit, ex contractibus eius ea exercitoria actione ad similitudinem institoriae tenetur.

[And if a *magister navis* [a captain] was appointed by a woman, she is held liable for his contracts, by way of *exercitoria actio ad similitudinem institoriae.*]

C. 4.29.6 *Alexander Torquato* (228) (nn. 68, 98)

Si mater, cum filiorum suorum gereret patrimonium, tutoribus eorum securitatem promiserit et fideiussorem praestiterit vel pignora dederit, quoniam quodammodo suum negotium gesisse videtur, senatus consulti auxilio neque ipsa neque fideiussor ab ea praestitus neque res eius pigneratae adiuvantur. 1. Sin autem tutore se excusare volente ipsa se interposuit indemnitatem ei repromittens, auxilio senatus consulti uti minime prohibetur. 2. Sin vero tutores petiit et sponte periculum suscepit, quominus teneatur, auctoritate iuris tuetur.

[When a mother, while administering the property of her children, promises security to their *tutores* and furnishes a *fideiussor* or gives pledges, neither she nor the *fideiussor* furnished by her nor her pledged item will be supported by the *senatusconsultum,* since she somehow seems to have conducted her business. 1. But if the *tutor* desired to excuse himself and she interposed herself by promising him indemnity, she will by no means be prevented from using the aid of the *senatusconsultum.* 2. If, however, she demanded *tutores* and voluntarily has assumed the risk, she by the authority of the law will be protected from becoming liable.]

C. 4.33.4 *Diocletianus et Maximianus Aureliae Iulianae* (n. 64)

Cum proponas te nauticum fenus ea condicione dedisse, ut post navigium, quod in Africam dirigi debitor adseverabat, in Salonitanorum portum nave delata fenebris pecunia tibi redderetur, ita ut navigii dumtaxat quod in Africam destinabatur periculum susceperis, perque vitium debitoris, nec loco quidem navigii servato, illicitis comparatis mercibus quae navis continebat fiscum occupasse: amissarum mercium detrimentum, quod non ex marinae tempestatis discrimine, sed ex praecipiti avaritia et incivili debitoris audacia accidisse adseveratur, adscribi tibi iuris publici ratio non permittit.

[As you bring forward that you have granted a maritime loan under the condition that after the voyage, which your debtor asserted he was about to make to Africa, the ship having anchored in the harbor of Salona, the loan would be repaid to you, so that you would only bear the risk of the voyage to Africa—and that through the fault of the debtor the course of the vessel was not directed toward the stipulated place, and, illicit goods having been purchased, the *fiscus* confiscated the cargo of the ship. The rule of public law does not permit that you end up with the loss of the goods, which, so it is asserted, was caused not by the peril of the sea storm, but by the precipitant avarice and undue boldness of the debtor.]

C. 5.35.1 *Alexander Otaciliae* (224) (nn. 49, 61)

Tutelam administrare virile munus est, et ultra sexum femineae infirmitatis tale officium est.

[To administer a tutelage is a male task, and such a responsibility is beyond the sex of womanly feebleness.]

D. 1.5.4 pr.–1 *Florentinus 9 institutionum* (n. 12)

pr. Libertas est naturalis facultas eius quod cuique facere libet, nisi si quid vi aut iure prohibetur. 1. Servitus est constitutio iuris gentium, qua quis dominio alieno contra naturam subicitur.

[pr. Freedom is one's natural power of doing what one pleases, unless it is ruled out either by coercion or by law. 1. Slavery is an institution of the *ius gentium,* whereby someone is, against nature, made subject to the ownership of another.]

D. 1.5.10 *Ulpianus 1 ad Sabinum* (n. 2)

Quaeritur: hermaphroditum cui comparamus? et magis puto eius sexus aestimandum, qui in eo praevalet.

[Question: with whom is a hermaphrodite comparable? I rather think each one should be ascribed to that sex that prevails in him [her].]

D. 2.4.10.5 *Ulpianus 5 ad edictum* (n. 59)

Liberos parentesque patroni patronaeque utriusque sexus accipere debemus.

[One must understand children and parents of patrons and patronesses as of either sex.]

D. 3.1.1.5–6 *Ulpianus 6 ad edictum* (nn. 7, 61, 74)

5. Secundo loco edictum proponitur in eos, qui pro aliis ne postulent: in quo edicto excepit praetor sexum et casum, item notavit personas in turpitudine notabiles. sexum: dum feminas prohibet pro aliis postulare. et ratio quidem prohibendi, ne contra pudicitiam sexui congruentem alienis causis se immisceant, ne virilibus officiis fungantur mulieres: origo vero introducta est a Carfania improbissima femina, quae inverecunde postulans et magistratum inquietans causam dedit edicto. . . . 6. Removet autem a postulando pro aliis et eum, qui corpore suo muliebria passus est. si quis tamen vi praedonum vel hostium stupratus est, non debet notari, ut et Pomponius ait. . . .

[5. Next comes an edict against those who are not to make application on behalf of others. In this edict the praetor debarred (them) on grounds of sex and disability. He also blacklisted exceptionally disreputable persons. On the grounds of sex, he forbids women to make applications on behalf of others. There is a reason for this prohibition, to prevent them from involving themselves in the cases of other people contrary to the modesty in keeping with their sex and to prevent women from performing male duties. Its introduction goes back to a shameless woman called Carfania who by brazenly making applications and annoying the magistrate gave rise to the edict. . . . 6. He [the praetor] excludes also that one from making applications for others who has submitted his body in the female manner. And as Pomponius says, if someone was raped by robbers or enemies, he must not be denounced. . . .]

D. 3.5.3.1 *Ulpianus 10 ad edictum* (n. 58)

Haec verba 'si quis' sic sunt accipienda 'sive quae': nam et mulieres negotiorum gestorum agere posse et conveniri non dubitatur.

[The words "if someone" must be understood as "or if a female." For there is no doubt that women can file a claim or be sued for *negotia gesta.*]

D. 5.1.12.2 *Paulus 17 ad edictum* (nn. 22, 106)

Non autem omnes iudices dari possunt ab his qui iudicis dandi ius habent: quidam enim lege impediuntur ne iudices sint, quidam natura, quidam moribus. natura, ut surdus mutus: et perpetuo furiosus et impubes, quia iudicio carent. lege impeditur, qui senatu motus est. moribus feminae et servi, non quia non habent iudicium, sed quia receptum est, ut civilibus officiis non fungantur.

[Not everybody may be appointed judge by those with the right to appoint judges. For some are prevented by statute from being judges, some by nature, and some by custom. Prevented by nature are, for example, the deaf and the mute, the permanently insane, and the *impubes,* since they lack judgment. A person expelled from the senate is prevented by statute. Women and slaves are prevented by custom, not because they lack judgment, but because it is accepted that they do not perform civic duties.]

D. 5.2.29.3 *Ulpianus 5 opinionum* (nn. 21, 51)

Quoniam femina nullum adoptare filium sine iussu principis potest, nec de inofficioso testamento eius, quam quis sibi matrem adoptivam falso esse existimabat, agere potest.

[Since a woman cannot adopt a son without *iussum* of the *princeps,* someone cannot file an action for *inofficiosum testamentum* of a person who he wrongly believed to be his adoptive mother.]

D. 14.1.1.16 *Ulpianus 28 ad edictum* (n. 81)

Parvi autem refert, qui exercet masculus sit an mulier, pater familias an filius familias vel servus: pupillus autem si navem exerceat, exigemus tutoris auctoritatem.

[But it is of little importance whether the person who manages the ship is a man or a woman, a *pater familias* or a *filius familias* or a slave. But if a minor-age child manages the ship, we require the approval of the *tutor.*]

D. 15.1.1.3 *Ulpianus 29 ad edictum* (n. 58)

De eo loquitur, non de ea: sed tamen et ob eam quae est feminini sexus dabitur ex hoc edicto actio.

["He" is mentioned, not "she." Nevertheless, on the basis of this *edictum* the *actio* is also granted because of a person of feminine sex.]

D. 15.1.3.2 *Ulpianus 29 ad edictum* (n. 81)

Parvi autem refert, servus quis masculi an mulieris fuerit: nam de peculio et mulier convenietur.

[It is of little importance whether the slave belongs to a man or a woman. For by way of *actio de peculio* also a woman will become liable.]

D. 16.1.1.1 *Paulus 30 edictum* (n. 71)

Nam sicut moribus civilia officia adempta sunt feminis et pleraque ipso iure non valent, ita multo magis adimendum eis fuit id officium, in quo non sola opera nudumque ministerium earum versaretur, sed etiam periculum rei familiaris.

[For just as by custom civic duties have been taken away from women, and most [of such activities] are invalidated by the law itself, so much the more had that office to be taken away from them in which was concerned not only their work and mere employment but even the risk of the family property.]

D. 16.1.2 pr. *Ulpianus 29 ad edictum* (n. 75)

Et primo quidem temporibus divi Augusti, mox deinde Claudii edictis eorum erat interdictum, ne feminae pro viris suis intercederent.

[And first in the reign of the deified Augustus, then in the reign of Claudius, it was forbidden through their edicts that women intercede for their husbands.]

D. 16.1.2.2 *Ulpianus 29 edictum* (n. 70)

Verba itaque senatusconsulti excutiamus prius providentia amplissimi ordinis laudata, quia opem tulit mulieribus propter sexus inbecillitatem multis huiuscemodi casibus suppositis atque obiectis.

[And so let us examine the words of the *senatusconsultum*, having first praised the foresight of the most illustrious assembly [the Senate], because it brought help to women, seduced and deceived in many cases of this kind, on account of the weakness of their sex.]

D. 16.1.31 *Paulus 1 ad Neratium* (n. 77)

Paulus: si mulier quod ex intercessione solvit nolit repetere, sed mandati agere et cavere velit de indemnitate reo, audienda est.

[Paulus: If a woman does not want to reclaim what she paid on an *intercessio*, but wants to file the *actio mandati* and provide security to the debtor as regards indemnification, she must be heard.]

D. 23.3.2 *Paulus 60 ad edictum* (n. 96)

Rei publicae interest mulieres dotes salvas habere, propter quas nubere possunt.

[It is in the public interest that women have secure dowries, owing to which they can get married.]

D. 24.3.1 *Pomponius 15 ad Sabinum* (n. 96)

Dotium causa semper et ubique praecipua est: nam et publice interest dotes mulieribus conservari, cum dotatas esse feminas ad subolem procreandam replendamque liberis civitatem maxime sit necessarium.

[The issue of dowries is paramount, always and everywhere. It is also of public interest that dowries be preserved for women, because it is utterly necessary that women have dowries to bear offspring and replenish the community with children.]

D. 26.1.18 *Neratius 3 regularum* (n. 48)

Feminae tutores dari non possunt, quia id munus masculorum est, nisi a principe filiorum tutelam specialiter postulent.

[Women cannot be appointed as *tutores* since this is a responsibility of males [*munus masculorum*], unless they specifically request the tutelage of their children from the emperor.] (trans. Frier and McGinn, *Casebook on Roman Family Law* [2004] 461)

D. 32.62 *Iulianus liber singularis de ambiguitatibus* (n. 58)

Qui duos mulos habebat ita legavit: 'Mulos duos, qui mei erunt cum moriar, heres dato': idem nullos mulos, sed duas mulas reliquerat. respondit Servius deberi legatum, quia mulorum appellatione etiam mulae continentur, quemadmodum appellatione servorum etiam servae plerumque continentur. id autem eo veniet, quod semper sexus masculinus etiam femininum sexum continet.

[A person who had two *muli* made a *legatum* as follows: "The heir should give the two *muli,* which I will own when I die." The same person left no *muli,* but two *mulae.* Servius gave the *responsum* that the *legatum* was owed, because *mulae* would be included by the term *muli.* Likewise, slave women are generally included in the term *servi.* This follows from the point, that the masculine sex always comprises the feminine sex.]

D. 32.81 pr. *Modestinus 9 differentiarum* (n. 60)

Servis legatis etiam ancillas quidam deberi recte putant, quasi commune nomen utrumque sexum contineat: ancillis vero legatis masculos non deberi nemo dubitat. sed pueris legatis etiam puellae debentur: id non aeque in puellis pueros contineri dicendum est.

[When *servi* are disposed of by way of *legatum,* some hold correctly that also the *ancillae* [slave women] are owed. But if *ancillae* are disposed of by way of *legatum,* nobody doubts that male slaves are not owed. But if *pueri* [slave boys] are disposed of by way of *legatum,* also the *puellae* [slave girls] are owed. It is not equally to be said that the *pueri* are included in the [term] *puellae.*]

D. 38.16.13 *Gaius 10 ad legem Iuliam et Papiam* (n. 38)

Nulla femina aut habet suos heredes aut desinere habere potest propter capitis deminutionem.

[No woman either has *sui heredes* or can cease having them because of a *capitis deminutio.*]

D. 43.29.3.1 *Ulpianus 71 ad edictum* (n. 59)

Haec verba 'quem liberum' ad omnem liberum pertinent, sive pubes sit sive impubes, sive masculus sive femina, sive unus sive plures, sive sui iuris sit sive alieni: hoc enim tantum spectamus, an liber sit.

[The words "the freeborn" relate to all freeborn—be they adults or minors, male or female, one or more, *sui* or *alieni iuris,* since here we look only at the point whether someone is freeborn.]

D. 48.19.38.3 *Paulus 5 sententiarum* (n. 6)

Qui nondum viripotentes virgines corrumpunt, humiliores in metallum damnantur, honestiores in insulam relegantur aut in exilium mittuntur.

[Those who corrupt immature *virgines,* if they are of low rank, are sentenced to labor in the mines; if they are of high rank, they are relegated to an island or exiled.]

D. 50.16.56.1 *Ulpianus 62 ad edictum* (n. 59)

"Liberorum" appellatione continentur non tantum qui sunt in potestate, sed omnes qui sui iuris sunt, sive virilis sive feminini sexus sunt exve feminini sexus descendentes.

[By the term *liberi* are comprised not only those who are in *potestas* but all who are *sui iuris,* of male or female sex or descendants of female sex.]

D. 50.16.152 *Gaius 10 ad legem Iuliam et Papiam* (n. 58)

"Hominis" appellatione tam feminam quam masculum contineri non dubitatur.

[It is not doubted that the term "person" comprises the woman as well as the man.]

Gaius Institutiones 1.143–45 (nn. 40, 41)

143. *Ac prius dispiciamus de his, quae in tutela sunt.* 144. *Permissum est itaque parentibus liberis, quos in potestate sua habent, testamento tutores dare; masculini quidem sexus inpuberibus, feminini autem tam inpuberis quam puberis, his quoque, cum nuptae sint. Veteres enim voluerunt feminas, etiamsi perfectae aetatis sint, propter animi levitatem in tutela esse.* 145. *Itaque si quis filio filiaeque testamento tutorem dederit et ambo ad pubertatem pervenerint, filius quidem*

desinit habere tutorem, filia vero nihilo minus in tutela permanent; tantum enim ex lege Iulia et Papia Poppaea iure liberorum tutela liberantur feminae. Loquimur autem exceptis virginibus Vestalibus, quas etiam veteres in honorem sacerdotii liberas esse voluerunt; itaque etiam lege XII tabularum cautum est.

[1.143. But first we should look at those who are in *tutela.* 144. It is allowed that fathers appoint by way of testamentary *tutores* for the children whom they have in their power [*potestas*]—for minor-age males, but for females both for minor-age children and for adults, even when they are married. For the *veteres* held that women, even when they have come of age, because of the levity of their spirit should be under *tutela.* 145. Thus, if someone appoints in his will a *tutor* for his son and for his daughter and both come of age, the son ceases having a *tutor* whereas the daughter stays in *tutela.* For only under the *lex Iulia et Papia Poppaea* are women freed from *tutela* by way of the *ius liberorum.* We mention also the exception for the Vestal Virgins, whom even the *veteres* wanted to be free in honor of their priesthood. Such is also the provision of the Twelve Tables.]

Gaius Institutiones 1.190–91 (nn. 12, 46)

190. *Feminas vero perfectae aetatis in tutela esse fere nulla pretiosa ratio suasisse videtur. Nam quae vulgo creditur, quia levitate animi plerumque decipiuntur et aequum erat eas tutorum auctoritate regi, magis speciosa videtur quam vera; mulieres enim quae perfectae aetatis sunt, ipsae sibi negotia tractant, et in quibusdam causis dicis gratia tutor interponit auctoritatem sua; saepe invitus auctor fieri a praetore cogitur. 191. Unde cum tutore nullum ex tutela iudicium mulieri datur. . . .*

[190. There is, to be sure, no very good reason for adult women being in tutelage. The reason that is commonly given, namely, that since they are frequently deceived through their weak judgment [*levitas animi*], they are rightly controlled by the authority of *tutores,* seems more specious than true, since adult women handle their business matters for themselves, and in certain situations the *tutor* grants his authorization [merely] as a matter of form. Often he is compelled by the praetor to give authorization even against his will. 191. For this reason a woman with a *tutor* has no action on tutelage . . .] (trans. Frier and McGinn *Casebook on Roman Family Law* [2004] 450).

Gaius Institutiones 2.274 (nn. 83, 85)

Item mulier, quae ab eo, qui centum milia aeris census est, per legem Voconiam heres institui non potest, tamen fideicommisso relictam sibi hereditatem capere potest.

[Likewise a woman, who under the *lex Voconia* cannot be appointed heir by a person census-listed in the category of one hundred thousand, is able nevertheless to take an inheritance [*hereditas*] that is bequeathed to her by way of *fideicommissum.*]

CHAPTER 10

*An Anthropology of Fault at Rome**

SALVO RANDAZZO

Fault and Liability in a Chain of Imputation

An anthropological and legal analysis of individual fault and its repercussions in a given social context must, without doubt, be conducted in "contextualized" terms, that is, evaluated in relation to a specific society in a given historical moment. This method is certainly as obvious as it is indispensable. In any case, on a methodological level, it is undeniable that the conceptual categories from which we depart and that tend to characterize also our emotional—well before our intellectual—approach to this issue may reflect how we perceive the idea of "fault" in its various connotations before it becomes an object of study. And this "idea" of ours is the result of complex cultural layering, reflected in the terminology used to describe the phenomenon, with consequences that inevitably end up (more or less consciously) being "decontextualizing" at the level of historical research. Nevertheless, the use of words and concepts we perceive as modern and to which we entrust the formation and exposition of our thinking about an ancient society not only cannot be avoided but, quite the contrary, if weighed against the sources, can contribute perhaps to an improved mediation between the ancient context and our modern understanding of it.

By acknowledging this and anchoring ourselves in simple observations drawn from experience, we can begin to approach the idea of an "anthropology of fault" as an expression of a connection between the individual and the

* In preparing this essay, I have intentionally maintained the discursive, colloquial tone of my talk, except for the addition of a limited number of notes. For Franca La Rosa.

social context in question—in our case, that of archaic and republican Rome—without giving up our own semantic and cultural categories of reference. Within this framework, we can attempt to proceed by tracing the connection, close and meaningful, that ties the principle of fault to that of "liability,"[1] in a conceptual pattern very well established in the common perception, so much so as to create the sense that there is liability for a given action to the degree that there is fault arising from that action. This widely accepted association should not, however, prevent us from observing how individual liability, in its conceptual expression linked to fault, assumes a multiplicity of meanings, to whose diverse possibilities legal scholars should pay particular attention.

First of all, that person who commits what is considered a "blameworthy" act—for example, the author of a crime—is certainly "liable" or "responsible": the identification of "guilty" with "liable" is a matter of common usage. Further, anyone who takes it upon himself or herself to answer, objectively and subjectively, for a broader range of violations is "liable." An example would be the case of the publisher of a newspaper, who answers for his or her own actions as well as for those of the individual editors, in a dynamic whose borderlines are not always so clear but where Italian jurisprudence has witnessed its Supreme Court of Appeals (Corte di Cassazione) basing its decisions on a conception of fault, which is not so much (or only) objective as it is subjective and direct, according to an approach shared by the Constitutional Court (Italy has two high courts, one that hears constitutional issues, the Corte Costituzionale, and another that functions as a court of last resort for other appeals, the Corte di Cassazione).

The Italian Constitutional Court, called to rule (sent. no. 3/1956) on the constitutionality of article 57, no. 1, of the Criminal Code and article 47, no. 3, of the law of February 8, 1948, regulating the press, focused its own analysis on the possibility of establishing, in the case presented to it regarding the liability of a newspaper publisher, either a standard of personal liability or a standard of vicarious liability. The court highlighted the fact that the publisher's liability "is based on the circumstance, *particular to him*, of not having observed the duties

1. "Liability" here translates the Italian word *responsabilità,* which can mean "liability, "responsibility," or both in what follows. The use of the term in this sense is, unlike the expression "responsible" (*responsabile*), rather recent. In fact, it can be traced to the end of the eighteenth century, when it takes on a technical significance only in the wake of the French Revolution. See Henriot, "Note sur la date et le sens" (1977).

of supervision and oversight to which he is held as publisher—duties which it is not necessary to set forth in detail in a legislative text, but which can be inferred from the practical context, as in this case of the newspaper publisher, a position whose characteristics, and so rights and obligations, are well defined." The level of the publisher's liability appears so pronounced as to center not so much on a standard of liability "without fault" but, rather, on a standard of liability in which his or her fault is assumed, and so the court upheld a ruling made by the Supreme Court of Appeals (the Corte di Cassazione). In fact, the Constitutional Court affirmed that "liability does not accrue through the acts of others," noting that "an authoritative holding of the Supreme Court of Appeals has affirmed that the liability of the publisher is *based on fault*."

Revisitation of the subject by the Italian legislature, as called for in the same decision and realized in a new statute (art. 1 of L. March 4, 1958, no. 127), although clarifying the liability of the newspaper publisher (and extending the principle to television—Const. C. no. 42/1977—but, it may be observed, still tolerating a serious lacuna with reference to Internet service providers, despite the implications of L. 249/1997, introduced by the Communications Regulatory Authority, and the resulting variations in court holdings on the subject) in a manner more consistent with a standard of criminal liability, has nevertheless seen the Constitutional Court essentially continue in the same direction. Most recently, with decision no. 198/1982, the court confirmed, albeit within an altered normative framework (represented by a new version of art. 57 and by the entirely new art. 57bis of the Criminal Code, both the product of L. 127/1958), the underlying principles of the 1956 decision by still requiring the publisher to respond *as personally liable,* with the basis of his or her fault being more specifically identified, pursuant to the legislative reform of 1958, in the violation of a particular rule of conduct, as prescribed precisely by the very same norm when it establishes that the publisher must "exercise over the content of the periodical under his management the oversight necessary to prevent criminal offenses being committed through publication."

At other times, even in this latter application, the concept of "liability" in the meaning that is most familiar to us, one that is connected with potential punishment, weakens as it is linked with the characterization of a prominent position within a business, for example, the "manager" of a commercial branch, a sales manager, or a public relations or human resources manager. This same holds, to give another instance, for the "person in charge" of a call center, who coordinates the activities of a group of telephone operators and who, unlike them, can authorize certain services or function as a link between customer and management and so on. In each of these scenarios, we use the term *responsible* in a sense that appears considerably broader with respect to its more specific connotation regarding a subject from whose "blameworthy" activity—however we might want to consider it—derives a consequence that is immediately vulnerable to criminal sanction.

In fact, in the cases I have set forth as generic examples, such a correlation between fault and liability does not always appear with clarity, since it is rather common that, given a possible legal case for damages deriving from bad service or an act of negligence, the "liability" technically falls on the business as a legal entity and not on the so-called responsible party. In such cases, even where his or her "fault" may be postulated, it is more likely that he or she would answer not directly to a third party but to his or her superiors on the basis of the labor contract and, ultimately, to the business for which he or she works. In such cases, therefore, a "chain of imputation" is set in motion, which, moving from the subject to whose behavior, whether characterized by commission or omission, a harmful act is connected, turns to others, often proceeding beyond the individual applicability of the act giving rise to liability, which, at least at the level of common experience, will head in the direction of resolutions as varied as the multiple situations it embraces. In these, as in so many other cases, the strength of the meaning—to a certain degree, exposed to sanction—connected to the "liability" of the agent weakens or intensifies in an impressively broad range of connotations and not even necessarily coherently with the strict link between fault and liability, to the degree that the latter also takes on the elevated sense attributed to one who is "responsible" because he or she is trustworthy,[2] mature, and worthy of occupying a certain role, such as a position of leadership in a family, in a society or, more generally, in the infinite gamut of interpersonal relations.

This commonly accepted meaning of responsibility does not always appear immediately applicable as a reference category in a more strictly legal context. From a theological perspective, for example, Karl Rahner inverts the relationship between "fault," "responsibility," and (subsequent) punishment, placing

2. Thus serving to guarantee, to a certain degree, future events. This last has a meaning that refers back to Roman law and remains present in seventeenth-century language, according to Villey, "Esquisse historique" (1977) 46.

responsibility before fault.[3] At the foundation of his view on the matter, Rahner ascribes to "responsibility" the sense of an individual's ability to discern possible behaviors and to choose among them freely. If this approach can be justified on a theological level, it does not seem immediately translatable into a generalized reading of the relationship between fault and responsibility. In truth, the role attributed to human will (and to the related "responsibility" in making choices) must necessarily be connected with that complex of effects that derive from the violation, as such, of a rule of conduct. Therefore, obedience to such a rule by those subjects bound to uphold it does not take into account the individual's ability to choose at all or to choose "with due consideration." Either we choose the approved behavior (or we abstain from the prohibited behavior) or we are "responsible," meaning, in legal terms, "liable." If we abide by the rule, we are not blameworthy; therefore, we are not liable.

Consequently, the mere fact of a violation that is accomplished and thus "certain" marks behavior as "blameworthy" and connects with it the punitive consequences already laid down. If, as in Rahner's case, we want to follow a vision theologically informed by such concepts, placing the accent on the individual's freedom of choice, this should probably be restricted to that context alone and not pushed toward a general definition of the phenomenon.[4] In this context, one has only to reflect on how this view, rigidly anchored in the freedom to determine individual behavior, cannot begin to explain (if applied to the field of law) an objective standard of liability, where the connection with freedom in determining one's own actions is manifestly problematic.[5]

The criterion of responsibility/liability is thus interwoven in very different ways with that of fault, allowing us to determine the qualities of its technical character without losing sight of the need for constant comparison with social reality and its own rules. This comparison is necessarily variable over time and iridescent, to be sure, in relation to the exact nature assumed by the object under observation, even if such observation is made in the same historical moment but in different spatial contexts.

---

3. Rahner, "Colpa-responsabilità-punizione" (1989).
4. In the context of a correspondence with those the author defines as the "material norms of the objective and universal type" (Rahner, "Colpa-responsabilità-punizione" [1989] 157).
5. On the cultural connotations of the concept of "fault" and its influence on the history of European society, see Delumeau, *Il peccato e la paura* (1987).

The Central Role of Fault in the Objective Measure of Archaic Religious Liability

In ancient societies, the specific anthropological significance of the connections that unfolded between the elements of fault (rule/violation) and its effects (liability/punishment) must be captured in the link that firmly binds rules of conduct, in the broad sense, to religion and its precepts. Religion, to follow the analysis of Emile Durkheim,[6] aims to maintain in a positive manner the normal course of life and thus to ensure for the community, tightly coalesced around its religious practice, a regularity of positive behaviors (i.e., for Durkheim, "normal" behaviors).

In this context, according to the father of modern sociology, religion takes on rational aspects, while its very ritual appears to function as a way of achieving objectives that are anything but abnormal or "magical"[7] but, rather, are held to be "natural" and therefore able to be pursued rationally. So it is that religious precept and the notion of divinity, although theoretically traceable to the same sensibility, maintain their independence from each other. Moreover, from the start, many of the rules in the Old Testament lead us to this conclusion: for example, the isolation of women during menstruation[8] or childbirth,[9] the prohibition against wearing clothing made of both hemp and linen,[10] or the many

6. Durkheim, *Les formes élémentaires* (1912/1963). On the influence of the French sociologist's work on our field(s), see Randazzo, "Emile Durkheim e gli storici" (2000).
7. So religion can perhaps be seen, in its general outlines, as the public, social, and collective expression of the relationship with the divine, whereas magic is the private, intimate, and secret aspect.
8. Lev. 15.25.
9. Lev. 12. The impure state of a woman giving birth was connected to the blood of childbirth, which placed an obstacle in the relationship between human and divine. On the level of "ritual" impurity, this state was analogous to that of menstruation and continued for forty days (eighty if the newborn was female). During this period, the woman lived in isolation, particularly in regard to religious activities, from which she was completely prohibited. At the end of this period, the woman was obliged to carry out a ritual, expiatory sacrifice, offering the priest a lamb or, if she did not have such means, a dove or a turtledove. This situation has some parallels also with the Greek world (Moulinier, *Le pur et l'impur* [1952], esp. 66) as well as with the Mesopotamian (Van der Toorn, *Sin and Sanction* [1985] 31).
10. Deut. 22.10, 11.

restrictions on food (found in almost all religions).[11] Rules such as these do not connect directly with faith in God, even though they are certainly religious. Therefore, religious precept and the notion of divinity do not seem inseparable.

Within this framework, archaic religious formalism, a prototype of legal formalism, sees in its rituals a way to achieve a result that is the ritual in and of itself, in its predetermined articulation of gesture and word, and to achieve this, moreover, without divine intervention—whether invoked or presumed—ensuring its successful function. All of this produced the effect of consolidating around ritual and its supportive system of shared practices a moral community that became a collective and political entity.[12] The fetial, in his role as *pater patratus,* was, therefore, the *publicus nuntius populi romani,* acting on a mandate from the Roman *populus,* not a divine one. The formula he pronounced on leaving Rome and preparing himself to meet the enemy at the borders is manifest proof of this point: *Audi Juppiter, audite Fines, audiat Fas. Ego sum publicus nuntius populi romani, iuste pieque venio verbisque meis fides est.*[13]

The parameters of religious practice are choral, popular, and objective and include what, as already outlined in the ancient, mysterious initiation ritual of the *in Lupercali sacra,*[14] is later described by Festus in terms of the *publica*

11. All of the major religions (except Christianity) lay down what are often rigorous prohibitions or restrictions on food. For example, devout Hindus believe that a human being, according to his or her actions in life, is reincarnated as a human or transmigrates into another living being. As a consequence, to kill and eat any animal, in which a soul resides or could reside, is considered a gravely blameworthy act. Anyone who kills a cow in particular is punished very severely. In fact, in order to leave the cycle of reincarnations and reach nirvana and perfect happiness, the soul must face a series of transmigrations, passing from demon, the lowest level, to cow, the state immediately preceding the human. For Judaism (Deut. 14.21 lists pure and impure animals, and the Hebrew sources overall provide a vast range of restrictions and prohibitions) and for Islam (Koran 2.173, 6.145, 16.115), pigs are impure animals par excellence. Pork is probably banned because it is linked to the idea of contamination and impurity, which is connected, in turn, to ancient hygienic and sanitary restrictions.
12. This also holds for microcommunities, interpreters of a subcategory of the "religious," such as the *sodalitates,* in which the element of *religio,* in the "social" and "political" sense, is a very ancient source of cohesion and a recurring basis of their own legitimacy. On these aspects, see my works on the law of organizations: "*Senatus consultum*" (1991–1992); "I *collegia tenuiorum*" (1998); "*Collegia iuvenum*" (2000); and "Per la storia del diritto" (2001/2005).
13. Liv. 1.32.6: "Hear, O Jupiter; hear, O boundaries, may divine justice hear! I am the public representative of the Roman People; I come duly and religiously commissioned; my words merit credence."
14. Varro *Lingua Latina* 5.83–86: *Luperci, quod Lupercalibus in Lupercali sacra faciunt* (*Luperci,*

sacra quae publico sumptu pro populo fiunt.[15] Here is a *populus*—namely, the Roman—so anchored in religion and its public significance that it fears foreign religions as sources of conflict with the divine, as we find in an episode in 427 BCE, recounted by Livy, in which severe drought and resulting pestilence came to be linked precisely to new sacrificial rites, *peregrina atque insolita piacula*, causing the intervention of the aediles "*ut animadverterent ne qui nisi Romani dii neu quo alio more quam patrio colerentur.*[16]

There is no god, Livy recalls, who is not Roman, no ritual except that of the homeland (*patrio*).

This is the conceptual context in which religion assumes the role of a social entity that can prohibit and punish, that can contrive the broad framework of reference that sees the sacred and the profane as converging domains, aspects of the same perceptible universe in which religion and its (by now) "institutional" organs regulate the roles and behavior of individuals. This is the cornerstone of the social dimension of Roman religion, and it is not just Roman. What comes to mind is a choral ode in *Antigone,* the most "political" story line among those that Sophocles adapted from the mythographic tradition for his tragedies. In this choral ode, the author takes on the contrast between divine and secular laws. It ends with a reference to a man who can turn sometimes to evil, sometimes to good, but who finds in the laws "of the homeland" and in "faith sworn" to the gods of his land a point of reference that orients him and differentiates him from those who, precisely because they are "without a country," turn inevitably to evil.[17] This, over a long arc of time, forms the basis for the development of Western legal thought on these themes, like the sequence

because they carry out the rituals of the *Lupercalia* during the ceremonies in honor of the god Pan).

15. Festus 284L s.v. *publica sacra:* "that are held for the people at public expense." On the text, see, most recently, Fiorentini's *Ricerche sui culti gentilizi* (1988) 106, to which I refer for the literature concerning Festus's source, identifiable as probably Capito (ibid., 106 n. 5).

16. Liv. 4.30.12–13: "[The aediles were then charged] with ensuring that none other than Roman gods were worshiped, nor by any other ritual than that of the Roman people." See also, for the obvious similarities, Liv. 5.46.2 and the story of the *sacrificia* by the Fabii, as well as, continuing the theme of cults described as *gentilicia,* the story of the *sacrificia* conducted by the Claudii, which Festus again provides (274L s.v. *propudialis porcus*). On the religious practices of the *gentes,* see Fiorentini, *Ricerche sui culti gentilizi* (1988) with literature.

17. This is the man who, according to his free choice, " . . . now he turns to wickedness, and now to virtue. If he honors the laws of the ancestors, and the oath sworn to the Gods of the Underworld, he brings honor to his land. But no land has he who, full of audacity, clings to wickedness" (Sophocles *Antigone* 3.364–71). See the 1996 trilingual version of the *Antigone* edited by Hönderlin and Lombardo Radice (1996).

of dichotomies proposed by Lévi-Strauss in the wake of Durkheim and, from a perspective more markedly political and economic in nature, by Weber in the wake of Marx.[18]

It is in this general framework of the "settling" of the phenomenon of religion that key concepts of fault and responsibility, observable as immediate consequences of the precipitation of religious rules and understood as tools of social cohesion and collective regulation, emerge and are consolidated. Religious precept and legal precept flow from the same social source and respond to the same needs: the responsibility or liability of someone who violates a rule, whether intentionally or merely through carelessness or negligence, always springs from the violation of a social order of conduct that is collective and individual at the same time and becomes an objectively observable act. We know well how the restoration of religious equilibrium violated by blameworthy behavior prompts the community in its entirety to act. The community "responds" either by physically removing the guilty party or indirectly as in sacrificial rites by which either human sacrifice or its surrogate in the form of animal sacrifice[19] serves to placate the anger of the gods, thereby reconnecting a physiological thread broken by the blameworthy act, or fault.

Fault, *this* fault, is the consequence of conduct that violates religious precept and, therefore, is blameworthy conduct for that reason alone, without requiring an investigation into an actual intention to cause harm or into the presence of simple negligence from which loss arises. Responsibility/liability is a consequence that, in its unyielding implementation, outstrips this distinction and ignores it. Imputability, from this perspective, thus becomes the flip side of a wrongful act, understood as an action contrary to the accepted rule, without drawing a distinction between religious and legal rules or, even less, between civil and criminal rules affecting the general nature of imputability.

This network of rules makes it very difficult to define the boundaries between religious fault and fault in the legal sense. This is perhaps the reason why the appearance of *culpa* in classical Roman law seems blurred, becoming clearer in its outlines only gradually up until Justinian's conception, with its distinctions among wrongful act, liability, and negligence. But, even in what is, by now, a mature legal framework, the variety of connotations we observe among the various accepted meanings of fault casts a reflection on the nature of the very concept of liability, whose conceptual configuration, broad as it is (and

18. According to Bourdieu's point of view: see "Genèse et structure" (1971).
19. Cicero *De har. resp.* 32 speaks of the *sacrificia gentilicia*, performed by senators.

which, as already mentioned, lives on in modern usage) is perhaps the result of the compression into a merely legal meaning of an assumption that derives its reason for being from an indefinite series of rules and social conduct—rules and conduct that should be read, at any rate, in their precise historical and social contexts in order to allow us to follow that "situational approach," in the terms proposed by Geoffrey MacCormack,[20] which guides us in our attempt to grasp in the archaic legal experience the application of precepts appropriate to the case in point, in the constant search for that point of equilibrium (ever challenging to locate precisely) between concrete events, "criteria," and problematic standards of liability. MacCormack does well to shed light on how the conceptual development of the notion of fault in the archaic period—disengaged from an obligatory search for a deliberate element, that is, an aspect of intentionality on which the imputability of an event to and, consequently, punishment of a notionally liable subject would depend—does not at all imply ignorance of the distinction between "intentional, careless, and accidental acts" but instead postulates it and reconnects a range of consequences to it.[21] The "situational" peculiarity of the archaic rule (therefore, one not generally applicable) lies, for MacCormack, in the absence of a body of rules in written form and is thus suited to overcoming the particularity, in a practical sense, of oral norms, linked (albeit in the light of shared and general social and legal principles) as they are to the individual case.

If MacCormack's perspective succeeds in illuminating important elements of archaic law, disengaging our evaluation of them from concepts developed only later, it seems to me, that connecting them in terms of social history to the advent of a literate society, in which writing determined the definition of detailed written rules, risks leading to a reductionist view of the complexity of archaic legal experience—understood in the syncretistic terms I believe I have identified for this period—as if this phase of antiquity were characterized by law that was still immature in the development of its rules, where "that" law was the mirror of "that" society, a faithful mirror whose reflection was a legal system tied to custom and religion in terms so narrow as to appear, precisely, "syncretistic" on the level of shared and protected values and, consequently, on the level of the legal forms and arrangements on which this protection was based.[22] The genesis of liability for fault is, therefore, bound up with the sacred-

20. MacCormack, "*Dolus, Culpa, Custodia,* and *Diligentia*" (1994).

21. MacCormack, "*Dolus, Culpa, Custodia* and *Diligentia*" (1994) 190.

22. In a different way, MacCormack's view seems isolated where, in reference to the rules dat-

religious genesis of its source and its character as social, collective, and, in the last analysis, "political" regulation. I am bound by a religious precept that is the way it is because it is a socially meaningful fact. My personal belief in the ethical validity of the precept and my adherence to prescribed forms of conduct is not taken into account, especially in the ancient world. What is taken into account is the fact in itself of the violation of a rule that is social and religious and that objectively binds all members of a community, who, for the very fact that they live in the same city or area, are bound to the religion of the community and its rules. Ethnoanthropological research has shown how all of this is very commonly found in ancient societies in which "membership" in a religion is not a free choice but obligatory and objective, just as membership in the group into which one is born is objective and highly obligatory.

What determines archaic liability is the violation or omission of archaic religious ritual, which thus constitutes behavior the opposite of an act in keeping with the ritual, therefore instrumental, by means of precise adherence to ritual formalism, to a positive outcome. This breach therefore requires that the previous equilibrium of the situation violated by the *culpa* (fault) of the wrongdoer be restored in ritually appropriate terms. Archaic Roman society employed to this end, as does every other religious community, rituals of expiation and atonement that served to solicit the favor of the gods, especially Jupiter and Quirinus, divinities predisposed to maintaining the social and political status quo of the community that had been disturbed, in its entirety, by the blameworthy act or omission. From all of this, then, derives a need for the public to witness the restoration of the equilibrium broken by the *culpa*, an itinerary of expiation and atonement that is objectively and formally visible, appreciable, and, as a result, able to effect the objective need to reestablish the collective equilibrium that has been upset. In other words, liability becomes a formal ritual restorative of the violated order, aimed at objectively healing the wound created, in a "blameworthy" manner by the act or omission in question, in the social equilibrium, in its "order," and therefore in its "system." If, then, an individual initiative reacts to

---

ing from before the Twelve Tables as well as to the Twelve Tables themselves, the scholarship seems inclined to accept a reading evidently receptive, more than to a "situational approach" of this kind, to a perspective that ends up flattening fault in terms of the intentionality of the harm caused. In this line, see Martinez Sarrión, *Las raíces romanas de la responsabilidad* (1993), on which see de los Mozos Touya, "Recensión de Ángel Martínez Sarrión" (1996). See likewise MacCormack's "Fault and Causation" (1981); and "Standards of Liability" (1985); and, for a more general perspective on classical law, his "*Culpa*" (1972).

the wrong suffered, it is precisely "the principle of fault" that, in this context, becomes the central point of reference.

To quote the words of Rudolf von Jhering in his famous 1867 essay on the *Schuldmoment,* cited here in Francesco Fusillo's useful translation,[23] it is precisely "the principle of fault that shatters this general mechanism of compensation, through which the same very direct uniqueness of the individuals involved constituted the means of establishing a community's legal system." Affirms Jhering, "the entire *Schuldmoment* [i.e., the advent of the conception of fault] reconstructs this sea change in Roman law, which more than any other, has determined the history of law throughout the world. What legal formalism simply cannot in any way embrace is precisely this discontinuity which a substantially ethical requirement introduces into the development of law, causing the concept of fault to predominate over the external contingency of the act." Jhering's words capture the essential importance of this "advent of fault" from which arose the very construction of fault that, in his view developed into, at a more advanced stage of Roman law, "the general criterion of liability in all legally-defined relationships." But more than the effects of the *Schuldmoment,* it is precisely its genesis that I think should be taken into consideration in order better to decipher the very "discontinuity" of which Jhering writes.[24]

Objective Elements of Obligation: *Culpa* in the Dialectic between *Fides* and Archaic Dutifulness

It is well known that the possibility of discerning in classical Roman law an adequately defined concept of fault (*culpa*), embracing both the intentional

23. Jehring, "Das Schuldmoment" (1867/1879). I quote from the introduction to the Italian translation of this work by Fusillo (*Il momento della colpa* [1990] xxix): "il principio della colpa che spezza questo meccanismo generale di compensazione, per il quale la stessa immediata singolarità degli individui costituiva il mezzo di realizzazione dell'ordinamento della comunità. Tutto lo Schuldmoment ricostruisce questo passaggio epocale del diritto romano, che più di ogni altro ha determinato la storia universale del diritto. Ciò che il formalismo giuridico non può in alcun modo comprendere è appunto questa discontinuità che un'istanza essenzialmente etica introduce nello sviluppo del diritto, facendo valere l'idea della colpa rispetto al momento esteriore del fatto."

24. The essay is a version of a lecture given by Jhering while dean during his last year of teaching at Giessen (familiar to us also because the municipal library holds the only surviving fragment of the *Constitutio Antoniniana*), the city from which he departed when he moved to Vienna the following year for his last four years of university teaching.

infliction of harm and negligence, has been the occasion of much doubt in the scholarship,[25] which consequently shows a great variance of opinion over its nature in contrast to the better-documented concepts of *dolus* and *custodia*. Likewise, we know that, even in the Justinianic compilation, a definition of *culpa* powerful enough to capture its unifying outlines (if they are really capable of being "captured") is lacking. Even this much stands as a result that can contain a certain significance, despite the fact that the method of the Roman jurists favors the concrete case and is certainly not prone to conceptualizations.[26]

In the generally accepted definition of *culpa* (in the sense most familiar to and used by us), the expression suggests "the specific connection between the breach of an obligation, in contractual liability, or between the emergence of the obligation (*ex delicto*), in non-contractual liability, and conduct on the part of the debtor, a specific connection which entails the liability of the debtor him- or herself."[27] By this route, we arrive at a level of abstraction such as to identify as *culpa* the simple imputability of an act of the debtor, totally emptying the expression of its connotation of intent.[28] This is a circumstance that, besides being difficult to reconstruct in historical terms, certainly stands in contrast with Justinian's system, in which, in addition to imputability, *culpa* indicates "the criterion on the basis of which such imputability is judged."[29]

But the genetic lines of *culpa* can be traced back to a moment when the injustice caused by the infliction of harm not only has significance if linked to the conduct of the actor—and, thus, to imputability in the sense (if we want to use the expression) of mere "ascribability" of the harmful occurrence to one or another specific subject—but also has significance in its own right, because of the intensely negative social valence that even a violation in the "private" sphere of obligatory relationships entails. This occurs in the context of an entirely ancillary and contingent estimation of the intention of the actor to cause the harmful act as such, while this is circumscribed by the "objective observation of the existence of a causal connection between the outward behavior of the

25. A critical examination of the various scholarly positions is not possible here. For a detailed bibliography of scholarship on the topic, see de Robertis, "Responsabilità contrattuale (1988). For that regarding wrongful acts, see Crifò, "Illecito" (1962).
26. Telling, and certainly not classical, is the division of fault into its degrees of *lata* and *levis*, then divided into three in the *Glossa accursiana* as *lata*, *levis*, and *levissima*.
27. Talamanca, "Colpa civile" (1960).
28. This comes close to linking imputability to the subject's capacity to discern, thus excluding the possibility of attributing an act and its consequences to someone who was not able to form an intent at the moment the act was committed.
29. See, precisely, Talamanca, "Colpa civile" (1960) 518.

person in question and the harmful act."[30] What emerges, then, in a perspective that moves within the generally complex categorization of fault and liability is an objective parameter that, although less visible and conspicuous than what can be identified in the sphere of criminal liability, is nevertheless deeply rooted in the community's sensibility. It is the loss *caused unjustly*, not just any loss, that prompts a reaction at law and the demand to concretize the liability of the party responsible for the act. And this, as we know, turns out to be the criterion that endures, not only when the actor is aware of the harmful effects of his or her conduct, but also when the occurrence causes, in any case, loss, even without such awareness on the part of the actor.[31]

If we accept this premise as a possibility, we can propose a reconstruction that recognizes in the archaic articulation of the relationship between the intentional and the negligent infliction of harm, as both are assimilated to the objective moral rejection of the conduct liable to punishment, the key to a *culpa* that is strictly linked to the occurrence, an integral part of an act that, as such, absorbs the subjective element on the level of a necessary redress of the state of affairs that has endured a wrong. Ultimately, the same "elasticity" of *culpa* in the sphere of contracts in classical law seems to derive from a valuation that was originally undifferentiated—I would be tempted to define it as "syncretistic"—of archaic *culpa*.[32] Such a characterization, which does not, in any case, prevent fault from assuming specific connotations in its usage in the area of criminal law and, perhaps, that of delicts,[33] is reflected in the standardized nature of fault in the law of contracts,[34] which is indissolubly linked to what Emilio Betti lucidly defines as "deviation from an objective criterion of

30. See Crifò, "Illecito" (1962) 155.

31. See esp. Ulp. *D.* 9.2.27.9, along with Paul. *D.* 9.2.31; Gaius 3.202, 211; Ulp. *Collatio* 12.7.7.

32. And thus in such a way as not to find itself focused on one or more unifying terms, a circumstance that could perhaps explain the absence of the term *culpa* in the Twelve Tables: see Luzzatto, "Colpa penale" (1960).

33. On this, see the *leges* of Numa 16 and 17 (*FIRA* 1.13–14).

34. And perhaps already in *culpa in contrahendo*, so much so that, if our approach were to gain favor, the main reference on the topic, expressed in Ulp. (25 *ad edictum*) *D.* 11.7.8.1 concerning the sale of a *locus religiosus* and developed by Modestinus (*D.* 18.1.62.1) with the more detailed terms of *loca sacra vel religiosa vel publica*, might be viewed from a perspective that allows its characteristics to be regarded as very ancient, whereas one has the impression that these cases of liability tend to be read in terms of a conceptual framework that is Justinianic (see, e.g., *Inst.* 3.23.5), if not in the light of modern perspectives. See Winkel's "*Culpa in contrahendo*" (2002) and Federico Procchi's contribution in the present volume.

social conduct."[35] From this derives the possibility of adapting a judgment to a varied range of situations treatable at law that seem to have, precisely as their common denominator, reference to the blameworthy act "in itself" as the act's specific, subjectively significant nature. This seems clear in the *iudicia stricti iuris,* in which fault is considered as the product of "an act of commission," as the "act of the debtor," and has importance as such.

But the same nature of fault, in origin undifferentiated and objective, seems to be captured, on closer scrutiny, also in the efforts of the jurists to reconcile the *diligentia debitoris* with the logical and structural particularity of each binding from which it is seen to emerge. To a certain degree, precisely the effort to "subjectivize" *culpa* in the range of possible acts of negligence on the part of the debtor brings us back to a system that, at its origins, was essentially undifferentiated. In this system, fault, starting out as a fact that was socially significant and objectively evaluated, in terms of *Erfolgshaftung,* began gradually to assume differentiated nuances, in an attempt to distinguish liability as a function of what the actor does. The first literary evidence of this complicated itinerary, whose deepest roots trace back to Greek philosophy,[36] is already in Cicero.[37] And as Mario Talamanca notes,[38] *diligentia* develops as a concept precisely in a solid relationship with *fides.*[39]

The gradual departure from archaic *fides,* a formidable tool of cohesion around the rules while at the same time a constraint on their evolution, is thus caught up with the appraisal of *diligentia,* a fact that probably, precisely in its role as an element of differentiation among the various standards of care, becomes the principle element of innovation in the system. This system reinvents the fundamental connection between *fides* and human conduct, initiating

35. Betti, *Diritto romano* (1935) 423.

36. On this point, see Foddai, "Tracce di responsabilità" (2007). For an overview of research on the relationship between Roman law and Greek philosophy, see, among other sources, Sokolowski, *Die Philosophie im Privatrecht* (1907); Stroux, "*Summum ius summa iniuria*" (1926); Stroux, "Griechische Einflüsse" (1934); Stroux, *Römische Rechtwissenschaft und Rhetorik* (1949); Georgescu, *Études de philologie juridique* (1940); Coing, "Zum Einflusse der Philosophie des Aristoteles" (1952); Wieacker, "Griechische Wurzeln des Institutionen-Systems" (1953); Viehweg, *Topik und Jurisprudenz* (1953); and the essays in *La filosofia greca* (1976). In particular, on the relationship between Stoic culture and Roman jurisprudence, see Pohlenz, *Die Stoa* (1949) 535; Frezza, review of Pohlenz, (1951).

37. Cicero *Pro Roscio Amerino* 38.111–12; Cicero *Pro Quinctio* 3.11–13.

38. Talamanca, "Colpa civile" (1960) 523.

39. For a close examination of *fides* in relation to *diligentia,* see Voci, "*Diligentia, custodia, culpa*" (1990/2007) 79.

a process that leads, by way of an acknowledgment of the various manifestations of the standard of care, to a more flexible and essentially secularized role for *fides* itself.

Conclusion

The path that lay ahead for the jurists was increasingly free of the archaic legacy of *fides,* but from that *fides* derived the inspiration for mapping out a system of secular duty that finds in Justinian[40] and in his distinction between *culpa lata* and *levis*[41] an important stage in the itinerary that medieval commentators later completed with the tripartite division of *culpa* and the elaboration of the concept of *culpa levissima.* It is an itinerary that, as it continued, came to diverge further from the threefold classification in Accursius's *Glossa ordinaria* and in Azo's *Summa*[42] and, through the intervention of the *doctores ultramontani* (primarily Jacques de Revigny) to arrive at Bartolus and his system of six *species* of *culpa.* But at this point, we find ourselves confronting a *culpa* defined, by now, in terms of the subjective element of the wrongful act, even though (and this is not an insignificant detail) it is still regarded by Pierre de Belleperche as a "deviatio a legis dispositione," with an objective nuance that recurs amid the contours of subjective variation that characterizes human behavior.[43]

Ultimately, the cornerstone of this solid link between rule and the subjective ascribability of its violation (and, at the same time, its social metaphor) can perhaps be grasped in the very nature of objective liability, a category that is certainly not religious but utterly legal in nature. Early on, it became important for the Romans, in my view, to maintain that in objectively defined liability, fault is, in some sort of way, assumed. The reading of fault, in cases of indirect or objective liability, can only be conducted in a public, collective register—the same register that includes, for example, an owner's liability for the loss caused by one of his animals, which, in such cases, functions as a mere trajec-

---

40. Justinian has three possible meanings of "fault" (*culpa*): wrongful act, responsibility, and negligence "in the general sense" (see Talamanca, "Colpa civile" [1960] 518).

41. As is well known, only Ulp. *D.* 9.2.44 pr. refers to *culpa levissima,* while the *magna culpa* mentioned by Paul. *D.* 50.16.226 can only be identified as *culpa lata,* as Talamanca ("Colpa civile" [1960] 520) correctly points out.

42. *Summa a C. depositi,* n. 27.

43. de Belleperche, *Lectura Institutionum* (1536/1972) 313.

tory for a loss that lies beyond psychological ascribability to the *dominus* and is characterized precisely as a source of objective liability, presenting itself as the prerequisite for a "compensatory ritual" that is public or, at any rate, possible to link to a valuation by a group or circle that is broader and more general than the individual who is objectively concerned. This arrangement is largely already present in the *actio de pauperie,* a remedy available to someone who has suffered loss through the behavior of an animal or through any object moved or dragged by it and that presents manifest elements of an objective nature.[44]

As a result, there is a definitive disconnect between the construction of fault—of this fault—and the idea that it can be described as "assumed" in all cases in which it is not possible to attribute it directly to the intention of the actor.[45] What comes to mind is the enormous importance that the principle of "no liability without fault"—elevated almost to the status of dogma in the late nineteenth century—has assumed especially in the American legal system,[46] which perhaps sets out a clear path in the scholarship and court decisions regarding the various torts,[47] a path that departs precisely from that rule heading off inevitably in the direction of current controversies over the "economic" reading of no liability. I trust that the historical reconstruction presented in this essay, beyond representing an attempt to offer a better reading of our past, may contribute to tempering the extremes of this perspective, by leading current thinking back onto the track of a balanced relationship between individual and liability.

---

44. The *actio de pauperie* shows characteristics of great interest that are addressed by an extensive scholarly literature. I limit myself to citing, for an initial orientation, Giangrieco Pessi, *Ricerche sull'Actio de Pauperie* (1995).
45. Maiorca, "Responsabilità" (1988) rightly speaks of "useless exaggeration."
46. Bessone, "Problemi attuali della responsabilità civile" (1989) 20. This article is particularly useful for an overview of the problems relating to liability in common-law systems.
47. The conceptual development of torts in American law, in the dialectic between torts and negligence, arises and takes shape in the context of the Industrial Revolution, assuming a markedly original character (as with, e.g., the principles of proximate cause and contributory negligence), through seeing in fault (just to take its implications for our subject) a violation of one's duties to society, according to a parameter of reasonableness, even as it displays a reluctance to develop a truly objective standard of liability. In the twentieth century, the substance of torts law views judges as its central protagonists and develops especially around the issues of liability connected with automobile traffic, a direction that winds up by promoting the development of a conception of liability without fault (i.e., no-fault liability) and the important trends (possessing great economic importance) of liability on the part of manufacturers (products liability) and of professional liability (malpractice), especially regarding doctors and hospitals, but extended also to other professionals by the courts.

Bibliography

Bessone, M. "Problemi attuali della responsabilità civile." In *La responsabilità civile nei sistemi di Common Law,* vol. 1, *Profili generali,* ed. F. Macioce, 20–32. Padua: CEDAM, 1989.

Betti, E. *Diritto romano: Parte generale.* Padua: CEDAM, 1935.

Bourdieu, P. "Genèse et structure du champ religieux." *Revue française de sociologie* 13.3 (1971): 295–334.

Coing, H. "Zum Einflusse der Philosophie des Aristoteles auf die Entwicklung der römischen Rechts." *Zeitschrift der Savigny-Stiftung (Romanistiche Abteilung)* 69 (1952): 24–59.

Crifò, G. "Illecito (diritto romano)." *Novissimo digesto italiano* 8 (1962): 15364.

de Belleperche, P. *Lectura Institutionum.* 3rd ed. In *Opera Iuridica Rariora,* ed. D. Maffei, E. Cortese, and G. Rossi, 7. Bologna: Forni Editore, 1972. Lyon: Apud heredes Simonis Vincentii, 1536).

de los Mozos Touya, J. J. "Recensión de Ángel Martínez Sarrión: Las raíces romanas de la responsabilidad por *culpa.*" *Zeitschrift der Savigny-Stiftung (Romanistiche Abteilung)* 113 (1996): 509–39.

Delumeau, J. *Il peccato e la paura: L'idea di colpa in Occidente dal XIII al XVIII secolo.* Bologna: Il Mulino, 1987.

de Robertis, F. M. "Responsabilità contrattuale (diritto romano)." *Enciclopedia del diritto* 39 (1988): 1054–60.

Durkheim, E. *Les formes élémentaires de la vie religieuse.* Paris: Alcan, 1912. Translated into Italian as *Le forme elementari della vita religiosa* Milan: Edizioni di Comunità, 1963).

Fiorentini, M. *Ricerche sui culti gentilizi.* Roma: La Sapienza Editrice, 1988.

Foddai, M. A. "Sulle tracce di responsabilità." *Diritto@Storia* 6 (2007). http://www.dirittoestoria.it/6/Monografie/Foddai-Tracce-di-responsabilit.htm

Frezza, P. Review of M. Pohlenz, *Die Stoa: Geschichte einer geistigen Bewegung. Studia et Documenta Historiae et Iuris* 17 (1951): 318–32.

Fusillo, F. *Il momento della colpa nel diritto privato romano.* Naples: Jovene Editore, 1990. Italian translation of R. von Jehring, "Das Schuldmoment."

Georgescu, V. *Études de philologie juridique et de droit romain.* Vol. 1, *Les rapports de la philologie classique et du droit romain.* Paris: Rousseau, 1940.

Giangrieco Pessi, M. V. *Ricerche sull'Actio de pauperie dalle XII tavole ad Ulpiano.* Naples: Jovene Editore, 1995.

Henriot, J. "Note sur la date et le sens de l'apparition du mot 'responsabilité.'" *Archives de philosophie du droit* 22 (1977): 59–63.

Hönderlin, F., and G. Lombardo Radice, eds. *Antigone.* Turin: Einaudi, 1996.

Jehring, R. von. "Das Schuldmoment im römischen Privatrecht." In *Vermischte Schriften juristischen Inhalts*, 155–240. Leipzig: Breitkopf und Härtel, 1879.

La filosofia greca e il diritto romano: Colloquio italo-francese dell'Accademia Nazionale dei Lincei. 2 vols. Rome: Accademia Nazionale dei Lincei, 1976–77.

Luzzatto, G. I. "Colpa penale (diritto romano)." *Enciclopedia del diritto* 7 (1960): 614–17.

MacCormack, G. "*Culpa*." *Studia et Documenta Historiae et Iuris* 38 (1972): 123–88.

MacCormack, G. "*Dolus, Culpa, Custodia,* and *Diligentia:* Criteria of Liability or Content of Obligations?" *Index* 22 (1994): 189–210.

MacCormack, G. "Fault and Causation in Early Roman Law: An Anthropological Perspective." *Revue internationale des droits de l'antiquité* 28 (1981): 97–126.

MacCormack, G. "Standards of Liability in Early Law." *Juridical Review* (1985): 166–77.

Maiorca, C. "Responsabilità (teoria generale)." *Enciclopedia del diritto* 39 (1988): 1004–40.

Martinez Sarrión, A. *Las raíces romanas de la responsabilidad por culpa*. Barcelona: Bosch, 1993.

Moulinier, L. *Le pur et l'impur dans la pensée des grecs d'Homère à Aristote*. Paris: Klincksieck, 1952.

Pohlenz, M. *Die Stoa: Geschichte einer geistigen Bewegung*. Göttingen: Vandenhoeck und Ruprecht, 1959. Translated into Italian as *La Stoa: Storia di un movimento spirituale* (Milan: Bompiani, 2005).

Rahner, K. "Colpa-responsabilità-punizione nel pensiero della teologia cattolica." In *La funzione della pena: Il commiato da Kant e da Hegel*, ed. L. Eusebi, 147–72. Milan: Giuffrè, 1989.

Randazzo, S. "*Collegia iuvenum:* Osservazioni in margine a D. 48.19.28.3." *Studia et Documenta Historiae et Iuris* 66 (2000): 201–22.

Randazzo, S. "Emile Durkheim e gli storici del diritto romano: Le radici di un'incomprensione." *Index* 28 (2000): 53–68. Reprinted in *Bollettino telematico di filosofia politica* (2001), http://bfp.sp.unipi.it/riviste/randazzo.htm.

Randazzo, S. "I *collegia tenuiorum* fra libertà di associazione e controllo senatorio." *Studia et Documenta Historiae et Iuris* 64 (1998): 229–44.

Randazzo, S. "Per la storia del diritto associativo tardoimperiale: La testimonianza di Tertulliano." *Atti dell'Accademia Romanistica Costantiniana* 15 (2005): 95–105.

Randazzo, S. "*Senatus consultum quo illicita collegia arcentur* (*D.* 47.22.1.1)." *Bullettino dell'Istituto di Diritto Romano* 94–95 (1991–92): 49–88.

Sokolowski, P. *Die Philosophie im Privatrecht*. 2 vols. Aalen: Scientia Verlag, 1959. Reprint of ed. Halle: Niemeyer, 1907.

Stroux, J. "Griechische Einflüsse auf die Entwicklung der römischen Rechtswissenschaft gegen Ende der republikanischen Zeit." In *Atti del Congresso Internazionale di Diritto Romano,* 1:113–32. Pavia: Fusi, 1934.

Stroux, J. *Römische Rechtswissenschaft und Rhetorik.* Potsdam: Stichnote, 1949.

Stroux, J. "*Summum ius summa iniuria:* Ein Kapitel aus der Geschichte der *Interpretatio iuris.*" In *Festschrift Paul Speiser-Sarasin zum 80: Geburtstag,* 115–56. Leipzig: Teubner, 1926.

Talamanca, M. "Colpa civile (diritto romano ed intermedio)." *Enciclopedia del diritto* 7 (1960): 517–34.

van der Toorn, K. *Sin and Sanction in Israel and Mesopotamia.* Assen: Van Gorcum, 1985.

Viehweg, T. *Topik und Jurisprudenz.* Munich: C. H. Beck, 1953. Translated into Italian as *Topica e giurisprudenza* (Milan: Giuffrè, 1962).

Villey, M. "Esquisse historique sur le mot responsable." *Archives de philosophie du droit* 23 (1977): 46–58.

Voci, P. "*Diligentia, custodia, culpa:* I dati fondamentali." In P. Voci, *Ultimi studi di diritto romano,* ed. R. Astolfi, 71–178. Naples: Jovene Editore, 2007. Originally published in *Studia et Documenta Historiae et Iuris* 56 (1990): 29–143.

Wieacker, F. "Griechische Wurzeln des Institutionen-Systems." *Zeitschrift der Savigny-Stiftung (Romanistische Abteilung)* 70 (1953): 103–37.

Winkel, L. "*Culpa in contrahendo* in Roman Law and in Some Modern Dutch Court Decisions." In *Viva vox iuris romani: Essays for E. Spruit,* 149–57. Amsterdam: J. C. Gieben, 2002.

CHAPTER 11

Roman Delicts and Criminal Law

Theory and Practice

COSIMO CASCIONE

A Fundamental Question

The scholar of ancient Roman law is confronted with a radical question when addressing the topic of Roman delicts and criminal law.[1] It concerns the general framework and very existence of a "Roman criminal law" as a normative system that functions (to a certain extent, independently) in order to classify and repress real-life situations considered to be socially damaging.

The radical nature of this question stems from at least two ways of viewing it. The first issue arises not just in terms of the general diachronic comparability of legal systems (thus it refers to the possibility of using our modern concept of "criminal law" to understand or a posteriori establish the Roman one) but also from a peculiar characteristic that is more relevant to this field than it would be, for example, to private law. This peculiarity derives from the existence in the history of Roman law (and thus from its persistence in Roman legal scholarship) of a significant divide in a category that today is assigned entirely to modern criminal law. The category consists both of private wrongs, which (to anticipate a simplification[2] based on a strong textual foundation and that carries a definite heuristic usefulness) we can start out by calling *delicta,* and of public wrongs (*crimina*). This division has produced a strong discontinuity discernible in the history of legal thinking. Since the Bolognese revival of Roman law, the control of criminal behaviors across different European contexts has

1. On these introductory aspects, see, for example, Humbert, "La peine en droit romain" (1991) 133–34.
2. See the discussion later in this chapter.

detached itself rather clearly from this perspective and from the procedural forms that sustain it (as had already partly occurred with the law of the late classical period onward),[3] drawing the *delicta* into penal spheres tied to the exercise of public or authoritative powers over individuals.

With regard to the many and serious challenges posed by this question, one can proceed only by selecting a few of the most relevant aspects for discussion here.

The Peculiarity of the Division between *Delicta* and *Crimina*

From the very start, the topic of Roman delicts and criminal law highlights, in line with a tradition strongly grounded in the Roman sources, these two perspectives on what has been described as "Roman criminal law." It lends immediate emphasis to the different repressive configuration of private delicts, achieved primarily through the structures of civil procedure, and to that of criminal offenses pertaining to public law, repressed since ancient times, as far as we can tell, through procedural forms describable in terms of a "public trial." These forms obviously differed greatly from one period to the next. It is then a question of evaluating in what way (and to what extent and since when) the Romans considered "legal" the exercise of truly criminal repression. I here intend the term *legal* in the sense of pertaining to the category of *ius* as consistent with that idea of rationality to which our conception of Roman law refers almost automatically and not without some measure of (over)simplification, particularly in relation to other ancient cultures.

The dichotomy just described expresses itself immediately through the alternative *delicta/crimina*. This dualism[4] represents a clear doctrinal distinc-

3. See, recently, Giglio, "Teodoro Mommsen e la repressione penale" (2006). Garofalo (*Fondamenti e svolgimenti della scienza giuridica* [2001/2005] 235–65) advances an interesting interpretation arguing for the continuity of European thinking about criminal law from the Romans onward. See also Ebert, "Mommsen und das Römische Strafrecht" (2005), esp. 55–56, 59, on some of the dynamics involved.

4. Along with the further articulation of *maleficia/flagitia/scelera*, which also takes particular details into account. For Albertario ("*Maleficium*" [1925/1936]), *maleficium* (in the classical period) corresponded to *delictum*, while according to Volterra ("*Flagitium*" [1934/1999] 269–88), *flagitium* (again in this period) denoted, in a technical sense, a moral or military offense, while *scelus* referred to the most ancient crimes (whether capable of being expiated or not): see, for example, Santalucia, *Diritto e processo penale* (1998) 6–7.

tion, emphasized during the period of radical interpolationism:[5] on the one hand, the *ius civile* generated a private penalty (it is mainly here that there comes into play the *obligatio,* the main theme of the conference on which the present volume is based); on the other hand, public penalties were a consequence of behaviors deemed by the legal system to be damaging to the most socially significant interests as identified by the community (or later by the authorities). In this system, the legal basis for penalties appears composite. On one side, there is the *ius civile,* followed by the praetor's edict; on the other is a line of development (in a certain sense, taking place within the civil law, when viewed in the context of the sources that determined its lawfulness) that embraces the ancient *mores* and successive legislation (extending from the much-debated *leges regiae,* to the Twelve Tables, and later to comitial legislation, with spikes of attempts at social control that crystallized in the laws of Sulla and, later, in the *leges Iuliae* promulgated by Julius Caesar and Augustus, when a sort of "public" criminal procedure code was devised together with consolidated acts relating to the different *crimina*).

This way of looking at the problem can be disarticulated historically and doctrinally, or rendered more detailed and nuanced in relation to particular contexts or to more closely defined periods. Along with the public repression enforced by the institutions of the *civitas* in ancient Rome, there at times coexisted, since the very beginnings of the community (actually it helped establish the community itself by entrusting the *rex* with the power to decide over conflicts among the different *gentes*), a response mechanism enacted in the civil trial for acts that we would usually consider ontologically criminal today. And the connection between "law" and "procedure," not being merely functional but structural as well, is extremely important.

Hence, one simplifies greatly (in a certain sense by bringing up to date) the frame of reference that can be found in the sources. This framework suggests both some fluidity from the very beginning (suffice it to think of *furtum* in the

---

5. On the precise division between *delictum* (= private wrong) and *crimen* (= public offense), see, above all, Albertario, "*Delictum e crimen*" (1924/1936); Volterra, "*Delinquere*" (1930/1999) 135–64. Lauria (*Contractus* [1938/1983] 636–41) was an early (and quite correct) critic of this thesis. Later, Longo also objected to it (see *Delictum e crimen* [1977] 7 n. 1 for earlier bibliography on this subject). Longo's book-length treatment, however, is seriously flawed, as well shown by the deeply critical reaction by Voci (review of Longo [1977]). Voci points out that Longo's argument is based on an editing of the texts no less drastic than that of the interpolationists who had constructed the dichotomy in such a clear way.

Twelve Tables, punished also through public intervention)[6] and the repressive mechanisms that involved the wider sphere of social control. Examples include revenge practices, vendetta (and therefore relations between social groups) as well as other forms of self-defense, the *pater familias*'s private powers over his dependents, and the punitive interventions of the censors.

The Problem in the Scholarship

The tradition of Roman law scholarship, being focused, as is well known, chiefly on private law, has usually considered private offenses (delicts) among its interests, situating them within the category of the law of obligations (as already had the ancient institutional perspective we see in, e.g., Gaius),[7] because the wrongdoing (as far as the general theory is concerned) is followed by the establishment of a relative right, articulated in the credit/debit dialectic.[8]

The work that marks the beginning of the systematic modern study of Roman criminal law, Theodor Mommsen's *Strafrecht,*[9] takes the opposite stance, incorporating private wrongdoings into the broader perspective of criminal law, though all the while keeping them conceptually distinct. The state of the scholarship in this area of Roman law was "neglected" in Mommsen's day, as has been recently and acutely remarked.[10] This state of affairs is easily explained in terms of the Pandectist school that dominated Roman law studies in nineteenth-century Germany. The Pandectists were exclusively interested, also for practical reasons, in building a private law system. Mommsen's choice of classification was not at all innocent. It had an important background, both political and ideological, that modern scholarship has not failed to investigate.[11] I would like to highlight here the premise Mommsen set as a foundation of his conception of Roman criminal law. On the one hand, the benchmark for the (re)construction of that legal experience was the idea of "moral duty";[12] on the

6. See Cascione, *Tresviri capitales* (1999) 134–36.
7. Gaius 3.88, 182, on which see the discussion later in the present chapter.
8. On this question, see the discussion later in this chapter.
9. Mommsen, *Römisches Strafrecht* (1899). For recent discussion of Mommsen's views, see, for example, Ebert, "Mommsen und das Römische Strafrecht" (2005); Liebs, "Mommsens Umgang mit den Quellen" (2005).
10. Ebert, "Mommsen und das Römische Strafrecht" (2005) 53.
11. See, at minimum, Masiello, *Mommsen e il diritto penale romano* (1995); Venturini, *Processo penale e società politica* (1996) 3–84.
12. To quote Bassanelli Sommariva, "Ricerca nel diritto criminale" (1986) 333.

other, Mommsen assumed an ahistorical "Staat"[13] that served as the guardian of public order that derived from that moral duty. As a result, on a practical level, it became necessary for Mommsen to deal with the category of private delicts together (as we have seen) with criminal law and to treat substantive law and procedure simultaneously. On a hermeneutical level, there arose the "Zwischenstellung des Strafrechts zwischen Jurisprudenz und Geschichte."[14] In fact, Mommsen's work, perhaps even because of its intended purpose (by which I mean its publication in the *Handbuch des Strafrechts* edited by the criminal law scholar Binding), favors thematic over diachronic treatment, or system over history. That is why, in doctrinal terms, the work remains flawed—which I say with all the respect due to an outstanding scholar.[15]

Beginning in the 1960s, in the wake of important developments in Roman law scholarship, Wolfgang Kunkel put himself forward as the anti-Mommsen. He dismantled Mommsen's reconstruction, both by reconnecting the criminal repression of the Twelve Tables (apart from the simplified and barely regulated forms of vendetta, particularly in cases involving the shedding of blood, as well as "high treason," *perduellio,* which was punished by public institutions) to the civil procedure (*legis actiones*)[16] and by speculating that as the population grew enormously in the midrepublican period, the praetor began to exercise a significant criminal jurisdiction together with the *tresviri capitales.* The latter (upon the praetor's mandate) established a form of criminal repression, using the summary and simplified forms of a *Polizeijustiz* against the urban poor, foreigners, and women.[17] Until the recent works of Ebert and

13. Mommsen, *Römisches Strafrecht* (1899) 3–4. It is hardly casual that Mommsen considered the *Strafrecht* to be the "completion" of his most important work dedicated to the Roman law of the state, the celebrated *Römisches Staatsrecht.* See Höbenreich, "Leopold Wenger" (1989–1990) 382–83; Liebs, "Mommsens Umgang mit den Quellen" (2005) 199 and n. 3.

14. Mommsen, *Römisches Strafrecht* (1899) vii.

15. On this point, with a telling example on the topic of homicide, see Archi, "Gli studi di diritto penale romano" (1981) 1429–30, in which Archi makes reference to Ferrini's improved, but still not entirely acceptable, reconstruction. See Ferrini, "Esposizione storica e dottrinale" (1905) 38–62.

16. For a summary, see Kunkel, *Linee di storia giuridica romana* (1973) 38–43; for discussion at greater length, Kunkel, *Entwicklung des römischen Strafverfahrens* (1962) 97–130; for a specific case, Kunkel, "Ein direktes Zeugnis" (1967/1974).

17. See Kunkel, *Entwicklung des römischen Strafverfahrens* (1962), esp. 48–51, on the jurisdiction of the praetor. For subsequent scholarship on this subject, see Cascione, *Tresviri capitales* (1999) 91 n. 24. On the *tresviri capitales,* see Kunkel, 71–79. For subsequent criticism of Kunkel's reconstructions, see Cascione, *Tresviri capitales* (1999), esp. 85–93.

Liebs,[18] these points were cited as proofs of breaches in Mommsen's carefully crafted argument. This criticism has even greater force if one considers how, for example, *furtum*, which is (correctly) labeled a "private offense," was in some cases—from the republican period onward—punished by public institutions (sometimes by the aforementioned *tresviri*).[19] This scholarly approach, in my opinion, cannot be followed by imagining the activities of the *tresviri* as a true and proper "jurisdiction,"[20] a point suggested partly by the reevaluation of some sources (and entire types of sources, such as Plautus's comedies). However, this new direction accounts for an aspect of the problem that, as the subtitle of this chapter suggests, ought not to be omitted from consideration, namely, practice—a practice involving the violent exercise of power, the interventions of the plebeian tribunes (who were selective in choosing which statuses of "delinquents" they would protect), and the weakness of the *provocatio ad populum* that cannot be understood (except by oversimplifying) as a constitutional guarantee of the citizen's *libertas*. Indeed, apart from the formal limits of the system of penalties (these included death and, later, monetary fines and physical chastisements, but not *prensio* or *ductio in carcerem*), one must take into account the practical difficulties involved in carrying them out, a fact that has, for example, encouraged some historians to consider as necessary for this purpose a concurrent action of the *tribuni plebis*.

Yet we must at this point return to Gaius's schematization, which justifies the relationship between *delicta* and *obligationes*.

Obligationes ex Delicto

The private law connection between *delictum* and *obligatio* is very clear in Gaius's famous categorization in the *Institutiones*.

> Gaius *Institutiones* 3.182: *Transeamus nunc ad obligationes, quae ex delicto nascuntur, veluti si quis furtum fecerit, bona rapuerit, damnum dederit, iniuriam commiserit.*

18. See Ebert, "Mommsen und das Römische Strafrecht" (2005); Liebs, "Mommsens Umgang mit den Quellen" (2005).
19. Cascione, *Tresviri capitales* (1999) 134–35.
20. Cascione, *Tresviri capitales* (1999) 85–117.

> [(Gaius in the third book of his *Institutes*): Now let us pass on to obligations arising from delict, as where theft or robbery is committed, or damage to property is done, or injury to the person.] (trans. F. De Zulueta)

This perspective—considered exhaustive for the *obligationes ex delicto* by some and merely illustrative by others[21]—is commonly recognized to encounter complications, in the first instance, through the interweaving of civil and praetorian consequences (e.g., with theft and the extensions of the sanctions of the *lex Aquilia de damno*). But for now, we can accept the immediate application of Gaius's representation, which corresponds in detail to the general outline he puts forth in the passage with which he opens his discussion of obligations in the *Institutiones.*

> Gaius *Institutiones* 3.88: *Nunc transeamus ad obligationes, quarum summa divisio in duas species diducitur: omnis enim obligatio vel ex contractu nascitur vel ex delicto.*

> [(Gaius in the third book of his *Institutes*): Let us now proceed to obligations. These are divided into two main species, for every obligation arises either from contract or from delict.] (trans. F. De Zulueta)

This, too, is a very famous text, a starting point for scholars (particularly during the first half of the twentieth century) in their search for the origins of *obligatio,* a problem that has literally obsessed generations of Roman law scholars. Even this passage possesses a doctrinal structure: *obligatio* (every obligation, *omnis enim obligatio,* and thus all possible obligations) arises either from contract or from delict. This means not only that *contractus* and *delictum* are clearly distinct but also that the two levels cannot overlap. This fact was embraced by the interpolationists, some of whom believed (not incorrectly) that linguistic expressions could validate doctrinal structures,[22] while others argued that these principles of law were in substance stable and universally shared throughout the so-called classical period (this cannot be accepted, however).

---

21. See, for example, Kaser, *Das römische Privatrecht* (1971) 1:611 n. 15.

22. As an element of a more developed scholarly perspective, see, in particular, Biondi, "Terminologia romana" (1953); Kaser, "Terminologie" (1965/1976). See, further, Daube, *Roman Law* (1969) 1–63.

Perspectives on the Origins of *Obligatio*

Another point to emphasize is that the history of *obligatio* itself is very obscure. First of all, one must consider the never-ending debate regarding its origins, which was particularly heated during the first half of the twentieth century. There were two basic positions: the concept of *obligatio* took its point of departure either from contractual agreement (thus as a bond for the fulfillment of a promised performance) or from a wrongful act (therefore serving as a bond of liability). Roman law scholars split into two teams. Bonfante, Perozzi, Albertario, Marchi, and Luzzatto (I am generalizing here, as they do not agree on all details) point to the primary social importance of wrongful behavior over licit behavior; similarly, Max Weber maintains that every "judicial" remedy was necessarily one *ex delicto*.[23] Betti, De Visscher, Segrè, Pugliese, Monier, Grosso, Kaser, and Scherillo give precedence to the contract as a source of obligation (or better still, as Talamanca emphasizes,[24] to those abstract elements that blend together in the contract). We should add here the religious (for some, magical) background that lies behind the ancient repression of infractions against the *pax deorum* and also behind the oath that substantiated the original means of making a binding commitment.[25]

To this dilemma, we can, moreover, append the doubt surrounding the moment at which, starting from concrete figures (the *obligatus*), the abstract notion of obligation came of age. Although there is a scholarly consensus over an ancient stabilization ("ancient" meaning it had already occurred at the time of the Twelve Tables), some very careful and stimulating recent studies date the conceptualization of the obligatory relationship much later, up to and including the classical period.[26]

23. Weber, *Economia e società* (1995) 6.
24. Talamanca, "Obbligazioni" (1979) 4–13.
25. In this context, it is impossible to give an adequate account either of these individual theses (in all of their detail) or of the other theories (like that which reduces the issue to a religious context). For the older literature on the controversy, see the summary in Luzzatto, *Obbligazioni romane* (1934) 8–26; for subsequent developments, see Talamanca, "Obbligazioni" (1979) 2 n. 7, 3 n. 11; Gaudemet, "Naissance" (2001). See also Gioffredi, *Antiche forme giuridiche romane* (1955), esp. 2–25. On oaths in particular, see Calore, *Per Iovem lapidem* (2000).
26. Gaudemet, "Naissance" (2001) 145–54. Santoro, "Per la storia dell'*obligatio*" (2009). See also Zimmermann, *Law of Obligations* (1990) 2 and n. 6 (with bibliography).

The Reuniting of *Delicta* and *Crimina* in the Semantic Field of *Obligatio*

On the crucial point of the distinction between delicts and crimes, the sources are not always as precise as a somewhat Manichean trend in the scholarship, ever ready to resort to the deletion of texts, would have them. We can take as an immediate illustration a passage from Papinian that might, in terms of its content, appear extreme.

> Pap. (1 *def.*) *D.* 1.3.1: *Lex est commune praeceptum, virorum prudentium consultum, delictorum quae sponte vel ignorantia contrahuntur coercitio, communis rei publicae sponsio.*
>
> [(Papinian in the first book of *Definitions*): A comitial law is a communal directive, a resolution of wise men, a repression of offenses committed either voluntarily or in ignorance, a collective covenant of the community.] (trans. A. Watson [adapted])

Here is a text written in a very general[27] and perhaps insufficiently technical manner, one that is certainly configured as a definition and that obviously has important connections with Greek philosophical thought. Critics clearly mishandled it during a period in which one approached the challenge of understanding legal principles with scissors in hand. The passage contains explicit reference to "contracting delicts." Delicts thus appear to constitute the object of human action (whether voluntary or involuntary, *sponte vel ignorantia*), as suggested by the use of the verb *contrahere.* We must in this context pass over the relationship between *contrahere* (*contractum*) and *contractus,*[28] the object of recent and ample scholarly discussion. The same holds for the meaning of *delicta* in this passage from Papinian, about which much could be said. This is because "private law" terminology is being used fairly obviously in order to convey the sense of a public criminal offense,[29] in defiance of the other approach,

27. On which, see, most recently, Stolfi, "Osservazioni su Pap. (1 *def.*) *D.* 1.3.1" (2004) 441–79 (with full bibliography); see also Stolfi, *Introduzione* (2006) 134–51 (and the notes at 228–36).
28. See, recently, the summary offered by Burdese, "Panoramica sul contratto" (2007).
29. As in other Severan texts that are also suspect and probably not without problems. See, for example, two passages that deal explicitly with the *coercitio* of the *delicta.* The first is, like the

previously mentioned, that would hold the two distinct. Thus it would seem that the text is saying that (even) "crimes" can be "contracted."

Admittedly, this suggested reading of Papinian's text (which requires a deeper analysis than can be offered here) is intended to be a bit provocative. Let us return, therefore, to what today appears to be the scholarly consensus on the origin of *obligatio,* between delict and contract. According to Talamanca,[30] liability as subjection to a penalty does not define obligation. The characteristic that "makes the difference" for him is that liability is connected with an unfulfilled satisfaction of an expectation, so there must be a period in which the same liability is suspended until one has ascertained whether or not the creditor's expectations have been met. To better understand the obligation, one must look to a state of contingency, not to an immediate subjection (as would be the case for a person responsible for a delict), whereas the terminology relating to *obligare* could be adopted even "beyond an 'obligation' in its true sense," keeping in mind that in its "original meaning," such terminology expressed bond or subjection.

The expression *obligatio furti* would not then date back to the most ancient period of Roman law, because it corresponds substantially to the standard scheme of the *obligatio ex delicto.* This scheme recurs again and again in Gaius. From what we know by reading (as Talamanca suggests) the *Vocabularium Iurisprudentiae Romanae,* it previously occurred only in Iavolenus Priscus.[31]

---

one quoted in the text, also from Papinian's *Definitiones* (Pap. [2 *def.*] *D.* 48.19.41): *Sanctio legum, quae novissime certam poenam irrogat his, qui praeceptis legis non obtemperaverint, ad eas species pertinere non videtur, quibus ipsa lege poena specialiter addita est. Nec ambigitur in cetero omni iure speciem generi derogare, nec sane verisimile est delictum unum eadem lege variis aestimationibus coerceri* (The sanction of the statutes, which in very recent times has imposed a fixed penalty on those who fail to comply with the provisions of a law, is not deemed to apply to those special cases to which a penalty is specifically attached by the statute itself. There is no doubt that in all other (aspects) of the law the particular derogates from the general, nor indeed is it likely that a single offense should be punished by different assessments under the same statute) (trans. A. Watson [adapted]). The second is from Paul's commentary on the Augustan *lex Iulia et Papia* (Paul. [3 *ad legem Iuliam et Papiam*] *D.* 50.16.131.1: *Inter 'multam' et 'poenam' multum interest, cum poena generale sit nomen omnium delictorum coercitio, multa specialis peccati, cuius animadversio hodie pecuniaria est* . . . (There is a considerable difference between a fine and a penalty, since a penalty is a general term for the punishment of all wrongful acts, while a fine refers to a particular one whose punishment today takes monetary form. . . .). (trans. A. Watson [adapted]).

30. Talamanca, "Obbligazioni" (1979) 3 with nn. 12–14.

31. See Iav. (6 *epist.*) *D.* 39.5.25.

But we must not forget that this work of reference does not contain a full catalog of juristic evidence. If one considers all of this literature, including texts that have come down to us from so-called nontechnical sources, the expression seems to date back at least to Quintus Mucius Scaevola and so to a relatively early period of the history of Roman juristic literature. We can find it in a (very famous) excerpt from his *libri* on the *ius civile.*

> Gell. 6.15.2 (frg. 2 Huschke/Seckel-Kübler, 1 Bremer, 11 Lenel): *Itaque Q. Scaevola in librorum quos de iure civili composuit XVI verba haec posuit: 'Quod cui servandum datum est si id usus est sive quod utendum accipit ad aliam rem atque accepit usus est, furti se obligavit'.*
>
> [(Aulus Gellius in the sixth book of his *Attic Nights*): Accordingly Quintus Scaevola, in the sixteenth book of his work *On the Civil Law,* wrote these words: "If anyone has used something that was entrusted to his care, or having borrowed anything to use, has applied it to another purpose than that for which he borrowed it, he is liable for theft."] (trans. J. C. Rolfe)

This text is particularly interesting for our purpose. We find it under the heading regarding the severity of punishment (expressed by the verb *vindicare*) for theft, according to the *mores maiorum.* It follows another fairly famous text by Labeo (who quotes the republican jurist Iunius Brutus), from his commentary on the Twelve Tables.

In the text under discussion, *obligare* is the result of actions not by the person who determines or enforces sanctions but by the party responsible for a blameworthy behavior: for example, using an object entrusted to one's care or using it for a purpose other than that for which it was received. This shows that we are facing not a metaphor for the *vindicta* but the belief that someone who behaves in a certain way imposes on himself or herself a bond. One can easily move back in time, tracing the same use of the *genetivus incommodi* from Quintus Mucius to Plautus, who wrote, *homo furti sese adstringit* (By theft a man binds himself).[32] The semantic content of *adstringere* (like that of *adligare*) is very close to that of *obligare.* Similarly close (also in the syntactical construction) in a more strictly criminal field are *se scelere obligare,/obstringere,*

32. Plautus *Poen.* 737.

alligare, and *adstringere.* As noted recently by Brachet,[33] the crime is expressed in the instrumental ablative of the bond: one places one(self) in a bond (the shackles) as consequence of a crime (or, more generally, of a wrongful act). Perhaps this argument, though expressed in synthesis, can help our understanding of what it originally meant to be under an obligation. It is not a mere metaphor, especially for the most ancient age when the ideological foundations of the system were determined.

A Greek Myth

The imposition of physical bonds means merely to make manifest a situation at whose root there is already the fact that "binds" the agent. One can draw a comparison with a well-known image (particularly fraught with meaning) taken from Greek mythology:[34] we find it in Homer's *Odyssey,*[35] in the context of a story told by an *aoidos,* a "singer of tales," in the court of Alcinous. Ares, guilty of adultery with Aphrodite and caught in the act, is restrained along with her in a web of unyielding chains forged by Hephaestus, her cuckolded husband and blacksmith to the gods, who seeks redress. The Homeric passage, which also contains an intervention by Poseidon on behalf of Ares, has been put to good use by scholars of Greek law in order to improve our understanding of *enguē* (a form of guarantee for debt).[36] Most relevant for us is the binding image: the guilty party (who is only liable "privately," meaning he merely owes compensation to the husband) remains enmeshed in the net. The situation corresponds to a rule of the so-called Gortyn Code: the detention of the adulterer is a guarantee for payment of compensation, while the failure to give satisfaction places the guilty party at the husband's discretion.[37] Hephaestus's symbolic net is invisible, woven from a metal as thin as a spider's web, but indestructible—it is Poseidon's

33. Brachet, "Observations morphologiques et sémantiques" (2005) 27. On assertions about the Indo-European origins of the bind/oblige relationship, see, at minimum, Onians, *Le origini del pensiero europeo* (1998).
34. As Brachet has done recently in "Observations morphologiques et sémantiques" (2005) 37–40.
35. *Odyss.* 8.226–366. For an indispensable guide, see Huebeck, West, and Hainsworth, *Commentary on Homer's "Odyssey"* (1988) 370–71.
36. See Cantarella, "La *enguē* nell'Odissea" (1964); Cantarella, "Obbligazioni in Omero" (1988), with full bibliography and persuasive conclusions.
37. Gortyn Code 2.20. The situation is similar in Attic law, but the adulterer caught in the act might be lawfully killed: see Lysias 1.25–27.

subsequent guarantee that allows the lovers to be freed. The net is the poetic metaphor for fault and for the liability that flows from this.[38]

Liability, Obligation, Punishment, Freedom

The Roman conception assigns to the wrongdoer an even greater level of liability. At Rome, the debtor, guilty party, or criminal tied himself in a bond through his behavior. The objective result (not the intention) already defined the nature of the bond. There was no divine intervention, nor was the creditor the active party. This is made clear by the constant use of *se* as the direct object of the verb *obligare* (and of its semantic equivalents). The mechanism appears in a fairly early context, for example, in Varro.

> Varro *Lingua Latina* 7.105: *Liber qui suas operas in servitutem pro pecunia quam debebat nectebat, dum solveret, nexus vocatur, ut ab aere obaeratus.*
>
> [(Varro in the seventh book of his *Latin Language*): A free man who, for money which he owed, 'bound' (*nectebat*) his labor in slavery until he should pay, is called a 'bond slave' (*nexus*), just as a man is called 'indebted' (*obaeratus*), from 'money-debt' (*aes*).] (trans. R. G. Kent)

In this passage, Varro is concerned with drawing definitions. The free man (*liber*) who "owed" a sum, in lieu of which (*pro pecunia*) he "tied" his capacity for work to the creditor against payment (*dum solveret*), putting himself in a slave-like condition, is called a *nexus*. I find it very interesting that Varro uses the term *obaeratus* to explain the link *suas operas . . . nectebat* (in which, it is well worth remembering, *operae* has a meaning of subordinate work and thus of a subjection in functional terms). This term (like *obligatus*) is made up of the prefix *ob-*, which evokes an image of the debtor as almost immobilized (bound)

38. It might be interesting to examine the next episode featuring Aphrodite, maligned by her husband, who, in the passage under discussion, calls her "face of a bitch, lovely, but unfaithful" (*Odyss.* 8.319–20). The goddess, after being freed, disappears and goes to Cyprus. There, at Paphos, the Graces wash her, anoint her with an everlasting oil, and dress her in enchanting clothes, evidently a true and proper rite of purification for what she had done, because the goddess could not remain "sullied" by the illicit act (*Odyss.* 8.362–66).

by the quantity of *aes* owed to the creditor that has been imposed on him.[39] The party obligated suffers by being bound, a restriction of his personal freedom.

Just as shackles are provided for the *nexus* (literally, the "bound one") and the *addictus,* so, too, in the earliest public procedure for repressing wrongful behavior, dating to the regal period (traditionally dated to 753–509 BCE), that of the so-called *lex horrendi carminis,* the order given to the *lictor* (*nomen agentis,* he who "binds")[40] is—according to well-known sources—precisely *i lictor colliga manus* (go, *lictor,* bind his hands),[41] *deliga ad palum, lictor*[42] (*lictor,* bind him to the stake). It is as if the declaration made by the *duumviri perduellionis* and the related order of the *rex* had as a consequence the actual physical binding of the guilty according to a strict legal ritual.[43] In this context, the bound man becomes the image and symbol of the loss of space where freedom was exercised (which can be called *ius*).[44] There is a movement from "public" (the *rex-lictor*) to private control (the creditor, empowered by the legal system)—to tie, that is, while waiting for the punishment or for compensation (but if the compensation fails, we must recall that in the older law, matters proceed to the *partes secanto*). It is not, then, by chance that Livy records two "beginnings" of *libertas* at Rome: the end of the *regnum*[45] (the beginning of "constitutional" *libertas,* because with the yearlong term for public officials and the *provocatio,* there is no further room for tyrannical power, capable of deciding matters of life and death *ad libitum*)[46] and the *lex Poetelia Papiria* (featuring a "private law" *libertas,* intended mainly for the indebted plebs): *Eo anno plebi Romanae velut aliud initium libertatis factum*

---

39. On Varro's *obaerarius* (*Res rustica* 1.17.2), see Lo Cascio, "Dipendenza in Varrone" (1982) with full discussion of the scholarship.
40. See the etymology in Plut. *Quaest. Rom.* 67.
41. Cic. *Pro Rab.* 13; Liv. 1.27.7, 11.
42. Liv. 8.7.19 (see also 9.11.13).
43. I discuss this in Cascione, "*Lege agere* e *poena capitis*" (2001).
44. I am put in mind of the interpretation of Dumézil, *Idee romane* (1969/1987) 40–45 (quotation at 41): *ius* equals the "widest sphere of action or of a claim flowing from the natural definition or from the agreed-upon status of an individual or a group" (area di azione o di pretesa massima risultante dalla definizione naturale o dallo statuto convenzionale di un individuo o di un gruppo).
45. Liv. 2.1.1–2, 7. On *libertas* (and the *homo liber*), see, most recently, Garofalo, "*Homo liber* et *homo sacer*" (2009), esp. 318–22.
46. It would be interesting to examine in detail the tradition reported by Plutarch (*Quaest. Rom.* 82), according to which the rods that made up the lictors' *fasces* and were placed at the disposition of the consuls and praetors were tied in order to restrain the resort to violence on the part of these officials: the need for their unloosing to allow physical chastisement to proceed would have provided time for reflecting on this punishment.

est quod necti desierunt (In that year the liberty of the Roman *plebs* had as it were a new beginning; for men ceased to be imprisoned for debt).[47] This law, however, did not abolish resort to *compedes* and *nervus, (ni)si qui noxam meruisset* ([save] those who have been guilty of some crime).[48]

Everything that binds—either literally or figuratively—limits freedom. This also holds true for the paradigm of the inverted enchainment of the *flamen Dialis* and the taboos that marked his status. This ancient priest of Jupiter suffered a series of behavioral and practical restrictions and, at the same time, created a space of freedom for "those who were bound," precisely by being the living and manifest sign of the impossibility of being bound. Tellingly, a scholar who has devoted a lengthy analysis to Gellius's chapter on the *flamen Dialis*[49] entitles the part dedicated to the prohibitions that this priest had to tolerate "*Libertas sine vinculis.*"[50] Two points from the chapter are relevant to our discussion: first, according to notions of *fas,* it was impossible for the —*flamen* to swear an oath,[51] which meant, in the earliest legal system, "voluntarily" obligating oneself;[52] second, in the edict, the praetor declares that he will not (i.e., he cannot) subject Jupiter's priest to an oath, as with the Vestals.[53] The *fides* implied by the *iusiurandum,* of which the *flamen* is a witness in his role as a priest of Jupiter, constructs hierarchical ties to which the *flamen* himself cannot be subjected.[54] *Vinculum fidei* is the relationship that describes, in Livy, the position of the *nexi* before the passage of the *lex Poetelia Papiria.*[55] Also relevant is the fact that one finds in Gellius's list a series of rules, prohibitions, and rituals that keep the *flamen* away from the bonds that could "tie" him: he could not

47. Liv. 8.28.1 (trans. B. O. Foster). See also 8.28.9: . . . *Ita nexi soluti, cautumque in posterum ne necteretur* (So those in confinement were released, and it was forbidden any should be confined thereafter) (trans. B. O. Foster).
48. Liv. 8.28.8.
49. Gell. 10.15. On the textual tradition, see, for example, Gioffredi, "Frammento di Fabio Pittore" (1976). On the position of the *flamen Dialis,* see, most recently, Garofalo, "*Homo liber* et *homo sacer*" (2009) esp. 321–22.
50. Simón, *Flamen Dialis* (1996) 89–139. The combination *libertas sine vinculis* does not appear in the sources, but it is well suited for outlining the position of the *flamen.*
51. Gell. 10.15.5. See also Gell. 10. rubr.; Plut. *Quaest. Rom.* 44.
52. See, for example, Fiori, *Homo sacer* (1996) esp. 164–66.
53. Gell. 10.15.31. Lenel, *Das Edictum Perpetuum* (1927) 236 (§ 95)
54. So Fiori, "*Fides e bona fides*" (2008).
55. Liv. 8.28.8. There is no room here for discussion of the problematic etymology of *fides,* but, at least from a scholarly perspective, the link with some derivative of the wicker vase and thus of the bush whose branches were used to bind is important; see, for example, Gioffredi, "Religione e diritto" (1954) 277 and n. 58.

look at an army marshaled for battle (*classis procincta*);[56] he could not wear unbroken rings;[57] his hat, belt, and clothing could not contain any knots;[58] he could not walk beneath intertwined vines or touch or even name ivy,[59] as noted in the epitome of Festus—because *edera vincit* (ivy binds).[60] Then there were situations in which the mere presence of the *flamen* frees one, albeit temporarily, from a bond: if someone in bonds (*vinctum*) took refuge in his house (the *flaminia domus,* which shares this very peculiar *status* with its inhabitant), the chains were immediately struck off, conveyed through the *impluvium* to the roof, and hence cast down into the street;[61] and if a criminal (bound, obviously) on his way to be physically punished met the *flamen* and fell suppliant at his feet, he could not be punished on that day.[62]

This is the clearest proof we possess for an archaic system of prescriptions that defined the essential *libertas* of the *flamen Dialis* with respect to all of the constraints of the secular world as well as to his capacity to free others.[63] It provides us with tools to understand the nature of the symbolism and the values (and flaws) at the root of the signs and behavior that suggest subjection through binding.

The Importance of Earlier Household Structures and Progressive Developments regarding the Public Bodies Responsible for Social Control[64]

Despite the diversity of scholarly approaches that have been taken, the importance of household structures in the control of some behaviors considered to be socially reprehensible appears now to be widely accepted as a feature of life in

56. Gell. 10.15.4. See also Paul. Fest. 295 L s.v. *procinctam classem.*
57. Gell. 10.15.6.
58. Gell. 10.15.9. For the last two provisions, see also Paul. Fest. 72 L s.v. *ederam.*
59. Gell. 10.15.13.
60. Paul. Fest. 72 L s.v. *ederam.*
61. Gell. 10.15.8. See also Serv. auct. *ad Aen.* 2.57.
62. Gell. 10.15.10. See also Serv. auct. *ad Aen.* 3.607.
63. See, at minimum among the vast literature that examines this priesthood, Simón, *Flamen Dialis* (1996) 135–38.
64. I have a fuller treatment of the themes of this and the following section (9 and 10), with more bibliography, in an article, now forthcoming, entitled "Antichi modelli familiari e prassi corrente in età protoimperiale" given as a paper on 5 June 2008 at the XIV Convegno internazionale di Diritto romano di Copanello, a conference held under the theme "*Ubi tu Gaius:* Modelli familiari, pratiche sociali e diritti delle persone nell'età del principato."

the earliest days of the Republic and has been projected by some historians back to the regal period or even earlier. In the first place, given what we know to have been true for the period for which we possess reliable sources, it was the *pater familias* who performed this social (and, to a certain point, political) function through the exercise of his powers, which extended to the possibility of putting to death those in his *potestas*. In fact, in the earliest system, the entire household was subject to him, including the women who had entered the family by virtue of his acquisition of *manus* over them, his descendants, and the household slaves. Some situations (though the picture presented by the sources is neither uniform nor completely clear) were subjected to examination by a *consilium* of family members (probably the agnates of the *pater* himself, but the sources make some mention of *cognati* and also of senators chosen ad hoc),[65] considered by some scholars to be an enactment of a judicial procedure. The emergence of the dependent's liability to someone outside the group produced the *noxae deditio*. The terminology is not incidental: as previously noted, *noxa*-fault is connected with *nectere*-binding.[66] It is possible that—on an interhousehold level and in rivalry with the centralized structures of the community—the *gentes* may have been able to mediate conflicts. The vestiges of solidarity within *gentes*, traced by some scholars[67] to as late as the first century BCE, might attest to this.

The community's primitive criminal law aimed at maintaining the *pax deorum*.[68] It developed between the end of the regal period and the age of the Twelve Tables, with the identification of acts detrimental to a public interest, distinguished, in turn, from those that determined *sacratio*.[69] Punishment of acts deemed detrimental to public interest was removed from the sphere of private vengeance (vendetta) and entrusted first to the *rex* and later to elected public officials, in contention with the people at least from the time that the *provocatio* was established.[70]

65. Regarding the *consilium* and the so-called household court, the position taken by Volterra in "Il preteso tribunale domestico" (1948/1991) is well known: taking a cue from Mommsen (*Römisches Strafrecht* [1899] 17), he argues against situating paternal powers in the context of a household "court." The older view is revived by Kunkel in "Das Konsilium im Hausgericht" (1948/1974). On procedure and penalties in the context of the *consilium*, see, particularly, Thomas, "Remarques sur la juridiction domestique" (1990).
66. Brachet, "Observations morphologiques et sémantiques" (2005) 30–37.
67. See Hinard, *Les proscriptions* (1985) 219; Glotz, *La solidarité* (1904).
68. See Burdese, "Repressione penale romana" (1996).
69. On the subject of the *homo sacer*, see, above all, the extensive monograph *Homo sacer* by Fiori (1996).
70. See, recently, Tassi Scandone, *Repressione criminale e garanzie costituzionali* (2008).

Censorial Control (of Public and Private Wrongdoing)

Over time, the exercise of social control, at first divided between the power of the *pater* within the household and the "political" balancing of relations among "family" groups (mainly the *gentes*), became a problem that involved the public structures of the city. On one side—as already noted—were the annually elected public officials operating as organs of coercion. On the other, and with a more functionalized competence, were the censors.

The interference by the censors (perceptible above all until the midrepublic) was significant, as they were responsible for monitoring the *mores* in both the private and public lives of the citizens.[71] The censorship, in part through the personal influence of some who held this office (suffice it to think of Cato the Elder), built up, over time, what has been defined as a true and proper "ethical model."[72] This model became normative as generations of Romans were subjected to it, a subjection achieved through an effective system of sanctions. Thus a remarkable *Sozialer Druck* developed through the exercise of the powers associated with the censorship, that is, one that was no longer interhousehold or intrahousehold in nature but that identified and codified models of behavior and imposed itself as obligatory.

We can sufficiently understand the scope of control exercised by these officials and its intersection with our idea of "criminal law" by glancing at a list of their responsibilities. In their control of moral behavior, they handled (among other things) misbehavior by soldiers in the field, refusal to obey the orders of officers, avoidance of conscription, misdeeds in the exercise of public duties (including those of juror), bearing false witness, perjury, theft and *captio* of *pecunia*, breaking of *fides* in business transactions, attempted suicide, abusive exercise of *patria potestas*, and so on.[73] The overlap between criminal and civil jurisdictions is crystal clear even in the sources. The man who promised his daughter in marriage had better follow through—otherwise, he faced conse-

---

71. On the *regimen morum* of the censors, see, at minimum, Astin, "*Regimen morum*" (1988); Baltrusch, *Regimen Morum* (1989) 9–30.

72. See Humm, "Censure chez Valère Maxime" (1998), esp. 82–88.

73. This list, which is not comprehensive, is taken from Mommsen, *Römisches Staatsrecht* (1887) 2:377–82 (with references to the sources).

quences before both the praetor and the censors.[74] The *populi iudicio damnatus* was ordered by the censors to sell his horse.[75]

As Masi Doria shows,[76] the procedure followed by the censors—originally a free expression of the vast powers of this office—was formalized at least from the middle of the second century BCE, if not before, taking on the features of the criminal procedure of the *quaestiones.* The *lex Clodia de censoria notione* led to a further restriction of the censors' power regarding exclusion from the Senate and the infliction of *ignominia.*[77] It accomplished this by codifying a procedure that used the language of the courts, required a formal accusation, and defined the final step taken by the censorial pair as a *sententia* (sentence), which produced a *damnatio* (i.e., a declaration of guilt).[78]

The history of social control at Rome in the regal and republican periods, along with the early, weak forms of public repression, seems almost a gradual unwinding of the exercise of power within the household group, yielding to a public control managed by the community representatives over aspects involving "moral" behavior and then to the legal formalization ("purification," isolation, and rationalization) of control itself.[79]

On the one hand, Cicero speaks in the past tense when he recalls the censors' judgments on oaths;[80] on the other, he emphasizes the weakness, in his day, of the censorial sanctions (*notae*) imposed by Cn. Lentulus and L. Gellius for *furtum* and *captae pecuniae.* This is evidence of the decline of the office in the first century BCE and also of the *vis attractiva* of the judicial decisions that were "rational"[81] and, by their nature, regulated by fixed procedure (meaning both the praetor's private law verdicts and the criminal verdicts pronounced

74. Varro *Lingua Latina* 6.71.

75. Liv. 29.37.9.

76. See the essay by Masi Doria in this volume.

77. According to the important evidence of Ascon. 8C: *Ne quem censores in senatu legendo praeterirent, neve qua ignominia afficerent, nisi qui apud eos accusatus et utriusque censores sententia damnatus esset* ([The law laid down] that the censors not expel anyone while reviewing the roll of the Senate, nor inflict anyone with civic disgrace, if he had not been formally accused before them and condemned by a sentence of both censors). See Tatum, "*Lex Clodia*" (1990).

78. Even if later invalidated in 52, by a *lex Caecilia.*

79. See Weber, *Economia e società* (1995) 6–17.

80. Cic. *De off.* 3.31.111.

81. Cic. *Pro Cluentio* 42.120. The censors are those from 70 BCE: see Broughton, *Magistrates* (1952) 2:126–27.

in the jury courts). Praetorian *infamia* becomes a substitute for the atechnical *ignominia*.[82] It is not, then, by chance that in the *Pro Cluentio*, immediately after putting before the jury the acquittals of those who had been punished by Lentulus and Gellius, Cicero states the principle behind that rationalized procedure: *neminem voluerunt maiores nostri non modo de existimatione cuiusquam sed ne pecuniaria quidem de re minima esse iudicem, nisi qui inter adversarios convenisset* (It was the intention of our ancestors that no one should act as a judge in a question involving not just someone's reputation but even the slightest monetary interest, unless the litigants agreed to accept him) (trans. H. Grose Hodge [adapted]).[83]

The Evolution of Criminal Law before the Principate

In light of this forceful exercise of social control on the part of heads of households and magistrates, the collective response to illicit or dangerous behavior on Roman territory (apart from the sphere of the military, which was strictly subject to official *imperium* until passage of the Porcian laws) remained rather weak in terms of its structural aspects, at least until the Second Punic War. Without doubt, the highest public officials had at their disposal coercive powers, which, according to the sources, corresponded—albeit with the significant limitation imposed by the *provocatio ad populum*—to those once held by the kings. Apart, however, from the ancient pair of *duumviri perduellionis* (whose responsibilities seem to have been merely declarative in nature) and (insofar as we know) the investigative role played by the *quaestores* (*parricidii*), criminal repression was part of a set of powers that lacked clear definition from a functional point of view. Until the introduction of the *tresviri capitales* (these differ, in my view, from the earlier *tresviri nocturni*, appearing, at first in a supplementary role, only at the beginning of the third century BCE),[84] there was no public office with specific police duties or able to provide consistent support in the organization of criminal repression (e.g., supervision of prisons and supervision of capital punishment). Meanwhile, regarding the category of delicts that was taking shape, we see a "degradation" of punishment. Concurring fac-

82. See, most recently, Wolf, "Das Stigma ignominia" (2009).

83. Cic. *Pro Cluentio* 43.120.

84. Cascione, *Tresviri capitales* (1999) 1–24.

tors were the abolition of the possibility of shackling insolvent debtors and the whole development of civil procedure from the *legis actiones* to the *formulae* (the type of sentence was consistently pecuniary, leading to the development of the idea of a pecuniary punishment as a compensatory mechanism).[85]

Over time, different factors (economic, social, spiritual, and cultural) transformed the deep structures of Roman life. New forms of criminality became widespread. In the city, they were the result of the urbanization of proletarian masses; in the countryside, of an increase in banditry, fostered by changes that were predominantly economic. The *ethos* of the ruling class no longer managed to contain political corruption, which came also to be defined in a series of new criminal offenses.

The ever-increasing spread of violence in daily life became, at the end of the Republic, much more than a sign of the times: the law (both praetorian and legislative) devised solutions to hold back its rise. On the one hand, courts were established: thus criminal repression emerged from the dualism between popular trial (developed starting with the *provocatio*), with its political coloring, and mere coercion by public officials. First, extraordinary courts were set up at the time of a political alignment between the Senate and leading public officials. Later, permanent courts were established by law, functioning with juries made up of members of the upper classes: at first senators, then members of the equestrian order, then—with a fluctuation itself a product of the political tensions we see between the end of the second and the first centuries BCE—senators again, and still later a mixture of members of both orders (with the inclusion also of the *tribuni aerarii*). On the other hand, the praetor's court, through the protection granted by awarding interdicts and the identification of illicit behaviors as *vis,* contributed to the enucleation of most of the instruments of social control for a society whose political and moral connective tissue was in the process of dissolving.[86] At the same time, *delicta* were being drawn into the sphere of repression *per quaestionem,* as the delict of *iniuria,* beginning with the *lex Cornelia,* was endowed with a particular criminal procedure.[87] The ultimate outcomes of the chaotic flow of history that formed the backdrop to

85. For a fundamental study on the "degradation" of the illicit act, taking as a point of departure a conceptualization entirely criminal in nature, see Albanese "Illecito" (1970/1991) 804–8.

86. From different points of view, see Lintott, *Violence in Republican Rome* (1968/1999); Labruna, *Vim fieri veto* (1971); Labruna, "*Iuri maxime . . . adversaria*" (1992); and, recently, Harries, *Law and Crime* (2007) 106–17.

87. Santalucia, *Diritto e processo penale* (1998) 151–53; Ermann, *Strafprozeß* (2000) 77–84.

these developments were the crisis of the republican constitutional system, civil war, and the establishment of the Principate.

The Augustan constitution was also based on the definitive stabilization of the courts (*ordo iudiciorum publicorum*),[88] at the same time it supported the organization of new procedures: the *cognitiones* would gain ground and overtake the traditional jury courts, before ultimately replacing them. From Augustus on, a new and more flexible system for policing Rome was established, which hinged on the prefects responsible (among other things) for maintaining public order (*urbi, praetorio,* and *vigilum*).[89] These new positions, established by the first emperor, produced profound changes—through the exercise of their jurisdictions and the command of the urban troops at their disposal—in the practical aspects of repressing criminal activities, and they later had consequences also for the formal structures of the criminal trial.

Only at the end of the Republic and the advent of the Principate does Mommsen's idea of the impossibility of a criminal law without a criminal trial strike me as plausible. This perspective is one that is entirely modern, progressive, rational, and even liberal.[90] But the earlier forms of vendetta and the *Selbsthilfe* accepted by the legal system, the full powers enjoyed by the *pater,* the violent powers of the creditor, and the oversight exercised by the censors (ultimately arbitrary if not moderated by the collective nature of their judgment) escape this precise framework.

The Juristic Literature Comes into Its Own

Here we see why the field of criminal law, which had for a long time remained beyond the purview of the jurists, was gradually taken up by the jurists under the Principate. At least under the profile of interpretation as it is reflected in the jurists' writings, we have very little evidence of their engagement from the Republic.[91] We know—mostly from Cicero, who may exaggerate the state of affairs—how the laws that regulated the procedure of the *quaestiones* were

88. On the system of the *quaestiones* in the late republican period and the Principate, see, for example, Robinson, *Criminal Law* (1995) 2–9.
89. Guizzi, *Praefectura urbi* (1981), esp. 25–40.
90. Mommsen, *Römisches Strafrecht* (1899) vii; see, recently, with emphasis on Mommsen's metaphor of the knife handle without a blade, Ebert, "Mommsen und das Römische Strafrecht" (2005) 71–77.
91. See, most recently, the outline in Giuffrè, "Diritto criminale" (2001) 64.

controlled by the *scribae*[92] and therefore not exclusively by the officials who presided over the courts and were supposed to guarantee that the proper procedure was followed and who were sometimes even manifestly ignorant of the same, with consequences in its application.[93] Of course, legal experts also sat on the *consilia* of *praetores* and *quaesitores.* And perhaps (though we lack full and accurate evidence) the legal literature on "public law" that begins in the second half of the second century BCE, dealing with the *potestates,* also contained discussion of criminal procedure (concerning trials *per populum* and the organization of the *quaestiones,* the forms and limits of *coercitio*). The *vetus commentarius anquisitionis,* passed down to us from Varro, is more a working manual than literature.[94]

At the time that the Principate was established, with the Augustan reordering of the *quaestiones,* we find some indications of interest on the part of the jurists (Capito, Labeo, Proculus, and later perhaps also Aristo) concerning the topic of the *publica iudicia.* Silence (either absolute or partial, if compared with the rhetoric's unrestrained interest in the topics of law and, above all, criminal procedure)[95] ensues down to Volusius Maecianus. Only in the Severan period do the most important jurists (who were by then, however, an organic part of imperial administration) dedicate their attention also to criminal law—to the *iudicia publica,* especially to penalties,[96] and to the individual types of crimes (as they appeared in the ancient republican *leges,* in the *senatusconsulta,* and in criminal law praxis). This was also a result of the interest taken by the emperors themselves in a subject constantly brought to their attention in the *cognitio,* in a symbiotic connection between the reaction to the case in question and the construction of a paradigm. With regard to the comprehensive framework suggested by Giuffrè a few years ago, one can add the importance of Ulpian's commentary *De officio proconsulis,*[97] with its books devoted to provincial jurisdiction. Imperial *cognitio* and provincial repression attract delicts more and more into the criminal sphere.[98] New abstract cases arise and receive legal rec-

92. Cic. *De leg.* 3.20.48.

93. A striking example, drawn from the account of M. Caelius Rufus (Cic. *Fam.* 8.8.3), is discussed recently by Masi Doria in *Quaesitor urnam movet* (2007) 96–112.

94. Varro *Lingua Latina* 6.90–92.

95. Giuffrè, "Diritto criminale" (2001) 66–71. On the relationship between jurists and criminal law, see the earlier discussion by Ferrini in *Diritto penale romano* (1899) 1–24.

96. See Bauman, *Crime and Punishment* (1996) 115–40.

97. The recent monograph by Nogrady, *Römisches Strafrecht nach Ulpian* (2006) is of great interest.

98. Santalucia, *Diritto e processo penale* (1998) 266–67. See, recently, on theft in particular, Harries, *Law and Crime* (2007) 54–58, esp. 58.

ognition.[99] At that time (and then even more so in late antiquity), the jurists must include in their technical perspective (suffice it to think of Gaius's *omne ius*)[100] this important aspect of social regulation, with all its challenges of systemic coherence, its chaos and its cruelty, as by then something both necessary and functional to the imperial legal organization.

Bibliography

Albanese, B. "Illecito (storia)." In *Scritti giuridici,* 1:791–833. Palermo: Palumbo, 1991. Originally published in *Enciclopedia del diritto* 20 (1970): 50–90.

Albertario, E. "*Delictum* e *crimen.*" In *Studi di diritto romano,* vol. 3, *Obbligazioni,* 141–95. Milan: Giuffrè Editore, 1936. Originally published in Milan: Vita e pensiero, 1924.

Albertario, E. "*Maleficium.*" In *Studi di diritto romano,* vol. 3, *Obbligazioni,* 197–208. Milan, Giuffrè Editore, 1936. Originally published in *Studi in onore di Silvio Perozzi nel XL anno del suo insegnamento,* 221–27. Palermo: Arti Grafiche G. Castiglia, 1925.

Archi, G. G. "Gli studi di diritto penale romano da Ferrini a noi: Considerazioni e spunti di vista critici." In *Scritti di diritto romano,* vol. 3, *Studi di diritto penale, Studi di diritto postclassico e giustinianeo,* 1395–432. Milan: Giuffrè Editore, 1981. Originally published in *Revue internationale des droits de l'antiquité,* 3rd ser., 4 (1950): 21–60.

Astin, A. E. "*Regimen Morum.*" *Journal of Roman Studies* 78 (1988): 14–34.

Baltrusch, E. "*Regimen morum*": *Die Reglementierung des Privatslebens der Senatoren und Ritter in der römischen Republik und frühen Kaiserzeit.* Munich: C. H. Beck, 1989.

Bassanelli Sommariva, G. "Proposta per un nuovo metodo di ricerca nel diritto criminale (a proposito della sacertà)." *Bullettino dell'Istituto di Diritto Romano* 89 (1986): 327–77.

Bauman, R. A. *Crime and Punishment in Ancient Rome.* London: Routledge, 1996.

Biondi, B. "La terminologia romana come prima dommatica giuridica." In *Studi in onore di Vincenzo Arangio-Ruiz,* 2:73–103. Naples: Jovene Editore, 1953.

Brachet, J. P. "*Obligare et obnoxius:* Observations morphologiques et sémantiques." *Glotta* 81 (2005): 25–44.

Broughton, T. R. S. *The Magistrates of the Roman Republic.* 3 vols. New York: American Philological Association; Atlanta: Scholars Press, 1951–84.

Burdese, A. "Panoramica sul contratto nelle dottrine della giurisprudenza romana."

99. Santalucia, *Diritto e processo penale* (1998) 267–68.

100. Gaius 1.1.

In *Fides, Humanitas, Ius: Studii in onore di Luigi Labruna,* 1:565–80. Naples: Editoriale Scientifica, 2007.

Burdese, A. "Riflessioni sulla repressione penale romana in età arcaica." *Bullettino dell'Istituto di Diritto Romano* 69 (1966): 342–54.

Calore, A. Per Iovem lapidem: . . . *Alle origini del giuramento: Sulla presenza del "sacro" nell'esperienza giuridica romana.* Milan: Giuffrè Editore, 2000.

Cantarella, E. "La *enguē* nell'Odissea." *Studi italiani di filologia classica* 36 (1964): 199–214.

Cantarella, E. "La garanzia personale delle obbligazioni in Omero: Ripensando all'adulterio di Afrodite." In *Atti del seminario sulla problematica contrattuale in diritto romano: Milano, 7–9 aprile 1987,* 1:261–72. Milan: Cisalpino-Goliardica, 1988.

Cascione, C. "*Lege agere* e *poena capitis:* Qualche spunto ricostruttivo." In *Iuris vincula: Studi in onore di Mario Talamanca,* 1:511–36. Naples: Jovene Editore, 2001.

Cascione, C. *Tresviri capitales: Storia di una magistratura minore.* Naples: Editoriale Scientifica, 1999.

Daube, D. *Roman Law: Linguistic, Social, and Philosophical Aspects.* Edinburgh: Edinburgh University Press, 1969.

De Zulueta, F. *The "Institutes" of Gaius.* 2 vols. Oxford: Clarendon, 1951, 1953.

Dumézil, G. *Idee romane.* Trans. M. Gabellini Baiardi. Genoa: Il Melangolo, 1987. Originally published in French as *Idèes romaines.* Paris: Gallimard, 1969.

Ebert, U. "Strafrecht ohne Strafprozess ist eine Messergriff ohne Klinge: Theodor Mommsen und das Römische Strafrecht." In *Theodor Mommsen: Gelehrter, Politiker und Literat,* ed. J. Wiesehöfer, 51–79. Stuttgart: Franz Steiner, 2005.

Ermann, J. *Strafprozeß: Öffentliches Interesse und private Strafverfolgung.* Cologne: Böhlau, 2000.

Ferrini, C. *Diritto penale romano: Teorie generali.* Milan: Hoepli, 1899.

Ferrini, C. "Esposizione storica e dottrinale del diritto penale romano." In *Enciclopedia del diritto penale italiano,* ed. E. Pessina, 1:1–428. Milan: Società Editrice Libraria, 1905.

Fiori, R. "*Fides* e *bona fides:* Gerarchia sociale e categorie giuridiche." In *Modelli teorici e metodologici nella storia del diritto privato,* ed. R. Fiori, 3:237–59. Naples: Jovene Editore, 2008.

Fiori, R. *Homo sacer: Dinamica politico-costituzionale di una sanzione giuridico-religiosa.* Naples: Jovene Editore, 1996.

Garofalo, L. "Concetti e vitalità del diritto penale romano." In L. Garofalo, *Fondamenti e svolgimenti della scienza giuridica,* 235–65. Padua: CEDAM, 2005. Originally published in Iuris Vincula: *Studi in onore di Mario Talamanca,* 4:73–106. Naples: Jovene Editore, 2001.

Garofalo, L. "*Homo liber* et *homo sacer:* Deux archétypes de l'appartenance." *Revue historique de droit français et étranger* 87 (2009): 317–36.

Gaudemet, J. "Naissance de la notion d'obligation." In *Iuris Vincula: Studi in onore di Mario Talamanca*, 4:135–57. Naples: Jovene Editore, 2001.

Giglio, S. "Teodoro Mommsen e la repressione penale nell'impero Romano." *Studia et Documenta Historiae et Iuris* 72 (2006): 355–68.

Gioffredi, C. *Diritto e processo nelle antiche forme giuridiche romane.* Rome: Apollinaris, 1955.

Gioffredi, C. "Il frammento di Fabio Pittore in Gell. N.A. 10.15.1 e la tradizione antiquaria dei testi giuridico-sacrali." *Bullettino dell'Istituto di Diritto Romano* 79 (1976): 27–47.

Gioffredi, C. "Religione e diritto nella più antica esperienza romana." *Studia et Documenta Historiae et Iuris* 20 (1954): 259–302.

Giuffrè, V. "Il diritto criminale secondo la giurisprudenza del principato." *Seminarios Complutenses de derecho romano* 13 (2001): 59–92.

Glotz, G. *La solidarité de la famille dans le droit criminel en Grèce.* Paris: Fontemoing, 1904.

Grose Hodge, H. *Cicero: The Speeches (Pro lege Manilia, Pro Caecina, Pro Cluentio, Pro Rabirio perduellionis reo).* Cambridge, MA: Harvard University Press, 1927. Reprint, 1966.

Guizzi, F. *Per la storia della praefectura urbi.* Camerino: Università degli Studi di Camerino, 1981.

Harries, J. *Law and Crime in the Roman World.* Cambridge: Cambridge University Press, 2007.

Heubeck, A., S. West, and J. B. Hainsworth. *A Commentary on Homer's "Odyssey."* Vol. 1, *Introduction and Books I–VIII.* Oxford: Clarendon, 1988.

Hinard, F. *Les proscriptions de la Rome Républicaine.* Rome: École française de Rome, 1985.

Höbenreich, E. "Leopold Wenger und das Studium des römischen Strafrechts." *Bullettino dell'Istituto di Diritto Romano* 92–93 (1989–90): 377–460.

Humbert, M. "La peine en droit romain." In *La Peine/Punishment.* Vol. 1, *Antiquité/Antiquity,* 133–83. Brussels: De Boeck Université, 1991.

Humm, M. "L'image de la censure chez Valère Maxime: Formation et évolution d'un paradigme." In *Valeurs et mémoire à Rome: Valère Maxime ou la vertu recomposée,* ed. J.-M. David, 73–93. Paris: de Boccard, 1998.

Kaser, M. *Das römische Privatrecht.* 2nd ed. 2 vols. Munich: C. H. Beck, 1971–75.

Kaser, M. "Zur juristischen terminologie der Römer." In *Ausgewählte Schriften,* 1:35–83. Naples: Jovene Editore, 1976. Originally published in *Studi in onore di Biondo Biondi,* 1:95–142. Milan: Giuffrè Editore, 1965.

Kunkel, W. "Das Konsilium im Hausgericht." In *Kleine Schriften: Zum römischen Strafvehrfahren und zur römischenVerfassungsgeschichte,* 117–49. Weimar: Böhlau, 1974. Originally published in *Zeitschrift der Savigny-Stiftung (Romanistische Abteilung)* 83 (1966): 219–51.

Kunkel, W. "Ein direktes Zeugnis für den römischen Mordprozeß im altrömischen Recht." In *Kleine Schriften: Zum römischen Strafvehrfahren und zur römischen Verfassungsgeschichte,* 111–16. Weimar: Böhlau, 1974. Originally published in *Zeitschrift der Savigny-Stiftung (Romanistische Abteilung)* 84 (1967): 382–85.

Kunkel, W. *Linee di storia giuridica romana.* Trans. T. Spagnuolo Vigorita and B. Spagnuolo Vigorita. Naples: Edizioni Scientifiche Italiane, 1973. Originally published as *Römische Rechtsgeschichte: Eine Einführung,* 6th ed. (Cologne: Böhlau, 1972).

Kunkel, W. *Untersuchungen zur Entwicklung des römischen Strafverfahrens in vorsullanischer Zeit.* Munich: Verlag der Bayerischen Akademie der Wissenschaften, 1962.

Labruna, L. "*Iuri maxime . . . adversaria:* La violenza tra repressione privata e persecuzione pubblica nei conflitti politici della tarda repubblica." In *Illecito e pena privata in età repubblicana: Atti del Convegno Internazionale di diritto romano, Copanello 4–7 giugno 1990,* ed. F. Milazzo, 253–74. Naples: Edizioni Scientifiche Italiane, 1992.

Labruna, L. *Vim fieri veto: Alle radici di una ideologia.* Naples: Jovene Editore, 1971.

Lauria, M. "*Contractus, delictum, obligatio* (A proposito di recenti studi)." In *Studii e ricordi,* 619–44. Naples: Jovene Editore, 1983. Originally published in *Studia et Documenta Historiae et Iuris* 4 (1938): 163–92.

Lenel, O. *Das Edictum Perpetuum: Ein Versuch zu seiner Wiederherstellung.* 3rd ed. Leipzig: Tauchniz, 1927.

Liebs, D. "Mommsens Umgang mit den Quellen des römischen Strafrechts." In *Theodor Mommsens langer Schatten: Das römische Staatsrecht als bleibende Herausforderung für die Forschung,* ed. W. Nippel and B. Seidensticker, 199–214. Hildesheim: Olms, 2005.

Lintott, A. *Violence in Republican Rome.* 2nd ed. Oxford: Oxford University Press, 1999.

Lo Cascio, E. "*Obaerarii (obaerati)*: La nozione della dipendenza in Varrone." *Index* 11 (1982): 265–84.

Longo, G. *Delictum e crimen.* Milan: Giuffrè Editore, 1976.

Luzzatto, G. I. *Per un'ipotesi sulle origini e la natura delle obbligazioni romane.* Milan: Giuffrè Editore, 1934.

Masi Doria, C. *Quaesitor urnam movet e altri studi sul diritto penale romano.* 2nd ed. Naples: Editoriale Scientifica, 2007.

Masiello, T. *Mommsen e il diritto penale romano.* Bari: Cacucci, 1995.

Mommsen, T. *Römisches Staatsrecht.* 3rd ed. Vol. 2.1. Leipzig: Hirzel, 1887.

Mommsen, T. *Römisches Strafrecht.* Leipzig: Hirzel, 1899.

Nogrady, A. *Römisches Strafrecht nach Ulpian: Buch 7 bis 9 De officio proconsulis.* Berlin: Duncker und Humblot, 2006.

Onians, R. B. *Le origini del pensiero europeo.* Trans. P. Zaninoni. Milan: Adelphi,

1998. Originally published in English as *The Origin of European Thought,* 2nd ed. Cambridge: Cambridge University Press, 1954.

Robinson, O. F. *The Criminal Law of Ancient Rome.* Baltimore: Johns Hopkins University Press, 1995.

Rolfe, J. C. *The "Attic Nights" of Aulus Gellius.* 3 vols. Cambridge, MA: Harvard University Press, 1927.

Santalucia, B. *Diritto e processo penale nell'antica Roma.* 2nd ed. Milan: Giuffrè Editore, 1998.

Santoro, R. "Per la storia dell'*obligatio:* Il *iudicatum facere oportere* nella prospettiva dell'esecuzione personale." In *Scritti minori,* 2:557–747. Turin: Giappichelli, 2009. Originally published in *Iuris Antiqui Historia* 1 (2009): 61–124.

Simón, F. M. *Flamen Dialis: El sacerdote de Júpiter en la religión romana.* Madrid: Ediciones Clásicas, 1996.

Stolfi, E. *Introduzione allo studio dei diritti greci.* Turin: Giappichelli, 2006.

Stolfi, E. "*Lex est . . . virorum prudentium consultum:* Osservazioni su (Pap. 1 *def.*) D. 1.3.1." *Studia et Documenta Historiae et Iuris* 70 (2004): 441–79.

Talamanca, M. "Obbligazioni (storia: diritto romano)." *Enciclopedia del diritto* 39 (1979): 1–78.

Tassi Scandone, E. *Leges Valeriae de provocatione: Repressione criminale e garanzie costituzionali.* Naples: Jovene Editore, 2008.

Tatum, W. J. "The *Lex Clodia de censoria notione.*" *Classical Philology* 85.1 (1990): 34–43.

Thomas, Y. "Remarques sur la juridiction domestique à Rome." In *Parenté et stratégies familiales dans l'antiquité romaine,* ed. J. Andreau and H. Bruhns, 449–74. Rome: École française de Rome, 1990.

Venturini, C. *Processo penale e società politica nella Roma repubblicana.* Pisa: Pacini Editore, 1996.

Voci, P. Review of G. Longo, *Delictum e crimen. Iura* 28 (1977): 216–19.

Volterra, E. "*Delinquere* nelle fonti giuridiche romane." In *Scritti giuridici,* 7:135–64. Naples: Jovene Editore, 1999. Originally published in *Rivista italiana per le scienze giuridiche* 5 (1930): 117–46.

Volterra, E. "*Flagitium* nelle fonti giuridiche romane." In *Scritti giuridici,* 7:269–88. Naples: Jovene Editore, 1999. Originally published in *Archivio giuridico* 111 (1934): 39–58.

Volterra, E. "Il preteso tribunale domestico in diritto romano." In *Scritti giuridici,* 2:127–77. Naples: Jovene Editore, 1991. Originally published in *Rivista italiana per le scienze giuridiche* 85 (1948): 103–53.

Watson A., ed. *The "Digest" of Justinian.* 4 vols. Philadelphia: University of Pennsylvania Press, 1985.

Weber, M. *Economia e società*. Vol. 3, *Sociologia del diritto*. Trans. P. Chiodi. Milan: Edizioni di Comunità, 1995. Originally published in *Rechtssoziologie*, ed. J. Winckelmann, 2nd ed. Neuwied: Luchterhand, 1967.

Wolf, J. G. "Das Stigma ignominia." *Zeitschrift der Savigny-Stiftung (Romanistische Abteilung)* 126 (2009): 55–113.

Zimmermann, R. *The Law of Obligations: Roman Foundations of the Civilian Tradition*. Cape Town: Juta, 1990.

CHAPTER 12

Roman Delicts and the Construction of Fault

MARIA FLORIANA CURSI

Introduction: Fault and the *Lex Aquilia*

How did the Romans come to construe the notion of "fault" in the field of delict? The regime surrounding the *lex Aquilia* provides an excellent case study for examining this question. This essay begins by considering the construction of the notion of *culpa* in the juristic treatment of *damnum iniuria datum* (loss wrongfully given) under the *lex Aquilia.* I next examine intentional fault as a subjective criterion of liability both in the original conception of Aquilian loss and in the other delicts. We can trace a historical development in juristic views on Aquilian loss in terms of the increasing emphasis on the compensatory interest, a phenomenon linked, in turn, to what can be described as the "reification" of the slave as well as to the mixed nature of the Aquilian action itself. One can see a parallel in the emergence of rules for *culpa in vigilando* and *culpa in eligendo* in the field of quasi delict. Key elements here are the subdued role played by the notion of a penalty and the valuation of (meaning the assignment of a monetary value to) the body of a free man in the *actio de effusis vel deiectis.* I conclude that just as we can trace a development over time from intentional fault to presumed negligence, so we see a similar move away from an emphasis on penalty toward one placed on compensation for wrongful loss.

I thank Francesca Rosati, of the University of Teramo Foundation, Mike Riddell, and Tom McGinn for help with the translation of this essay from Italian.

The Jurists and *Culpa:* Current Views

According to the currently dominant view,[1] the notion of *culpa* outside the terms of a contract emerged from the context of juristic treatment of the *lex Aquilia,* specifically in cases where the application of the statute initially may have seemed doubtful. Such well-known cases include the resort to self-defense in a manner deemed excessive,[2] the abuse of an instructor's disciplinary authority that results in permanent physical damage to a student,[3] injury to passersby inflicted by careless tree trimmers,[4] and the intentional infliction of harm on an animal grazing illegally on one's property.[5] In these cases, the legal authorities came to construe fault in a manner that transcended the strict illegality of the behavior and that gave a new meaning to *iniuria* in the context of this delict.

It is generally accepted that *iniuria,* as an expression of the illegal nature[6] of damage, was initially conceived in a way that was completely independent of the subjective element of conduct—*culpa.* Gradually, however, the original division was overcome, thanks to the interpretative work of the jurists, which, in the very case of uncertain application of the *lex Aquilia,* led to an emphasis on the reprehensibility of the conduct in question and allowed the emergence of the "modern" notion of *culpa.* Sandro Schipani, for example, observes that *culpa* is "linked to a subjective criticism, even if this does not only concern dispositions of an intentional nature, but likewise the lack of control—measured against a standard—over one's own dispositions" (connessa a un rimprovero soggettivo, anche se questo non colpisce soltanto gli atteggiamenti intenzionali, ma altresì il mancato controllo—in rapporto ad un modello—dei propri atteggiamenti).[7] On this view, it was the Severan jurists who, toward the end of the classical period, accomplished the definitive equivalence of the two notions,

1. See, for all of these, Schipani, *Responsabilità 'ex lege Aquilia'* (1969) 133–34.
2. See Gaius (7 *ad edictum provinciale*) *D.* 9.2.4.
3. Ulp. (18 *ad edictum*) *D.* 9.2.5 pr. and 3, 7 pr. = Ulp. (32 *ad edictum*) *D.* 19.2.13.4.
4. Paul. (10 *ad Sabinum*) *D.* 9.2.31.
5. Pomponius (17 *ad Q. Mucium*) *D.* 9.2.39 pr.
6. I use the term here to indicate, in an extremely broad sense, the situation of nonconformity to the law, without going into the hoary problem of defining the object on which the value judgment of illegal nature falls. For a similar problem, though without definite result, see Dell'Andro, "Antigiuridicità" (1958) 542–43.
7. Schipani, *Responsabilità 'ex lege Aquilia'* (1969) 131.

stating that *iniuria* consists in *quod non iure fit . . . id est culpa quis occiderit* (what does not occur rightfully . . . that is, [if] someone should slay with fault).[8]

Intentional Fault as a Subjective Criterion of Liability in the Original Conception of Damage under the *Lex Aquilia* and the Other Delicts

The point of departure for this approach—the objective nature of *iniuria*—does not appear to be based on any actual evidence.[9] In fact, an examination of the scholarship on the origins of the notion of illegality shows that the interpretation of *iniuria* under the *lex Aquilia* in the terms previously described is best understood as the projection of a modern category onto a Roman concept.

While attempting to discover another meaning for the term *iniuria* in the texts reporting the terms of the *lex Aquilia,* I have been able to trace, in the logic of Roman relations of dependency, the key to the meaning of the term as used by the legislator. In fact, a connection emerges between the case of the killing of a slave (in all probability, the most ancient provision of the *lex Aquilia*) and that of injuring a slave, both conceived of as *iniuria.* The common denominator is the offense to the *dominus,* viewed in the context of the logic of dependent relations within the *familia:* as with the delict of *iniuria,* the injury done to the slave amounts to an offense against the *dominus* (*iniuria per alias personas*), consistently with the conception of abstract *iniuria* as insult. This means that also under *damnum iniuria datum,* the killing of the slave amounts to (wrongful) loss for the owner. This may seem like an obvious point, but the interesting fact is that the Romans in both cases (and in a way that is completely novel compared with the system of damages prevailing before the *lex Aquilia*) defined this offense with the word *iniuria.* Evidently they believed that *iniuria* was done to a *dominus* not only when a slave was injured but also, and with greater reason, when the slave was killed.

It is clear, however, that the decision to borrow the notion of *iniuria* from the delict of the same name ("injury") could only lead to its "comprehensive" adoption. The killing of the slave determines, as far as the *dominus* is concerned, not only a financial loss but also, as in the case of injury to the slave, an impair-

8. Ulp. (18 *ad edictum*) *D.* 9.2.5.1.

9. Here I depend on my previous work: see Cursi, *Iniuria cum damno* (2002).

ment of his status. This is because the giver of loss, through his behavior, usurps the place of the *pater familias* in his exercise of the power of life and death over his slaves, so claiming a *potestas* that was not his to wield and wronging the legitimate possessor of that power. Worth noting also is that the legislator of the *lex Aquilia,* in taking the notion of *iniuria* from the delict of injury, could not omit an integral element of that delict (and one that was especially prominent in its new praetorian form), namely, the requirement of intentional fault. Abandoning this requirement would have resulted not in a reception of the concept of *iniuria* but in a complete perversion thereof.

Thus, in the text of the *lex Aquilia,*[10] *iniuria* is linked to the wish to cause harm—here the killing of the slave—with the awareness of thereby causing offense to the *dominus.* At bottom, the original conception of *iniuria* in the *lex* amounts to intentional fault or, rather more accurately, to a "specific" fault.

The voluntary nature of the prejudicial behavior was, as we have seen, borrowed from the delict of *iniuria.* This delict underwent a praetorian revision of the original system of the Twelve Tables, which probably took place before the advent of the *lex Aquilia,* that is, between the end of the third and beginning of the second centuries BCE.[11] This was a radical innovation, in which some of the features of the ancient delict presumably survived unchanged, features that are attested for certain in a later period but that most probably were already present under the regime of the Twelve Tables. Without doubt, intentional conduct was required for liability to be present, which was defined in the later praetorian formulation as *contumelia.*

The same observation can be made regarding the subjective criterion of liability in the case of two other delicts, theft and robbery. There is no need here to dwell on the fact that both theft and robbery (classified as a violent form of theft)[12] involve the wish to gain possession of another's goods with the further

10. Gaius (7 *ad edictum provinciale*) *D.* 9.2.2 pr.: *Lege Aquilia capite primo cavetur: 'ut qui servum servamve alienum alienamve quadrupedem vel pecudem iniuria occiderit, quanti id in eo anno plurimi fuit, tantum aes dare domino damnas esto'* (The first chapter of the *lex Aquilia* provides as follows: "If anyone kills unlawfully a male or female slave belonging to someone else or a four-footed beast of the class of cattle, let him be condemned to pay the owner the highest value that the property had attained in the preceding year") (trans. Watson, *"Digest" of Justinian* [1998] [adapted]).

11. Cursi, *Iniuria cum damno* (2002) 221–68.

12. This holds even though, as regards robbery, the juristic sources show differences over the mixed nature of the action, in that it was both penal and reipersecutory (see Gaius 4.8; *Inst.* 4.6.19).

aim of profiting from them. From the traditional fourfold scheme of Roman delicts, there emerges a common denominator that renders intentional fault the subjective criterion of liability. This is also present in the concept of loss under the *lex Aquilia,* at least in its original form.[13]

If we examine the pre-Aquilian rules regarding the wrongful infliction of harm to another's property, evidence for which is found scattered throughout the sources for the Twelve Tables,[14] an additional point emerges that I think is interesting as far as the subjective criterion of liability for loss is concerned. When describing situations of fact involving setting fire to a building or sheaves of wheat beside a dwelling, Gaius[15] distinguishes between a case of intentional action and one of unintentional action. In the first instance, criminal liability arises, while in the second, in which the action is carried out *casu, id est negligentia* (by chance, that is, through negligence), compensation for damages is prescribed under the regime of delict (*noxiam sarcire*).

We may question whether Gaius here actually quotes the text of the Twelve Tables,[16] particularly when he uses the term *negligentia* to refer to chance (*casus*).[17] Such reservations aside, there can be no doubt that the distinction he

13. For a more general description of the transition from intentional fault to differing forms of subjective liability, see Gioffredi, "L'elemento intenzionale nel diritto penale romano" (1970) 37–38.

14. See the law concerning an ill-defined *ruptio,* according to the affirmations of Festus 320L s.v. *rupitias: rupitias . . . XII significat damnum dederit* (*rupitias* . . . in the Twelve Tables means causing damage); the provision of the *actio de pastu* against a person who has grazed his herds on another's property, as attested by Ulp. (41 *ad Sabinum*) *D.* 19.5.14.3; the disposition on the *actio de pauperie* that Ulp. (18 *ad edictum*) *D.* 9.1.1 pr. attributes to the Twelve Tables; and the fine of twenty-five *asses* imposed on a person who has cut down, *iniuria,* another's trees, reported by Pliny *NH* 17.1.7. However, on the genuine nature of the reference to *iniuria* in the text of the law, see Cursi, *Iniuria cum damno* (2002) 274 n. 6.

15. Gaius (4 *ad legem XII tabularum*) *D.* 47.9.9: *Qui aedes acervumve frumenti iuxta domum positum conbusserit, vinctus verberatus igni necari iubetur, si modo sciens prudensque id commiserit. si vero casu, id est neglegentia, aut noxiam sarcire iubetur aut, si minus idoneus sit, levius castigatur. appellatione autem aedium omnes species aedificii continentur* (A person who burns down a building or a pile of grain set beside a dwelling is directed to be bound, flogged, and put to death by fire, if, that is, his act was deliberate and conscious. If, however, he did it by chance, that is, through negligence, he is to make good the wrong, or if his means be inadequate, be more lightly punished. The expression "dwelling" covers every form of edifice) (trans. Watson, *"Digest" of Justinian* [1998] [adapted]).

16. Twelve Tables 8.10. See MacCormack, "Criminal Liability for Fire" (1972) 382–83.

17. This sounds like a gloss inserted to give a technically accepted meaning to a term, *casus,* which perhaps already for Gaius had multiple connotations: see, in this sense, MacCormack, "Criminal Liability for Fire" (1972) 393–94 n. 6; MacCormack, "Fault and Causation in Early Roman Law" (1981) 117; Wacke, "Fahrlässige Vergehen im römischen Strafrecht" (1979) 553; Molnár,

draws between the intentional and unintentional (in the restricted meaning of unpremeditated)[18] lighting of a fire and their relative sanctions are indeed genuine. The provision of compensation in the case of a fire that was set unintentionally, already present in a stage dating back to the initial formulation of redress for loss, can be seen as a starting point for a more general reflection on the emergence of the notion of fault in relation to purely compensatory requirements.

Aquilian Loss and the Assertion of Compensatory Interests: The Reification of the Slave and the Composite Nature of the Aquilian Action

There is no doubt that the provisions of the Twelve Tables on arson[19] are the first evidence for a connection between unintentional action and the compensation for loss deriving from such action. That Gaius refers to this in his commentary on the Twelve Tables attests to the survival of the rule, notwithstanding the Aquilian provision for damage carried out by means of the *urere* that was set forth in the third chapter of the law.[20]

The continued existence of this provision of the Twelve Tables leads us to believe that a case of *damnum iniuria datum* was pursuable at law along independent lines compared to those of the precedents deriving from the Twelve Tables on wrongful loss.

"Erfolgshaftung oder typisierter *dolus malus*" (1986) 481–82 and n. 53. For arguments that the precise statement is not Gaius's, see Gioffredi, "L'elemento intenzionale nel diritto penale romano" (1970) 40 with n. 11, 50; Wittmann, *Die Körperverletzung an Freien* (1972) 21–22 with n. 89; Pólay, "*Iniuria*" (1984), 179–80 with n. 55, 184–85.

18. This interpretation, probably that of Gaius, conforms to the logic supporting both general and particular compensation for loss in the case of fire. Cf. Gaius 3.211, which, while recognizing the possibilities of intentional fault and negligence in Aquilian *iniuria*, excludes the infliction of a penalty in the case of damage caused *casu*. Also, more specifically concerning arson, a fragment of Callistratus (*D.* 48.19.28.12) and, along much the same lines, a passage from Marcian (*D.* 47.9.11) reaffirm the distinction between deliberate arson and involuntary starting of a fire *per negligentiam*.
19. Twelve Tables 8.10.
20. Ulp. (18 *ad edictum*) *D.* 9.2.27.5: *Tertio autem capite ait eadem lex Aquilia: 'ceterarum rerum praeter hominem et pecudem occisos si quis alteri damnum faxit, quod usserit fregerit ruperit iniuria, quanti ea res erit in diebus triginta proximis, tantum aes domino dare damnas esto'* (In its third chapter the *lex Aquilia* says: "In the case of all other things apart from slaves or cattle that have been slain, if anyone causes loss to another by wrongfully burning, breaking, or rending his property, let him or her be condemned to pay to the owner whatever the loss shall prove to be worth in the next thirty days") (trans. Watson, *"Digest" of Justinian* [1998] [adapted]).

It is likely that the original nucleus of the law, probably enacted during the third century BCE,[21] consisted of only the first two chapters,[22] to which was later added the third, of wider scope, since its purpose was to complete the rubric of damage to property. Within the layered structure of the text of the *lex Aquilia,* it is quite probable that the oldest part was that preserved in the first *caput,* concerning the *iniuria* of killing a slave. The connection between this provision and the injuring of a slave in the delict of *iniuria* has already been stressed, and I have assumed a form of doubling of the first section of the law on *iniuria/contumelia,* which shares the same structure and the same criterion of liability—intentional fault. The subsequent extension of the first *caput* to *pecus quadrupes*—by virtue of the essential similarity between humans and animals, the only objects that can be killed, since they are living things—and the introduction of the third *caput,* which widens the protection for damage to inanimate *res,* are without doubt significant additions to the content.

I believe that the extension of protection to inanimate *res* introduces a substantial novelty. For the first time, an explicit reference to *damnum* appears in the text of the law. Perhaps the reference to the slave (and subsequently to the *pecus quadrupes*) was still too closely linked to the logic of *iniuria* to be able to talk of *damnum.* By including inanimate *res,* a new level is introduced, involving a new definition of conduct to which pertain the scenarios provided for in the first *caput,* laying the foundation for distinguishing between *iniuria* and *damnum iniuria datum.* This phenomenon is a reflection, in both social and legal terms, of the progressive reification of the slave. The scenario derived from the delict of *iniuria,* in the first chapter of the law, derives from domestic slavery—where, even if there are differences in the monetary payments required, the injured slave is placed on the same level as a free man. But in commercial slavery, the slave is equated with inanimate objects in the common case of *damnum.*[23]

At this point, the emphasis on the property aspect of Aquilian loss is sup-

---

21. Cursi, *Iniuria cum damno* (2002) 147–65.

22. Cursi, *Iniuria cum damno* (2002) 208–12.

23. Serrao, *Diritto privato, economia e società* (2006) 206–7, maintains that the slave under consideration in the *lex Aquilia* is merely an element of the property of the *dominus* and thus an object of compensation. As described in the text, the movement away from the domestic idea of slavery—which sees the *servus* as a person, equivalent in important respects to a free man in some areas of the law, such as *iniuria* in the Twelve Tables—to the commercial concept was a more gradual one. Again the first section of the *lex Aquilia* reflects the same legal *ratio* as *iniuria,* which is only modified upon the introduction of the third section, where the compensatory features are emphasized for the first time.

ported by the introduction of fault as a subjective criterion that can justify compensation in cases where damage is not done deliberately. This is not only a temporal coincidence linked to the juristic interpretation of the *lex Aquilia;* the two innovations are connected to each other. The need to compensate loss, understood not only as an offense to the *dominus* but as a material loss to property, led to the extension of cases of application of protection by means of the subjective requirement of *culpa,* which did not allow the blameworthy, though involuntary, conduct of the agent to go unpunished.

This innovation, moreover, has the effect of extending Aquilian protection to instances that were not previously included in the application of the law. Originally, the intentional injuring of a slave was covered by the delict of *iniuria,* and it was therefore pointless to have a legal provision that punished such a case as *damnum iniuria datum.* The third *caput* of the *lex Aquilia* was thus originally limited to the destruction of *ceterae res,* that is, all the "other" *res* apart from the slaves and animals identified in the first *caput.* However, when Aquilian *iniuria,* originally equal to intentional fault, was transformed into *culpa,* the protection *ex lege Aquilia* became subjectively wider than that guaranteed by the delict of *iniuria;* at this point, the *prudentes* decided to insert also the cases of unintentional injury of a *servus* and *pecus quadrupes* among the *ceterae res* of the third *caput.*

A transformation of this kind could only lead to a coherent modification of the nature of Aquilian action from penal to mixed, by adding a specific compensatory feature to the original penal intent. As in the rule in the Twelve Tables for arson, in the Aquilian concept of loss, the material aspect of damage introduces the evaluation of negligence as a subjective criterion of liability in addition to intentional fault.

Culpa in Vigilando and *Culpa in Eligendo* in Quasi Delict: The Diminished Character of Penalty and the Valuation of the Body of a Free Man in the *Actio de Effusis vel Deiectis*

A further stage in the process that, in the area of delicts, links the emergence of negligence to cases of compensation is represented, to my mind, by the assertion of *culpa in vigilando* and *culpa in eligendo* among the quasi delicts. The Roman jurists closely connected this form of third-party liability with the need to guarantee positive compensation for damages in circumstances where the damage originated in the lack of surveillance or supervision by the person responsible for such; the *habitator* in the *actio de effusis vel deiectis* comes to mind, as well as the *nauta, caupo,* and *stabularius* in the *actio furti* and *actio damni.* The creation of a similar form of liability arises directly from the adaptation of known cases to the new ones that the praetor was beginning to handle.

The *actio ex lege Aquilia* obviously provided the main reference model regarding the subjective criterion of liability. In other words, *culpa*[24] is expressly named as such with *culpa in eligendo* and *culpa in vigilando.* The adaption of Aquilian negligence to these scenarios is, however, not entirely innocuous. To presume culpability on the part of a person who may be different from the

24. Thus, for the *actio de effusis vel deiectis,* Ulpian ([23 *ad edictum*] *D.* 9.3.1.4) in similar terms to what we find with Paul (*D.* 9.3.6.2) in explaining why the action is allowed against the *habitator* and not against the *dominus* of the house, maintains that *culpa* accrues to the former: *Haec in factum actio in eum datur, qui inhabitat, cum quid deiceretur vel effunderetur; non in dominum aedium culpa enim penes eum est* (This *actio in factum* is given against him or her who occupies the house when anything is thrown down or poured out and not the owner; for the fault rests with the former) (trans. Watson, *"Digest" of Justinian* [1998] [adapted]). Consequently, he establishes a parallel with the action for wrongful loss under the *lex Aquilia,* emphasizing the difference between the two actions, in that there is no mention in the *actio de effusis vel deiectis,* as there is in the former, of *culpa* or *infitiatio,* because there an *actio in duplum* is permitted: . . . *nec adicitur culpae mentio vel infitiationis, ut in duplum detur actio, quamvis damni iniuriae utrumque exiget* (. . . . nor is there added any mention of fault or of the defendant denying the facts, so that he or she becomes liable for double the damages although these are both factors of liability in an action for unlawful loss") (trans. Watson, *"Digest" of Justinian* [1998] [adapted]). The reference to the Aquilian action is expressed in terms of not only a general derivation but also a protection added to that offered by the praetor and which is granted in cases where a free man has caused damage by throwing something out of a building, for which the *habitator* is responsible: a kind of action of recovery against the real culprit (Ulp. *D.* 9.3.5.4). In the *actio damni adversus nautas, caupones, stabularios,* Ulpian ([18 *ad edictum*] *D.* 4.9.7.4) traces the liability of the *exercitor* for damages caused by one's dependents to the negligence involved in having employed them: . . . *haec autem actione suo nomine exercitor tenetur: culpae scilicet suae, qui tales adhibuit* (. . . moreover, the person in charge of the ship is liable under this action on his own account, of course, in respect of his fault in employing such persons) (trans. Watson, *"Digest" of Justinian* [1998]); see also Ulp. (28 *ad edictum*) *D.* 14.1.1.2, for the *exercitor navis.* Paul refers to this action for damages as *actio damni iniuriae* (*D.* 4.9.6.4). In the corresponding *actio furti,* again Ulpian ([38 *ad edictum*] *D.* 47.5.1.5) alludes to an equal liability of the *exercitor* for having placed trust in a dependent (in this case, a *servus*) who is *malus: Cur ergo non exercitor condemnetur, qui servum tam malum in navem admisit?* (now why is the shipper not condemned personally since he allows so evil a slave on his ship?) (trans. Watson, *"Digest" of Justinian* [1998]). But according to Ulp. (38 *ad edictum*) *D.* 47.5.1.6, the *caupo* does not appear to be held liable for theft committed by *viatores* (in other words, his customers), because *viatorem sibi eligere caupo vel stabularius non videtur* (the innkeeper or manager of a lodging house is not deemed to choose the passing traveller for himself) (trans. Watson, *"Digest" of Justinian* [1998] [adapted]).

actual author of the illicit deed obviously means perverting such a criterion, through the introduction of a form of liability that is measured objectively.

Scholars have already shown that key features of these actions do not correspond precisely to those of penal actions. For Serrao,[25] the *actio* deriving from the edict *de effusis vel deiectis* is of the type he defines as "of diminished penalty," meaning that because they establish third-party liability, they have not, since antiquity,[26] had the features characteristic of penal actions.[27] The legal system, reflecting social values, would not, in fact, give permission "to carry to extreme consequences the penal character of actions directed against parties other than those who commit the delict" (condurre alle estreme conseguenze il carattere penale[28] di azioni che si dirigevano contro soggetti diversi dagli autori del delitto).[29]

25. Serrao, *Impresa e responsabilità a Roma* (1989) 139. But already Wittmann (*Die Körperverletzung an Freien* [1972] 69) places the *actio penalis, quae rei persecutionem continet* (a penal action that has a reipersecutory character), in a different category than does Levy (*Privatstrafe und Schadensersatz im klassischen römischen Recht* [1915] 22–23). Contrary to this view, Voci (*Risarcimento e pena privata* [1939] 103–4) criticizes the "processo di decantazione del concetto di *actio poenalis*" (the process of leaching out the concept of penal action), begun by scholars who refer to the possibility that an action might be penal in some of its aspects and reipersecutory in others. According to Voci, *l'actio de effusis vel deiectis* is of an exclusively penal nature. Sanfilippo ("Il risarcimento del danno per l'uccisione di un uomo libero" [1950–1951] 118–19) recognizes, in the cases of personal injury to or death of a free man, a purely penal outcome, with no element of compensation.
26. Marchi ("Il risarcimento del danno morale"[1904] 224) prefers to imagine a situation where an attenuation over time of the original penal features of the action has taken place, favoring its reipersecutory nature. In the end, it became impossible to claim compensation for the injury caused to the passerby as well as any nonmaterial damage. However, it would perhaps be better to think of particular actions as having ambiguous features that are hard to categorize as either penal or reipersecutory, seeing that it does not appear possible to trace in the sources the attenuation that Marchi claims took place.
27. In other words, the features of noxal liability, cumulative liability, and a year's window in which to bring the action.
28. Gaius (3 *aureorum*) *D.* 44.7.5.5: *Is quoque, ex cuius cenaculo (vel proprio ipsius vel conducto vel in quo gratis habitabat) deiectum effusumve aliquid est ita, ut alicui noceret, quasi ex maleficio teneri videtur: ideo autem non proprie ex maleficio obligatus intellegitur, quia plerumque ob alterius culpam tenetur aut servi aut liber* (Also a person from whose upper floor [whether it is his or her own or a hired place or even one in which he or she is living rent free] something has been thrown or poured down with the result that it caused harm to another is regarded as liable in quasi delict; but because generally here he or she is liable for the fault of another, either of a slave or a child, he or she is not properly considered to be liable in delict) (trans. Watson, *"Digest" of Justinian* [1998] [adapted]).
29. Serrao, *Impresa e responsabilità a Roma* (1989) 104.

I am inclined to agree with the idea that the objective criterion of liability contributed to the modification of the nature of penal actions, especially as far as the aspect of noxality[30] is concerned, but I also think that the compensatory function itself, linked to the objective nature of the liability, had an influence on the notion of compensable damage.

In the *actio de effusis vel deiectis,* the object of legal protection was not limited to the *res* alone, as set out in the *lex Aquilia,* but was extended to *personae* as well. One has only to read the text of the edict quoted by Ulpian on this subject to understand this key point.

> Ulp. (23 *ad edictum*) *D.* 9.3.1 pr.: *Praetor ait de his, qui deiecerint vel effuderint: "Unde in eum locum, quo volgo iter fiet vel in quo consistetur, deiectum vel effusum quid erit, quantum ex ea re damnum datum factumve erit, in eum, qui ibi habitaverit, in duplum iudicium dabo. si eo ictu homo liber perisse dicetur, quinquaginta aureorum iudicium dabo. Si vivet nocitumque ei esse dicetur, quantum ob eam rem aequum iudici videbitur eum cum quo agetur condemnari, tanti iudicium dabo. si servus insciente domino fecisse dicetur, in iudicio adiciam: 'aut noxam dedere.'"*
>
> [(Ulpian in the twenty-third book on the Edict): Concerning those who throw or pour out, the praetor says: "Whence something is thrown or poured out onto a place where persons commonly go or stand, against the occupant I will give a trial for double the loss inflicted or done by this act. If a free man allegedly dies from this blow, I will give a trial for fifty gold coins; if he lives and is allegedly injured, I will give a trial for as much as it will seem right to the *iudex* that the defendant be condemned for this thing. If a slave allegedly acted without his master's knowledge, I will add in the trial: "or make noxal surrender."] (trans. Frier, *Casebook* [1989]).

The action for what is thrown or scattered on the street is allowable with respect to the *habitator,*[31] even in the case where he is not the material author of the

30. See Cursi, "Tra responsabilità per fatto altrui e logica della nossalità" (2007) 657–81.

31. A similar criterion of liability correlates exactly with the public safety of the streets according to Glück (*Ausführliche Erläuterung der Pandecten* [1808]) 395–96 [= *Commentario alle Pandette,* 88–89 (§ 707)]). Casavola (*Studi sulle azioni popolari romane* [1957] 156–57) draws attention to the multiple connotations of the word *popularis,* which is attributed, in one sense, to a single member of the population and, in another, to sections of the populace who exert

damage, which is normally quantified at double the value of the damaged object. The interesting part comes immediately afterward, in the hypothetical situation in which the object thrown causes the death of a free man. Here, the penalty is not double the value but a fixed sum of fifty gold coins. In the scenario where the free man is injured rather than killed, however, the praetor authorizes an outcome based on equitable criteria. The passage ends with a reference to noxal liability.

The innovation consists in the fact that compensation for loss deriving from the death or injury of a free man is placed on the same level as that for loss produced by the destruction of *res*. In a way, the two are conflated in a common notion of *damnum*[32]—even if this is accompanied by a series of correctives dictated by respect for the principle that forbids the quantification of the body of a free man.

An example of this is the sanction that provided for compensation for loss following the death of a free man. As Ulpian specifies in a commentary on a lemma of the text of the edict,[33] in applying the principle that prohibits the evaluation of a (free) body, the sanction must be rigorously fixed at a determined sum. The equitable criterion behind allowing compensation for loss deriving

social pressure to obtain recognition and protection for the particular conditions under which they live. On the innovation involved in introducing this instrument of protection, compared to the Aquilian action, see Wołodkiewicz, "*Deiectum vel effusum* e *positum aut suspensum*" (1968) 365–66; Wołodkiewicz, "*Obligationes ex variis causarum figuris*" (1970) 201–2. More recently, see Rodriguez-Ennes, "Los actos ilícitos de derecho honorario" (1994) 905–6, on the usefulness of the praetorian remedy to the public interest. Rossi ("In tema di tutela pretoria della viabilità" [1999] 409–10) emphasizes the undoubted advantage for the injured party of being exonerated from the burden of proof.

32. Ulp. (23 *ad edictum*) *D.* 9.3.1.6: *Haec autem verba 'si vivet nocitumque ei esse dicetur' non pertinent ad damna, quae in rem hominis liberi facta sunt, si forte vestimenta eius vel quid aliud scissum corruptumve est, sed ad ea, quae in corpus eius admittuntur'* (These words "if he or she lives and is allegedly injured" do not refer to damage which is done to the property of a free person, if, for example, his or her clothes or anything else belonging to him or her is torn or spoilt, but apply only to matters affecting his or her body) (trans. Watson, *"Digest" of Justinian* [1998] [adapted]). The text defines as recoverable loss injuries inflicted on a free person from the throwing of objects from *insulae*. See De Visscher, *Le régime romain de la noxalité* (1947) 557 with n. 95.

33. Ulp. (23 *ad edictum*) *D.* 9.3.1.5: *Sed cum homo liber periit, damni aestimatio non fit in duplum, quia in homine libero nulla corporis aestimatio fieri potest, sed quinquaginta aureorum condemnatio fit* (When a free person is killed, there is no doubling of the amount of loss because in the case of a free person no valuation of his or her body is possible, but the condemnation will be for fifty gold coins) (trans. Watson, *"Digest" of Justinian* [1998] [adapted]).

from injury to the body of a free man[34] appears to follow the same principle. In this case, too, the penalty does not follow the rule of double the value of the object but defers to the principle of *bonum et aequum*, which is well known as the criterion used for the quantification of the penalty for *iniuria*. In this latter case, the jurists have identified some criteria for the guidance of the judge. On the one hand, Gaius[35] reports that medical expenses are reimbursed in their entirety, as are damages deriving from the nonperformance of work and loss of working capacity—consistently with juristic guidelines developed for Aquilian loss concerning compensation for injuries inflicted on the *filius familias* and possible *impensae* sustained for medical treatment.[36] On the other hand, deformities or scars cannot be compensated, because of the aforementioned principle that prohibits the quantification of the body of a free person.

When we compare the two solutions—one for the death of and the other

34. Ulp. (23 *ad edictum*) *D.* 9.3.1.6.

35. Gaius (6 *ad edictum provinciale*) *D.* 9.3.7: *Cum liberi hominis corpus ex eo, quod deiectum effusumve quid erit, laesum fuerit, iudex computat mercedes medicis praestitas ceteraque impendia, quae in curatione facta sunt, praeterea operarum, quibus caruit aut cariturus est ob id, quod inutilis factus est. cicatricium autem aut deformitatis nulla fit aestimatio, quia liberum corpus nullam recipit aestimationem* (When a free person sustains bodily injury by something which is thrown down or poured out, the *iudex* takes account of the cost of medical services and other expenses incurred in his or her recovery as well as the value of any employment which he or she has lost or is going to lose because of his or her disability. However, no account is taken of scars or disfigurement, because the body of a free person is not susceptible of valuation) (trans. Watson, *"Digest" of Justinian* [1998] [adapted]).

36. On the case of the wounding of a free man by an animal, Gaius ([7 *ad edictum*] *D.* 9.1.3) reports, *Ex hac lege iam non dubitatur etiam liberarum personarum nomine agi posse, forte si patrem familias aut filius familias vulneraverit quadrupes: scilicet ut non deformitatis ratio habeatur, cum liberum corpus aestimationem non recipiat, sed impensarum in curationem factarum et operarum amissarum quasque amissurus quis esset inutilis factus* (There is now no doubt that under this law an action can be brought even in the name of free persons, if, for example, an animal wounds a head of a household or a son-in-power, but that is not to say that disfigurement can be taken into account, because the body of a free person is not susceptible of valuation. Nevertheless, account can be taken of the expenses for medical treatment and the loss of employment and of the opportunity of taking a job which were caused by the party being disabled") (trans. Watson, *"Digest" of Justinian* [1998] [adapted]). In the case of injury to the *filius familias*, Ulpian ([18 *ad edictum*] *D.* 9.2.7 pr.) writes, *Qua actione patrem consecutum ait, quod minus ex operis filii sui propter vitiatum oculum sit habiturus, et impendia, quae pro eius curatione fecerit* (And in this action the father will recover the amount of his loss of prospective profit from his son's services, of which he is deprived through the eye being damaged, and also the expenses incurred for medical attention) (trans. Watson, *"Digest" of Justinian* [1998]).

for injury to a free person—it appears that they seem animated by two different criteria. In the case of injury, the jurists can count on well-established guidelines, developed for Aquilian loss, that they can apply to our case. In the case of death, however, they choose not to draw on the criteria relevant to compensation for injury. They prefer instead to take an independent line that consists in the provision of a fixed penalty, as in the *edictum aedilicium de feris.*[37] This solution also corresponds, evidently, to the logic of combining the prohibition on *aestimatio* of the body of a free person with the new need for compensation, a compromise whose difficulties did not pass unnoticed by later interpreters. I refer in particular to Placentinus, who, in the *additio* to the gloss *libertas inestimabilis res est* of Bulgarus,[38] solves the problem by holding that the penalty in question should be conceived *in vindictam* and *non nomine aestimationis.*

This observation brings us back to the problem of the nature of the action, whose characteristics are related by Ulpian in his commentary on the edict.[39]

---

37. Ulp. (2 *ad edictum aedilium curulum*) *D.* 21.1.40, 42: *Deinde aiunt aediles: 'ne quis canem, verrem vel minorem aprum, lupum, ursum, pantheram, leonem . . . qua vulgo iter fiet, ita habuisse velit, ut cuiquam nocere damnumve dare possit. si adversus ea factum erit et homo liber ex ea re perierit, solidi ducenti, si nocitum homini libero esse dicetur, quanti bonum aequum iudici videbitur, condemnetur, ceterarum rerum, quanti damnum datum factumve sit dupli'* (The aediles then say: "No one is to have a dog, any wild boar, wolf, bear, panther, lion . . . where there is frequent traffic and it might injure someone or cause loss. The penalty for any contravention of this provision is, if a free person's death results from it, two hundred *solidi*; if a free person be said to have been injured, what a *iudex* regards as right and proper; in all other cases, double the value of the loss inflicted") (trans. Watson, *"Digest" of Justinian* [1998] [adapted]).
38. Beckhaus, *Bulgari: Ad Digestorum titulum de diversis regulis iuris antiqui* (1856) cvi (*ad D.* 50.17.106): *Paulus libro secundo ad Edictum. Libertas inestimabilis res est,* 88. Placentinus: *Quippe libertas pecunia aestimatur, licet interdum poena aliqua in vindictam, non tamen nomine aestimationis iniungatur, puta ubi per id quod in subgrunda positum erat periculose, liber homo periit, quinquaginta aurei praestantur. Item si per feras bestias in loco prohibito liber homo periit, ducenti aurei dantur. iure enim nostro, id est Romano, liberi hominis occisi nulla fit aestimatio . . .* (Freedom is a precious thing 88. Placentinus Since freedom can be valued in monetary terms, it is sometimes allowed to insert some penalty as a form of punitive damages, not, however, as a valuation: for example, in the case where something was placed dangerously on a gutter and a free person is killed, fifty gold coins must be paid. In the same way, if a free person is killed by wild animals in a forbidden place, two hundred gold coins must be paid. According to our law, that is, Roman law, there is no valuation for the free person killed . . .).
39. Ulp. (23 *ad edictum*) *D.* 9.3.5.5: *Haec autem actio, quae competit de effusis et deiectis, perpetua est et heredi competit, in heredem vero non datur. quae autem de eo competit, quod liber perisse dicetur, intra annum dumtaxat competit, neque in heredem datur neque heredi similibusque personis: nam est poenalis et popularis: dummodo sciamus ex pluribus desiderantibus hanc*

The text, as has been justly noted,[40] is written in a convoluted fashion, although there is no reason to believe that there have been interpolations of substance.[41]

In his definition of the characteristics of the action, Ulpian rehearses the various examples contained in the text of the edict, referring first to damage to a *res,* where the action is treated as private, because, unlike "popular" actions,[42] it is described as not being barred by lapse of time and as transmissible to the heirs of the injured person. This latter feature is proof of a material interest in compensation for loss, which is guaranteed not only to the victim but also to his (or her) heirs. The reipersecutory nature of the action explains the exception to the rule indicated by Cassius[43] for praetorian penal actions, which applies here. Praetorian penal actions are, in fact, subject to a prescriptive time period of a year, while these terms do not apply for actions of a reipersecutory nature.[44]

---

actionem ei potissimum dari debere cuius interest vel qui adfinitate cognationeve defunctum contingat. sed si libero nocitum sit, ipsi perpetua erit actio: sed si alius velit experiri, annua erit haec actio, nec enim heredibus iure hereditario competit, quippe quod in corpore libero damni datur, iure hereditario transire ad successores non debet, quasi non sit damnum pecuniarium, nam ex bono et aequo oritur (This action which is available in the case of things poured out or thrown down cannot be barred by lapse of time and is available for the heir of the plaintiff, but not against the heir of the defendant. But the action which lies in the matter of an allegation that a free person has been killed is available only for one year and is not granted against an heir, nor can it be brought by an heir or successors generally, for it is a penal action and one which anyone may bring, though we are aware that where a number of people wish to bring this action, preference should be given to one who has a special interest in the matter or who was related to the deceased by blood or marriage. But if a free person was injured, his or her own action will not be barred by lapse of time, though if anyone else wishes to pursue the matter it will expire in a year; nor is it available to the heirs by virtue of hereditary right because the rule is that when any injury is done to the body of a free person, no claim can pass to his successors by hereditary right, as it is not a matter of pecuniary loss and the action is based upon justice and fairness" (trans. Watson, *"Digest" of Justinian* [1998] [adapted]). See also, with similar language, *Inst.* 4.5.1.

40. See Casavola, *Studi sulle azioni popolari romane* (1957) 160.
41. See Fadda, *L'azione popolare* (1894) 157.
42. Lozano y Corbi ("Popularidad y regimen de legitimación" [1984] 317–18) holds the opposite view, namely, that the action is "popular," arguing for an interpolation, at a later date than Hadrian or the Antonines, of the reference to the perpetual nature of the actionable protection of the plaintiff. See also Van Hoek, "D. 9, 3, 5, 4" (2000) 463–64.
43. See, in this latter sense, Serrao, *Impresa e responsabilità a Roma* (1989) 130. Here, however, I do not think it is necessary to believe that there is an imitation of the *actio civilis legis Aquiliae,* as is supposed by Voci (*Risarcimento e pena privata* [1939] 153) and Casavola (*Studi sulle azioni popolari romane* [1957] 161).
44. Compare the rule formulated by Cassius and reported in Paul. (1 *ad edictum praetorium*) *D.* 44.7.35 pr.: *In honorariis actionibus sic esse definiendum Cassius ait, ut quae rei persecutionem*

An action for the killing of a free person is available only for a year and cannot be transferred to or against the heirs. The action, explains Ulpian, is, in fact, penal and popular. This latter aspect obviously concedes a public interest in the action, but the logic of private penal actions continues to be important in this type of action, at least as far as transmissibility to heirs is concerned.

Proof of this is to be found, in my opinion, in the clause immediately following. A popular action does not accrue *iure hereditario* to the heir of the decedent victim, since—apart from the legal impossibility of transferring a right that has not matured during the life of *de cuius*—the action, by its very nature, pertains to anyone.[45] Despite this, Ulpian makes a list of people with an interest in the decedent still being alive—the *is cui interest,* meaning generally the heir, blood relatives, or in-laws. This list is introduced by a concessive conjunction, as if to say that the action cannot be transferred to the heirs although (*dummodo*) it usually is conceded following a precise hierarchy of interests.[46] In other words, keeping in mind that the trial, despite the public nature of the interest protected by means of a popular action, remains private and that the pecuniary *aestimatio* is acquired by the plaintiff,[47] Ulpian specifies a classification of parties with an interest in the payment of the monetary penalty,[48] which substantially reflects the expectations of the heirs of the plaintiff.[49] These

habeant, hae etiam post annum darentur, ceterae intra annum (Cassius says that in praetorian actions the following must be laid down, namely, that those which involve recovery of the thing should be allowed even after a year, and the others only within a year") (trans. Watson, *"Digest" of Justinian* [1998] [adapted]).

45. It is not necessary here to resort to the notion of actions *vindictam spirantes,* as does Rodriguez-Ennes ("Los actos ilícitos de derecho honorario" [1994] 913).

46. Cf. the similar provision of the *edictum de positis vel suspensis*—at least according to the interpretation I believe to be the most likely, where the action does not concern the heir *iure hereditario* but is available to him or her as the most interested person. See Casavola, *Studi sulle azioni popolari romane* (1957) 165–66; Wołodkiewicz, *"Deiectum vel effusum* e *positum aut suspensum*" (1968) 383–84; Ulp. (23 *ad edictum*) *D.* 9.3.5.13: *Ista autem actio popularis est et heredi similibusque competit, in heredes autem non competit, quia poenalis est* (This action also is open to anyone and is available for an heir and successors generally, but it cannot be brought against the heir of the defendant because it is penal) (trans. Watson, *"Digest" of Justinian* [1998]).

47. See, on this point, Bruns, "Le azioni popolari romane" (1882) 534; Fadda, *L'azione popolare* (1894) 269–70; *contra* Serrao, *Impresa e responsabilità a Roma* (1989) 131.

48. See Fadda, *L'azione popolare* (1894) 157; Botta, *Legittimazione, interesse ed incapacità all'accusa nei 'publica iudicia'* (1996) 164–65.

49. I do not agree with Casavola (*Studi sulle azioni popolari romane* [1957] 161), who argues that the central part of the passage, from *dummodo* to *contingat* should be expunged because of the

expectations, considering this preferential treatment reserved for the relatives of the deceased, could also be compensatory in nature, despite the time-limited aspect of the action, determined by its "popular" character. Notwithstanding the prohibition on the quantification of the body of a free man, in fact, the provision for the fixed penalty might have been a satisfactory solution in (almost) every case of compensation for loss suffered by close relatives.

In the second provision—that referring to the injury to a free man—the action is not barred by lapse of time if pursued directly by the plaintiff. Such a feature, which is not consistent with the praetorian nature of the delict, can be explained, as in the case of damage to *res*, as a reflection of the reipersecutory nature of the action.[50] If the injured party does not take action, then the action, now popular and therefore available for only a year, is open to everyone and, as in the case of the killing of a free man, is not transmitted *iure hereditario* to the heirs.[51]

All the complexity of a legal protection that oscillates between reipersecutory and penal emerges here.[52] In the case of injury to a free man, in fact, the nontransmissibility of the action to an heir is justified by the fact that the injury in question cannot be considered to be pecuniary loss (*quasi non sit damnum*

---

difficulty of logically coordinating the active nontransferability of the action with the hierarchy of interests in the action, introduced by the concessive *dummodo.* The author maintains that whoever wrote this passage committed a serious error, assuming that *neque heredi* refers not to the heir of the one who advances the popular action but to the heir of the deceased person, without realizing that the decedent could not transfer the action to his own heir. Lozano y Corbi ("Popularidad y regimen de legitimación" [1984] 319) claims an error here on the part of the compilers.

50. So argues Casavola (*Studi sulle azioni popolari romane* [1957] 162). In his opinion, moreover, the action, as in the case of the killing of a free man, is popular, for reasons of logical symmetry within Ulpian's argument (ibid., 163–64). See also Lozano y Corbi, "Popularidad y regimen de legitimación" (1984) 320–21; *contra* Fadda, *L'azione popolare* (1894) 157, relying on substantive arguments linked to the time-limited nature of popular actions.

51. Casavola (*Studi sulle azioni popolari romane* [1957] 164) maintains, on the basis of a comparison with the edict *de sepulchro violato,* that the action would be exclusively allowed to the injured party until the time of his or her death and that only afterward, up to a year later, would a third party be qualified to sue. See Serrao, *Impresa e responsabilità a Roma* (1989) 134; Botta, *Legittimazione, interesse ed incapacità all'accusa nei 'publica iudicia'* (1996) 182–83; Ankum, "L'édit du préteur *de his qui deiecerint vel effuderint*" (2003) 13. The entire section of text referring to the freedom to act of the *alius* is the result of an interpolation, according to Longo ("I *quasi delicta*" [1983] 445–46).

52. Palmirski, "*Effusum vel deiectum*" (2000) 680, justly points out that it is impossible to classify the action in question within a specific category, because of its numerous applications.

pecuniarium), but this injury represents, I think, a type of loss nearer to that in the delict of *iniuria*[53] than to Aquilian loss, since it is evaluated on the basis of *bonum et aequum*. The parallel with *iniuria* is incomplete, however, because of at least two insurmountable difficulties. One is the deliberate nature of the offense in *iniuria,* which is absent in the case we are examining. The other, regarding the *actio iniuriarum,* is that the nontransmissibility to the heir(s) of the *actio vindictam spirans* is at variance with the popular nature of the action.

Leaving aside the comparison with *iniuria,* I think that the principle of nontransferability to heir(s) of this legal protection depends more on the popular nature of the action.[54] While the action is not available to the heir of the victim, he or she is allowed, like any (other) *alius,* to raise the action *iure proprio* and perhaps, as with killing, in the manner of a privileged *quivis de popolo.* This interpretative solution seems to me confirmed, for other reasons, by Ulpian's use of the fiction—*quasi non sit damnum pecuniarum*—which he uses to shift the level of discourse from the nontransmissibility of the action to the nontransferability of the loss.[55] The loss is indeed pecuniary, but it is not considered so because of the personal nature of the offense. Gaius, too, in identifying the criteria for the quantification of the damage suffered by the injured party, uses certain parameters that are useful in evading the prohibition of the valuation of the body of a free man.

The impression remains that the jurists, especially in these cases where the

53. See Voci, *Risarcimento e pena privata* (1939) 153, regarding active and passive nontransmissibility; Serrao, *Impresa e responsabilità a Roma* (1989) 136; Giménez-Candela, *Los llamados cuasidelitos* 1990, 98; Ankum, "L'édit du préteur *de his qui deiecerint vel effuderint*" (2003) 13–14.

54. Serrao (*Impresa e responsabilità a Roma* [1989] 136) emphasizes the contrast between the private nature of the action reserved for the plaintiff, which derives from its perpetuity, and the popular nature of the same protection for third parties. I believe, however, that this logical confusion can be resolved by imagining a situation that brought about the transformation of the original praetorian action, from a time-limited one to one without a time limit, when it became much more closely linked to cases involving compensation.

55. Casavola (*Studi sulle azioni popolari romane* [1957] 167) maintains that the fact that the action does not pass to the heirs means only that the loss has not affected property, not that the loss suffered by the injured party is not in itself, within certain limits as regards the injured party, capable of being represented in material terms. I do not see the connection postulated by Serrao (*Impresa e responsabilità a Roma* [1989] 136) between the motivation concerning the nontransmissibility of the action, by dint of the almost nonpecuniary nature of the loss, and his conclusion about the non-time-limited nature of the action reserved to the plaintiff, which Serrao links to the appearance of the fundamentally compensatory function of the action, as regards the Cassian rules on *honorariae actiones.*

penal character of the action is reduced to the advantage of its reipersecutory nature, have difficulty in respecting a principle that, probably originating in the penal sphere and linked to intentional conduct (e.g., *iniuria,* the injury to a free person, a delict unrelated to the logic of a reipersecutory action that punishes the intentional fault of the defendant) does not align with delicts (i.e., quasi delicts) where the offense to a free man is not deliberate, as in the case of the *actio de effusis vel deiectis.*[56] Presumably from this arose the attempt to get around the prohibition of the quantification of the body of a free man with devices such as legal fictions and the identification of alternative criteria to obtain the same results on a concrete level.

Conclusion: From Intentional Fault to Presumed Negligence, From Penalty to Compensation

At this point, we can draw together the threads of our argument and outline the event that possibly led to the emergence of negligence in Roman delicts, connecting it, as far as can be sustained, to compensation. In the provision regarding arson in the Twelve Tables, the legislator had already distinguished between two applications: intentional and unintentional arson. Only the second instance entailed compensation.

This same pattern was reproduced in the regime for the *lex Aquilia.* The emergence of negligence is linked to the emphasis placed on the compensatory aspect, which, as I have attempted to show, did not fall within the scope of the *lex Aquilia* at the time of its enactment but began to be embraced by the statute when the third section was added, which, not by chance, contains the only express reference to loss to be found in the text of the law. The penal action—probably an original feature of the statute—becomes mixed, combining the two aspects of penalty and compensation.

The Aquilian model of liability is adopted also in the quasi delicts, but with an important new feature: negligence becomes presumed negligence, as we see with the concepts of *culpa in vigilando* and *culpa in eligendo,* and as such corresponds to strict liability. As we have seen, this modification had an effect on the nature of the action, diminishing its penal force, and not just with respect to the character of noxality. In the *actio de effusis et deiectis,* the logic of compensation

56. See Feenstra, "L'application de la loi Aquilia en cas d'homicide d'un homme libre" (1993) 144.

not only includes the *res* but is extended to include the damage suffered by a free person, something traditionally bound up with the prohibition of placing a value on his or her body. In deference to this prohibition, jurists are cautious in providing for compensation for such loss and avail themselves of legal fictions or alternative criteria that, even if they do not contravene the prohibition on valuation, have the effect of ensuring compensation at a practical level. It appears obvious that the material need to redress damage is indissolubly linked to the criterion of negligence, especially in its strict sense.

In the later juristic tradition, the connection between negligence and the reipersecutory character of the action begins to be emphasized by the glossators, for whom, as regards Aquilian liability, *culpa* is located in the context of civil actions and understood in a purely reipersecutory sense, while the term *dolus* is more and more used in criminal cases.[57] This "reification" of the purpose behind the Aquilian action involves the progressive recognition of compensation for damage brought about by the killing of or injury to a free person. In the period separating the commentators from the humanists, the role played by judicial procedure seems to be decisive; sensitive to the law and to local custom, it spawned interesting developments, especially on the subject of the identification of persons legally entitled to compensation, in the *interesse civile pro homicidio*.[58]

On these foundations was based the synthesis of Grotius, who, in developing the theory of *damnum per iniuriam datum*, placed the general notion of *maleficium* at the center of his reflections, corresponding to the culpable conduct that requires compensation for damage.[59] Damage here embraces a category of goods decidedly larger than that protected by the *actio legis Aquiliae:*

57. See Rasi, "*L'actio legis Aquiliae* e la responsabilità extracontrattuale" (1968) 736–37 and particularly n. 36, with citations of evidence and literature.

58. See, on this matter, Cursi, *Iniuria cum damno* (2006) 66–77. See also the work of Montel ("La legittimazione attiva nell'azione di risarcimento" [1930] 43–44), who attempts to separate the modern logic of compensation for the death of a relative from the Roman prohibition of the valuation of the body of a free person, reexamining those texts dealing with the action *de effusis vel deiectis* that already recognize such a possibility.

59. Grotius (Van Groot), *De iure belli ac pacis libri tres* (1773), 512–13 (2.17.1–2): *Maleficium hic appellamus culpam omnem, sive in faciendo, sive in non faciendo, pugnantem cum eo, quod aut homines communiter, aut pro ratione certae qualitatis facere debent. ex tali culpa obligatio naturaliter oritur, si damnum datum est, nempe ut id resarciatur* (We call *maleficium* every fault, depending on an act of commission or neglect, against the duties required to men commonly or according to their condition. From this fault, if damage is done, rises by nature an obligation to compensate").

vita . . . corpus, membra, fama, honor, actiones propriae.[60] This recognition—at least with respect to life, the body, its limbs—creates the conditions for compensation for indirect loss deriving from the killing of or injury to a free person.[61]

A similar configuration of Aquilian liability is widely shared and amplified by natural law authorities—I refer especially to the system of Pufendorf, particularly his recognition of the absolute legal protection of the person[62]—becoming a reference model of modern European legal codes, above all the French, which connects extracontractual liability to the notion of *faute.*[63]

The recognition of a general principle of liability, such as negligence, in the common-law systems—which recently has assumed an autonomous configuration as "tort of negligence"—brings the common-law system closer to the French model,[64] creating the basis for a common theory of liability.

Bibliography

Ankum, H. "L'édit du préteur *de his qui deiecerint vel effuderint.*" *Studia iuridica* 41 (2003): 7–26.

Beckhaus, F. W. C. *Bulgari: Ad Digestorum titulum de diversis regulis iuris antiqui Commentarius et Placentini ad eum additiones sive exceptiones.* Bonn: Henry und Cohen, 1856.

Botta, F. *Legittimazione, interesse ed incapacità all'accusa nei "publica iudicia."* Cagliari: AV, 1996.

Bruns, K. G. "Le azioni popolari romane." Trans. V. Scialoia. *Archivio Giuridico* 28 (1882): 166–213. Originally published in German as "Die römischen Popularklagen," *Zeitschrift für Rechtsgechichte* 3 (1864) 341–415.

Casavola, F. *Studi sulle azioni popolari romane: Le "actiones populares."* Naples: Jovene Editore, 1957.

---

60. Grotius (Van Groot), *De iure belli ac pacis libri tres* (1773) 513 (2.17.2.1): "Life . . . body, limbs, reputation, honor, freedom of movement." See also 32 (1.2.5): *Nam vita, membra, libertas, sic quoque propria cuique essent, ac proinde non sine injuria ab alio impeterentur* (For life, limbs, freedom belong to each person in such a way that they cannot be infringed upon by others without wrongfulness). See, similarly, Grotius (Van Groot), *Jurisprudence of Holland* (1953) 471 (3.33.1).

61. Cursi, *Iniuria cum damno* (2006) 77–88.

62. Cursi, *Iniuria cum damno* (2006) 88–96.

63. Cursi, *Iniuria cum damno* (2006) 110–16.

64. See, in general, Zweigert and Kötz, *Introduzione al diritto comparato* (1995) 295–96; see, specifically, Gallo, *L'elemento oggettivo del tort of negligence* (1988) 10–11, 65–66.

Cursi, M. F. *Iniuria cum damno: Antigiuridicità e colpevolezza nella storia del danno aquiliano.* Milan: Giuffrè Editore, 2002.

Cursi, M. F. "Per una storia critica della tutela aquiliana del credito." In *Modelli teorici e metodologici nella storia del diritto privato,* 2:23–126. Naples: Jovene Editore, 2006.

Cursi, M. F. "Tra responsabilità per fatto altrui e logica della nossalità: Il problema della cosiddetta *exceptio noxalis.*" In *Filìa: Studi per G. Franciosi,* ed. F. M. d'Ippolito, 1:657–81. Naples: Satura Editrice, 2007.

Dell'Andro, R. 1958. "Antigiuridicità." *Enciclopedia del diritto,* 2:542–59. Milan: Giuffrè Editore, 1958.

De Visscher, F. *Le régime romain de la noxalité.* Brussels: A. De Visscher, 1947.

Fadda, C. *L'azione popolare: Studio di diritto romano ed attuale.* Vol. 1. Turin: UTET, 1894.

Feenstra, R. "L'application de la loi Aquilia en cas d'homicide d'un homme libre, de l'époque classique à celle de Justinien." In *Mélanges F. Wubbe,* 141–60. Fribourg: Fribourg University Press, 1993.

Frier, B. W. *A Casebook on the Roman Law of Delict.* Atlanta, GA: Scholars Press, 1989.

Gallo, P. *L'elemento oggettivo del tort of negligence: Indagine sui limiti della responsabilità delittuale per negligence nei paesi di Common Law.* Milan: Giuffrè Editore, 1988.

Giménez-Candela, T. *Los llamados cuasidelitos.* Madrid: Editorial Trivium, 1990.

Gioffredi, C. "L'elemento intenzionale nel diritto penale romano." In *Studi G. Grosso,* 3:35–53. Turin: Giappichelli, 1970.

Glück, C. F. *Ausführliche Erläuterung der Pandecten nach Hellfeld: Ein Commentar.* Vol. 10. Erlangen: J. J. Palm, 1808. Translated into Italian as *Commentario alle Pandette,* vol. 9 Milan: Leonardo Vallardi Editore, 1905.

Grotius (van Groot), H. *De iure belli ac pacis libri tres.* 2 vols. Utrecht: Ioannis a Schoonhoven, 1773.

Grotius (van Groot), H. *The Jurisprudence of Holland.* Trans. R. Warden Lee. Oxford: Oxford University Press, 1953. Originally published in Dutch as *Inleidung de Hollandsche Rechtsgeleertheyd.* Haarlem: A. Roman, 1631.

Levy, E. *Privatstrafe und Schadensersatz im klassischen römischen Recht.* Berlin: F. Vahlen, 1915.

Longo, G. "I *quasi delicta: Actio de effusis vel deiectis / Actio de positis ac suspensis.*" In *Studi C. Sanfilippo,* 4:399–469. Milan: Giuffrè Editore, 1983.

Lozano y Corbi, E. "Popularidad y regimen de legitimación en la *actio de effusis et deiectis.*" *Studi A. Biscardi,* 5:311–27. Milan: Istituto Editoriale Cisalpino, 1984.

MacCormack, G. "Criminal Liability for Fire in Early and Classical Roman Law." *Index* 3 (1972): 382–96.

MacCormack, G. "Fault and Causation in Early Roman Law." *Revue internationale des droits de l'antiquité* 28 (1981): 97–126.

Marchi, A. "Il risarcimento del danno morale secondo il diritto romano." *Bullettino dell'Istituto di Diritto Romano* 16 (1904): 282–89.

Molnár, I. "Erfolgshaftung oder typisierter *dolus malus* im archaischen römischen Recht." *Bullettino dell'Istituto di Diritto Romano* 89 (1986): 465–90.

Montel, A. "La legittimazione attiva nell'azione di risarcimento per la morte di una persona." *Temi Emiliana* 7 (1930): 1–68.

Palmirski, T. "*Effusum vel deiectum:* Au-delà des frontières." In *Mélanges W. Wołodkiewicz,* 2:667–83. Warsaw: Liber, 2000.

Pólay, E. "*Iniuria:* Tatbestände im archaischen Zeitalter des antiken Rom." *Zeitschrift der Savigny-Stiftung (Romanistische Abteilung)* 101 (1984): 142–89.

Rasi, P. "*L'actio legis Aquiliae* e la responsabilità extracontrattuale nella glossa." In *Atti del convegno internazionale di Studi Accursiani (Bologna, 21–26 ottobre 1963),* ed. G. Rossi, 2:723–75. Milan: Giuffrè Editore, 1968.

Rodriguez-Ennes, L. "Los actos ilícitos de derecho honorario: Derecho romano de *obligationes.*" In *Homenaje J. L. Murga Gener,* 903–20. Madrid: Centro Estudios Ramon Areces, 1994.

Rossi, D. "In tema di tutela pretoria della viabilità: A proposito di D. 9.3.5.12." *Index* 27 (1999): 409–22.

Sanfilippo, C. "Il risarcimento del danno per l'uccisione di un uomo libero nel diritto romano." *Annali Catania* 5 (1950–51): 118–31.

Schipani, S. *Responsabilità 'ex lege Aquilia': Criteri di imputazione e problema della 'culpa.'* Turin: Giappichelli, 1969.

Serrao, F. *Diritto privato, economia e società nella storia di Roma.* Vol. 1, *Dalla società gentilizia alle origini dell'economia schiavistica.* Naples: Jovene Editore, 2006.

Serrao, F. *Impresa e responsabilità a Roma nell'età commerciale.* Pisa: Pacini, 1989.

van Hoek, J. B. M. "D. 9, 3, 5, 4: Übersetzungsfragen im Bereich der *actio de deiectis vel effusis* als Popularklage." *Zeitschrift der Savigny-Stiftung (Romanistische Abteilung)* 117 (2000): 454–72.

Voci, P. *Risarcimento e pena privata nel diritto romano classico.* Milan: Giuffrè Editore, 1939.

Wacke, A. "Fahrlässige Vergehen im römischen Strafrecht." *Revue internationale des droits de l'antiquité* 26 (1979): 505–66.

Watson, A. *The 'Digest' of Justinian.* Rev. ed. 2 vols. Philadelphia: University of Pennsylvania Press, 1998.

Wittmann, R. *Die Körperverletzung an Freien im klassischen römischen Recht.* Munich: Beck, 1972.

Wołodkiewicz, W. "*Deiectum vel effusum* e *positum aut suspensum* nel diritto romano." *Rivista italiana per le scienze giuridiche* 95 (1968): 365–91.

Wołodkiewicz, W. "*Obligationes ex variis causarum figuris:* Ricerche sulla classificazione delle fonti delle obbligazioni nel diritto romano classico." *Rivista italiana per le scienze giuridiche* 97 (1970): 77–227.

Zweigert, K., and H. Kötz. *Introduzione al diritto comparato.* Vol. 2, *Istituti.* Milan: Giuffrè Editore, 1995. Originally published in German as *Einführung in die Rechtsvergleichung,* vol. 2, *Institutionen* (Tübingen: J. C. B. Mohr, 1984).

CHAPTER 13

The Byzantine Law of Obligations

BERNARD STOLTE

Se vogliamo che tutto cambi, bisogna che tutto rimanga com'è.

Roman Law and Byzantine Law

Byzantine law is, at heart, Roman law. The Byzantine Empire is the Roman Empire. The Byzantine emperors considered themselves the rightful successors of Augustus—indeed, of Aeneas.[1] The word *Byzantine* is a late Western concept. So what do we mean by Byzantine law?

The crucial period is, of course, the Justinianic age, when Roman law, as we know it, went through two transformations. The first is the result of Justinian's codification of 529–34, which hardly needs to be illuminated in detail. Suffice it to say that not only did it abrogate the existing sources of Roman law insofar as not incorporated in the *Digest* and *Code* and monopolize legislation for the imperial throne, but it also, by its very existence, influenced the transmission of the older Roman legal texts. I will return to the latter aspect shortly. The second transformation is the subsequent translation and explanation of the Latin codification into Greek. This, I would suggest, is the real starting point of Byzantine law, since, on the one hand, it made possible the use and development of a body of law for the Greek-speaking population and, on the other hand, it is the first moment in which a separate development was irrevocably started—separate from Latin-speaking, Western legal thought. Justinian's *Novels* belong to this Eastern development.

1. See the *prooimion* of *Nov.* 47, in the version of the Latin *Authenticum: nosque Aenaeadae ab illo vocamur* (and after him we are called the sons of Aeneas).

What we know of Roman law largely depends on the Justinianic codification. Its use of existing legal writing and legislation eternalized the voices of Paul, Ulpian, and Papinian, whose works ceased to be copied separately since they had lost legal force with the compilation of the *Digest.* When we speak of "classical" Roman law, we speak of a legal *universum* mainly reconstructed from Justinianic sources. Many Romanist lawyers (as I, in order to avoid confusion, would call the modern students of Roman law) find themselves standing in the sixth century and looking at the preceding centuries. There is, of course, nothing wrong with that position, as long as they are aware of what they are doing. It is slightly curious that, when in doubt about text or explanation, they should pay, as a rule, little or no attention to the writings of the so-called *antecessores,* the law professors of the Justinianic age, who, as the compilers and commentators of the codification, were its best connoisseurs and whose writings have been preserved by subsequent Byzantine legal compilations, above all the so-called *Basilica.*

Byzantinist lawyers find themselves on the same spot but gazing in the opposite direction. Contrary to their Romanist colleagues, they need not bother about interpolations, the conscious changes effected in the "classical" texts by the compilers of the Justinianic codification. They may do as the Byzantines themselves have done, that is, consider the Justinianic texts as the points of reference that would be repeated, reformulated, summarized, and so on and so forth, but hardly ever really changed. That is not to say that Byzantine law did not change; it is just that the Byzantines did not always use legislation as their preferred vehicle for legal change.

Byzantine Law

If one wishes to speak of Byzantine law, one therefore needs to start, first and foremost, with Justinianic Roman law. At least Justinianic Roman law has been described adequately, you may think. Well, I am not so sure. Existing treatments of the subject are few and far between and never incorporate the entire body of material: their aim usually is to describe "classical" Roman law and mention Justinianic developments by way of an appendix.[2] A textbook of Byz-

2. The standard handbook of Roman law, Kaser's *Das römische Privatrecht* (1971), is an example: the second volume describes the "nachklassische Entwicklungen" (postclassical developments), in which the Justinianic legislation is characterized as not only the pinnacle but also the conclusion of "eastern Roman classicism" ([1975] 32).

antine law that is based not only on the *Institutes, Digest,* and *Code* but also on the Justinianic *Novels* and the Greek commentaries as preserved in the so-called *Paraphrase of Theophilus* and, above all, the scholia on the *Basilica* and that takes account of subsequent Byzantine compilations and sources from legal practice is, alas, lacking, with the noble exception of Zachariä von Lingenthal's *Geschichte des griechisch-römischen Rechts,* in its third edition of 1892, published when Zachariä was eighty years of age.[3] Nobody has undertaken a similar attempt for more than a century, and no one is expected to do so in the near future.[4] It should be mentioned, however, that we now have infinitely better editions of the sources and considerably more material than Zachariä did and that his views on many points have been superseded.

One more ghost to dispel is the idea that Byzantine law should be the product of a felicitous marriage of Roman law and Hellenistic, Christianized philosophy, a notion popular with some Greek scholars.[5] I am not convinced. Indeed, our sources present a remarkably "pure," Justinianic form of Roman law for the duration of the Byzantine Empire; such deviations as may be observed cannot be attributed to the other partner of that hypothetical marriage. Reflection on law and on its role in society is rare: the preface to the *Eisagoge,* a short manual of ca. 900, associated with the patriarch Photius,[6] is an isolated exception.

Purely Christian reform is another ghost but rarely seen. The most-quoted example is the law of "marriage property" (*Ehegüterrecht*), which supposedly had been reformed in the *Ecloga* of 741 into a system of joint ownership under the influence of the *mia sarx* (one flesh) doctrine.[7] H. J. Scheltema and, later, Dieter Simon and Ludwig Burgmann have exorcised that devil for good, I hope.[8] To be sure, there is Christian influence to be observed in Byzantine law, but for examples, we must consult the Theodosian and Justinianic Codes: in other words, most of it was already there with the inception of Byzantine law.[9]

In short, Byzantine law is predominantly Justinianic Roman law that went through "normal" development during the remaining nine hundred years of the Byzantine Empire. In that respect, Byzantine law may be compared with

3. Zachariä, *Geschichte des griechisch-römischen Rechts* (1892).
4. See Stolte, "Balancing Byzantine Law" (2005) 74–75.
5. See, e.g., Yiannopoulos, "Historical Development" (1993).
6. On this preface, see now the commentary of W. J. Aerts et al. in Stolte and Meijering, "The Prooimion of the Eisagoge" (2001), with literature.
7. Ephesians 5:31, for example.
8. See Burgmann, "Reformation oder Restauration" (1992), with literature.
9. The classical treatment is still Biondi, *Il diritto romano cristiano* (1952–1954).

continental European law between 1100 and 1800. One would be tempted to reverse the words of the Prince of Salina: the more things needed to be changed, they had to remain the same.[10]

The first question to be asked is, what are our sources for information about this Byzantine development that built on the basis of the Justinianic legislative program?[11] Little is to be gained from the translations and abbreviations into Greek that have been preserved in Theophilus's paraphrase of the *Institutes* or the text of the *Basilica,* where one might look at passages going back to the pertinent titles of the *Corpus iuris civilis.* The reason is that they usually just translate and summarize what we already know from their Latin counterparts. At the end of the day, valuable as these Greek equivalents are (they sometimes supplement or correct our Latin sources), they represent the Justinianic texts. If we want to know how Byzantine lawyers interpreted and applied these texts, we have to look elsewhere. A first port of call would be the scholia on the *Basilica*—the "glosses," as they are called in the Western tradition. The annotations in the margins and between the lines of the *Basilica* manuscripts have been edited in the *Basilica* edition in separate volumes.[12] Usually, two layers may be distinguished. One is the so-called "older" scholia, commentaries in Greek on the *Corpus iuris* in the Justinianic age, which later were appended to the corresponding *Basilica* passages. The other is the "younger" scholia, annotations written after the *Basilica* had been compiled and mostly dating to the eleventh century and later. On the whole, the older scholia are more numerous and have been studied more intensively.

Our information may be distorted by the fortunes of the transmission of the text of the *Basilica,* which have not always been generous. Sixteen books out of sixty have been lost altogether, and a number of the forty-four preserved books have reached our day without scholia. What has been preserved is thus very uneven in terms of information.

Although, therefore, we may learn more about one subject than another,

10. Cf. the original wording in G. Tomasi di Lampedusa, *Il Gattopardo* (first published in 1958): "Se vogliamo che tutto rimanga com'è, bisogna che tutto cambi."

11. For the history of the sources of Byzantine law, see Pieler, "Byzantinische Rechtsliteratur" (1978); van der Wal and Lokin, *Delineatio iuris graeco-romani* (1985) Troianos, *Oi peges tou buzantinou dikaiou* (2011).

12. *Basilicorum libri LX,* edited in eight volumes of text and nine of scholia by Scheltema, Holwerda, and van der Wal (1953–88). There is no modern translation: some help may be found in the old edition by Heimbach, which contains the Greek text with facing Latin translation, but the latter is, of course, based on a Greek text, which is sometimes very defective.

I am confident that we are offered, altogether, a representative and reliable picture of Byzantine legal scholarship. Ideally, we would wish to confront this scholarship with sources stemming from legal practice. However, these are few and far between, especially as far as early and middle Byzantium are concerned. True, for the early period, there are the papyri from the desert, but after the Arab conquest of Egypt in the seventh century, their information is no longer related to what was happening in the capital. Apart from the papyri, our sources are not very numerous; even in the later period, the situation does not improve all that much. Some precious documents have been published in the volumes of *Fontes Minores,* with an emphasis on the law of marriage property. Precisely for the law of obligations—to be more precise, of obligations arising from contract—we are somewhat better served.

The Byzantine Law of Contractual Obligations

It would, of course, be preposterous to pretend to offer, in this place, a comprehensive treatment of the Byzantine law of obligations. After what has been said so far, the starting point would, in any case, have to be the Justinianic codification. Byzantine lawmakers never lost sight of the fourfold division made by Justinian's *Institutes* into obligations arising from contract, quasi contract, delict, and quasi delict;[13] the further subdivision of contractual obligations into the four categories of *re, verbis, litteris,* and *consensu;* and the sub-subdivision of consensual contractual obligations into four—from *emptio venditio, locatio conductio, societas,* and *mandatum.*[14] However, in Byzantium just as in the later Western, Latin tradition, this rigid scheme left the problem of the status of so-called *pacta,* agreements not fitting into the traditional scheme. *Pacta sunt servanda,* as we learn, with somewhat different phrasing, from the mouth of Ulpian.[15] This is certainly so, but how? Any discussion of this problem tends to develop into a general theory of contract. This has been true in Byzantium just as much as in the Western legal tradition.

The aforementioned division of contractual obligations into various types is, in fact, rooted in the classical Roman law of civil procedure, which offered to a prospective plaintiff the possibility of bringing an *actio* in a limited number of

13. *Inst.* 3.13.

14. *Inst.* 3.22 pr.

15. Ulp. *D.* 2.14.7.7.

situations: the procedure *per formulam.* In principle, if an agreement had been made outside the standard situations, as a mere *pactum,* no action was available. A defendant, however, could invoke such a *pactum* as a legitimate defense by way of an *exceptio.* To that extent, *pacta* were recognized. Gradually, certain *pacta* were also recognized as a ground for an action. For example, *pacta* made at the same moment as and in addition to a recognized type of contract, the *pacta ex continenti,* could lead to an action, in contradistinction to those that were made later, the *pacta ex intervallo.* Certain other *pacta* were made enforceable, too. However, *pacta* were never raised to equal status with the original standard contracts.

It is well known how, under the influence of canon, natural, and Germanic law, Western legal systems based on Roman law came generally to recognize the principle of enforceability of any contractual promise, howsoever made.[16] I will here confine myself to the Byzantine development and take my cue from the standard view in Romanist circles as formulated by Max Kaser.[17]

According to Kaser, who usually categorizes late and Eastern developments with the notion "oströmische Schuldoktrin" (East Roman law school teaching), the opposition between *contractus* and *pacta* was maintained in the East but mitigated by making the *pacta* enforceable. Having set out the result, Kaser then concludes that " . . . one may start from the assumption of a general rule of enforceability of *pacta,* so that the opposition of *contractus* and *pacta* in the East, too [just as in the West], ceases to be meaningful. . . ."[18] I beg to differ. Of course, Kaser was not primarily (and mostly not at all) concerned with post-Justinianic developments, and it is a moot point whether some of what he sees as *nachklassisch* is not already "classical." In my opinion, when looking at post-Justinianic texts, we should stress that, until the end, the Byzantines adhered to the principle that *pacta* were not enforceable independently, unless certain conditions were met. In that respect, the Byzantines remained true to what they considered themselves to be: *Rhoomaioi.* Even so, one might ask oneself whether the ways in which a *pactum nudum,* a mere "informal" agreement, could be "upgraded" to a formal, recognized, and therefore enforceable type of contract were not so numerous as to render the old distinction devoid of sense. Apparently they were not, or at least not yet in the eleventh century.

If we look at the state of our sources, it is striking that the textual tradition

16. Zimmermann, *Law of Obligations* (1990) 537–45.

17. Kaser, *Das römische Privatrecht* (1975) 2: § 261.

18. Kaser, *Das römische Privatrecht* (1975) 2:364.

has been extremely generous with information about *pacta*. True, fortune may have played its part, but the numbers are too striking to be just coincidence. The *Digest* title *De Pactis, D.* 2.14, is represented in the *Basilica* in title *B.* 11.1, which contains a vast amount of scholia. The latter fact is a strong indication that it was taken seriously as a subject, not only when the *Digest* was used as a teaching text in the sixth century, but also after the compilation of the *Basilica,* in the tenth century, when the so-called old scholia were added, and still later, when "new" scholia were written. I am inclined to interpret this interest in *pacta* as a sign that the Byzantines remained prisoners of the classical opposition between *contractus* and *pacta,* to such an extent that *pacta* attracted a disproportionate interest.

Also from the sixth century, we have a papyrus that discusses *pacta* and repeatedly quotes *Digest* 2.14 in Greek paraphrase.[19] It has been debated to whom the text may be ascribed.[20] To me, it seems more significant that we find precisely the subject of *pacta* treated in one out of the three surviving sixth-century Egyptian juristic papyri, strengthening the impression of a sixth-century interest in the doctrine of *pacta.*[21]

No doubt some scholars would claim the sixth century for Roman, rather than for Byzantine, law—which is entirely acceptable as long as we are agreed that Roman lawyers of the sixth century were predominantly writing in Greek. Let us therefore proceed to the undisputedly Byzantine centuries and cast a look at some stepping-stones in the subsequent development.[22]

Two strands may be distinguished. One is a preference for written agreements and witnesses, which is understandable as far as it concerns proof of what actually has happened. The other is the old discussion on the status of *pacta* within the framework of contractual obligations. The two strands are not always kept separate. The first can be documented in legislation by the emperors Irene (797–802)[23] and also Leo VI (886–912). Leo's *Novel* 72 covers both these lines of thought and, if taken seriously, makes any *pactum nudum* into an enforceable agreement when it is written down and when the parties have

19. *PSI* 55.

20. Most recently Brandsma, *Dorotheus and His Digest Translation* (1996) 113–18, with literature.

21. The other two are *PSI* 1350, pertaining to *D.* 9.2 *De lege Aquilia,* and an unpublished Oxyrhynchus papyrus relating to the first book of the *Digest.*

22. See the general overview by Zachariä, *Geschichte des griechisch-römischen Rechts* (1892) 283–99.

23. See Burgmann, "Die Novellen der Kaiserin Eirene" (1981) 16–25, with German translation.

appended the sign of the cross to their words.[24] At the same time, *Novel* 72 is witness to the force of the classical doctrine, since Leo complains in his preamble of some people who still maintain that unless a *stipulatio poenae* has reinforced it, a mere *pactum* can at best produce an *exceptio.*

Pace Leo the Wise, to take this classical view was still an entirely respectable line of argument in the eleventh century. Our source is an interesting text, little known to Romanists. From this last period of flourishing of Byzantine secular law, which also saw the "refounding of the law school of Constantinople" in 1045, we have a *Melete peri psiloon sumphoonoon.*[25] The usual Latin version of the title, *Meditatio de nudis pactis,* suggests a scholarly and unworldly "treatise on mere agreements,"[26] but the work is, in fact, a note by a judge from the imperial high court of Constantinople, addressed to his colleagues (one in particular),[27] on the occasion of an actual case in which the point had arisen. The note represents in writing what had been said in session a little while earlier.[28]

The case itself is unrecoverable in its full details.[29] A Byzantine of high social standing (*protospatharios*) had agreed to pay a certain amount to a monastery on the condition that he would be received into the monastery on the same footing as a monk but without actually becoming a monk. We are therefore dealing with a *do ut des et facias.* The *protospatharios* had paid the money, and the monastery had fulfilled its part of the agreement for some years. Then,

24. See Noailles and Dain, *Les Novelles de Léon* (1944), with French translation; Troianos, *Oi Neares Leontos* (2007), with translation into modern Greek.

25. Edited with translation into French and extensive commentary by Monnier and Platon in *La Meditatio de nudis pactis* (1915); the edition is found at pp. 28–64 and has been divided into titles and paragraphs, after which I will quote here. See also Zachariä, *Geschichte des griechisch-römischen Rechts* (1892) 296; Pieler, "Byzantinische Rechtsliteratur" (1978) 467–68; van der Wal and Lokin, *Delineatio iuris graeco-romani* (1985) 103; Troianos, *Oi peges tou buzantinou dikaiou* (2011) 292–93.

26. Already Leunclavius, whom we have to thank for the *editio princeps* (Leunclavius, *Iuris graeco-romani tomus secundus* [1596] 192–202), noted (at 192) on *Meditatio, Licebit et declamationem dicere,* and the header over the text says *Responsum.* Reinsch ("Eustathios Rhomaios' Opusculum über das Hypobolon" [1986] 249) notes, in a similar case (*Peira* 66,1), that it was, in fact, a synonym for *semeiooma,* meaning something like "(draft) sentence." In any case, it is clear that we have to understand *melete* in a procedural context—if not actually as "draft sentence," then as "legal opinion" or memorandum.

27. He addresses his fellow judges in the *prooimion,* and from the third title onward, he addresses one in particular with whom he differs.

28. *Melete* 6.29.

29. Monnier and Platon, *La Meditatio de nudis pactis* (1915) 141–86.

apparently, there arose a dispute, the precise nature of which does not become entirely clear. On the basis of the information in the text, Monnier conjectures that after some time, a second agreement had been made, in which additional money had been promised, about which the *protospatharios* later had second thoughts, refusing to pay the agreed-on sum. The monastery was now claiming this. The legal point at issue was whether the subsequent agreement could be enforced. To answer this question, our author argues that it is necessary first to establish the nature of the second agreement, which he set out to do in his note by developing a theory of *pacta nuda,* which he then applied to the case in hand. We do not know the final judgment of the court.

Whatever the occasion and outcome, this treatise's author, about whose identity there has been some discussion,[30] wished to instruct "those who are ignorant of the doctrine of *pacta.*"[31] I will restrict myself to a brief overview of his argument. The author distinguishes *pacta* in various ways. First, he deals with *pacta legitima, pacta* sanctioned by a law or constitution (title 1). In title 2, he mentions *pacta iuris gentium* with an individual name, by which he apparently means the *contractus consensu* and *re;* the *pacta* without a name but with a *causa* and indicated by a the general name of contract (*synallagma*), that is, the *contractus innominati re;* and, also originating in the *ius gentium,* but neither carrying a special name nor falling under the general name of contract, the so-called *pacta nuda.* He proceeds to "subdivide"[32] (2.3) these agreements into those that never give rise to an action but only generate an affirmative defense (*exceptio*). Examples are the remission of a debt and all *pacta* made *ex intervallo.* He then intercalates a parenthesis (title 3) in which he directly addresses his opponent, to conclude preliminarily that "*nuda* and *psila*—the Latin and Greek words for 'naked' are used—are the *pacta* that are made *ex intervallo*" (3.5).

The argument of 2.3 is resumed in title 4: all *pacta ex intervallo* give rise to an *exceptio,* not to an action. To such *pacta* are now added those that have been made later "against the nature of the contract." If I am not mistaken, the author

30. Monnier and Platon, *La Meditatio de nudis pactis* (1915) 186–236; van der Wal and Lokin, *Delineatio iuris graeco-romani* (1985) 103; Troianos, *Oi peges tou buzantinou dikaiou* (2011) 293.

31. *Melete* prooim., 1.

32. *Melete* 2.3: *hypodiaireitai.* In fact, it is not yet so much a subdivision as an elaboration of various examples of *pacta nuda,* concentrating on those made *ex intervallo.* The subdivision announced here does not occur until titles 4 and 5, as discussed shortly.

means agreements that extend the original contract into an arrangement significantly diverging from the standard contract (4.4).[33] But not only are there *pacta nuda ex intervallo;* there are also *ex continenti* (5 pr.–1). *Pacta nuda* give rise to an *exceptio* (5.3), but sometimes they transform the nature of the *actio bonae fidei* (5.4), provided that these *pacta* have been made *ex continenti,* in which case they also serve the plaintiff (5.5). The *pactum nudum,* therefore, is twofold in nature, embracing all *pacta ex intervallo* and, under certain conditions, also the *pacta ex continenti* (5.6–10). Sometimes, however, there are agreements to resolve a contract *re nondum secuta* (i.e., *integra re*), which extinguish the action (5.20). What about partial resolution? Such *pacta* serve the defendant. Examples from sale are given: a diminution of the price speaks for itself; it is further pointed out that an increase in the price is in fact a diminution of the thing bought. It thus works also in favor of the *actor,* by transforming the action (5.31) into a claim of receiving a higher payment in exchange for the same thing, and could be compared with *novatio* of a debt (5.34).

Having set forth the nature of the *pactum nudum,* the author anticipates, in title 6, the question of his opponent: "where is this to be found in the *Basilica*?" (6 pr.). The proper question is, where is a rule that contradicts this? Indeed, all this is in conformity with the *Basilica* (6.12), as a quotation from that work demonstrates.[34] All this only holds *re nondum secuta;* if one part of the agreement has been fulfilled, there is no going back, either in part or in full (6.22). As for "according to the nature," this should be understood, more precisely, as "anything agreed upon to diminish or increase the preceding arrangements" (6.23). The author concludes this part with a plea for the use of the *Digest* rather than the *Basilica.*

This, then, is the theory of *pacta nuda* as set forth by the author. The remainder of the treatise, titles 7 and 8, refers to the case in hand. Briefly, it is established that there has been a contract *do ut des et facias,* potentially leading to an *actio praescriptis verbis,* but now completed in full, with the result that no *actio* could be available to either party. The second agreement is seen as an additional *pactum,* which, in the light of what has preceded, can be of no value (7.14). There can be little doubt about what the court should decide, in the view of our author.

If a distinction no longer existed between *contractus* and *pacta* in Byzan-

33. See Kaser, *Das römische Privatrecht* (1975) 2:366 with n. 32.

34. *B.* 11.1.7.6 = *D.* 2.14.7.6.

tium in the eleventh century, a treatise such as this could not have been written. It is worth noting that the distinction ultimately originated in a law of procedure long obsolete. Many of the points made would not have been out of place several centuries earlier. If the maxim *pacta sunt servanda* applied without qualification, the treatise would make no sense.

Much else could be said by way of comment on the *Meditatio de nudis pactis* (or *Melete*). One may say that one is not convinced by this exposition of the *pactum nudum;* one may find fault with the composition of the argument, its verbosity, and so on. One may voice surprise that not once are we told that enforceability of the second agreement might easily be secured by putting it into a *stipulatio.* One may observe that the treatise is halfway between a general theory of contract and a specialized treatment of *pacta.* I would probably agree with these observations and objections. However, rather than isolating the treatise from its context, I should like to make a few remarks of a general nature.

First, the fact that these jurists still discuss the law in terms familiar to us from the Justinianic *Corpus iuris civilis* and even keep to the Latin technical terms is more interesting than the question of whether these jurists still understood their Roman law correctly. After all, they were under no obligation to adhere to pure Roman law.

Second, the detailed discussion in the note speaks for a high level of the deliberations in this eleventh-century Byzantine court case. We do not know whether it was the rule or an exception, but at least it proves that judges were capable of a fairly sophisticated legal debate.

Third, it is not without profit to contrast the previous observation with current scholarly opinion about the nature of Byzantine litigation, which seems to have swung in an entirely different direction thanks to a very influential paper of 1973 by Dieter Simon about the *Peira.*[35] The *Peira* is a collection of cases in (what is evidently) the same eleventh-century high court of Constantinople, in which are reported several opinions of the judge Eustathios Rhoomaios. Simon rejects any suggestion of doctrinal debate taking place and infers instead the presence of a "totale Kasuistik" (pure case law method), thus an approach "arguing with, rather than from, the law." Whichever of the two approaches, doctrinal or case law, was the rule, it cannot have operated without exceptions.

35. Simon, *Rechtsfindung am byzantinischen Reichsgericht* (1973). On Eustathios and the *Peira,* see also Schminck, "Vier eherechtliche Entscheidungen" (1979); Oikonomides, "The 'Peira' of Eustathios Rhomaios" (1986); Simon, "Das Ehegüterrecht der Pira" (1986).

The *Meditatio* represents an attempt at resolving a dispute through the adoption of a doctrinal method.

Fourth, interestingly, our author reproaches his opponent for exclusively relying on the *Basilica,* whereas, in his view, the proper method of understanding the law was to go back to the *antecessores* of the sixth century, in particular to the immensely popular and influential Stephanus. This has been interpreted to mean that in the eleventh century, the *Basilica* were not yet seen as an exclusive and exhaustive codification.

Conclusion

It is time for a conclusion on Byzantium and (the place of *pacta* in) the law of obligations. The main point seems to me that in Byzantium, in contrast with certain developments that may be observed on the western half of the European continent in the late Middle Ages, an attempt was made to maintain the Justinianic system and substance of the law, with, on the whole, little scope for other influences. Many scholars would think of Byzantium as an inextricable whole of church and state, but I have not there found the Gospel according to Matthew used as an argument for extending the *pacta sunt servanda* rule into a general rule of binding and enforceable agreements, as was the case in the West. Perhaps we might say that if we want to understand Justinian's law of obligations, we should study Byzantine sources. I gladly leave to the reader's judgment whether this is a future for the law of obligations.

Bibliography

Biondi, B. *Il diritto romano cristiano.* 3 vols. Milan: Giuffrè Editore, 1952–54.

Brandsma, F. *Dorotheus and His Digest Translation.* Groningen: Egbert Forsten, 1996.

Burgmann, L. "Die Novellen der Kaiserin Eirene." In *Fontes Minores,* vol. 4, ed. D. Simon, 1–36. Frankfurt am Main: Vittorio Klostermann, 1981.

Burgmann, L. "Reformation oder Restauration? Zum Ehegüterrecht der Ecloga." In *Eherecht und Familiengut in Antike und Mittelalter,* ed. D. Simon, 29–42. Munich: Oldenbourg, 1992.

Kaser, M. *Das römische Privatrecht.* 2nd ed. 2 vols. Munich: Beck, 1971–75.

Leunclavius, J. *Iuris graeco-romani tomus secundus.* Frankfurt: Heredes Petri Fischeri, 1596.

Monnier, H., and G. Platon. *La Meditatio de nudis pactis.* Paris: Recueil Sirey, 1915. Reprinted in H. Monnier, *Études de droit byzantin,* (London: Variorum Reprints, 1974), as no. III with the original pagination.

Noailles, P., and A. Dain, eds. *Les Novelles de Léon VI le Sage.* Paris: Les Belles Lettres, 1944.

Oikonomides, N. "The 'Peira' of Eustathios Rhomaios: An Abortive Attempt to Innovate in Byzantine Law." In *Fontes Minores,* vol. 7, ed. D. Simon, 169–92. Frankfurt am Main: Vittorio Klostermann, 1986.

Pieler, P. E. "Byzantinische Rechtsliteratur." In *Die hochsprachliche profane Literatur der Byzantiner,* ed. H. Hunger, 341–480. Munich: Beck, 1978.

Reinsch, D. "Eustathios Rhomaios' Opusculum über das Hypobolon." In *Fontes Minores,* vol. 7 , ed. D. Simon, 239–52. Frankfurt am Main: Vittorio Klostermann, 1986.

Scheltema, H. J., D. Holwerda, and N. van der Wal, eds. *Basilicorum libri LX.* Series A, *Textus,* 8 vols. Series B, *Scholia.* 9 vols. Groningen: Bouma's Boekhuis/ Wolters-Noordhoff, 1953–88.

Schminck, A. "Vier eherechtliche Entscheidungen aus dem 11: Jahrhundert." In *Fontes Minores,* vol. 3, ed. D. Simon, 221–79. Frankfurt am Main: Vittorio Klostermann, 1979.

Simon, D. "Das Ehegüterrecht der Pira: Ein systematischer Versuch." In *Fontes Minores,* vol. 7, ed. D. Simon, 193–238. Frankfurt am Main: Vittorio Klostermann, 1986.

Simon, D. *Rechtsfindung am byzantinischen Reichsgericht.* Frankfurt am Main: Vittorio Klostermann, 1973.

Stolte, B. H. "Balancing Byzantine Law." In *Fontes Minores,* vol. 11, ed. L. Burgmann, 57–75. Frankfurt am Main: Vittorio Klostermann, 2005.

Stolte, B. H., and R. Meijering, eds. "The Prooimion of the Eisagoge." *Subseciva Groningana* 7 (2001): 91–155.

Troianos, Sp. N. *Oi Neares Leontos S' [VI] tou Sophou.* Athens: Erodotos. 2007.

Troianos, Sp. N. *Oi peges tou buzantinou dikaiou.* 3rd ed. Athens-Komotini: Sakkoula, 2011.

Van der Wal, N., and J. H. A. Lokin. *Delineatio iuris graeco-romani: Les sources du droit byzantin de 300 à 1453.* Groningen: Forsten, 1985.

Yiannopoulos, A. N. "Historical Development." In *Introduction to Greek Law,* ed. K. D. Kerameus and Ph. J. Kozyris, 1–12. 2nd ed. Deventer-Boston: Kluwer, 1993.

Zachariä von Lingenthal, K. E. *Geschichte des griechisch-römischen Rechts.* 3rd ed. Aalen: Scientia Verlag, 1955. Originally printed in Berlin: Weidmann, 1892.

Zachariä von Lingenthal, K. E. "Practica ex actis Eustathii Romani [Peira]." In *Jus Graecoromanum,* vol. 4, ed. J. Zepos and P. Zepos, 7–260. Aalen: Scientia Verlag, 1962. Originally published in *Jus Graecoromanum,* vol. 1, ed. Zachariä von Lingenthal (Leipzig: T. O. Weigel, 1856).
Zimmermann, R. *The Law of Obligations: Roman Foundations of the Civilian Tradition.* Cape Town: Juta; Deventer: Kluwer, 1990.

CHAPTER 14

Looking Ahead to the Roman Law of Obligations

Reflections on Opportunities in Research and Pedagogy

THOMAS A. J. MCGINN

Implications for Research

One common criticism of published collections of papers from conferences is that they lack a certain coherence with respect to each other. Perhaps enough has been written in chapter 1 to dispel that notion in this case, but let me point out a few more relevant details, because I believe that the interconnections between the papers collected in this book are among its particular strengths. Masi Doria, for example, uses a theoretical approach derived from the nineteenth century (mostly that of Henry Sumner Maine, though Savigny is also important) in a novel way, while Fiori shows some of the limits inherent in scholarship from that period. Procchi suggests how the intellectual tradition of that day, especially as represented by Jhering, might function as an extension of the Roman, while Randazzo makes broad use of anthropological methodologies from both the nineteenth and twentieth centuries: Jhering asserts himself here too. Cascione moves in a similar way, from a nineteenth-century analysis of criminal conduct (chiefly that of Mommsen) to much more recent evaluations based on considerations of social control.

Like Fiori with regard to contracts, Metzger explores the implications of a lack of a general concept (in his case, a "law of procedure") for the development of legal rules. Benke, too, is able to suggest how complexity (in this case, complexity operating to the point of contradiction) can sustain the development of a legal system deeply penetrated by considerations of gender. New institutional economics, like gender studies, presents the legal historian with a relatively new methodology and is ably deployed by Kehoe to advance our understanding of some traditional problems in the relationship between Roman law and society. This relationship is a theme explored by du Plessis in his examination of the connection between legal theory and practice. A similar concern is evident in Rainer's contribution, which constructs a parallel universe of contracts in the public realm, parallel, that is, to those examined by a number of our contributors under the heading of private law. It is fair to say that none of the contributors to this book ignores the problem of historical development, though some opt for a closer focus, such as Cursi, who unites an analytical understanding of Aquilian liability (i.e., loss wrongfully inflicted on another's property) to an understanding of how this developed over time. In a similar fashion, Stolte explores the significance, on both a macrolevel and a microlevel, of what the words *Roman* and *Byzantine* really stand for in terms of the content of legal rules, specifically relating to the law of contracts. His focus on the central question of what agreements can and cannot be enforced takes up a theme raised by Fiori and touched on by some of the other contributors.

There is a great deal of contemporary interest in the field of Roman law, an interest that reaches far beyond any reasonable boundaries we can set for the discipline itself. It is true that this interest is frustrated at times by perceptions that specialist (i.e. Romanist) writings on the subject are inaccessible to outsiders, in part because they are couched in highly technical terms, assume a great deal of information, and are published in journals and collections that are unfamiliar to most classicists and ancient historians. This collection presents a genuine opportunity for both sides to set aside that perception (which is to some extent justified, truth be told). A group of highly regarded specialists offers here a set of essays designed to open up their subject to a general audience of interested scholars from a diversity of fields. This collection will, I believe, interest not only Roman law specialists on both sides of the Atlantic but also ancient historians and students of anthropology, economic history, and gender studies.

Regarding the interest of nonspecialists, we contributors operate on the basis of a double premise. First, it seems likely that few are well acquainted with current discussions and controversies in the field of Roman law. Second, many of them are deeply interested in learning more about the current state of play. We trust that this collection offers them a sophisticated yet accessible point of entry to a discipline that has long seemed out of reach, even to those with an interest in the subject.

Opportunities in Pedagogy: The Case Method

We contributors further anticipate that this collection can play a role in Roman law pedagogy. For the sake of example, I cite the case method of teaching Roman law. I do this for three reasons. First, it is the method personally most familiar to me. Second, it enjoys, by all indications, an increasing popularity in various countries, notably, Austria, Spain, and the United States. Third, the utility of the collection for the purpose of offering seminars will, one trusts, be reasonably obvious. Teaching from a casebook or, more precisely, relying on the instant collection of essays while doing so perhaps requires a bit more exposition of this pedagogical approach.

There is no need to offer a full justification for the method in this place, in part because almost every casebook contains one in its preface. A few words of description may suffice instead. The case method was introduced in 1870 by an administrator and professor at Harvard Law School named Christopher Columbus Langdell. Langdell practically invented this method out of nothing, inspiring, in the end, a revolution in the practice of American legal pedagogy.[1] Instead of listening to lectures by professors, the students read and discussed decisions delivered by appellate courts. This material was presented to the students through the mechanism of question and answer, the Socratic method of instruction, something Langdell insisted on. He viewed the law as an exercise in the application of reason through the deployment of a system of axioms and corollaries, privileging logic above experience.[2] These cases were put together in textbooks published as casebooks, the first of which was published by Langdell himself.[3]

As in almost all revolutions, there was a strong and determined resistance. The new, strange, and, for many, deeply disturbing teaching methods promoted by Langdell provoked a very bitter reaction, even (or especially) at Harvard. With the passage of time, however, the opposition abated sufficiently so that the casebook method defeated all of its rivals.[4] By the late 1920s, it was practically

1. On Langdell's appointment as Dean of the Harvard Law School and his introduction of the case method, see LaPiana, *Logic and Experience* (1994) 7–28; Kimball, *Inception* (2009) 18–19, 32–39, 65–66, 87–90, 193–232 (the precedents for Langdell's method are revealed as very thin).
2. Kronman, *Lost Lawyer* (1993) 184.
3. Langdell, *Selection of Cases on the Law of Contracts* (1871).
4. Langdell's pedagogy has outlasted the influence of his scholarship, which was decisively

universal in American law schools.[5] It still dominates the field, above all in the first year (of three) in the typical U.S. law school curriculum. It must be said that the contents of twenty-first-century casebooks differ in important ways from the type known to Langdell, as they contain a great deal of explanatory material that is not strictly legal in nature but drawn from the fields of economics, history, and sociology.[6]

There are perhaps three basic characteristics of the method. First, students are confronted with actual problems and legal texts. The emphasis is decidedly placed on how to treat these problems instead of on learning abstract systems of legal rules. Second, the students are encouraged to develop their skills in reading the legal materials with a critical eye and in exercising their judgment. They are discouraged from concluding that problems in a legal context have solutions that are unique and optimal in nature. Third, classroom teaching focuses on an exploratory dialogue between the instructor and individual students. The instructor uses the dialogue format in order to push the students to think more deeply about the cases that they have prepared as assignments for class and also to reflect on their assumptions and beliefs about law.

These ideas are reflected in the three main traditions of Roman law casebooks, the American, the Austrian, and the Spanish.[7] The latter is the oldest, introduced over eighty years ago by José de Castillejo and later taken up by one of his students, Alvaro D'Ors.[8] The tradition developed further out of the expe-

---

rejected by the Realists in the 1930s. In the latter, Langdell set out to deploy scientific and even mathematical (meaning chiefly geometrical) methods to accomplish what the exponents of nineteenth-century codification movements aimed at, namely, to render the law rational, transparent, and manageable. See Kronman, *Lost Lawyer* (1993) 170–225; LaPiana, *Logic and Experience* (1994) 55–70. On the (largely unsuccessful) codification movement in the antebellum United States, see Cook, *American Codification Movement* (1981).

5. According to Konop ("Case System" [1931] 276), it was "generally used" in all law schools belonging to the Association of American Law Schools. On the spread of the case method in the early twentieth century, see LaPiana, *Logic and Experience* (1994) 148–52, 160–61.
6. On the evolution of casebooks from 1871 to the early twenty-first century, see Maxeiner, *Educating Lawyers Now and Then* (2007) 44–46. The basic elements remain edited versions of appellate cases: see Mertz, *Language of Law School* (2007) 53; Sullivan et al., *Educating Lawyers* (2007) 55.
7. In what follows, I rely in part on personal communications from Jorge Adame Goddard, Manuel Jesus García Garrido, Teresa Giménez-Candela, Herbert Hausmaninger, and Bruce Frier. I am happy to express my gratitude to all of them.
8. Castillejo's *Ejercicios y casos de derecho romano* (1930) has 115 invented or (at minimum) freely adapted cases devoted to various areas of the law. See Giménez-Candela, "Il diritto romano in Spagna" (2007) 501.

rience of Manuel Jesus García Garrido, teaching first at Santiago de Compostela and later at the Universidad Nacional de Educación a Distancia. García Garrido published his first casebook in 1965.[9] The current version has appeared in five editions between 2004 and 2010.[10] This contains cases on the law of property, obligations, and family law.[11] It has been translated into Italian and Russian.

The other two traditions are, to an extent, interconnected. The Austrian took its point of departure from the experience of Professor Herbert Hausmaninger from the University of Vienna as a faculty visitor at the University of Virginia Law School beginning in the academic year 1971–72, when he had the opportunity to observe the U.S. method of first-year law teaching.[12] The almost immediate result was his casebook on Roman property law, the *Casebook zum römischen Sachenrecht,* published for the first time in 1974 and still accessible in its tenth edition (with Richard Gamauf as coauthor), published in 2003. Meanwhile, Hausmaninger's casebook on Roman contract law, the *Casebook zum römischen Vertragsrecht,* appeared for the first time in 1976 and witnessed its sixth edition in 2002.

Hausmaninger's interest in the method, while initially inspired by his experience teaching in the United States, was rendered more acute by discussions related to a crucial curriculum reform that took place in Austria in the years 1979–81. One outcome of this reform was that Roman law remained central in the first-year legal curriculum with regard to both lectures and small discussion

9. García Garrido, *Casuismo y jurisprudencia romana* (1965).

10. The most recent full version is García Garrido, *Casuismo y jurisprudencia romana (Responsa)* (2008), now available in abbreviated form as *Casos prácticos de derecho romano* (2010).

11. A significant difference between the Spanish casebooks (at least the ones known to me), on the one hand, and the American and Austrian ones, on the other, is that the latter include the Latin text of the case while the former do not. The reason has to do with the cost of publishing (personal communication, Prof. T. Giménez-Candela). There is a companion volume that serves as a textbook, García Garrido's *Derecho privado romano* (2008). On the teaching of the case method in Spain see also García Camiñas, "Metodología casuística" (2005); García Camiñas, "El método del caso" (2008).

12. A fascinating and much earlier connection between the case method in the U.S. and Austria is represented by the work of Josef Redlich, professor of civil law at the University of Vienna and author of the 1914 Carnegie Foundation report on legal education, published under the title *The Common Law and the Case Method in American University Law Schools* and reprinted in Maxeiner, *Educating Lawyers Now and Then* (2007). Redlich was chosen for this task because continuing controversy over the method made appointment of an American scholar difficult. He came away from his experience with the case method with some criticism but otherwise so impressed by it that he resolved to see it implemented in German-speaking countries (Redlich in Maxeiner, *Educating Lawyers,* 73).

sections. Hausmaninger and his colleagues at Vienna exploited this opportunity to install the case method in a fundamental way for the teaching of Roman law. In the lectures, the cases serve, for the most part, as illustrations of the core material. In the small discussion sections, his casebooks are employed more or less on the classic Langdell model, using the Socratic method of question and answer for the purpose of analyzing the legal texts. Today, the examinations for Roman law consist no longer of purely of oral exams, as in the past, but of essay questions prompting the written analysis of cases.

The crucial role of Roman law in Austrian legal education was confirmed by a later reform that took place in 1999. The year before that reform, another Austrian casebook appeared, devoted to the law of property and obligations (contract and delict) and prepared by Michael Rainer and Johanna Filip-Fröschl.[13] Hausmaninger's casebooks have been translated into Bulgarian and form the base of a textbook written with Peter Blaho for the teaching of Roman law in Slovakia and the Czech Republic. One has appeared in English in 2012, as we shall see in a moment.

The Austrian experience exerted a strong influence on the American. In the academic year 1972–73, Bruce Frier, while studying at the law school at the University of California at Berkeley, had the idea of designing a course on Roman law based on the case method. When he returned to teaching at the University of Michigan the next year, he taught a course on Roman law using a traditional lecture format. The results of the course evaluations, however, suggested a different direction might be taken that was more consistent with the interests and needs of the students. Many of the students who responded to these evaluations intended to proceed to law school after completing their undergraduate degree. They had taken the course in Roman law because they were interested in law and not because they were interested in learning about the Romans, their history, and culture. Very few of them had much knowledge of the ancient world or the least inclination to remedy this state of affairs. Most valued those aspects of the course emphasizing methods of juristic thinking and had little use for descriptions of the cultural and historical context of Roman law or appreciations of its merits.

In response, Frier began preparation of a casebook on Roman contract law. But precisely at this point, in the academic year 1976–77, Frier had a sabbati-

13. Rainer and Filip-Fröschl, *Texte zum römischen Recht* (1998). Yet another is scheduled to appear in late 2012: Kossarz and Pichler, *Casebook Römisches Recht* (forthcoming).

cal year in Salzburg, where he first encountered Hausmaninger's casebooks on contract and property law. Given their clever design and level of sophistication, Frier thought it best simply to translate them into English, with the permission of the author, for use in his courses at Michigan. When he returned to Ann Arbor, he began a new version of the contracts book, which has never been published, and started work on a casebook on delicts, which appeared in 1989.[14] In the fall of 2003, Frier and McGinn published a second casebook on Roman family law, embracing such subjects as marriage, *patria potestas,* succession, guardianship, and the status of women.[15] A third casebook in English, a translation by George Sheets of the property law textbook by Hausmaninger and Gamauf, has appeared in 2012, as previously mentioned.[16]

To state this record of successful application is not to deny that, despite its considerable merits, there are difficulties with the case method. The method is an inefficient means of conveying substantive information, a fact long ago emphasized.[17] It is a problematic way of teaching statutes, an increasingly important source of modern law.[18] It has been taught in many different ways in different law schools, often in a manner that—allegedly—focuses on the holdings of cases at the expense of an understanding of the principles that underlie them. Another way of putting this criticism is to observe that the Socratic method ideally central to this approach has been many things to many people.[19]

14. Frier, *Casebook on the Roman Law of Delict* (1989).

15. Frier and McGinn, *Casebook on Roman Family Law* (2004). While this book appeared in 2003, the official publication date is 2004.

16. Hausmaninger and Gamauf, *Casebook on Roman Property Law* (2012). I do not mean to imply that Spain, Austria, and the U.S, are the only countries where the case method is used to teach Roman law. For recent developments in Mexico, see Adame Goddard, "¿Sirve la discusión de casos?" (2003) and the other materials collected at www.jorgeadame.com.

17. Llewellyn ("Current Crisis in Legal Education" [1948] 215) wrote, " . . . [I]t is obvious that man could hardly devise a more wasteful method of imparting *information about subject matter* than the case-class" (his emphasis). See also Llewellyn, "On What Is Wrong with So-Called Legal Education" (1935) 676. For a polemic that is lively if highly indiosyncratic, see Watson, *Shame* (2006).

18. Llewellyn, "Current Crisis in Legal Education" (1948) 212; Moskovitz, "Beyond the Case Method" (1992) 249, 259.

19. Llewellyn, "Current Crisis in Legal Education" (1948) 212–13; Moskovitz, "Beyond the Case Method" (1992) 244–45 ("Under the case method, the holding is less important than the way the court gets to it"); Blasi, "What Lawyers Know" (1995) 359, 386; Leslie, "How Not to Teach Contracts" (2000) 1295–99. One might well question whether, in recent years, there has existed a "pure" case method and, if so, how widespread this has been: see Leslie, "How Not to Teach Contracts," 1290. Garrett ("Becoming Lawyers" [1998] 200–201) points out that the case method and the Socratic method are not precisely the same thing.

Yet the experience of the method is remarkably similar from one law school to the next.[20]

The method has also been attacked as an instrument of ideology.[21] Students are often disappointed to discover that understanding the law requires them to de-emphasize or even to set aside commonly accepted moral norms or ideals of fairness.[22] One anthropologist's remarkable study of contracts classes in eight law schools—differing from each other in terms of geography, rank, and type—finds that the case method inculcates an elitist legal epistemology, an ideology of language, that marginalizes morality and social context while indeed preparing students for legal practice, but only in a very dark sense.[23]

One of the biggest criticisms has taken aim at a perceived disconnect between the focus on reconstructing the principles behind appellate court opinions central to the tradition of the case method as taught in American law schools and what most lawyers actually do most of the time, which is to attempt to solve problems of various—but fairly predictable—kinds.[24] One proposed

20. See Sullivan et al., *Educating Lawyers* (2007) 186. In her survey of eight contracts classes, Mertz (*Language of Law School* [2007] 26–28, 41, 86–93, 109, 141–44, 154, 169, 189, 201, 210, 265) finds that despite great variety in the deployment of the Socratic method, "... there is still an approach that shares many of the underlying tenets of the classic Socratic method, conveying the same core metalinguistic features through a variety of discursive styles" (quotation at 41). Even so, definitions of "Socratic method" can vary significantly (see Mertz, *Language of Law School,* 144, 265).

21. For assertions of class bias, see Wright, "Whose *Phronesis*?" (1996) 828–32, in response to the positive view in Kronman, *Lost Lawyer* (1993) 154. On concerns with perceptions of justice and ideology more generally, see Maute, "Response: The Values of Legal Archaeology" (2000) 234.

22. Sullivan et al., *Educating Lawyers* (2007) 24, 57, 78, 132–44. The authors of this report regard professional education as "inherently" ethical in nature (30).

23. Mertz, *Language of Law School* (2007), largely accepted in O'Neill, review of Mertz (2008). Mertz's proposed solutions, however, are vague to the point of evanescent.

24. For sustained presentation of this criticism, see Frank, "Why Not a Clinical Lawyer School?" (1933); Llewellyn, "Current Crisis in Legal Education" (1948) (Llewellyn believed that the method was often taught badly and yet was redeemable, whereas Frank thought it fundamentally flawed); Blasi, "What Lawyers Know" (1995); Heriot, "Songs of Experience" (1995); Leslie, "How Not to Teach Contracts" (2000); Sullivan et al., *Educating Lawyers* (2007) 56–57. A century ago or so, the case method was widely perceived to connect pedagogy with legal practice, even to the point of serving as a kind of clinical education: see Konop, "Case System" (1931); LaPiana, *Logic and Experience* (1994) 103; Maxeiner, *Educating Lawyers Now and Then* (2007) 13–21. This view, in a moderate form, has been recently defended by Garrett ("Becoming Lawyers" [1998] 201–4, 207) and J. B. White (*From Expectation to Experience* [1999] 178–79).

remedy has been to offer a clinical legal perspective that would teach how juries decide cases, as well as impart a sense of the potential "instability" of the facts in cases tried in an adversarial process, the unreliability of witness testimony, and so on.[25]

Another solution has been to introduce new methods for teaching "cases," such as adopting an approach more influenced by the social sciences, for example.[26] A way of summarizing this solution is to say that it advocates more background and less holding in the teaching of cases. One source of inspiration are the much more detailed cases used in business school pedagogy.[27] In fact, there is a striking variety in the approaches taken by the adherents of this pedagogy, which is usually described as the problem method.[28] Finally, there is the enriched case method, whose proponents take certain landmark cases found in traditional casebooks and subject them to detailed scrutiny, with careful attention to the legal and historical (meaning the full social, economic, political, and cultural) context, often calling attention to the instability of the facts behind the holdings.[29] A key premise is that a true doctrinal understanding depends on a correct comprehension of the facts behind a given case and a focus on improving the lawyering skills of students. A central aim is to foster a community among legal historians, jurists, and students who later become practitioners

25. Frank, "Why Not a Clinical Lawyer School?" (1933) 916–19; Blasi, "What Lawyers Know" (1995) 327, 367, 373, 378; Maute, "Response: The Values of Legal Archaeology" (2000) 230. The recent Carnegie Foundation report on legal education recommends a "pervasive method" of teaching practical skills and legal ethics extending throughout the three years of law school: see Sullivan et al., *Educating Lawyers* (2007) 59, 91–100, 120–22, 151–52, 159–60. This 2007 report recommends a clinical model drawn from medical school practice, a suggestion repudiated, on financial and practical grounds, by Maxeiner, *Educating Lawyers Now and Then* (2007) 25–38.

26. As long ago advocated by Frank, "Why Not a Clinical Lawyer School?" (1933). For a list of various approaches, see Teich, "Research on American Law Teaching" (1986) 171–72.

27. For a discussion of the business school case method, see Stapleton and Stapleton, "Teaching Business Using the Case Method and Transactional Analysis" (1998).

28. See Moskovitz, "Beyond the Case Method" (1992) esp. 258–63; Blasi, "What Lawyers Know" (1995), esp. 387; Heriot, "Songs of Experience" (1995); Wright, "Whose *Phronesis*?" (1996); Leslie, "How Not to Teach Contracts" (2000), esp. 1308.

29. This approach is also known as the enhanced or reconstructed case method or "legal archaeology." See Maute, "Response: The Values of Legal Archaeology" (2000) 223–25, 229, 240, 244–45; P. D. White, "Afterword and Response" (2000) 301–2; Sullivan et al., *Educating Lawyers* (2007) 76, 199; Clermont, "Civil Procedure Archaeology" (2008) 5–12. The unreliability of facts as established by courts was a theme dear to the Realists: see Frank, "Why Not a Clinical Lawyer School?" (1933) 918–19; Llewellyn, "Current Crisis in Legal Education" (1948) 214.

of law. The method has received strong support from the Law Stories series launched by Foundation Press in 2003, two of whose volumes I use for the introduction of comparative material in chapter 1. The enriched case method traces its roots to developments in scholarship and textbook development over the last couple of decades or so.[30]

One might anticipate, from all this, the long-delayed triumph of Realist pedagogy, at least in that form represented by Karl Llewellyn, who wanted to rock the boat of Langdellian method, if not that advocated by Jerome Frank, who wanted to sink it. But the victory has, at best, been highly qualified. The case method continues to reign supreme in American first-year law classes, to all appearances.[31]

Scholars have asserted a variety of reasons for the continued survival or even success of the method in the teeth of such withering criticism. Some have either celebrated or deplored its ideological implications, a theme I have already explored. Frank long ago pointed to a disconnect between the experience of most law professors, who were not practicing attorneys, and the perceived needs of their students.[32] Critics have claimed the method as better suited to train law teachers, scholars, clerks, review editors, and appellate advocates, rather than the vast majority of lawyers.[33] A Romanist might be forgiven for viewing the controversy as turning, in no small part, on the distinction between

30. For example, the essays by Maute, Sanger, Simpson, and Threedy in Baird's *Contracts Stories* (2007) trace their genesis to law review articles published during this period. See also Simpson, *Leading Cases in the Common Law* (1995); Maute, "Response: The Values of Legal Archaeology" (2000) 228. For textbooks, see Linzer, *Contracts Anthology* (1995); Davies et al., *Torts Anthology* (1999); Danzig and Watson, *Capability Problem in Contract Law* (2004); Chirelstein, *Concepts and Case Analysis in the Law of Contracts* (2006). For an early application to the field of medieval English law, see Donahue, "Siebenthaler Lecture" (1991–92).

31. It has evidently declined somewhat in use in second- and third-year courses, relative to the situation almost a century ago: see Frank, "Why Not a Clinical Lawyer School?" (1933) 921; Llewellyn, "Current Crisis in Legal Education" (1948) 216; Leslie, "How Not to Teach Contracts" (2000) 1297; Sullivan et al., *Educating Lawyers* (2007) 50.

32. Frank, "Why Not a Clinical Lawyer School?" (1933) 909. See also the fascinating rant in Llewellyn, "On What Is Wrong with So-Called Legal Education" (1935) which anticipates, in some measure, the aforementioned enriched case method.

33. Frank, "Why Not a Clinical Lawyer School?" (1933) 915; Blasi, "What Lawyers Know" (1995) 315–16, 386; Sullivan et al., *Educating Lawyers* (2007) 60, 89, 95 (the only true mentoring in law schools benefits top students at top schools who go on to become law review editors, clerks for appellate judges, and then appellate advocates, teachers and scholars, or judges themselves).

educating jurists (*iuris consulti*) and trial lawyers (*causidici*).[34] It is claimed that among the benefits to its teachers are precisely that it privileges legal thought above practice, consistently with what is perceived by some as a general aversion to empirical research on the part of law school faculty.[35] Another view explains its survival in terms of the inherent conservatism of law teachers following the example of their own teachers.[36] Yet another is that it has no clear successor. It has been argued that, in both law and especially nonlaw contexts, different methods for teaching groups of students do not produce appreciably better results.[37] Other possible explanations that have been raised are that teaching doctrine in this manner fills out the curriculum; is necessary for testing in courses, important for a student's career as a lawyer, and essential for the bar examination; or even develops skills in analyzing precedent and generating arguments from law and policy.[38]

Without wishing to question the validity of any or all of these explanations, I would rank among the most important reasons for the continued popularity of the case method the utility and intellectual satisfaction it provides its instructors. They face the challenge of training students, often in large classes, who have no previous knowledge of the law. By insisting that the students construct solutions rather than simply receive answers and by inviting them, at times, to reflect on the nature of legal reasoning itself, teachers are able to see a marked improvement in a matter of months on the part of most of their novice students in the analytical thinking they need to succeed in law school and legal practice. This improvement is perceptible not only in the students' ability to think about law but also in their confidence about that ability.

This challenge, reenacted every year, is one that the teachers themselves find stimulating and even fun. They are often senior, well-respected faculty who presumably have some choice over what classes they teach and how they teach them. The experience of teaching the case method is unlike other methods of pedagogy most teachers encounter—lectures, seminars, and (for some of us) language courses. Diversity matters, as does a good challenge. One might

---

34. See the observations and recommendations made in Blasi, "What Lawyers Know" (1995) 386, 395–96; Heriot, "Songs of Experience" (1995), 1736; Leslie, "How Not to Teach Contracts" (2000) 1294, 1311; and Sullivan et al., *Educating Lawyers* (2007) 98, 111.
35. Blasi, "What Lawyers Know" (1995) 391; Sullivan et al., *Educating Lawyers* (2007) 82–83.
36. Moskovitz, "Beyond the Case Method" (1992) 241.
37. Teich, "Research on American Law Teaching" (1986).
38. All five reasons are canvassed in Leslie, "How Not to Teach Contracts" (2000) 1291–94.

describe the Socratic method as the instructional equivalent of working the high wire without a net. But the demonstrable benefit to students and the sheer challenge enjoyed by faculty are not the only rewards the case method brings. It constantly repays the teachers themselves with fresh insights into the cases they teach.

Lessons for Roman Law

All of this holds for the teaching of Roman law, and it is my hope that aside from a point of entry into the field of Roman obligations for classicists, ancient historians, and scholars in other fields, the present volume will offer an aid to pedagogy, not only in seminars of a traditional type, but precisely in courses using the case method.[39] The existing possibilities for casebooks available in various languages have already been canvassed. I recommend resort to a more traditional type of textbook to supplement the student's understanding of the cases (provided it is reasonably concise), as well as a resource to facilitate the development of legal reasoning.[40] Midterms and short papers prompting the analysis of a Roman case enable students to make great strides in developing skills in analytical thinking and in their understanding of law. For most of us who use it to teach Roman law, writing about law is an essential component of the case method.[41] Some instructors ask students to apply Roman law to the facts of a modern case for a long paper assignment. There is no question, all the same, that more can be done with a comparative approach, and it is hoped that some of the material in the first chapter in this volume can point the way in that direction.

Within the broad scope of the case method, different approaches are possible. This collection of essays might well serve to develop (or more fully to develop) an enriched case pedagogy for the Roman law of obligations. Ideally,

39. The teaching of Roman law itself might serve to assuage what is criticized as the insularity of American legal science: see Maxeiner, *Educating Lawyers Now and Then* (2007) 54.

40. English language examples of the first include Nicholas, *Introduction to Roman Law* (1987) and du Plessis, *Borkowski's Textbook on Roman Law* (2010). For the second, one cannot do better than Levi, *Introduction to Legal Reasoning* (1949).

41. In most U.S. law schools, legal writing is reserved for courses separate from the first-year doctrinal classes that teach the case method, while in the latter there is only one examination, a three-hour final at the conclusion of the course: see Sullivan et al., *Educating Lawyers* (2007) 108, 162–70.

this means to teach Roman law in its historical context, recognizing it as a distinct cultural product, without losing sight of the fact that its true pedagogical value is precisely as law.

Bibliography

Adame Goddard, J. "¿Sirve la discusión de casos en las aulas para la formación jurídica?" *Ars Iuris* 30 (2003): 13–38.

Baird, D. G., ed. *Contracts Stories.* New York: Foundation Press, 2007.

Blasi, G. L. "What Lawyers Know: Lawyering Expertise, Cognitive Science, and the Functions of Theory." *Journal of Legal Education* 45 (1995): 313–97.

Castillejo, J. *Ejercicios y casos de derecho romano.* Madrid: Librería General de Victoriano Suárez, 1930.

Chirelstein, M. A. *Concepts and Case Analysis in the Law of Contracts.* 5th ed. New York: Foundation Press, 2006.

Clermont, K. M. "Civil Procedure Archaeology." In *Civil Procedure Stories,* ed. K. M. Clermont, 1–20. 2nd ed. New York: Foundation Press, 2008.

Cook, C. M. *The American Codification Movement: A Study of Antebellum Legal Reform.* Westport, CT: Greenwood, 1981.

Danzig, R., and G. R. Watson. *The Capability Problem in Contract Law: Further Readings on Well-Known Cases.* 2nd ed. New York: Foundation Press, 2004.

Davies, J. A., et al. *A Torts Anthology.* 2nd ed. Cincinnati: Anderson, 1999.

Donahue, C. "Siebenthaler Lecture: A Legal Historian Looks at the Case Method." *Northern Kentucky Law Review* 19 (1991-92): 17-47.

du Plessis, P. *Borkowski's Textbook on Roman Law.* 4th ed. Oxford: Oxford University Press, 2010.

Frank, J. "Why Not a Clinical Lawyer School?" *University of Pennsylvania Law Review* 81 (1933): 907–923.

Frier, B. W. *A Casebook on the Roman Law of Delict.* Atlanta: Scholars Press, 1989.

Frier, B. W. "The Discourse of Roman Law: Should Our Students be Told?" *Journal of Roman Archaeology* 24.2 (2011): 564–66.

Frier, B. W., and T. A. J. McGinn. *A Casebook on Roman Family Law.* New York: Oxford University Press, 2004.

García Camiñas, J. "El método del caso en la cultura jurídica occidental." *Anuario da Facultade de Dereito da Universidade da Coruña* 12 (2008): 1173–1282.

García Camiñas, J. "Metodología casuística: Un proyecto de investigación y práctica docente." *Anuario da Facultade de Dereito da Universidade da Coruña* 9 (2005): 329–34.

García Garrido, M. J. *Casos prácticos de derecho romano (Responsa)*. 5th ed. Madrid: Ediciones Académicas, S.A., 2010.

García Garrido, M. J. *Casuismo y jurisprudencia romana: Pleitos famosos del Digesto.* Santiago de Compostela: Librería, 1965.

García Garrido, M. J. *Casuismo y jurisprudencia romana (Responsa)*. 4th ed. Madrid: Ediciones Académicas, S.A, 2008.

García Garrido, M. J. *Derecho privado romano: Casos, acciones, instituciones.* 16th ed. Madrid: Ediciones Académicas, S.A., 2008.

Garrett, E. "Becoming Lawyers: The Role of the Socratic Method in Modern Law Schools." *Green Bag,* 2nd ser., 1 (1998): 199–208.

Giménez-Candela, T. "Il diritto romano in Spagna: Università e società." *Studia et Documenta Historiae et Iuris* 73 (2007): 497–518.

Hausmaninger, H. *Casebook zum römischen Vertragsrecht.* 6th ed. Vienna: Manzsche Verlags- und Universitätsbuchhandlung, 2002.

Hausmaninger, H., and R. Gamauf. *A Casebook on Roman Property Law.* Trans. G. A. Sheets. New York: Oxford University Press, 2012.

Hausmaninger, H., and R. Gamauf. *Casebook zum römischen Sachenrecht.* 10th ed. Vienna: Manzsche Verlags- und Universitätsbuchhandlung, 2003.

Heriot, G. "Songs of Experience." *Virginia Law Review* 81 (1995): 1721–51.

Kimball, B. A. *The Inception of Modern Professional Education: C. C. Langdell, 1826–1906.* Chapel Hill, NC: University of North Carolina Press, 2009.

Konop, T. F. "The Case System: A Defense." *Notre Dame Lawyer* 6 (1931): 275–83.

Kossarz, E., and A. Pichler. *Casebook Römisches Recht.* Vienna: Facultas Universitätsverlag, forthcoming.

Kronman, A. T. *The Lost Lawyer: Failing Ideals of the Legal Profession.* Cambridge: Harvard University Press, 1993.

Langdell, C. C. *A Selection of Cases on the Law of Contracts.* 1st ed. Boston: Little, Brown, 1871.

LaPiana, W. P. *Logic and Experience: The Origin of Modern American Legal Education.* New York: Oxford University Press, 1994.

Leslie, D. L. "How Not to Teach Contracts, and Any Other Course: Powerpoint, Laptops, and the Casefile Method." *St. Louis University Law Journal* 44 (2000): 1289–316.

Levi, E. H. *An Introduction to Legal Reasoning.* Chicago: University of Chicago Press, 1949.

Linzer, P. *A Contracts Anthology.* 2nd ed. Cincinnati: Anderson, 1995.

Llewellyn, K. N. "The Current Crisis in Legal Education." *Journal of Legal Education* 1 (1948): 211–20.

Llewellyn, K. N. "On What Is Wrong with So-Called Legal Education." *Columbia Law Review* 35 (1935): 651–78.

Maute, J. L. "Response: The Values of Legal Archaeology." *Utah Law Review* 2000 (2000): 223–47.

Maxeiner, J. R. *Educating Lawyers Now and Then: An Essay Comparing the 2007 and 1914 Carnegie Foundation Reports on Legal Education.* Lake Mary, FL: Vandeplas, 2007.

McGinn, T. A. J. Review of A. M. Riggsby, *Roman Law and the Legal World of the Romans* (2010). 2010.12.39. bmcr.brymawr.edu/2010/2010-12-39.html.

Mertz, E. *The Language of Law School: Learning How to "Think Like a Lawyer."* New York: Oxford University Press, 2007.

Moskovitz, M. "Beyond the Case Method: It's Time to Teach with Problems." *Journal of Legal Education* 42 (1992): 241–70.

Nicholas, B. *An Introduction to Roman Law.* 3rd ed. Oxford: Oxford University Press, 1987.

O'Neill, K. Review of E. Mertz, *The Language of Law School. Journal of Legal Education* 58 (2008): 579–86.

Rabin, R. L., and S. D. Sugarman, eds. *Torts Stories.* New York: Foundation Press, 2003.

Rainer, M., and J. Filip-Fröschl. *Texte zum römischen Recht: Fallbeispiele für das Studium (Schuld- und Sachenrecht).* Vienna: Springer-Verlag, 1998.

Riggsby, A. M. *Roman Law and the Legal World of the Romans.* Cambridge: Cambridge University Press, 2010.

Simpson, A. W. B. *Leading Cases in the Common Law.* Oxford: Oxford University Press, 1995.

Stapleton, R. J., and D. C. Stapleton. "Teaching Business Using the Case Method and Transactional Analysis: A Constructivist Approach." *Transactional Analysis Journal* 28 (1998): 157–67.

Sullivan, W. M., et al. *Educating Lawyers: Preparation for the Profession of Law.* San Francisco: John Wiley and Sons, 2007.

Teich, P. F. "Research on American Law Teaching: Is There a Case against the Case System?" *Journal of Legal Education* 36 (1986): 167–88.

Watson, A. *The Shame of American Legal Education.* 2nd ed. Lake Mary, FL: Vandeplas, 2006.

White, J. B. *From Expectation to Experience: Essays on Law and Legal Education.* Ann Arbor: University of Michigan Press, 1999.

White, P. D. "Afterword and Response: What Digging Does and Does Not Do." *Utah Law Review* 2000 (2000): 301–3.

Wright, R G. "Whose *Phronesis*? Whose *Phronimoi*? A Response to Dean Kronman on Law School Education." *Cumberland Law Review* 26 (1996): 817–41.

Contributors

Nikolaus Benke teaches Roman law at the University of Vienna, where he is university professor and chair of the Department of Roman Law and Ancient Legal History. He is the author of a number of books and articles on Roman private law. His most recent book is *Exempla Sequimur: Untersuchungen zur Exemplum als normenbildender Größe im klassischen römischen Recht, unter spezieller Berücksichtigung kaiserlicher Entscheide* (in press).

Cosimo Cascione teaches the history of Roman law at the University of Naples (Federico II). He is the author of various books and articles on Roman public and private law and on the history of Roman law scholarship. Since his first monograph, *Tresviri capitales* (1999), he has been deeply engaged in the study of criminal law in ancient Rome. His most recent book is *Studi di diritto pubblico romano* (2010).

Maria Floriana Cursi teaches at the University of Teramo, where she is professor of institutions of Roman law. She is the author of a number of books and articles on *postliminium* and captivity, land law, damage to property, and Aquilian liability in the Roman experience. Her most recent books are *L'eredità dell'actio de dolo e il problema del danno meramente patrimoniale* (2008) and *Danno e responsabilità extracontrattuale nella storia del diritto privato* (2010). Her latest article about the *lex Aquilia* ("What Did *Occidere Iniuria* in the *Lex Aquilia* Actually Mean?") has recently been published in the journal *Roman Legal Tradition* (2011).

Paul du Plessis is a legal historian at Edinburgh University, whose research interests include Roman law, medieval interpretations of Roman law, Roman-

Dutch law, the historical development of the civilian tradition in mixed jurisdictions, and the relationship between law and history as well as between law and society in a historical context. His secondary research interests include the development of European private law, comparative law, and international private law.

Roberto Fiori is professor of Roman law at the University of Rome Tor Vergata. He is the author of a number of books and articles on criminal law, public law, contract law, and civil procedure in Roman law and in the civilian tradition. His most recent book is *Bonus vir: Politica filosofia retorica e diritto nel De Officiis di Cicerone* (2011).

Dennis Kehoe teaches at Tulane University, where he is professor of classical studies and Andrew W. Mellon Professor in the Humanities (2010–13). He has written on the economy and law of the Roman Empire, and his publications include *Investment, Profit, and Tenancy: The Jurists and the Roman Agrarian Economy* (1997) and *Law and the Rural Economy in the Roman Empire* (2007).

Carla Masi Doria is professor at the University of Naples (Federico II), where she teaches the history of Roman law. From 2005, she has been chair of the Department of Roman Law, History, and Theory of Law, named in honor of Francesco De Martino. She has published books and articles on slavery and the legal status of freed persons, as well as on the political and institutional history of the Roman Republic, with particular reference to political office and to criminal law. Her most important works include *Bona libertorum* (1996), *Spretum imperium* (2000), and *Quaesitor urnam movet e altri studi sul diritto penale romano* (2nd ed., 2007).

Thomas A. J. McGinn teaches at Vanderbilt University, where he is professor of classical studies, religion, and women's studies. He is the author of a number of books and articles on marriage, divorce, prostitution, women, and the family in ancient Greece and Rome. His most recent book is *Widows and Patriarchy: Ancient and Modern* (2008).

Ernest Metzger is the Douglas Professor of Civil Law at the University of Glasgow, Scotland. He writes on Roman law, especially Roman civil procedure, and the jurisprudence of Adam Smith. He is the author of *A New Outline of the Roman Civil Trial* (1997) and *Litigation in Roman Law* (2005).

Federico Procchi teaches Roman law at the University of Pisa, where he is researcher with tenure. He is the author of various articles on investment in real estate, forensic rhetoric, and precontractual liability in ancient Rome. His monograph *Licet emptio non teneat: Alle origini delle moderne teoriche sulla cosidetta culpa in contrahendo* has recently been published (2012).

J. Michael Rainer teaches Roman law at the University of Salzburg, where he is university professor. He is the author of numerous books and articles on Roman private law, including *Einführung in das römische Staatsrecht: Die Anfänge und die Republik* (1997) and *Römisches Staatsrecht: Republik und Prinzipat* (2006).

Salvo Randazzo teaches Roman law at the LUM Jean Monnet University of Bari. He is the author of numerous books and articles on Roman private law and legal theory. His latest book is on mandate. He is also editor of *Legal Roots: The International Journal of Legal History and Global Comparative Law.*

Bernard Stolte is professor of Byzantine law at the University of Groningen and directed the Netherlands Institute in Rome from 2007 to 2012. His research interests concern the early history of Byzantine law, legal papyri, textual criticism of legal sources (currently especially of texts preserved in palimpsests), and the history of European legal scholarship. Recent publications include a 2010 edition (in collaboration with colleagues) of the Greek *Paraphrasis Institutionum* of Theophilus and a study of two palimpsests of the *Basilica* in *Quellen zur byzantinischen Rechtspraxis* (also published in 2010).

Index of Sources

Literary Sources

Epigraphical and Papyrological Sources

Legal Sources

Pre-Justinianic

Corpus Iuris Civilis

Post-Justinianic

Modern Legal Sources

Index of Persons

Index of Subjects